# STYLE & SOCIETY

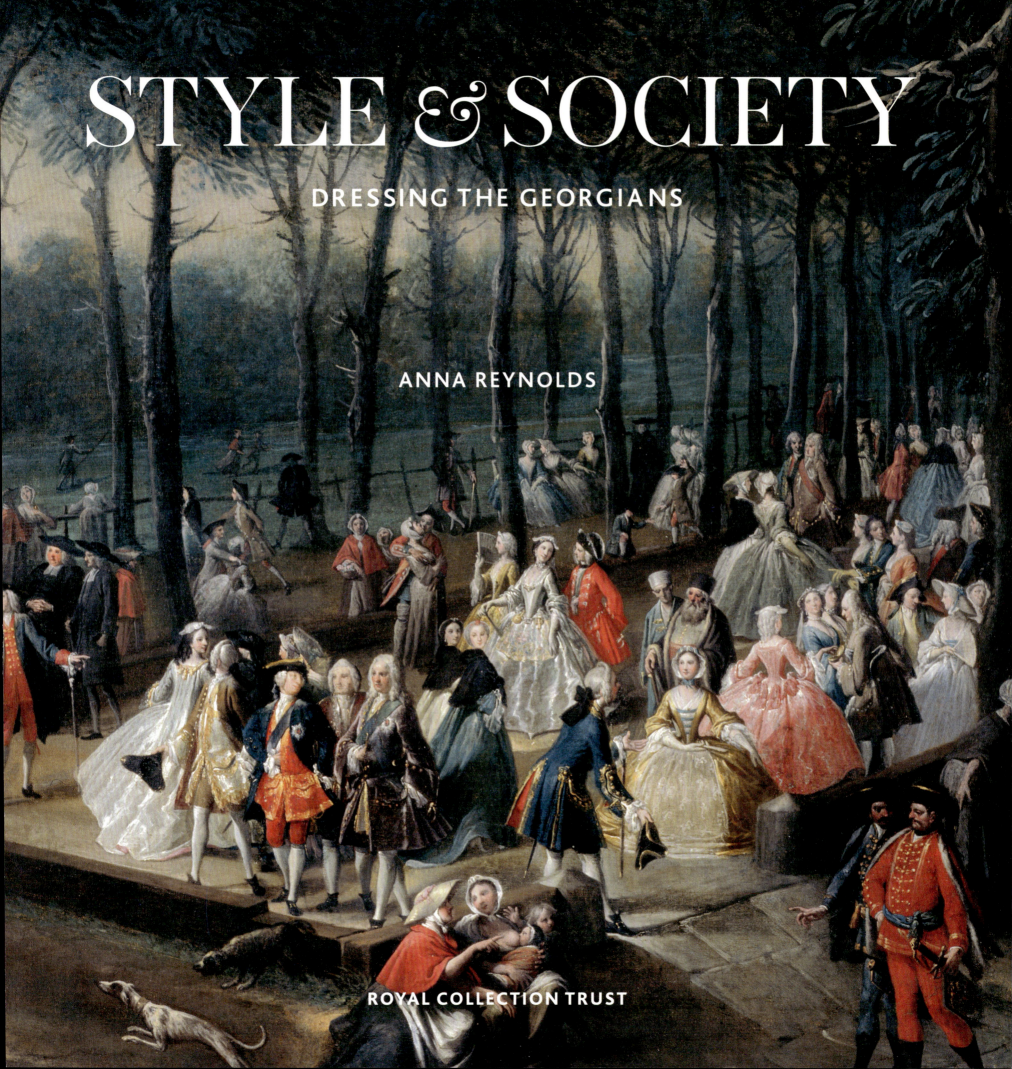

# STYLE & SOCIETY

## DRESSING THE GEORGIANS

ANNA REYNOLDS

ROYAL COLLECTION TRUST

# CONTENTS

# INTRODUCTION

This book uses portraiture to tell the story of fashionable dress in Britain, from the accession of George I in 1714 to the death of George IV in 1830. The thematic chapters serve as a guide to Georgian and Regency portraits in the Royal Collection, all interpreted through the lens of fashion history and with the aim of revealing what we can learn about life in Georgian Britain by examining the clothing worn. As might be expected, paintings by such well-known artists as Thomas Gainsborough, Johan Joseph Zoffany and William Hogarth are included. Alongside these, however, are quirkier and less well-known works, some produced by artists or craftspeople whose names are now lost to us, or depicting sitters whose identities are yet to be determined.

First, an explanation of scope, focus and terminology. This book introduces a wide range of themes and ideas that relate to eighteenth-century dress. It aims to provide an accessible guide for the general reader, and therefore assumes no prior knowledge of fashion history. It is hoped, however, that there will be something of interest to those for whom Georgian dress is a particular specialism. Here, the Georgian period is taken to refer to the reigns (and regency) of the four kings named George. The reign of William IV (1830–7) has been excluded, in part because the clothing of the 1830s is quite different from that of the decade before, in many ways feeling more like a prelude to the Victorian era than a conclusion of the Georgian. The terms Georgian and Hanoverian are both used to cover the period under discussion. Similarly, where the phrase 'eighteenth century' appears, it is often intended as shorthand for the 'long eighteenth century', thereby including the first three decades of the nineteenth century. Although many of the styles worn at this time were broadly consistent across western Europe, the focus here is explicitly on dress in Britain, with examples from other countries given where appropriate. This especially applies to France, it being the country that set fashions throughout much of Europe, at least until the eighteenth century's craze for Anglomania, which saw fashions flow over the Channel in the opposite direction. It is convenient that the period also happens to coincide almost exactly with regime changes in France, with the death of Louis XIV in 1715 and the end of the Bourbon dynasty in 1830.

It is impossible to cover every aspect of the subject exhaustively in a book of this size, and some chapters are perhaps best viewed as an appetiser, necessarily focused on one or two examples but, it is to be hoped, whetting the appetite for those who seek to know more (guidance on further reading can be found in the endnotes). For instance, while the impact of clothing worn outside Europe is discussed in Chapter 9, this is just a brief introduction to an enormous topic, using particular examples to highlight broader trends.

A final note on terminology: through the Acts of Union of 1707, the Hanoverian kings ruled the kingdoms of England (then including Wales) and Scotland, referred to together as Great Britain, as well as the Electorate of Hanover in what is now Germany. Throughout the text a reference to either England or Britain reflects the specificity of the original source material. Extrapolation beyond the original reference has not been inferred unless there is clear evidence to suggest this is a valid assumption. Details of clothing worn in Scotland are included in Chapter 12 within the section on the Jacobite risings.

The rich vocabulary used to describe dress and textiles demonstrates how clothing took its inspiration from across the globe, with components frequently transported many miles before reaching the wearer. In the process, some terms have changed their meaning: for example, nankeen was the name for a type of thick buff-coloured cotton first made in Nanjing in China, although it eventually came to refer to similar cottons produced in Britain. Items of dress were sometimes named after their supposed region of origin: *robe à la lévite, robe à la turque, robe à la polonaise*. As such names passed across borders, they were interpreted and adapted by new audiences, and occasionally their original defining features were misidentified or even completely forgotten. The Glossary explains the most common dress-related terms, with the caveat that terminology changed over time and was subject to different interpretations by different people.

Commissioning a formal oil portrait was an expensive undertaking, and visual sources of this kind therefore tend to represent elite sitters who wear styles of clothing suitable to their rank. A similar bias is seen in surviving eighteenth-century garments, with the most expensive and ornate examples more frequently saved for posterity than everyday clothing worn by the less well-off, which was usually recycled until it fell apart. Given that the majority of the source material for this book draws on items from the Royal Collection, the focus is naturally on dress worn by members of the royal family, as well as the aristocracy and the gentry. However, references to non-elite dress have also been included wherever possible, drawing on other types of visual material besides formal portraiture. In fact, during this period certain forms of clothing worn by lower classes were incorporated into the wardrobes of those of a higher social status, trousers and aprons being two specific examples of non-elite dress that were regularly worn by royalty.

Certain garments are more frequently represented in formal portraiture than others, with well-established styles favoured over those at the height of fashion, plain fabrics over patterns, and indoor clothing instead of protective outerwear, even if a sitter is depicted outside. The relative rarity of ultra-fashionable styles of clothing or seasonal textiles in portraits probably reflects a personal preference of many artists to avoid overwhelming a sitter with fussy detail at the expense of character, as well as a concern that a portrait not be quickly considered 'out of date'. For those wishing to sidestep the latter, a variety of alternative forms of dress were available, including fancy dress, or clothing that subconsciously alluded to tradition or history. For men, uniforms were a popular option, whether civilian or military, and ceremonial robes allowed artists to depict a range of expensive textiles while providing a sense of continuity with the past.

Although some artists of this period depicted dress with great accuracy – representing real clothing that was worn regularly – others modified it in portraits, whether for reasons of artistic effect or personal choice. Comparing two-dimensional images with three-dimensional garments is therefore illuminating, helping viewers determine to what degree dress has been adapted when portrayed in paint. Moreover, examining real garments reveals details of construction and marks of wear that are often invisible in portraits. In contrast, visual images demonstrate how clothes were combined and padded, and how they changed the deportment of the wearer.

Looking at a variety of sources informs an understanding of what was actually worn. In eighteenth-century Britain, the rise of the type of painting known as a 'conversation piece' (in which groups of people were informally arranged, often interacting in outdoor settings) provided an opportunity for sitters to be portrayed in a more natural form of everyday dress, from various angles. Prints, drawings and watercolours can contain small details that expose precise features of construction, and show people from a broader range of social classes and groups than are depicted in formal oil portraits. The extraordinary fashions of the eighteenth century were a gift for caricaturists, coinciding with what has become known as the golden age of the satirical print. Such prints were widely circulated, visible to all when hung in shop windows and other public social spaces. Despite their tendency for exaggeration, satirical prints reveal underlying attitudes towards dress and offer a contrast to sanitised and perfectly arranged formal portraits. Fashion periodicals are another invaluable source, although it is important to differentiate between what is suggested *should* be worn and what was *actually* worn. In this book the inclusion of images showing comparative garments from other collections is necessary because so little dress worn by the royal family survives.

Under the Tudor monarchs, a series of sumptuary laws had attempted to place restrictions on certain garments, fabrics and colours, with punishments for transgressors including confiscation, fines and imprisonment. The purpose of such laws – a form of which had been in existence since 1337 – was to ensure that clothing served as a clear demonstration of the wearer's status (therefore reinforcing established social hierarchies), to limit the importation of foreign luxury goods and to prevent excessive pride in appearance. In England, sumptuary laws had been officially repealed in 1604 after the accession of James I and VI, in part because they had proved so difficult to enforce. In reality such formal policies were replaced by an unspoken language of social etiquette that effectively served the same purpose of distinguishing those of noble birth from those lower down the social scale. For some occasions (generally ceremonial) the restriction of items of dress to certain groups remained in place, for example with peers' robes, which incorporated subtle details to emphasise the wearer's rank (see Chapter 8).

Despite the repeal of official sumptuary laws in the early seventeenth century in Britain, separate laws designed to protect and encourage the domestic economy (particularly the long-established and lucrative woollen industry) and prevent the outflow of currency continued in various forms. During the

1690s, for example, policies had been introduced to block the importation of patterned cottons from India, their popularity being considered a threat to the domestic textile industries. The ban on cottons culminated in the Calico Act of 1721, which forbade all imported cottons – legislation that would officially last until 1774. For imported items that were not prohibited outright, heavy duties were often imposed, an action that only served to make them even more exclusive and coveted.

The wearing of imported accessories and garments was particularly hard to justify when they were produced in countries considered enemies of Britain. French lace was prohibited for much of the century, and the laws were extended during the War of the Austrian Succession (1740–8) to include fine French linens such as cambric, which were hit with higher import duties before being banned entirely. After the second Jacobite rising (see Chapter 12), the Disarming Act of 1746, which forbade the wearing of Highland dress in Scotland, was another example of clothing proscription by law that was intended to serve as a public demonstration of patriotism and loyalty to the Crown. Laws designed to protect other established industries were also introduced at different times during the eighteenth century (often at the request of manufacturers such as wig-makers and button-makers, who appealed to the king), some of which passed into legislation. Other policies were aimed at maintaining quality standards: hair powder was subject to control measures for example, while the medieval guild system set out legal requirements for apprentices to receive sufficient training to maintain high levels of craftsmanship (see Chapter 1).

In reality most legal restrictions remained as hard to enforce as they had been under the Tudor monarchs, especially given that the laws tended to penalise suppliers rather than end users. The subtle but noticeable differences in quality of many foreign-made goods ensured they retained significant social cachet and commanded high prices – in fact, the restricted nature of such contraband items only enhanced their desirability. Smuggling was both lucrative and commonplace, even among the nobility.[1] In 1778 Horace Walpole described Lady Holderness (Lady of the Bedchamber to Queen Charlotte from 1770 to 1801) as 'Queen of the Smugglers'. Meanwhile, legal loopholes were liberally interpreted by shrewd merchants. Textiles intended for immediate export to British colonies, for example, were usually not subject

to the same restrictions and some of them found their way back to Britain rather than their declared destination.

The physical properties of fabric (light, non-perishable, non-breakable) combined with its intrinsic value made it an ideal trading commodity. Fashion was such an important element of life that subtle differences in quality were immediately noticeable to observers and had an appreciable impact on price, with discerning buyers prepared to pay extra for superior imported goods that proved impossible to imitate in Britain (lace from France, silks from China, cottons from India), even if they were subject to duties or legal restrictions. Wherever historical costs are given in this book, an approximate indication of equivalent value in 2021 is provided in the endnotes. In 1752 Britain adopted the Gregorian calendar in place of the Julian calendar. As a result, the start of the year was changed from 25 March (Lady Day) to 1 January. Dates in this book occurring before 1752 and falling between 1 January and 24 March have been converted to the Gregorian form (New Style) where appropriate.

In many ways the eighteenth century in Britain can be regarded as a period during which formal court structures saw a decline in influence, characterised as anachronistic and fossilised, out of step with the modern world and led by a sovereign whose executive powers were waning, set against an increasingly professionalised government growing in both independence and control. The reality was of course more nuanced, and activities at court continued to exert a powerful influence over political and cultural events. By attracting great scientists, artists and musicians, the Hanoverian monarchs and their consorts ensured the court acted as a focal point for sparkling conversation, intellectual curiosity and Enlightenment thinking, while royal patronage helped promote British craftsmanship in an increasingly globalised world. Although court dress provided a sense of continuity with the past and created a brilliant spectacle, it rarely set fashions for the future, its details governed by established rules of etiquette. Clothing did, however, play an influential role in demonstrating differences in status, wealth and taste, and could be used to build connections, cement relationships and codify allegiances. Though these signs could be subtle, they would have been more obvious to contemporary observers (see Chapter 8).

During the seventeenth century English dress had been characterised by its lack of national identity, with fashions from abroad being slavishly adopted or combined in unconventional ways.[2] With sartorial influence across borders closely linked to political power, the dominance of Spain in the sixteenth century had been usurped by France towards the end of the seventeenth century, and French fashions continued to dictate those worn across much of the Continent throughout the eighteenth century. As Carlo Goldoni wrote in 1787, it is the French 'who set the tone for all of Europe, whether in plays, in interior decoration, in dress, in finery, in jewels, in hairstyles'.[3] With their customary ambivalence towards their closest neighbour, while the English admired French fashions, by the eighteenth century they also prided themselves on a distinctive and self-consciously cultivated national style, which tended to be plainer and simpler than that worn in France. 'Not so gaudy', wrote one commentator, although the English 'wear Embroideries and Lace on their Cloaths on solemn Days … they do not make it their daily wear as the French do.'[4]

Although the English (unlike the Scottish) had no formalised type of national or regional dress, clothing worn by both men and women in England was renowned for a stylish naturalness, in contrast to the self-conscious artificiality of French fashion. Moreover, the English tended to prefer pragmatic and comfortable styles of clothing (often influenced by the dress of the working classes), which were more suitable for physical exercise: walking, hunting and shooting. Whereas French aristocratic life remained heavily centred on the court at Versailles, in England the elite spent a significant proportion of the year at their country estates, something indicated in portraiture, with English sitters frequently portrayed outside and the French within luxurious indoor settings. This conscious differentiation did not, however, prevent French silks, laces or hairdressers from being considered highly desirable in Britain, even during periods of conflict between the two nations.

French philosophers such as Jean-Jacques Rousseau linked this freedom and simplicity in dress with freedom of thought, and by the last quarter of the eighteenth century the English way of dressing was deemed to represent ideals of equality and patriotism. The period under discussion has often been termed the 'age of revolution', in both a political and a social sense, although with the introduction of a constitutional monarchy at the beginning of the eighteenth century the English already considered themselves post-Revolutionary, particularly in contrast to France.

As one of the most significant themes in the history of eighteenth-century dress centres on the increasing divergence between fashionable dress and that worn at court, we might be tempted to ask why the Royal Collection is well placed to tell this story. Is this not a distorted lens through which to view such broader trends? It is certainly true that many items within the Royal Collection reinforce a bias towards the old order, given that the majority were commissioned or collected by the monarch and their circle. However, *Style & Society* hopes to show that by looking more closely we can find an abundance of objects that also tell a story of revolution: Queen Charlotte adopting the aprons traditionally associated with working-class dress, the Prince of Wales wearing Whig buff and blue inspired by American Revolutionary ideals, and the contrast between simpler English dress and that worn in pre-Revolutionary France. It is perhaps ironic that the period under discussion ends with the restoration of the French royal family after a relatively brief intermission as a republic under Emperor Napoleon, who seized control of the first Republic in 1799 and established the first French Empire in 1804. And in Britain, with the coronation of George IV, we see an emphatic demonstration of spectacle (even within the confines of constitutional rule), with echoes of an absolutist monarchy more characteristic of earlier centuries.

Thomas Gainsborough (1727–88), *The Royal Family*, 1782.
Series of 15 portraits representing George III, Queen Charlotte
and their children.

Oil on canvas, each c.59.0 × 44.0 cm. RCIN 401006–20

**TOP ROW, LEFT TO RIGHT**
George III
Queen Charlotte
George IV when Prince of Wales
Prince William (later Duke of Clarence and William IV)
Charlotte, Princess Royal

**MIDDLE ROW, LEFT TO RIGHT**
Prince Edward (later Duke of Kent)
Princess Augusta
Princess Elizabeth
Prince Ernest (later Duke of Cumberland)
Prince Augustus (later Duke of Sussex)

**BOTTOM ROW, LEFT TO RIGHT**
Prince Adolphus (later Duke of Cambridge)
Princess Mary
Princess Sophia
Prince Octavius
Prince Alfred

# 1

# Setting the Scene

*The park is so crowded at times that you cannot help touching your neighbour. Some people come to see, some to be seen ... some of them magnificently attired, and all on the look-out for adventures.*

CÉSAR DE SAUSSURE WRITING OF ST JAMES'S PARK IN 1725[1]

T he history of dress rarely fits neatly into the arbitrary measure of a century, and the fashion industry in Britain under the early Hanoverian monarchs was, to a great extent, a continuation of that which developed at the end of the seventeenth century under the Stuarts. The fundamental materials used to make clothing were the same (linen, silk, wool and cotton, together with animal skins) and clothing remained a valuable commodity, prized for its raw materials more than for the way in which it had been cut, pinned and sewn together. Whereas the production of fabric was increasingly mechanised over the course of the eighteenth century, the process by which textiles were turned into garments was undertaken by hand, the invention of the sewing machine being many years away. As a result, the fundamental construction of most items in the male and female wardrobe was skilfully simple in conception. Elite dress was made bespoke for the wearer, and its production involved numerous processes, each undertaken by a different specialist: the silk for a dress might be woven, sold, embroidered, sewn together and trimmed by a weaver, mercer, embroiderer, mantua-maker and milliner, before it reached the body of its owner.

In Louis-Philippe Boitard's view of *A Tailor's Shop* (Fig. 1.1), a customer is being measured for a new coat in the outer room of the premises. The tailor, casually dressed in an elegant wrapping gown and soft fabric cap, his breeches unbuttoned at the knee for comfort, uses a strip of paper (known as a measure) to mark the key proportions of the figure.[2] Paper pattern pieces hang on the door, alongside measures relating to other customers, while in the workshop behind, 11 men sit cross-legged, sewing in the light of the large windows.

The intrinsic value of clothing was indicated by its manner of construction and the way in which it was cared for. Scraps of fabric were pieced together (for example in linings) to make full use of expensive material wherever possible. Shirts and shifts were recommended to be cut from lengths of linen in multiples of six and based on straight-sided shapes (squares, triangles and rectangles)

to avoid wastage.[3] Gowns were constructed (usually by female mantua-makers) using pleats to minimise the amount of cutting required and stitches that were simple to unpick, therefore making it easier to adapt existing dresses as fashions changed. Extra fabric was bought upfront to allow repairs or adjustments to be undertaken. The repurposing of garments, whether for practical or aesthetic reasons, was extremely common: eighteenth-century gowns often show evidence of alteration and it is not unusual to find a dress of a style that post-dates the design of the fabric by some decades.[4] Key outer garments such as a man's coat or a woman's gown could be retrimmed or modified to bring them up to date, as overall shapes of clothing changed much more slowly than fabric patterns and styles of trim.

Clothing was a valuable perquisite of the job for those in service. Members of the royal family gave their clothing away (including intimate personal linen) to their closest courtiers on a regular basis, while even the lady's maid of a middle-income household would expect to receive the cast-off clothing of her mistress. Garments were valuable enough to warrant itemisation and careful description in account books, marriage contracts, wills, posthumous inventories and newspaper adverts offering rewards for stolen goods.

There was a thriving second-hand clothing market: many tailors accepted unwanted clothing as part payment towards new items, rag fairs were held regularly, and traders selling garments and accessories found ready customers in towns outside the fashionable centres. Clothing was constantly recycled, until it eventually disintegrated and was used as rags or incorporated into the paper manufacturing process. While there are many more extant items of dress from the eighteenth century than from the seventeenth, those that survive today in their original form have done so largely because they were considered precious enough to pack away carefully and preserve (perhaps because of their association with a particular wearer) or were difficult to transform into something different. Petticoats, being constructed from sizeable amounts of uncut fabric, were easily reused or could be worn initially as outer garments and later as hidden underskirts for warmth, if the fabric had gone out of date. It was not so easy to give a second lease of life to an embroidered male court suit, cut tight to fit a specific person, after it had become unfashionable.

## MATERIALS

Raw materials for fabric were derived from animal and plant sources. Linen was extracted from the flax plant (*Linum usitatissimum*) via a series of labour-intensive manual processes that ranged from beating and twisting the stems, to rotting the stalks for several weeks. These steps were not simplified until the nineteenth century with the introduction of chemical processing.[5] The result was a strong thread that could be woven into linen cloth. Fibres from the stem of the hemp plant (*Cannabis sativa*) could

also be processed in a similar way to linen and produced fabrics with similar characteristics. The quality of linens varied greatly, the coarsest fibres being employed for heavy-duty sacking, so different from the fine, almost transparent textiles used for fashionable neckwear. The best linens came from Holland, which also became the name of a fine linen fabric itself regardless of its country of origin, while cambric, named after Cambrai in France, was favoured by the British elite for shirts, despite being officially banned by protectionist laws.[6] During the eighteenth century important linen industries also developed in Ireland and Scotland, which helped reduce the cost of the fabric.[7] Linen was most frequently used for underclothes (shifts and shirts) and as lining or stiffening layers in outer garments. While sometimes invisible in portraiture, layers of linen are often responsible for creating the stiff silhouette of a dressed figure, and strong linen thread was used for seams.

The staple textile industry in Britain – estimated to have employed close to a million people in 1741 – remained the wool trade, as it had been in the seventeenth century.[8] As a water-resistant yet breathable material, wool helped to regulate body temperature and was most frequently (but not always) derived from sheep. After the animal was sheared, the wool was combed, carded to break up clumps and align the fibres, then spun into thread which could be either woven into woollen cloth or knitted. Before the introduction of mechanisation during the second half of the eighteenth century, spinning was generally done by women and children within the home. Indeed, it was the most common form of paid female work, estimated to have provided employment for 75 per cent of all women over the age of 14 in 1770.[9] Although a spinning wheel was the fastest method to make thread, spinning the very finest yarn was achieved using a handheld distaff with a spindle and required great skill. In a chalk drawing by Paul Sandby (Fig. 1.2), a lady identified as Mrs Lane is shown spinning. She has pulled a piece of wool from the birdcage distaff at the top and is running it through her fingers before winding it onto the spindle below, which is attached to her waist leaving both hands free. Sandby's drawing demonstrates

that spinning was considered a valuable use of time for women from all walks of life. Mrs Lane's husband, John Lane of Hillingdon, was wealthy enough to have been able to acquire William Hogarth's *Marriage à-la-Mode* series of six oil paintings for 120 guineas in 1745 (equivalent to more than £22,000 in 2021), so presumably the couple did not depend on proceeds from spinning to earn a living.[10]

After being woven, woollen cloth often underwent a process known as fulling, which caused the fibres to become matted together, producing a more durable and waterproof material. This type of fabric was deliberately woven to a wider width, to allow for the shrinkage that occurred during the process, hence the origin of the name 'broadcloth'. The surface (nap) was then raised using the prickly seedheads of the teasel plant (*Dipsacus fullonum*) before being cut to produce a smooth, almost velvety surface. George Walker's *Costume of Yorkshire* (Fig. 1.3) depicts two men (known as croppers) working on the same piece of green cloth, raising the nap with teasels attached to small wooden handles, and on the right the 'preemer boy' who was responsible for 'detaching, by means of an iron comb or preem, the flocks or bits of wool from the teasels lately used'.[11] In another plate the croppers cut the surface of the fulled cloth with shears. Tailors exploited the fact that heavily fulled cloths did not fray after being cut, allowing them to create sharp edges for lapels and pocket flaps of coats.

Broadcloth was one of the most common fabrics used for male garments during the second half of the eighteenth century, worn on both formal and informal occasions. Many waistcoats that seem to be constructed entirely from silk in fact have woollen fabric at the back, which is usually concealed by a coat worn on top.[12] Stiffer and more hard-wearing glazed wool fabrics such as calamanco could be used for weather-proof shoes. Glazing involved applying a substance such as wax or starch to the surface of the material before passing it through hot rollers. Undergarments made of flannel (a woollen fabric with a fluffy raised surface) were worn for warmth, especially by the elderly and those convalescing from illness.[13] A much smoother and lighter fabric (worsted) required the fleece to be combed carefully before spinning so that long-staple fibres lay parallel with

each other, which resulted in a fine yarn that was woven into a lightweight and durable fabric. Norwich became especially well known for this type of fabric, hence it being named after the Norfolk town of Worsted.

Silk was another animal fibre, extracted from the cocoons of the silkworm (*Bombyx mori*) in a practice (known as sericulture) first established in China. In the early seventeenth century James I and VI had attempted to cultivate a domestic silk industry by importing 10,000 mulberry trees, a number of which were planted in the area around Buckingham House (now Buckingham Palace). The project was not a success, in part because black mulberry trees were planted rather than the white mulberry preferred by silkworms, although the cool climate was also a likely factor. Sericulture did, however, become established in France during the sixteenth century, and by the end of the seventeenth century France was the undisputed leader of the European silk textile industry, encouraged by government regulations and court patronage under Louis XIV and his chief minister Jean-Baptiste Colbert.

While the British weather made the cultivation of silkworms themselves untenable, raw silk could be imported and woven to domestic designs. Characteristic of these were the brightly coloured floral brocades set against a pale background, which during the 1740s became a distinctive national style. The most prolific designer was Anna Maria Garthwaite (1688–?1763), whose output peaked in the 1730s and 1740s. The proximity of established fruit, flower and vegetable

Fig. 1.3 George Walker (1781–1856), 'Preemer Boy', from Walker, *Costume of Yorkshire*, Leeds, 1813–14, pl. XXI.
RCIN 1075692

markets in the Spitalfields area provided abundant inspiration for designers based there. The English silk industry was aided by strict regulations on the importation and sale of foreign fabrics, together with the patronage of the court for rich, expensive silks even after fashions had begun to favour simpler, lighter styles. Queen Charlotte extensively patronised English silk makers: in 1765, for example, she specifically requested all ladies of the court wear only Spitalfields silk,[14] and in the same year George III passed an Act of Parliament prohibiting the importation of French silks. A collection of samples of dress fabric worn by members of the royal family in the 1790s survives intact (see Fig. 8.5), a number of which can be attributed to Spitalfields weavers due to their correspondence with designs in known pattern books.[15] Several of them can be directly associated with the outfits worn by Queen Charlotte and the four eldest princesses for events at St James's Palace during the 1790s. Silk was also used abundantly for small accessories such as ribbons, which were available to those lower down the social scale, and could quickly update an outfit.

The last key fibre during the period was cotton, derived from varieties of the *Gossypium* plant. This requires a temperate climate and was possibly first cultivated around the basin of the Indus River in 3200 BC.[16] In Maria Sibylla Merian's depiction of a cotton bush (*Gossypium barbadense*; Fig. 1.4), painted while the artist was living in Suriname in South America, the fibre-containing seed heads (bolls) are shown lower left.[17] Colourful Indian cottons (known as calico or chintz) entered European wardrobes via the East India trading companies, at first primarily as furnishing fabrics. The best were produced along the Coromandel Coast, involving a complicated sequence of steps to create the patterns. By the seventeenth century cotton was also being cultivated in the Caribbean and mainland North America for export to Europe: the origin of the large-scale plantations that exploited enslaved people for unpaid labour.[18] The growing popularity of cotton (alongside other colonial products such as sugar and tobacco) was a key factor driving the Atlantic slave trade, during which an estimated 12 million people were transported from Africa against their will and forced to work in inhumane conditions.

A significant market developed for these brightly coloured, lightfast and washable cotton fabrics – which came in a range of qualities and prices – to be used for clothing. In England the scale of the imports was considered sufficiently disruptive to the domestic woollen and silk industries that a number of protectionist laws were introduced, beginning in earnest in the 1690s.[19] Initially only painted, dyed or printed cottons were prohibited from importation, meaning plain fabrics could still be imported and printed domestically, often in imitation of foreign designs and colour schemes. A vociferous uprising by silk weavers – during which shops and printing workshops were vandalised and cotton-wearing members of the public assaulted, with clothing torn from their bodies – prompted the Calico Act of 1721, which forbade all imported cottons, even those printed in England.[20] Loopholes remained, however: plain cotton could still be imported and printed if intended for re-export, while mixed fabrics such as fustian (linen and cotton) were excluded from the ban entirely and could be printed and sold domestically.[21] The ban on imported printed cottons officially lasted until 1774, although in fact it was easily circumvented by inventive smugglers. The Calico Act provided an impetus to domestic weavers and printers in Britain to manufacture substitute products. The invention of the water frame, patented by Richard Arkwright in 1769, resulted in a cotton thread strong enough to be used as the warp instead of linen, enabling pure cotton fabrics to be woven in Britain for

Fig. 1.4 Maria Sibylla Merian (1647–1717), *Cotton bush with Helicopis Butterfly and Tiger Moth*, 1702–3.
Watercolour and bodycolour with gum arabic over lightly etched outlines on vellum, 36.0 × 26.8 cm (sheet). RCIN 921164

Fig. 1.5 Sir William Beechey (1753–1839), *Princess Sophia*, 1796–7.
Oil on canvas, 92.5 × 71.8 cm. RCIN 403417

Sophia's sixteenth birthday in November 1793, all the ladies 'were Dress'd in Muslin dresses, Round Gowns, with pale Blew, Sashess, & Blew ornaments, in their Heads, Feathers, Ribbons &c'.[23] Muslin was a type of plain woven cotton, initially made in India and later in Europe. Dresses similar to those in this description were represented by Sir William Beechey in his series of portraits commissioned by the Prince of Wales of his sisters at around the same time (Fig. 1.5). Princess Sophia's neo-classical gown of white cotton has a modest frilled collar, short sleeves gathered by gold ribbons and a high waistline emphasised by a blue sash, which matches the bandeau in her hair (here worn without feathers). Simple gold necklaces and bracelets complete the effect. The princess is clearly wearing an expensive cotton garment, which would have been prized for its quality and translucency. However, the mass production of cotton at a range of price points enabled a far greater proportion of the population to participate in the fashion industry, and even those on low incomes could buy small decorative accessories such as aprons or handkerchiefs on a regular basis.[24] By the first years of the nineteenth century, the value of Britain's cotton textile exports exceeded that of woollens, with quality that began to rival those from India.[25]

The most extravagant fabrics were sometimes embellished with metal threads (both silver and silver gilt, as well as cheaper metals), embroidered, woven or applied in the form of lace. Metal thread types were named after differences in their appearance, including filé (strips of metal spun around a silk core), frisé (curled for a crinkled effect), lamé (blade-like flat strips) and pulled wire, which could be tightly coiled to make purl. Embroidery might also incorporate precious metal paillettes in a variety of shapes, or spangles traditionally made by flattening circles of wire. Metal threads tended to be concentrated on the most visible areas of dress – around the neckline for example – with care taken to avoid wasting any precious metal on the back of the fabric. Minimal handling was required to avoid tarnishing, and the process of weaving with metal threads was much slower than with silk. The great expense of such raw materials meant that illicitly

the first time. The ban on their production was officially repealed five years later. By the end of the eighteenth century Lancashire had become the centre of the nation's cotton industry, weaving fabrics for both a domestic market and for export.[22] It was famous for making hard-wearing fabrics such as corduroy, known on the Continent as Manchester cloth.

Cotton fabrics were worn by all classes. At a ball held at Frogmore House, near Windsor Castle, on Princess

Fig. 1.6  Gottlieb Christian Doelitzscher (active 1769) (ed.), *Die Psalmen Davids*, manuscript, 1769.

23.0 × 18.0 × 4.7 cm. RCIN 1009364

The rich silk covering this psalter is brocaded with a variety of metal threads and may originally have been part of a piece of clothing. The design suggests it was made in the 1750s.

Fig. 1.7  Prince George and Prince Edward in George Knapton (1698–1778), *The Family of Frederick, Prince of Wales*, 1751 (detail).

Oil on canvas, 350.9 × 461.2 cm. RCIN 405741

imported goods containing metal threads seized at ports were burnt to recover the bullion.[26] A craze developed among the elite in France during the 1770s for a pastime known as *parfilage*, which involved unpicking metallic threads from fabric and trimmings in order for them to be sold to a gold dealer (hence the term 'purse money'). It subsequently spread to England where it was known as drizzling.[27]

Given their expense, fabrics decorated with metal threads were usually reserved for evening wear, the reflectiveness of the metals serving to catch whatever candlelight was available. Some indication of the sumptuous effect can be gleaned from an unusual source: a book titled *Die Psalmen Davids*, which was owned by Queen Charlotte and which is covered in a silk fabric brocaded with metal threads (Fig. 1.6). The design is typical of silks produced during the 1750s, with naturalistic flowers set against a more formalised framework.[28] The scale of the pattern, together with its quality, suggests the textile was taken from one of the queen's own dresses after it had passed out of use or fashion. Here the design elements are separated by colour, with two types of silver thread forming the background of undulating latticework bands, and three types of gold thread creating the flowers and trailing stems. The resulting variations in texture mean that each set of threads catches the light at different times, producing a glittering effect of constant movement as the book is moved. The interior of the book consists of a manuscript of the Psalms in German, while its slipcase and endpapers are both printed with patterns and colours evocative of printed cottons.

Unlike woven or embroidered metal threads, metal lace was easily transferable between garments. Its use was not as widespread during the eighteenth century as in the seventeenth, although metal lace was still retained for ceremonial occasions, uniforms and liveries. In George

Knapton's portrait of 1751 (Fig. 1.7), the future George III, aged 13, wears a blue coat abundantly decorated with bands of silver lace around the buttonholes and cuffs, while his younger brother Prince Edward wears a red coat with gold lace. Each sports a coordinating waistcoat decorated with similar lace of a narrower width. The expense of such trimmings is demonstrated by the fact that in 1733 Queen Caroline paid £25 11s for 11⅝ yards (10.6 m) of 'rich silver bone lace' for her nine-year-old daughter Princess Mary – the equivalent of approximately £4,600 today.[29] Gold lace was rarely used on coats and hats after the 1750s, although expensive fabrics continued to be woven with metallic threads.[30]

Animal skins in various forms were employed for dress throughout the eighteenth century. Leather, particularly buckskin, was traditionally used to make breeches for working men, as well as sporting or informal wear for the elite, although in the last decades of the century these were supplemented by breeches of thick cottons such as nankeen (the name was a corruption of Nanjing in east China from where the cotton fibres were imported). Fur was used for winter accessories such as muffs and scarfs, and for lining and trimming cloaks: in October 1800 the Prince of Wales acquired a 'large Sea Otter Muff' for £2 2s.[31] Animal welfare and conservation concerns did not influence the wearing of fur during the eighteenth century, and fur was sourced from a wide range of both exotic and native animals including rabbit, sable, wolf, skunk, bear, lynx and leopard.[32] Marie Leczinska wears a red gown possibly trimmed with skunk in her portrait after Jean-Marc Nattier (Fig. 1.8), perhaps a nod to her Polish ancestry, fur-trimmed garments being particularly popular in regions influenced by Turkish dress. Different furs varied in hair density and evenness of colouring, which had an impact on their value: fox pelts were cheap in comparison to the dense velvety fur from the back of a marten.[33] Ermine retained its elite status and continued to appear as a trimming on ceremonial robes. It was derived from the white winter coat of the stoat (*Mustela erminea*) with the black tails of the animal sewn in to form a pattern of black spots, known as powderings.

Sometimes these are flush with the white fur, while at other times the entire tail is used, as in the robe draped over a chair in Mary Green's miniature of Queen Adelaide when Duchess of Clarence (Fig. 1.9). Miniver, derived from the underbelly of the squirrel, is another white fur, but distinct from ermine in being plain. Bearskin had been a component of British military headwear since the late seventeenth century, but was given greater prominence in a variety of regimental uniforms under

Fig. 1.10  William Denune (c.1710–50), *Portrait of a Woman*, 1742.
Oil on canvas, 125.7 × 101.5 cm. RCIN 403933

Fig. 1.11  William Hogarth (1697–1764), *The Popple and Ashley Families*, 1730.
Oil on canvas, 63.1 × 75.1 cm. RCIN 400048

## COLOUR

Creating fabrics in deep colours that did not fade had long been a difficult process. However, the eighteenth century was a period of great innovation for the dyeing industry, particularly in France, with the invention of many new colours, as well as new techniques for their application. In general, animal fibres (wool, silk) take dyes better than those derived from plant sources (cotton, linen). Linen was especially difficult to dye, so was generally used in its natural or bleached state. Dyeing other fabrics often involved the addition of a mordant, a fixative derived from a mineral salt or metal that helped the colour develop and ensured its fastness, although some had the unwelcome side effect of corroding the fabric. One of the most important mordants in Britain was potassium alum (typically shortened to alum), and a significant alum industry flourished along the Yorkshire coast, with human urine contributed by the local population being a vital ingredient in the extraction process.

White was a popular colour for female clothing. In British portraits and conversation pieces of the 1730s and 1740s, women are often depicted in plain gowns of heavy white silk. William Denune's unidentified Scottish sitter provides an example of the style (Fig. 1.10), as does Sophia Popple (1704–78), seated on the far left in Hogarth's *The Popple and Ashley Families* (Fig. 1.11). Although perhaps representative of an artistic convention tending towards aesthetic simplicity, such a garment clearly indicated wealth due to the difficulty of maintaining its pristine appearance. White was favoured at important events for this reason, but not yet formalised as the colour worn by brides (see Chapter 8). The influence of neo-classicism on female dress during the last decades of the century encouraged the shift from silk towards pure white cotton, which came to dominate fashion and portraiture of the period.

Achieving a bright white colour involved bleaching, which was more effective on linen and cotton than on wool and silk. Haarlem, in the Netherlands, had become the centre of the bleaching industry in the seventeenth century and retained this reputation in the eighteenth,

the guidance of the Prince Regent after the Battle of Waterloo.[34] Perhaps painted to record his appointment as Colonel-Commandant of the 10th Light Dragoons, one miniature shows the prince wearing the eye-catching bearskin hat of the regiment, with a band of leopard skin around the base and plumes of white and red ostrich feathers (see Fig. 2.9). During the 1760s the influence of fur developed into a fashion for silks woven with patterns imitating animal print.[35]

although the French town of Cholet was also famous for the brilliant white of its textiles. The bleaching process took several months and required sunlight, so was seasonally limited. However, the discovery of chlorine in 1774, and the invention of a chemical bleaching process in 1785, revolutionised the bleaching industry – for both fabric and paper. In addition, imported cottons, which saw a dramatic increase during the same period, were whiter than wool in its untreated form, sheep in eighteenth-century Britain being naturally grey, brown or black rather than the white of today.[36] Household linens could also be whitened or 'bucked' as part of the regular laundry process, using lye (a strong alkali derived from wood ash) and sunlight.[37]

Dark sombre colours for male dress were popular in Britain from the 1730s, reflecting the tastes of an increasingly influential middle class, as well as a preference for practical country clothing by the gentry. The discovery in the seventeenth century of a method to increase the

colour fastness of the intense black derived from logwood, a tropical tree imported from Central America, provided an alternative to the previous laborious and expensive process of overdyeing multiple colours to achieve black. Logwood remained the quintessential black dye in the Georgian period, although the invention of a new black dye in the 1750s by the hosiery entrepreneur William Elliott (1707–92) provided a domestic source for the Midlands stocking industry – the recipe may have included tannins from oak trees in the nearby Sherwood Forest. While important throughout the century – notably during times of mourning – black became a fashionable colour towards the end of the eighteenth century for men, with Lord Byron (1788–1824) and George 'Beau' Brummell (1778–1840) helping to cement its popularity.

In the late seventeenth century, imported indigo (extracted from the *Indigofera* genus of plants) had replaced the domestic woad (*Isatis tinctoria*) as the most-used blue dyestuff in Britain. Notable for its intensity of colour and

LEFT
Fig. 1.12 Allan Ramsay (1713–84), *Princess Elizabeth Albertina, Duchess of Mecklenburg-Strelitz, c.*1769.
Oil on canvas, 127.7 × 101.7 cm. RCIN 403553

BELOW
Fig. 1.13 Daniel Woge (1717–97), *Princess Elizabeth Albertina, Duchess of Mecklenburg-Strelitz, c.*1750.
Oil on canvas, 80.0 × 63.5 cm. RCIN 402454

OPPOSITE
Fig. 1.14 Johan Joseph Zoffany (1733–1810), *Queen Charlotte*, 1771.
Oil on canvas, 162.9 × 137.2 cm. RCIN 405071

lightfastness, the popularity of indigo continued to rise during the eighteenth century and indigo harvested from plantations in India, North America and the Caribbean became the most important crop traded by the East India Company. Indigo dyeing was done in large vats and although the process, which involved the use of stale urine, was complicated, messy and pungent, it created a dark and fast blue. Up to ten times stronger than woad, indigo was even effective on linen.[38] The rise of indigo as a highly profitable export crop had a sinister side: it was a key driver in the institution of slavery, it was open to abusive labour practices and it reduced the availability of fertile ground to provide sufficient food for local populations. Prussian blue – first developed as an artist's pigment in Berlin in 1704 but utilised as a dye from the middle of the eighteenth century – was an

alternative to indigo, and enabled dyers to produce a much broader range of blues in the lighter end of the spectrum.[39]

By 1765 there were 24 commercially identifiable shades of blue,[40] and portraiture certainly indicates that pale blue was a popular choice for gowns, despite the fact that in his *Discourses* of 1778 Sir Joshua Reynolds referenced the established opinion that artists should avoid including large areas of blue, grey or green in a painting, in favour of warmer tones.[41] In around 1769 Queen Charlotte commissioned a posthumous portrait of her mother, Princess Elizabeth Albertina, from Allan Ramsay (Fig. 1.12). The artist apparently based the facial features on an earlier portrait by Daniel Woge (Fig. 1.13) and also copied exactly the sparkling diamond jewel pinned to the hair. The plain black scarf knotted under the chin,

however, has been transformed into a more delicate lace version, and although the open robe is comparable in both pictures, Ramsay – possibly in discussion with Queen Charlotte – has updated the stomacher to the newly fashionable buttoned style. The queen herself was painted in a remarkably similar (perhaps even the same?) dress by Johan Joseph Zoffany two years later (Fig. 1.14), while her sister-in-law, Princess Friederike of Hesse-Darmstadt, also chose to wear a blue gown in her portrait by Johann Georg Ziesenis of 1770.[42] Blue remained a popular colour throughout the Regency. One fashionable shade was named 'Clarence Blue' after Princess Adelaide who arrived in England in 1818 from Saxe-Meiningen to marry the Duke of Clarence (the future William IV), bringing with her a number of newsworthy fashions.[43] The duchess wears a velvet dress of her signature sapphire blue shade in the miniature by Mary Green (see Fig. 1.9) and the colour was frequently referenced in fashion periodicals of the 1820s.

The very brightest scarlet fabrics of the quality worn by Queen Marie Leczinska (see Fig. 1.8) were dyed with cochineal, a dyestuff derived from a scale insect (*Dactylopius coccus*) that lives on the prickly pear cactus and which had been imported to Europe from Mexico and Peru by the Spanish since the sixteenth century. Related dyes originating from different scale insects included lac in India and kermes in Europe. By the end of the eighteenth century cochineal had been successfully introduced in India, where it was cultivated as Madras cochineal and exported to England by the East India Company.[44] The plant root madder (*Rubia tinctorum*) was a cheaper alternative and could produce a range of colours depending on which mordant was used: orange, purple, black and brown, as well as a duller red than cochineal. Despite attempts to cultivate a domestic madder industry, the British climate was not favourable, and most was imported from the Netherlands and France. A method that used madder to achieve a bright and colourfast red suitable for dyeing cottons (so-called 'Turkey red') was introduced to France in the first half of the eighteenth century and was used in Britain by the 1780s, although the process was complicated, lengthy and noxious.[45] Such techniques, long used in the Levant

(eastern Mediterranean; see Chapter 9) and India to produce patterned cottons, became important in the textile centres of Manchester and Glasgow by the early nineteenth century.

Closely linked to red is the colour pink, which comes in a range of shades from the palest pastel to dusky rose but in the English language first appeared as a colour adjective only in 1733. Before that, the word was used to describe either the *dianthus* flower or decorative perforations in fabric. Pink is associated with the rococo period, when it was often combined with white as in Pietro Longhi's *Blind-Man's Buff* (Fig. 1.15). While portraits and surviving garments clearly demonstrate that pink was widely worn by men and boys, in women, pink was associated with fertility and deemed most appropriate from adolescence to the onset of middle age – then considered around 30. In Benjamin West's double portrait (Fig. 1.16, overleaf), Queen Charlotte, aged 32, still wears a dusky pink gown with white accessories, while the Princess Royal (aged 10) adopts a much brighter carnation shade, also echoed in the rosy glow of her cheeks; pink clothing was considered especially flattering to the complexion. During the 1770s and 1780s pink was a popular colour for wedding dresses,[46] and Princess Mary's trousseau from her marriage in 1740 included a gown of silver tissue and pink satin.[47] Madame de Pompadour was an enthusiast of pink, helping to popularise it across the decorative arts, notably the 'rose Pompadour' ground colour on porcelain introduced by Sèvres in 1758.

Gowns in a distinctive 'egg yolk' shade of yellow are regularly seen in museum collections (Fig. 1.17), and this is the colour chosen by Eva-Maria Veigel in Hogarth's double portrait (Fig. 1.18). The popularity of this shade around the middle of the century was perhaps influenced by the vogue for chinoiserie, the colour being revered in China where it was directly associated with the emperor. It was probably also appreciated for its similarity to gold, achieved without the expense of precious metal threads. A variety of plant species yield yellow dyestuffs: the Chinese foxglove (*Rehmannia glutinosa*) was reserved for imperial yellow, while in eighteenth-century Europe imported quercitron

Fig. 1.15 Pietro Longhi (*c*.1701–85), *Blind-Man's Buff*, 1744.
Oil on panel, 48.7 × 60.5 cm. RCIN 403030

Fig. 1.16  Benjamin West (1738–1820), *Queen Charlotte with Charlotte, Princess Royal*, 1776 (detail).
Oil on canvas, 168.2 × 205.7 cm. RCIN 404573

(from the bark of the American black oak tree, *Quercus velutina*) and turmeric (*Curcuma longa*) from India and south-east Asia were more frequently used. All these yellow dyes derived from plants were fugitive, fading on exposure to light, and where yellow has been overdyed with blue to produce green, the colour has often reverted to blue over time if the textile has not been protected from light.

With a proliferation of colours came more specific names to describe them. While these were increasingly linked to recognisable daily objects (*suie brûlée*, or burnt soot, being one evocative example), some were cryptic, with 'stifled sigh' and 'indiscreet complaints' two of the more obscure.[48] One of the most famous colours was popularised by Marie-Antoinette in 1775, and supposedly inspired by her husband, Louis XVI, who found her trying on a dress in a peculiar brown colour he likened to that of a flea: *couleur de puce*. That season variations of the shade included *tête de puce* (flea's head), *ventre de puce* (flea's belly) and *cuisse de puce* (flea's thigh). A fashionable Englishman represented in the *Cabinet des modes* demonstrates that the colour was still popular in the 1780s as his autumnal attire is described as cloth of puce (Fig. 1.19).[49]

## TECHNIQUE AND PATTERN

The appearance of a fabric depended just as much on the techniques employed in its production as the raw materials from which it was made. Fibres could be woven and combined in various ways. At a basic level the weaving process involved fixing warp threads into position and running weft threads back and forth across them. Silk threads in a plain weave pattern (over one warp thread and under the next) resulted in a stiff fabric (medium-weight silks woven in this way were called taffeta, probably derived from the Persian *tāftan*, 'to shine') that looked and felt quite different to a smooth silk satin, where weft threads crossed numerous warps at a time. In a brocaded fabric, additional coloured weft threads produced a pattern floating above the colour of the ground. Pattern effects in a damask (named after the city of Damascus) were created by varying weaving techniques, rather than including different coloured threads. This made damask fabrics reversible, and sometimes garments were turned to get more wear from the expensive material.[50] In velvets, additional weft threads were raised above the surface of the fabric into loops, which could then be cut or left uncut. Fabrics could be woven entirely from one material or combined: the widely used fustian was usually constructed from linen warp threads and cotton wefts.

Setting up the loom for a complex figured silk could take six weeks, with the actual weaving of enough silk for a dress (14 yards; 12.8 m) a week or longer.[51] The narrow width of woven silks was limited by the number of warp threads that could be accommodated: they usually ranged between 49 and 59 cm, or half an ell in Europe, with Chinese-woven silks up to 20 cm wider.[52] The flying shuttle, patented in 1733 by John Kay, greatly increased the speed of the weaving process and the width of fabric that could be woven, although the production of patterned fabrics remained extremely labour intensive until mechanisation brought about by the jacquard loom in the early nineteenth century, which used punched cards to automate the process. Throughout the eighteenth century Lyons retained its reputation as the city producing the finest quality and

widest range of silk fabrics in Europe, rivalled only by the industry centred around Spitalfields in London, originally set up by Huguenot exiles.[53] A portrait of Fredericka, Duchess of Saxe-Weissenfels, shows her wearing a dress probably made of French silk (Fig. 1.20), and alongside is a silk of similar design and date, with large pink flowers and leaves in shades of green against a well-preserved textured silver ground that includes the rare honeycomb and chevron patterns (Fig. 1.21).

Whereas the overall cut of clothing changed slowly during the eighteenth century, silk designs were innovative, with new patterns coming out from year to year and according to the season. While it was efficient for weavers to reuse existing compositions in new combinations and colourways, customers (and the mercers supplying them with fabric) expected innovation and exclusivity, and sometimes silks were woven to order for a particular customer and event. One important innovation in the 1730s, attributed to the Lyonnais designer Jean Revel (1684–1751), was *points rentrés*, which enabled more subtle shading effects by interlocking shades rather than having them meet with a sharp line, resulting in naturalistic and three-dimensional botanical motifs. This technique was adopted by Spitalfields weavers, with the distinction that patterned English silks of this date tended towards white backgrounds rather than the coloured grounds popular in France.

The popularity of imported printed textiles by the late seventeenth century prompted the development of a sizeable domestic printing industry in Britain. Printed fabrics were most frequently cottons, linens or cotton/linen mixtures. Patterns could imitate woven silk designs more cheaply, although silk itself could also be printed and hand-painted. European textile manufacturers do not appear to have mastered the complicated and labour-intensive processes developed in India and practised there since at least the thirteenth century, by which textiles were printed or painted by hand with a variety of different mordants and wax resists in successive stages. Instead, Europeans focused on the process of direct printing. Initially, wood blocks were used to transfer a mordant to

the fabric. In a polychrome design these needed to be carefully matched to ensure alignment of the colours. The fabrics produced by this 'direct impression' method in Europe were known as 'indiennes' in imitation of those made in India.

A new printing technique using engraved copper plates and a viscous dye was developed in Dublin around 1752 by Francis Nixon, and from there the technique was brought to England. Copperplate printed fabrics were usually monochromatic (black, red, sepia, purple or blue printed on white) due to the difficulties in aligning the plates exactly, but could result in an extraordinary level of detail. The fine pictorial and narrative designs included motifs and vignettes taken from a range of sources, such as mythology, the opera and contemporary political events (see Fig. 12.8). In so doing, European manufacturers

were able to capitalise on an existing and well-established paper-printing industry. Output was increased dramatically by the invention of cylinder printing in 1783, which was quickly adopted throughout Britain.

The most famous factory producing printed cottons was founded by Christophe-Philippe Oberkampf (1738–1815) at Jouy-en-Josas between Paris and Versailles in 1760, only one year after the ban on printed textiles imposed to protect the valuable silk industry in France had been lifted. Oberkampf refined the processes of woodblock printing – and later roller printing – to produce some of the most sophisticated printed cottons. The fabrics, which became known as toiles de Jouy, were used as both furnishings and dress fabrics, with idealised pastoral scenes especially popular. In 1783 Louis XVI awarded the company the status of 'Manufacture Royale' and it attracted

Fig. 1.22  Paul Sandby (1731–1809), *Encampment in St James's Park*, 1780 (detail).
Pen, watercolour and bodycolour, 26.9 × 47.5 cm. RCIN 451584

Fig. 1.23  English, Block-printed gown and petticoat, *c*.1780s.
Cotton and linen. London, Victoria and Albert Museum, T.274&A–1967

an affluent, courtly clientele – the drying fields were visible from carriages en route to Versailles.[55] Oberkampf also targeted the middle-class market with cheaper products, and cultivated a significant export market, particularly in colonial America during and after the Revolutionary War (1775–83).

Sandby's *Encampment in St James's Park* (Fig. 1.22) dates from the summer of 1780, when troops were stationed in the royal parks during the Gordon riots.[56] Despite their military intention, these encampments soon became popular venues for leisurely promenades and social interaction.

Among the elegant observers is a well-dressed woman wearing a printed cotton gown, similar to surviving examples (Fig. 1.23). The repeating pattern of small floral sprays on a white cotton ground is common to both, although in Sandby's drawing the gown is worn looped up over a plain white petticoat, with green ties across the bodice, whereas the extant garment has a matching petticoat. This would have been the perfect style of dress for a summer's day, although probably too informal for an evening event. Printed cottons worn as dress fabrics are rarely depicted in visual sources of the period, and

Fig. 1.24 Joseph Grozer (1753/5–98) after Sir Joshua Reynolds (1723–92), *Morning Amusement*, 1796.
Mezzotint, 49.3 × 61.4 cm (sheet). RCIN 641447

almost never in formal portraits. Where they do appear, they are most frequently shown being worn by working women – as in *Mrs Grosvenor, Landry [sic] Woman to the Queen* (see Fig. 1.30) – but in fact they were popular at all levels of society.

## LACE

Excluding jewellery, the most expensive element in an outfit was often lace, which was usually made from linen thread. The early years of the eighteenth century saw a shift away from the ornate Venetian lace accessories that had become fashionable under Charles II to simpler styles of transparent linen or muslin. A revived taste for lace coincided with the first years of the Hanoverian reign around 1715 and its popularity reached an apogee in Britain and France in the middle of the century. Both bobbin lace and needle lace continued to be produced as in the seventeenth century, although needle lace, being slightly thicker and weightier, was more frequently paired with winter attire or ceremonial dress, in contrast to the lighter, softly draping bobbin laces more akin to the transparent muslins worn during the summer season. Bobbin lace was also known as pillow or bone lace and this is what we see in *Morning Amusement* (Fig. 1.24). One young woman reads to her companions as each works on her piece of lace, using linen thread wrapped onto bobbins of bone or wood, and pins, to hold the stitches in place, set into a round cushion stuffed with straw.

Flemish lace was rightly famous in the eighteenth century, with important centres in Mechlin (now Mechelen near Antwerp) and Brussels. Mechlin bobbin lace was popular with members of the royal family: in the year of his accession George I ordered 3½ yards (3.2 m) of fine Mechlin lace for a cravat worn at his coronation, at a total cost of £19 5s (the equivalent of nearly £3,000 in 2021).[57] This is perhaps the cravat in Sir Godfrey Kneller's state portrait (Fig. 1.25), although the artist has not depicted the motifs with the strong raised outlines that are a characteristic feature of Mechlin bobbin lace. The cravat is worn on top of the Robes of State and simply knotted to

show off the expensive lace to best effect.[58] Valenciennes was another key centre for bobbin lace. Although technically part of France, its lace remained Flemish in style. Characterised by exceptionally fine linen threads, a flat surface with no raised outlines and dense patterns (some requiring the management of up to 800 bobbins at once), Valenciennes lace was exceptionally time-consuming to make. One full-time lacemaker working from 5am to 8pm might produce approximately half a metre per year.[59] Sets of lace made 'by the same hand' were most highly prized due to their uniformity. An example of a lappet of Valenciennes bobbin lace is in the Bowes Museum (Fig. 1.26 and see Fig. 6.34).

Needle lace was made with a needle and thread instead of multiple bobbins. By the early eighteenth century the regions of Alençon and Argentan in Normandy dominated the needle lace industry. Queen Marie Leczinska wears a complete set of French needle lace in her portrait (Fig. 1.27). Consisting of a matching cap, scarf and sleeve ruffles, the clear ground, variety of motifs and well-defined outlines to the design (*cordonnet*) are characteristic of this type of lace. A surviving sleeve ruffle (Fig. 1.28), dating from slightly later, demonstrates many of these enduring design features, including the very fine hexagonal ground, which is portrayed in a much coarser diaper pattern in the queen's portrait – presumably this was easier and quicker to paint.[60] Madame de Pompadour also wears a set of French needle

Fig. 1.29  Johan Joseph Zoffany (1733–1810), *Queen Charlotte with her Two Eldest Sons*, 1764.
Oil on canvas, 112.2 × 128.3 cm. RCIN 400146

lace in her portrait by François-Hubert Drouais (1763–4; NG 6440), of which there is a smaller copy in the Royal Collection (see Fig. 9.17).[61] Consisting of a matching cap, dress robings, sleeve ruffles and tucker, the lace can perhaps be associated with the '*garniture d'une robe de chambre … le tout de point d'Argentan*' [set of trimmings for a house gown … all in Argentan lace] in Pompadour's probate inventory, which was valued at 3,000 livres, one of the most expensive items listed.[62]

Both needle lace and bobbin lace imitated each other throughout the period, and varieties of lace can be even more difficult to distinguish in paintings than in person. In Zoffany's portrait of 1764 (Fig. 1.29), Queen Charlotte is seen at her dressing table, which is draped with a toilette service of fine lace. In 1762 the queen had been supplied with a suit of superfine Flanders point lace 'to Cover a Toilet Table Compleat' by Priscilla MacEune, the royal milliner and lace woman, at a cost of £1,079 14s – the equivalent of more than £171,000 in 2021.[63] While it has been suggested that this is the lace depicted in the portrait (and it would make sense to record such a significant purchase), the lace for both the toilette and dress accessories appears more like French needle lace than Flemish bobbin lace.[64] By this date luxury goods from France would have been available for purchase again, normal trading having resumed after the end of the Seven Years' War in 1763.

A domestic bobbin lace industry also developed in England during the eighteenth century, particularly in the Buckinghamshire town of Newport Pagnell and in Honiton in Devon.[65] Less expensive than that produced in France and Flanders, it catered to the lower end of the market in Britain and North America, although attempts were instigated to encourage royal patronage. In 1761 George III was given a pair of lace ruffles made in Buckinghamshire, while Queen Charlotte was presented with a lace dress produced in Lyme Regis.[66] For the wedding of Princess Augusta (sister of George III) in 1764, all lace and silks were required to be of English manufacture, by order of the king. Portraiture, however, indicates that Queen Charlotte clearly bought French needle lace, even when it was prohibited.[67]

Although traditionally made from linen thread, lace could also be made from silk, in which case it was known as blonde, even when dyed black. Chantilly in France was well known for its high-quality blonde lace. This type of lace was popular from the 1760s and in portraiture it usually has a distinctive shine. A popular alternative to lace was whitework, which combined meticulously counted threads with delicate white thread embroidery to produce beautiful designs on semi-transparent fabrics. Easily confused with lace in portraiture, expensive whitework accessories were worn by the elite on formal occasions, while simpler examples could be made by the amateur at home. Originally developed in Saxony, this style of embroidery was commonly known as Dresden whitework in England. In a portrait by Ramsay (see Fig. 5.6), the two-year-old Prince William wears a whiteworked apron decorated with sinuous trailing stems, possibly trimmed at the hem with scalloped lace. While still decorative, whitework was a more practical alternative to lace for larger, functional children's garments of this kind.

## GUILDS

Across Europe craftspeople had traditionally been organised into a complex system of trade guilds, which protected the interests of their members by regulating the quality and price of goods, limiting the overlap of spheres of production and setting working hours and pay rates. Many of the most powerful guilds in London formed a significant part of the textile industry. For example, the Merchant Taylors represented tailors, the Clothworkers were involved in the finishing of woollen cloth, while the Weavers represented the silk-weaving trade. Others were linked to particular specialties, such as the Worshipful Company of Spectacle Makers, to which John Cuff was appointed Master in 1748 (see Fig. 7.7). The amalgamation or separation of companies over time gives an indication of the changing landscape of trades. The Company of Barber-Surgeons, which had merged in 1540, split into separate guilds in 1745, driven by the increasing professionalisation of medicine and the rising importance of hairstyling and wig-making. Access to guilds was either through patrimony (following the

Fig. 1.30 Anonymous, *Mrs Grosvenor, Landry [sic] Woman to the Queen*, c.1765
Mezzotint, 36.2 × 26.3 cm (sheet). RCIN 655552

father's trade), servitude (an apprenticeship lasting seven years) or payment of a fee. Those who had completed an apprenticeship became Freemen and could find work as independent journeymen if they had not set up their own business, or as master craftsmen if they were responsible for training apprentices themselves.

Women had traditionally been excluded from the medieval guild system, and many of the clothing trades predominantly employing women (for example, as seamstresses and milliners) did not have formal guilds in place. However, by the eighteenth century a number of women were serving in the Merchant Taylors Company in London, as both apprentices and freewomen, and widows of guild members often continued to run their husbands' businesses.[68] Guilds became less influential in England over time, with people increasingly working outside the confines of the city limits to avoid guild regulations, or in newly industrial towns without established guild systems. Elsewhere in Europe guilds remained important for longer, with many operating until the early nineteenth century.

## CLEANING

Cleanliness in dress had long been considered an indicator of underlying moral character, demonstrating good manners and respect for self and others: 'can any degree of finery compensate the want of cleanliness?' queried the preacher and poet James Fordyce in 1766.[69] Keeping clothing clean was a challenge, however. Although the conditions of the roads had improved since the previous century, walking through streets strewn with human waste, animal manure and rotting food was unavoidable for most people. Sparkling white linens were important, with one French guide from 1740 recommending that 'if your clothes are clean, and especially if your linen is white, there is no need to be richly dressed: you will feel your best, even in poverty.'[70]

Linen or cotton undergarments worn next to the skin could be washed regularly using hot water and harsh alkaline soaps, unlike the more expensive silk or wool outer layers, whose surfaces would be damaged by immersion in water. Instead, soiled woollen garments were cleaned by scourers who scrubbed them with teasels or used fuller's earth (a kind of clay) to re-full the material. The incorporation of additional decorative or reinforcing materials such as metal threads, pasteboard stiffening or whalebone also limited the washability of a garment.[71] These fabrics could instead be spot treated with cleaning agents like turpentine, lemon juice or urine. The *Dictionarium Domesticum* of 1736 offers solutions for a variety of laundry-related problems, including 'calcine sheep's trotters' reduced 'to a powder' to take a spot of oil out of satin.[72] While silk garments could sometimes be redyed to improve their longevity, this process could cause them to rot prematurely due to the chemicals involved. One of the key advantages of cotton was that it was washable and retained its bright colours.

In elite households the cleaning of linen was undertaken by a professional laundress or laundry maid. Queen Caroline's accounts reveal that in 1733 a Mrs Hetling was paid a quarterly allowance of £17 11s 'for washing Her Majesty's linen'.[73] A distinction was made between the heavy-duty 'wet laundering' located off-site, and delicate 'dry laundering' usually undertaken within the house by a personal body servant. The latter involved washing

Fig. 1.31  Anonymous, *Miss White, Clear Starcher to the Queen*, c.1765.
Mezzotint, 36.0 × 25.6 cm (sheet). New Haven, Yale Center for British Art,
B 1974.12.684

Fig. 1.32  William Henry Pyne (1769–1843), 'Welsh Peasants
Washing', from Pyne, *Costume of Great Britain*, London, 1808, pl. 9.
RCIN 1075693

with kerchiefs over their décolletage and quilted petticoats protected by bib-fronted aprons tucked into the waistband. These sanitised representations of the less arduous laundry tasks are in the style of paintings by Henry Robert Morland (1716–97) of around the same date, although his industrious maidservants ironing and soaping are nameless and more overtly coquettish.[75]

A similarly picturesque depiction of the cleaning process for the lower classes can be seen in 'Welsh Peasants Washing' from William Pyne's *Costume of Great Britain* (Fig. 1.32). The accompanying commentary describes how the clothes are first rinsed in a 'clear and rapid stream', before being beaten on a smooth flat stone then laid out to dry on rocks or grass. Scottish peasants were described as utilising a different process called 'bucking'. After soaking the clothes in a tub 'an active lass, with her clothes curiously tucked between her knees … treads the wash with her naked feet'.[76]

smaller, higher-value and more visible items such as caps and kerchiefs, as well as ironing and starching. Women apparently representing Queen Charlotte's laundry maids are identified in two mezzotints: *Mrs Grosvenor, Landry [sic] Woman to the Queen* (Fig. 1.30) and the aptly named *Miss White, Clear Starcher to the Queen* (Fig. 1.31). However, their names do not appear in official court documents in these capacities, with Deborah Chetwynd instead being listed as 'Laundress, Seamstress and Starcher' from 1761.[74] 'Mrs Grosvenor' is shown squeezing a bag of blue dye (usually smalt, a powder derived from blue glass, or indigo) into the wooden tub of water, a step during the final rinse that was designed to counteract the natural yellowing of linen over time and give the optical illusion of bright white. 'Miss White' shapes a piece of fabric, possibly a cap, in her hands. The item on the stand beside her has the appearance of lace, which was removed to be washed separately. Although stiffly pleated ruffs had long been out of fashion, the use of starch remained necessary to create a crisp and smooth surface. It also helped protect against stains and dirt. Both women are modestly – and spotlessly – dressed in fashionably flowered gowns (possibly printed cottons)

## THE MARKET FOR FASHION

Although dress remained an important indication of social status during the eighteenth century, the traditional codified fashion hierarchy determined only by wealth and position had become less explicit and more nuanced. In previous centuries it had been the monarch and their consort, together with the aristocratic elite making up the court, who had set and propagated fashions, which were imitated by the lower ranks. However, in Britain in the eighteenth century the most influential tastemakers were increasingly those lower down the social scale (actresses, soldiers, courtesans), while the court became associated with traditional styles of dress rather than cutting-edge fashion. Alongside this, a growing professional class, who had made their money in trade or the burgeoning financial industry in the City of London, was able to afford many of the same items of dress as those from the established elite, blurring the divisions between the classes. More women were earning wages themselves (particularly in the retail industry), raising average family incomes, with more money available to spend on luxuries such as dress, and creating a larger target audience for fashion.[77]

At the same time, important sources of inspiration for upper-class male and female wardrobes were the more informal and functional styles of dress worn by the masses, including the frock coat and trousers for men, and aprons and short jackets for women. From the later 1760s this was accompanied by a rise in anti-aristocratic literature and imagery (including caricature), representing the nobility at court as unworthy of imitation. The resulting confusion of conventional distinctions in class was a recurring motif in literature of the period, and visitors to England commented on their inability to distinguish one group from another: 'The rich man dresses frequently as if he had but a small income, and he, whose circumstances are very narrow, is desirous of being supposed to be in affluence.'[78] The Prince de Ligne remarked that 'Everyone, even the shoemaker, is dressed alike.'[79] Such blurring of class boundaries was a source of frustration for those who considered clothing a fundamental indicator of social status, resulting in complaints of deliberate deception and disruption of the natural order. Daniel Defoe lamented the lack of livery for female servants, recounting an occasion when 'being at a friend's house, and by him required to salute the ladies, I kissed the chamber-jade into the bargain, for she was as well dressed as the best'.[80]

This realignment of influence away from the traditional nobility towards the middle classes was accompanied by a more subtle code of behaviour, prizing taste in dress and manners above flagrant ostentation. It became important to understand the appropriate level of display for each social setting or occasion. The first etiquette guides, such as *Rules to be observ'd at Bath* written by Beau Nash, Master of Ceremonies for the city, explicitly laid out the guidelines of deportment for polite society and helped the nouveaux riches understand (and avoid breaking) what had previously been implicit and unwritten codes of behaviour, ingrained from birth.[81]

This period also saw the rise of the named tastemaker or fashion adviser: of the actress Frances Abington (1737–1815) it was written 'There never is a marriage or ball in which she is not consulted'.[82] This was quite an achievement for Frances 'Fanny' Barton, born in the slums around Covent Garden, who had started life as a flower seller before being taken on as a servant to a French milliner, from whom she presumably learnt the art of dress. In France the role of fashion stylist was recognised in the profession of the *marchande de modes*, for which a guild was formally established in 1776, separate from the seamstress or dressmaker who cut and sewed a gown together. Usually a young woman, whose own fashionable dress served as an advertisement of her good taste, the *marchande de modes* – misleadingly translated as milliner in England – was responsible for suggesting, sourcing and applying fashionable trimmings and accessories to her clients' attire. The most successful of such fashion stylists was Rose Bertin (1747–1813), who counted Queen Marie-Antoinette among her aristocratic clientele and whose witty, topical and exaggerated creations (particularly headdresses) brought both fame and notoriety.

Eighteenth-century Britain also saw the introduction of new commercial venues for fashionable display, which operated alongside the established (and increasingly archaic) royal court system. Regular attendance at the pleasure gardens, coffee houses, assembly rooms, theatre and opera formed an important component of the social and political arena: places to develop connections, cultivate political influence and demonstrate personal alliances. While such settings encouraged some degree of mingling between different social classes, and have been cited as being indicative of a more inclusive society overall, the elite often still maintained a deliberate physical and visual separation from the masses: by occupying supper boxes at the pleasure gardens for example, allowing them to remain spectators to the crowd rather than form part of it, thereby staying within a narrow social sphere.[83] The range of ticket prices available at the playhouses attracted a more diverse audience than at the opera, which was like a private club, with a seasonal subscription costing 20 guineas in 1780.

London shops were considered the best in Europe, one visitor writing in 1786 that 'It is almost impossible to express how well everything is organised in London. Every article is made more attractive to the eye than in Paris or any other town.'[84] In the seventeenth century fashion retailers had been centred around the Royal Exchange in the City of London and later Covent Garden and the Strand. The City continued to remain important to the fabric trade: Carr's was a silk mercer based at Ludgate Hill, which supplied the royal family, for example.[85] However, by the 1780s many had moved west to encompass the newly developed Oxford Street, which according to one guide had more fashion shops in a single street than anywhere else in Europe.[86] Many merchants stayed open until late in the evening and shopping became a popular leisure activity.

Very few people bought all their clothing brand new and made-to-measure. A thriving trade in second-hand clothing existed across the country. In London its epicentre was Rosemary Lane, as portrayed in Thomas Rowlandson's *Rag Fair* (Fig. 1.33). Situated just north of the Tower of London, it was later renamed Royal Mint Street. For around a century Rosemary Lane had housed a bustling market every day except Sunday, and Rowlandson himself knew the area and its occupants well, having lodged in the vicinity for a number of years. The drawing shows the huge variety of goods available, with gowns, breeches, shirts and coats hanging on flagpoles and beneath the awnings, while hats, stockings and shoes are laid out in the street and sacks overflow with linens. The population in this area of the East End was conspicuously varied, notably housing the majority of London's Jewish community, many of whom by this date (*c*.1800) were closely involved in the trade of second-hand clothing. The names above the shops ('Moses Monceco' and

Fig. 1.34 Jean-Baptiste Greuze (1725–1805), *'Silence!'*, 1759.
Oil on canvas, 62.2 × 50.5 cm. RCIN 405080

Fig. 1.35 Hieronymus van der Mij (1687–1761), *A Family Group*, 1728.
Oil on panel, 33.6 × 28.9 cm. RCIN 405055

'Widow Levy Dealer in Old Breeches') clearly reference this connection. Some of the dealers are represented with derogatory and anti-Semitic facial features intended to identify the Jewish population. Their long beards would also have been distinctive during a period when shaving was the norm. Several of the proprietors wear piles of hats and long coats, common conventions in eighteenth-century pictorial representations of Jewish merchants. Prices and quality were lower here than in the area around Covent Garden, and while the new shopping areas in the West End of London saw a shift towards fixed pricing, bartering would

have been expected in Rosemary Lane. It was also the place for unscrupulous robbers to turn booty into cash, and victims of theft to search for stolen goods. In addition to rag fairs, second-hand clothing could be acquired from tailors, many of whom accepted used clothing as part payment towards a new garment, and from itinerant traders, who offered easily transportable items of dress among their miscellaneous wares.

## NON-ELITE DRESS

Two paintings depicting family groups provide an opportunity to examine some of the features of clothing worn by the poorer members of society. In general, the less well-off wore the same types of garments as the wealthy and they were broadly similar in construction, the key differences being the material used and quantity of items owned.[87] In Jean-Baptiste Greuze's picture of a young mother with her three children (Fig. 1.34), the nursing infant is possibly around nine months old. He is dressed in a plain white short gown, here pulled up to reveal loose stockings and tiny leather shoes that might suggest he has started to walk. Slumped sleeping in a baby chair nearby is a slightly older boy, maybe around two, whose clothing is difficult to determine but seems to consist of a white shirt worn beneath a buff-coloured outer garment. The eldest boy, who is being reprimanded for playing a toy trumpet that might wake the sleeping children, is perhaps around four and has been breeched. He wears mismatching clothes – a brown coat, red waistcoat, blue breeches and white stockings – all without any surface decoration. The garments are patched and worn: with less money to spare for clothing, the poor often acquired it second-hand, and items would be worn for longer before being replaced. Moreover, they would have fewer changes of clothes, perhaps only an everyday outfit and a Sunday best. In Hieronymus van der Mij's *A Family Group* (Fig. 1.35), the quilted baby's cap with lace trim and green damask blanket set to one side are likely to have been precious possessions, while the inclusion of a pincushion suggests the mother has recently been mending.

The dark muted colours in both paintings are typical of non-elite dress. The fabrics were either left in their natural

unbleached greyish brown or coloured with cheaper dyes such as madder and woad. Each artist has incorporated striped and checked fabrics: these were inexpensive patterns to weave but provided an element of colour and interest, with the combination of blue and white most popular. Fabrics such as linsey-woolsey (a linen/wool mix) were favoured, being hard-wearing although of a coarser texture than finer linens and silks. As the century progressed, cotton became cheaper in price, making it available to a broader section of society. The paintings fall within an established convention for idealised images of the poor, with Van der Mij's *A Family Group* evoking traditional representations of the Holy Family, the older brother holding a dog like John the Baptist with the lamb. The personal linen (including each mother's cap) is spotlessly white, suggesting that, while poor, they are morally pure and beyond reproach.

Images of non-elite dress in the early nineteenth century can also be found in George Walker's *Costume of Yorkshire* (see Fig. 1.3) and William Pyne's *Costume of Great Britain* (see Fig. 1.32). Both books illustrate the activities involved in the production of clothing, and demonstrate dress worn by the industrial labouring poor. However, as sanitised depictions, intended to provide a generic and recognisable representation of working-class dress for an elite audience able to afford such expensive publications, we should be wary of considering them accurate records of social reportage.[88]

## THE FASHION PRESS

The publishing industry flourished in the eighteenth century, with the introduction of both daily newspapers and formal copyright law during the reign of Queen Anne (1702–14). By the 1770s a specialised fashion press had developed, with the publication of the first true illustrated fashion periodicals, initially in England and slightly later in France. Many included fashion plates alongside society notes, reviews and news. Published monthly by subscription and lasting only eight years (1794–1802), Nicolaus Heideloff's *Gallery of Fashion* was not the first, but was the finest and most famous of those produced in Britain. Each instalment

contained large-scale, competently etched and hand-coloured plates, highlighted with metallic pigments, a technique drawing on Heideloff's background as a miniaturist (see Fig. 3.26). The publisher claimed to select for representation 'only the latest designs of those dresses in which ladies of fashion appear at the routs, the opera, the play-houses and the concert rooms; as well as those elegant morning dresses for Hyde Park and Kensington Gardens'.[89] Rudolph Ackermann's *Repository of Arts* was slightly later and was innovative in that it included fabric swatches from British manufacturers alongside the designs. In France *La Galerie des Modes et Costumes Français*, published from 1778 to 1787, featured over 400 beautiful illustrations of fashions by talented artists, which were described as accurate representations of fashions of the day rather than speculative designs. The influential fashion magazine *Cabinet des modes* (see Figs 1.19, 3.12, 3.20, 3.27, 8.32 and 9.8) was a more affordable, frequent and compact alternative, although it ceased production during the Terror in 1793. The accompanying text describes both fabrics and colours and is useful in establishing the contemporary terms for different garments.

The proliferation of such magazines drove consumer demand for novelty, while also disseminating the most up-to-the-minute trends more widely. In so doing they provided an alternative to fashion dolls dressed in the latest styles (known as Pandoras, 'babies' or *poupées de mode*), which had been despatched regularly from France to the various courts of Europe. Soon after George II's accession in 1727, Lady Lansdowne sent a fashion doll from Paris, 'dressed by the person that dresses all the princesses', to Henrietta Howard, requesting that she show it to Queen Caroline and then pass it on to the milliner, Mrs Tempest.[90] On court occasions, newspapers recorded in detail the clothing worn by the royal family and aristocracy, helping spread novelties in dress and gossip. Reports about what was worn were sometimes conflicting, however, and evidently based on hearsay rather than direct observation.

During the last quarter of the century a wave of Anglomania in fashion swept through Europe, which saw the *Cabinet des modes* announce in the November 1786

edition that it was being renamed *Magasin des modes nouvelles, françaises et anglaises*. The *robe à l'anglaise* became the most popular style of dress for women in the 1780s (in England it had previously been known simply as a nightgown or tight-bodied gown), and French women also adopted English riding coats, calling them 'redingotes' (see Fig. 3.30). French men, too, adopted their own version of the English frock coat, which had been inspired by non-elite working dress, although the French version was more decorative than that worn in England and was known as a *frac*.

## THE SPREAD OF FASHION

The eighteenth century might be considered the first great age of foreign travel, with far greater numbers of people venturing beyond Britain than had ever done so before. Many of those travelling were elite young men, a Grand Tour being regarded as a formative component of their education. A Grand Tourist would be expected to expand their network of acquaintances and broaden their horizons by learning about other cultures and languages. While Italy remained the primary destination, it became increasingly common for these travellers to extend their journeys into the Near East where they would have had a chance to see styles of clothing quite different from those that were broadly consistent across much of western Europe.

Diplomatic visits by ambassadors were another important means by which an understanding of differences in clothing was transmitted across borders, and by which the fashions of one country will have influenced those worn in another. Over the course of the long eighteenth century a number of foreign ambassadors were welcomed to London, where they met with members of the royal family. One of the most celebrated was Mirza Abu'l Hassan Khan, envoy extraordinary to the Shah of Persia, whose first visit in 1809–10 was an occasion of great interest. During his stay he was commemorated in poetry and painted by several artists, most notably Sir Thomas Lawrence after whose portrait a print was made (Fig. 1.36). 'Indisposition' prevented the Persian ambassador from attending the

Birthday Ball for Queen Charlotte, although the queen's outfit had been designed especially in his honour, consisting of 'a rich dark-green velvet petticoat, superbly embroidered in gold sprigs', the train 'of a beautiful green and gold velvet tissue … agreeably to the costume of Persia … it was meant as complimentary to the Representative of the Persian Court'.[91]

One of the primary purposes of such visits was to strengthen trade between nations and generate interest in foreign goods for import. As a result, ambassadors brought gifts of the highest quality to demonstrate the riches available. Mirza Abu'l Hassan Khan, for example, presented Queen Charlotte with 'three boxes of jewels, several choice shawls and a curious carpet' from the Shah of Persia.[92] In 1795 the Ottoman ambassador had presented numerous gifts from the sultan, including a pair of gold pistols and a gold dagger with a belt set with pearls and diamonds for George III, and for the queen and the princesses, 'a chest of silks, embroidered with gold; a plume of feathers for the head-dress, supported with a band of solid gold, and the top of the feathers ornamented with diamonds'.[93]

# 2

# Royal Fashion

*Last Tuesday was the Queen's Birthday. A great deal of fussing*
*& dressing you know of Old is required on such days,*
*and a good deal of fatigue from Morning to Night …*
*We had a most splendid Drawing Room with*
*Magnificent Cloaths and a Dull Ball in the evening.*

PRINCESS AUGUSTA TO HER BROTHER AUGUSTUS, 22 JANUARY 1791[1]

———

T his chapter provides an introduction to the key members of the British royal family during the Georgian period, and highlights how royal attitudes to fashion differed between generations. The focus is not on the ceremonial clothing of monarchy, which is discussed in Chapter 8.

George I was not known for glamour. Arriving from Hanover in 1714 at the age of 54, without his estranged wife Dorothea of Celle, who remained imprisoned at Ahlden House, in Lower Saxony, the first Georgian king of Great Britain and Ireland favoured simplicity and practicality in dress over ostentatious splendour, and disliked the ritualised formality of court etiquette and protocol. Although most frequently portrayed in ceremonial robes or armour (a reference to his successful military career), a portrait by Georg Wilhelm Lafontaine, the king's court painter (Fig. 2.2, overleaf), is unusual in showing the monarch in what was probably his typical everyday dress, albeit here with the symbols of kingship displayed rather incongruously alongside. Likely to have been painted from life around 1725, the king wears a plain wool coat with huge boot-sleeve cuffs and a matching waistcoat, unadorned but for gold buttons and gold braided buttonholes. By wearing such a style, the king would have been in keeping with the overall

mood of the nation: one foreign visitor remarked in the 1720s that the English 'generally go plain but in the best cloths and stuffs'.[2] The knotted lock of hair on the sitter's right shoulder identifies this as a campaign wig, a ceremonial style favoured by soldiers, which by this date was rather old-fashioned. The coat is worn in the up-to-the-minute manner, however, with only two buttons fastened, and the king adopts the 'hand-in-waistcoat' pose that became a common feature of English eighteenth-century portraiture, a gesture linked to ancient notions of modesty in rhetorical speech.[3] His plain black hat has been removed with his right hand, as dictated by etiquette,[4] and he wears an expensive lace cravat, slightly different to that worn in his coronation portrait (see Fig. 1.25). He honours his role as Sovereign of the Garter by wearing a Lesser George badge edged with large diamonds on the blue silk riband, almost tucked out of sight. Notably private by nature, and never comfortable with the English language, George I relied heavily on his loyal Turkish servants, Mehemet von Königstreu (see Fig. 8.2) and Mustapha de Mistra, to serve as *valets de chambre*. Among his numerous duties, Mehemet was responsible for managing the king's personal accounts, which involved ordering his wigs, clothing and other accessories.

Unlike his father, with whom he had a strained relationship, George II aimed to be 'always richly dressed, being fond of fine clothes'.[5] Until the death of George I in 1727, the heir lived with his wife, Princess Caroline of Ansbach, at Leicester House in London and, in the summer, at Richmond Lodge, presiding over a rival, more lively court and being seen regularly in public. Hard-working and conscientious as king, George II did not like sitting for portraits, and most of his likenesses derive either from an early portrait by Sir Godfrey Kneller or a late one by John Shackleton.[6] In both he wears traditional Robes of State of powdered ermine, red silk velvet and gold braid. A portrait by Robert Edge Pine from 1759 (there is a reduced copy in the Royal Collection, Fig. 2.3) gives a better indication of the type of dress George II would have worn in his later years. The artist described how he circumvented the king's natural reluctance for having his portrait painted by taking the likeness 'unseen by the King, as he was speaking to one of his attendants at the top of the great Staircase at Kensington Palace'.[7] By this date the king's attire is still rich but notably unfashionable. As an older man of 76, he has clearly retained the styles from his youth. Stockings pulled up to cover the breeches had gone out of fashion in the 1730s, while most men had stopped wearing campaign wigs by the middle of the century. Behind his back, courtiers called the king 'Old Square-toes' in reference to his old-fashioned footwear, most having adopted a rounder toe and lower heel.[8] George II was attached to court protocol and etiquette and took a particular interest in insignia and uniform. He always wore the Garter star, sash and garter, and was also responsible for introducing uniforms into the British army and navy (see Chapter 11).

Queen Caroline, George II's consort, was clever, lively and attractive. After being orphaned at a young age, she had grown up within the enlightened Prussian court where she received a comprehensive education. After arriving in Britain she presided over a progressive court herself, taking an active role in political life and cultivating wide-ranging intellectual interests, while carefully crafting a royal role that promoted a benevolent monarchy within the confines of its recently established constitutional boundaries.

While Queen Caroline placed great importance on being well dressed, she was not considered flamboyant, tending to favour sombre colours for her gowns, although she did occasionally order more expensive flowered and striped silks.[9] The majority of her portraits, both as princess and queen, depict her in official Robes of State, trimmed with ermine and adorned with pearls, although in Kneller's painting of 1716 (Fig. 2.4) the red velvet robes are worn over a beautiful woven silk petticoat, with a fashionable pattern in the late bizarre style, and reminiscent of those by the Spitalfields-based designer James Leman (1688–1745) at around the same date (Fig. 2.5). The queen's clothing accounts reveal regular orders for new clothes, but she was prudent in her spending throughout her life. For gowns she favoured the more traditional English mantua over the French sacque, and frequent deliveries of new shoes were

Fig. 2.4 Sir Godfrey Kneller (1646–1723), *Queen Caroline of Ansbach, when Princess of Wales*, 1716.

Oil on canvas, 240.0 × 141.6 cm. RCIN 405313

Fig. 2.5  James Leman (1688–1745), Silk design, 1711.
Pencil, pen and ink, watercolour and bodycolour on laid paper.
London, Victoria and Albert Museum, E.1861:38–1991

This silk design by the master weaver James Leman is similar in both colour and pattern to the silk used for Queen Caroline's petticoat (opposite), and is characteristic of the second decade of the eighteenth century.

Fig. 2.6  Sir Joshua Reynolds
(1723–92), *George III when
Prince of Wales*, 1759.
Oil on canvas, 127.8 × 101.8 cm.
RCIN 401034

required due to her love of taking long walks in the royal parks.[10] She took care to promote items of domestic manufacture, including Midlands lace and Irish plaid, although occasionally also bought expensive Continental items such as a Brussels lace 'head' acquired for £105 in 1733 (more than £18,500 in 2021).[11]

The relationship between George II and his eldest son, Frederick, Prince of Wales, was again fractured and dysfunctional. Frederick had been left behind in Hanover as the representative of the family there at the age of seven, and upon arriving in England at 21 was disappointed to find both his independence and income severely restricted. The king also openly favoured his third son, William Augustus, Duke of Cumberland. While marriage to Princess Augusta of Saxe-Gotha in 1736 brought the Prince of Wales greater financial independence, the rift between generations grew wider, culminating in a complete separation of households, with an opposition court maintained by the

Fig. 2.7  John Hopkins (active 1803), *Queen Charlotte*, *c.*1803–13. Watercolour on ivory, 10.5 × 8.2 cm. RCIN 420192

Prince of Wales, initially at Norfolk House in London, and later at Leicester House. Frederick's modish appearance at around this time is demonstrated in a portrait showing him in a fashionable mismatching suit of blue velvet coat and silver waistcoat (see Fig. 2.1). During this period, dress worn at important court events was used as a subtle demonstration of allegiance to these rival factions. The separation was further exploited by politicians who sought to divide the royal family, and so dilute their power. Prince Frederick, who was supported by a number of leading Tory politicians as well as discontented Whigs, used dress to profess his patriotism, in November 1738 banning his courtiers from wearing fabrics or trimmings made outside England.[12] These prohibitions were reissued ten years later, with a more explicit focus on excluding French fashions. Prince Frederick inherited the Hanoverian love of uniforms and developed a new form of hunting dress (see Chapter 11).

Frederick, Prince of Wales, was never to become king, dying in 1751, ten years before his father. His eldest son acceded to the throne as George III, and although taking care to appear richly dressed when occasion necessitated, particularly in his younger years (Fig. 2.6), he was not considered a fashion leader, his natural inclination tending towards frugality. In daily life, the king's preference for plain clothing resulted in reports of him not being recognised by the populace, while he was noted for wearing 'ill-made coats' and showing a 'general antipathy to the fashion'.[13] George III seems to have welcomed the shift towards simpler clothing for men, forgoing decorative pastel-coloured silks for plainer English cloth in darker colours. As an older man, George III did not choose to be painted in formal court dress, and was instead represented wearing ceremonial dress or the Windsor uniform he was responsible for introducing (see Chapter 11).

After a rather hasty courtship, George III married Queen Charlotte of Mecklenburg-Strelitz in September 1761 (see Fig. 8.20), with their joint coronation taking place a fortnight later. The marriage was happy, although disrupted by the king's bouts of mental illness, and the couple remained devoted to each other, sharing a

traditional, family-oriented outlook and range of intellectual interests. Among the personal wedding gifts to Queen Charlotte were a pair of bracelets from her husband, 'consisting of six rows of picked pearls as large as a full pea; the clasps – one his picture, the other his hair and cipher, both set round with diamonds',[14] and her loyalty to him is indicated by their appearance in many of her portraits (see Fig. 1.14). Later, after his retirement from public duty, she also wore a larger portrait miniature of her husband on a long necklace (Fig. 2.7). The royal couple hosted Drawing Room assemblies at St James's Palace each week on Thursdays, after which they visited the theatre. They attended the opera on Saturdays, but otherwise spent their evenings quietly at home, reading, listening to music

Fig. 2.8  Style of Robert Dighton (1751–1814), *The Family of George III*, c.1787.

Pen and ink with wash over pencil, 16.8 × 24.6 cm. RCIN 913935

and playing cards. Although she spent significant sums on the finest lace and magnificent jewellery, Queen Charlotte is generally considered to have been conservative in her attitude to fashion. Most famously, she insisted on women at court wearing the old-fashioned hoop underskirt long after it had passed from the fashionable wardrobe and attempted – unsuccessfully – to introduce the 'stiff-bodied' gown as obligatory court wear, as it was on the Continent (see Chapter 8). However, a number of Queen Charlotte's more informal portraits show her in styles of clothing that are at the forefront of fashion. For example, the new inverted triangle style of stomacher (known later as a 'zone front') that she wears in Benjamin West's painting of 1776 (see Fig. 1.16) is more commonly seen in portraits of the 1780s, while the intertwined laurel leaf border on the fabric in her lap is an early example of a neo-classical motif in dress.

George III and Queen Charlotte were attentive parents to their 15 children, and the family was often seen walking around Windsor together (Fig. 2.8). History was to repeat itself, however, in the strained relationship between the heir, George, Prince of Wales, and his father. Frugal and traditional by nature, George III was exasperated by his son's profligacy and political inclinations: the prince's friendship group included many Whig revolutionaries, such as Charles James Fox (see Fig. 12.12) and Richard Brinsley Sheridan (see Fig. 6.15). Unlike his father, the Prince of Wales was also very interested in fashion and took great care and expense to be up to the minute in his attire. By the early 1790s this meant that he favoured the understated styles of male dress for which Britain had become renowned across Europe, a look inspired not by the excesses of France, but by the practical clothing of the English landowner: finely cut riding coats in dark colours, worn with buff breeches, boots and a round hat rather than the formal tricorne (see Fig. 4.19). The friendship between the Prince of Wales and his sartorial mentor Beau Brummell (see Chapter 4),

Fig. 2.9 Richard Bull (1721–1805), *George IV when Prince of Wales*, 1793.
Watercolour on ivory, 7.8 × 6.2 cm. RCIN 420984

which lasted from 1794 to 1812, encouraged this appreciation for exquisite tailoring that hugged (and sometimes cleverly enhanced) the body, including the newly fashionable trousers, all made of the finest fabrics. Stylish and svelte in his youth, the impact of the prince's indulgent lifestyle on his figure is suggested by the frequency with which his clothes required regular adjustment by ingenious tailors, and the difference in the waist measurement of three surviving waistcoats in the Museum of London.[15] According to the Duchess of Devonshire, 'He is inclined to be too fat and looks too much like a woman in men's cloaths, but the gracefulness of his manner and his height certainly make him a pleasing figure.'[16]

Rather surprisingly, given his reputation for extravagance in expenditure and enormous debts during the 1790s, the prince's wardrobe account books for the years 1800 to 1812 show that he stayed within the clothing budget granted to him by the Treasury: initially £500 per quarter and later reduced to £300, suggesting that someone within his household was keeping a close eye on his spending.[17] The largest payment (around 50 to 60 per cent of the quarterly total) went to his tailors, including Schweitzer and Davidson on Cork Street and Jonathan Meyer on Conduit Street. Additional creditors in 1800 included Mr Clarke, bootmaker; Mr Crowther, whipmaker; William Webb, robemaker; and Vincent and Co., spurmaker.[18] The prince was also concerned that he smelt appropriately fragrant and he spent significant sums at Amick & Son perfumers on Haymarket (£54 a quarter in 1801).[19]

George, Prince of Wales, was continually thwarted in his military ambitions by his father, who forbade the heir to the throne from active service, unlike his brothers, the Dukes of York and Clarence, who became Commander-in-Chief of the army and Admiral of the Fleet respectively. Nevertheless, the Prince of Wales was happiest in uniform. Above all, he was fascinated by the clothing worn by the Hungarian hussar regiments (see Chapter 11) and during the 1780s often dressed in tasselled boots, tight-fitting pantaloons, coats decorated with braided frogging and rich fur pelisses in imitation of their attire. This style of dress influenced the elaborately expensive (and frequently

redesigned) uniforms of his own regiment, the 10th Light Dragoons, later renamed the 10th Royal Hussars (Fig. 2.9). In a portrait by John Russell (Fig. 2.10), the prince wears another form of uniform that he himself introduced, this time civilian: that of the Royal Society of Kentish Bowmen. Unlike the archers in the background, the prince wears his coat (in the regulation 'grass green') stylishly half-buttoned, over a buff waistcoat and breeches. His Lesser George badge of the Order of the Garter is prominently displayed: it is very similar to one in the Royal Collection that was acquired by George IV (Fig. 2.11), although not exactly the same. The fashionably large buttons are each marked with the 'RKB' initials of the society and the Prince of Wales's feathers. The collar, of black velvet rather than plain silk, indicates that this is the winter version of the coat. Laid on the stone plinth is the black round hat with a small feather, 'without which no member was allowed to shoot'.[20] Fines were charged to members who appeared at shooting meets

LEFT, AND DETAIL OPPOSITE
Fig. 2.10  John Russell (1745–1806),
*George IV when Prince of Wales*, 1791.
Oil on canvas, 250.2 × 180.3 cm.
RCIN 405414

Fig. 2.11 English, *Order of the Garter Badge (Lesser George)*, 1800–37. Onyx, gold, enamel and diamond, 9.4 × 5.2 cm. RCIN 441156

without the appropriate uniform, although these were relaxed for those in mourning dress.[21]

In 1795 the Prince of Wales married his first cousin, Princess Caroline of Brunswick, but the marriage was stormy from the outset and the couple quickly separated after the birth of their daughter Charlotte the following year (see Fig. 5.11). Of her husband Princess Caroline remarked that 'He understands how a shoe should be made or a coat cut … and would make an excellent tailor, or shoemaker or hairdresser but nothing else'.[22] High-spirited, affectionate and brash, Princess Caroline did not find it easy to adapt to the strict etiquette at court. While she enjoyed a measure of popularity among the British public, with the prince increasingly vilified by the press, criticisms were raised about her immodest and eccentric style of dress ('shewing too much of her naked person'[23]) together with a lax attitude to personal hygiene: she boasted of the brevity of her toilette, and the Earl of Malmesbury (who in 1794 had been the court diplomat sent to Brunswick to escort Caroline to England) found it necessary to suggest she change her undergarments more frequently.[24] Her behaviour and attire were the focus of much attention at the 'trial' of 1820, during which her husband (by that time George IV) attempted to strip her of her title and position as queen. Despite being excluded from his coronation, she continued to draw public support, particularly from women, and received gifts from artisans including a 'splendid dress' from the lacemakers of Loughborough and a bonnet from the straw plait weavers of the Midlands.[25] Her supporters, considering her purity unfairly smeared, demonstrated their allegiance by wearing white dresses, accessorised with white cockades and sashes.[26] Rather ironically, the sale of her wardrobe after her death, which raised £972, highlighted her preference for bold colours, particularly red.[27]

After his death in 1830, George IV's collection of clothing and accessories was sold at auction over three days. The eclectic variety of lots included a Windsor uniform coat, a silver-laced hussar jacket, masquerade costumes and a complete Highland dress (see Fig. 12.6), the low prices (50 shillings for six white waistcoats, £6 6s for the silver-laced hussar jacket) accepted reflecting the sorry state of both the king's finances and reputation by the end of his life.[28]

# 3
# Dressing Women

*They are always laced, and 'tis as rare
to see a Woman here without her Stays on,
as it is to see one at Paris in a full Dress.*

KARL LUDWIG FREIHERR VON PÖLLNITZ, 1737[1]

I n the eighteenth century, elite female dress became noticeably more complex and decorative than that worn by men, marking a change from the previous century when the dress of both genders was equally ornamental. Whereas in the seventeenth century the number of types of garment was limited, the eighteenth century saw a proliferation of differently named styles for women, many with only slight variations from each other. Certain types of clothing became associated with particular times of the day, and the distinctions in formality of dress, dictated by occasion, become more sharply defined. The process of dressing itself took on greater significance, and the morning *levée*, during which visitors were received and business conducted, was adopted in England by other members of the elite besides the monarch.

## UNDERGARMENTS

The first item of dress a woman put on each morning was the shift, which was increasingly known by the French name of chemise as the century progressed. This was a knee-length garment usually made of linen, occasionally cotton, often with a drawstring neckline and full sleeves. Linen was strong enough to

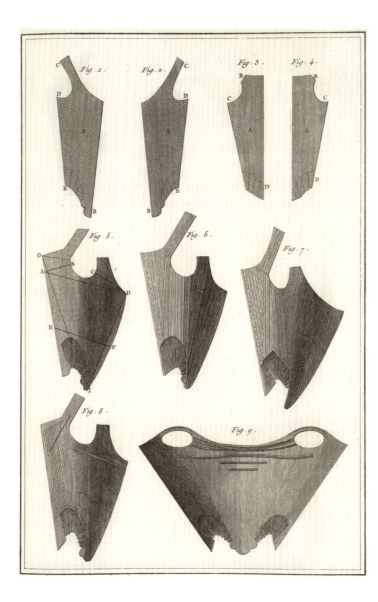

PREVIOUS PAGE
Detail of Fig. 1.10

Fig. 3.2  Denis Diderot (1713–84), *Encyclopédie*, [*t. 26, planches S–T*], Paris, 1771, Tailleur d'habits et tailleur de corps, pl. XXII.
RCIN 1195947

With regard to underwear for the lower half of the body, as many of the more explicit caricatures of the period demonstrate, drawers (initially known as trowsers) were not worn regularly by women until the early nineteenth century: being bifurcated, in Britain they were considered a masculine item of clothing and deemed immodest. Caroline of Brunswick's 'tight trowsers' were sufficiently remarkable to be commented upon during her divorce trial in 1820,[3] although her daughter Princess Charlotte had been wearing them since 1811.[4] Earlier in the eighteenth century, drawers for women seem to have been most frequently worn for warmth and modesty as part of riding dress. Princess Anne (eldest daughter of George II) took six pairs with her when visiting Ham House in the 1730s and these are listed in an inventory alongside her riding habit.[5] Unsurprisingly, drawers are never depicted in paintings, although they are sometimes shown in caricatures. A surviving pair of *c.*1820, made of lawn (fine linen), are associated with the Duchess of Kent.[6]

Just as the final effect of an eighteenth-century painting depends on the preparatory layers beneath, so the final appearance of an eighteenth-century woman was dictated by her underpinnings. Although the actual shape of these varied from decade to decade, resulting in significant differences in overall silhouette, the fundamental construction and types of garments remained the same. Over her linen shift a woman would wear a pair of stays, which by the early nineteenth century was increasingly known as a corset.[7] Stays provided comfortable support (like the modern bra) and shaped the torso, while also creating a smooth line for the garments above. Stay-making was a highly skilled trade, requiring a combination of attention to detail and strength. The pair of stays shown opposite (Fig. 3.1) indicates the sculptural quality of such garments. The tabs around the waistline would have spread outwards over the hips, preventing the straight edge from digging into the flesh, thereby making them comfortable to wear. The shaping of high-quality stays of this kind was achieved by inserting narrow strips of baleen (keratinous cartilage removed from the mouth of a whale) into stitched channels created between the layers of fabric. Baleen, which was also known as whalebone (although not actually a bone),

withstand regular washing and provided a comfortable layer next to the skin, helping to protect outer clothing from dirt and sweat. Although it would have been extremely unusual for a woman to go without her shift, paintings sometimes inaccurately suggest that this is the case, as it is concealed by the upper layers of clothing. If visible, the shift is usually only seen at the neckline and elbow, as in the portrait of an unknown woman by William Denune (see previous page and Fig. 1.10). The frill around the neckline here probably forms part of the shift, although decorative lace examples like that worn by the Princess Royal in the portrait by Christian Zincke (see Fig. 8.8) are likely to be a separate detachable 'tucker', which was sewn to the shift or gown. Instances of 'sleeve cheating' have been documented, with the sleeves of a shift being made of a finer-quality linen than the body – to suggest a higher-quality garment – or being detachable to indicate 'false' cleanliness.[2]

Fig. 3.3  Paul Sandby (1731–1809), *At Sandpit Gate, c.*1752.
Pencil, pen and ink and watercolour, 22.9 × 23.4 cm. RCIN 914329

Stays of the type depicted here would have been known as 'stitched stays' in contemporary accounts, and although in elite circles these would usually have been covered by upper garments, the workmanship is of the highest quality with regular rows of tiny stitches that would have taken days to complete. By contrast, 'smooth-covered stays' were constructed in the same way but then covered in a layer of more decorative fabric (usually silk), making them suitable to wear as an outer garment. They sometimes had sleeves and, rather counter-intuitively, could cost less than a well-made pair of stitched stays because the fabric could hide coarser stitching. In a portrait it is sometimes impossible to know whether we are seeing the stays worn as an outer garment or stomacher (see below) sewn or pinned on top.

In Britain, stays were almost universally worn by all classes, with less expensive versions differing in the quality of stitching and materials used. Imagery of the period indicates that stitched stays were considered acceptable outerwear for the lower classes. The two maidservants in Paul Sandby's watercolour, *At Sandpit Gate* (Fig. 3.3), wear their stitched stays with shifts and petticoats to scrub laundry and stoke the fire. The stays worn by both maids are strapless, which, although worn by women from across the social spectrum, were especially suitable for those undertaking manual labour, as they allowed for greater ease of movement. Sandby has included the tiny detail of a single lace threaded through the eyelet holes of the back-lacing stays worn by the kneeling figure. Back-lacing stays were more common than front-lacing stays in England, but tended to necessitate assistance during dressing, as ridiculed by Thomas Rowlandson in *A Little Tighter* (Fig. 3.4). Starting at the bottom, a single lace was passed through the offset holes and tied off at the top.

Stays were a key component in creating the fashionable body shape, which varied as the century progressed: the rather conical line of the early years was replaced by a much flatter profile by 1750. In Henry Fielding's *Amelia* (1751) it was remarked that 'no woman can be genteel… who is not entirely flat before'.[9] By the 1780s the rounded and prominent bosom had returned, with wadding and voluminous 'buffon' scarfs proving useful for the less

was prized because of its pliability, enabling it to mould to the body of the wearer over time with warmth, but 'bents' of stiff grass such as marram (*Ammophila*) were a cheaper alternative. Baleen varied naturally in thickness and stay-makers were advised to use the thickest pieces at the back to provide strength, saving the thinnest for the sides of the waist for comfort and flexibility.[8]

Although the exact method of making stays was a closely guarded secret passed from master to apprentice, Denis Diderot's *Encyclopédie* (Fig. 3.2) includes a variety of plates illustrating the process. The stay-maker (known in France as the *tailleur de corps*) drafted an individual pattern for each customer based on a series of standard measurements, taking care to account for asymmetries in the body, and making adjustments during a follow-up fitting. Until the end of the eighteenth century the stay-maker was almost always male due to the physical strength required to insert the whalebone into the narrow casings, although the stitching was usually completed by women. The intimate relationship between the stay-maker and his customers was a subject ripe for social comment and caricature.

Fig. 3.4  Thomas Rowlandson (1757–1827), *A Little Tighter*, 1791 (detail).
Hand-coloured etching, 39.0 × 31.2 cm (sheet). RCIN 810415

Fig. 3.5  William Hogarth (1697–1764), 'The Tavern Scene', from *A Rake's Progress, Plate 3*, 1735 (detail).
Engraving with etching, 36.6 × 42.2 cm (sheet). RCIN 811555.b

were a softer, unboned alternative that could be worn as a comfortable option at home or while pregnant or nursing. Fans included Mary Delany (see Fig. 8.29), a close friend of Queen Charlotte, who sent a pair of jumps to her sister in 1740, advising her against tight lacing.[12] Separate stays were an unnecessary addition with the 'grand habit', as the bodice itself was heavily boned (see Fig. 8.7). Riding stays were cut with a shorter peak below the waistline and no tabs, for comfort when sitting side-saddle.

The proportions of the lower half of the female body were modified by hoop petticoats, introduced around 1710 and popular until the 1780s in fashionable dress (although compulsory at the English court until 1820). The farthingales that had reached such extraordinary proportions during the reign of Elizabeth I (r. 1558–1603) in England had gone out of fashion in 1619 with the death of Anne of Denmark, but by 1709 sufficient time had passed for English women to be ready to accept 'the new-fashioned petticoats' described by the *Tatler*.[13] Early hoop petticoats were made using rings of baleen (the bowhead whale produced the longest strips suitable for hoops) or much cheaper rattan cane encased in strong fabric, usually linen. Unlike stays, hoops were not bespoke garments and many hoop-makers were women.

well-endowed. The bust was further emphasised by rising waistlines, and by 1811 one commentator remarked that the bosom had been 'shoved up to the chin, making a sort of fleshy shelf … most incommodious to the bearer'.[10] As this description indicates, it was not until the second decade of the nineteenth century that it became fashionable for the breasts to be visibly separated. This was achieved by a new style of long stays with shaped cups and a rigid supportive strip known as a busk, often made of wood, running down the centre line.

In literature and imagery of the period, a lack of stays can identify a character as a prostitute, or someone lacking in moral values. In the tavern scene from *A Rake's Progress*, the woman in the foreground has removed her stays, which lie on the ground at her feet (Fig. 3.5). William Hogarth clearly illustrates their three-dimensional quality: they retain the form of their owner, to whose body they have been carefully shaped. Despite the negative connotations of discarded stays, portraits indicate that during the neo-classical period around the turn of the nineteenth century some women do seem to have opted for a more natural look. Princess Caroline of Brunswick was known to leave her stays off regularly, according to her maid.[11] She might have replaced them with a pair of jumps, which

Fig. 3.6  Simon François Ravenet (1706–74) after William Hogarth (1697–1764), 'The Bagnio', from *Marriage à-la-Mode, Plate 5*, 1745 (detail).
Etching and engraving, 39.6 × 47.9cm (sheet). RCIN 811720.c

Fig. 3.7  Jointed wire hoop covered in silk taffeta, *c*.1740–80.
Iron, linen, silk and cotton. Toronto, Royal Ontario Museum, 2013.17.1

the skirt, each of which contained a large space suitable for storing essentials.

The reintroduction of hooped underskirts emphasised female physicality – women took up more space than men for much of the century. In the same way that the farthingale of the Elizabethan era had, to some extent, been balanced by the voluminous scale of padded breeches worn by men, male coats of the early eighteenth century included stiffened flaring skirts that echoed the shape of the hoop. However, by the 1740s a closer-fitting line was becoming more fashionable for men and the contrast in proportions between the two sexes in many couple portraits of the period is striking. The most enormous hoops were reserved for court occasions (see Fig. 8.10), their size (some more than 7 metres in circumference) providing an opportunity for the display of yards of expensive patterned fabric, trimmings and glittering embroidery, and making them a clear symbol of wealth and privilege. The sheer inconvenience of the most exaggerated examples also served to demonstrate conspicuous leisure, while simultaneously delighting satirists. Reported practical difficulties included having to move sideways through doors, accidentally knocking objects off tables and 'hurting Mens Shins'.[15] Hoops were also vocally criticised for more philosophical reasons, with some disapproving of their unnatural appearance and divergence from classical ideals of proportion: 'Nothing can be imagined more unnatural, and consequently less agreeable', wrote the *Weekly Journal* in 1718.[16] Moreover, the hoop had distinctly sexual overtones, exaggerating the width of the hips and accentuating a small waist, attributes traditionally associated with female fertility. Some considered hoops immoral, because they could help conceal or imitate pregnancy. The hoop petticoat allowed greater ventilation to the lower regions, and walking caused a slight tilting action that revealed the occasional female ankle beneath the gown. A powerful gust of wind or unpredicted movement had the potential to reveal far more. This moral ambiguity was compounded by the fact that the hoop provided a physical barrier to unwanted advances, underlining a woman's sexual autonomy. In *Clarissa* (1747) Anna Howe remarks that she wants a full hoop 'to keep ill-mannered fellows at a distance'.[17]

The shape of the hoop petticoat varied over time: initially conical, it gradually grew in circumference, forming a large circle in the 1730s. The shape then began to flatten at the front and back, creating a fan-shaped silhouette by the 1740s, as illustrated by the women in *St James's Park and the Mall* (see pp. 2–3). A print after Hogarth's *Marriage à-la-Mode* reveals what the understructure looked like off the body by 1745 (Fig. 3.6). The Countess's hooped petticoat lies on the floor, having been discarded along with her shoes, stays and masquerade mask during an assignation with Silvertongue, the lawyer. In the 1750s a squarer look was popular in England, although not admired in France, and this could be achieved through the recently patented jointed hoops (Fig. 3.7), usually constructed from hinged metal wires, which could be folded up so that a lady 'may go into a coach or chair without any manner of trouble or inconvenience'.[14] As a drawing by Sandby indicates (Fig. 3.8), hoops at this period were often short structures that supported the fabric at the hips and not at the hem, so that the gown was left to fall naturally. In this example the rather sharp corners of the understructure are revealed as the fabric is blown in the wind. Hoops were worn by women from all classes and a very practical alternative was a pocket hoop: a pair of paniers, one on each hip, to support

RIGHT

Fig. 3.8 Paul Sandby (1731–1809), *Two Ladies, Seen from Behind*, *c*.1751–2.

Red chalk, 18.9 × 13.8 cm. RCIN 914323

BELOW

Fig. 3.9 Thomas Rowlandson (1757–1827), *The Bum Shop*, 1785.

Etching printed in brown, 30.3 × 47.1 cm (sheet). RCIN 810134

In England the wearing of hoops as part of fashionable dress continued until the 1770s, by which time the softer, more rounded aesthetic with an emphasis on the posterior was increasingly achieved using a rump instead. This was a crescent-shaped pad, divided into sections and usually stuffed with fragments of cork or horsehair, which tied with tapes around the waist. Such pads could also be built into the sides and rear of a petticoat, which then turned it into a puff (or *bouffante* in France). Both types of support are depicted hanging on the wall of Rowlandson's *The Bum Shop* (Fig. 3.9). While the slender customer in the centre has the various options explained to her by the assistant, the lady on the right (possibly intended as an 'after' version of same person) admires her new silhouette using a pair of mirrors. On the left another departs, by now fully dressed, her bottom dramatically enhanced.

An eighteenth-century definition of a petticoat was much broader than a modern one. They ranged from purely practical items that were hidden by outer layers, to highly decorative garments worn as outerwear with an open gown or jacket. It would not have been uncommon for a woman to wear more than one petticoat at once: perhaps a quilted under petticoat for comfort or warmth, a hoop petticoat or puff to provide support, then finally a more decorative one for display. The construction of a petticoat was simple and involved pleating the length of fabric into the waistband (usually linen tape), rather than cutting it to shape, which

enabled it to be adjusted or the fabric reused later. In 1730 Mary Allen is listed as 'pettecoat maker' to Queen Caroline, charging 10 shillings to make each petticoat, and 3 shillings extra for ribbon.[18] One of the petticoats, made on 14 August, is described as of 'black lutstring [*sic*]': a lighter silk taffeta

suitable for summer. This is possibly the 'blk broad lustring'
provided by the mercer, Thomas Hinchliff, three days earlier
at a cost of 8s 6d a yard, a typical price for a plain silk of this
kind.[19] Each petticoat would have required at least 5 yards
(4.5 m) of fabric, demonstrating the significant expense even
for plain materials – far greater than the cost of the labour.[20]

## GOWNS

The main outer garment for women was the gown, which
took a variety of forms as the century progressed but
fundamentally consisted of a bodice and skirt, sometimes
cut in one piece, sometimes separate. For much of the
century gowns opened at the front and were put on rather
like a coat. Terminology at this date can be confusing and
fashion periodicals use alternative names for gowns that
seem very similar to modern eyes. One useful distinction
is between open gowns, which were designed to reveal the
petticoat beneath, and closed gowns, which circled the body
– the latter were also sometimes known as round gowns.

The mantua had been the most fashionable style of
gown at the end of the seventeenth century, and its use
continued for some decades. It was constructed from uncut
widths of fabric, with the fit achieved through pleating, so
preserving the material for future alterations. Originally
developed as an informal style of dress for women (reflected
in its etymology, derived from the French *manteau*, cloak),
the mantua gradually became more formal, and by the
1740s it was considered suitable for court where it was
worn over huge hoops. In Marcellus Laroon's *A Dinner
Party* (Fig. 3.10) the two women seated on the left of the
table wear mantuas of blue- and rust-coloured silk, their
seated positions revealing the stylised back drapery that
characterised this dress, created as the excess fabric at the
sides of the gown was looped up and arranged into folds
towards the back. A mantua was an open gown, so was
always worn with a petticoat, often of a matching fabric.
A rare complete ensemble survives in the Metropolitan
Museum of Art (Fig. 3.11), slightly earlier in date than
the rust-coloured gown in the Laroon painting, but of a

similarly coloured fabric and with the train laid out behind. As in the painting, the mantua sleeves end in narrow cuffs, and the shaping of the bodice is achieved by pleats in the front and back that created the tight fit at the waistline.

The confusingly named nightgown, originally an informal garment worn at home, was for much of the eighteenth century a stylish semi-formal woman's day dress, particularly popular in England. Consisting of a bodice and attached skirt, it was also known as a tight-bodied gown because it was fitted around the waistline. This is the style of dress that appears most frequently in English portraiture of the first half of the century, for example in Philippe Mercier's *The Music Party* (see Fig. 6.33), where all three princesses wear modest nightgowns. Queen Charlotte was noted as wearing 'an English nightgown and a white apron' while walking in the park in 1769.[21] By the 1780s this style of dress had also become popular in France, where it was renamed a *robe à l'anglaise*, in recognition of its popularity in England (Fig. 3.12), and was characterised by its sharply defined waistline that ended in an elegant point at the centre back; some gowns included internal tapes that tied around the waist to ensure a close fit. A surviving example at the Los Angeles County Museum of Art (Fig. 3.13) demonstrates the ubiquitous vogue for stripes in the late 1780s, as well as the fashionable fullness at the rear, enhanced with appropriate underpinnings. By this date the pleats in the bodice had often been replaced by seams (with patterns carefully matched and designed to resemble pleats), with the bodice cut separately to the skirt and usually closing in front.

The style of gown most associated with the mid-eighteenth-century rococo aesthetic is the *robe à la française*, also known as a sacque (anglicised to sack-back gown or sack), which originated in France but had become fashionable in England by the 1740s. A sacque can be differentiated from other styles of gown by its use of box pleats at the back neckline, which create an unbroken cascade of fabric where it merges with the skirt before the ground. In Sandby's *Two Ladies, Seen from Behind*

(see Fig. 3.8), the woman on the left wears a nightgown, while her companion is dressed in a sacque. The difference might be driven by age, a nightgown being considered more suitable for a younger girl than a sacque, although both were worn simultaneously in England and abroad. In contrast to their French equivalents, English women were known for their preference for tightly fitting garments to cover the torso; even when adopting the sacque, English women tended to wear a more structured version.

Eva-Maria Veigel also appears to be wearing a sacque in Hogarth's double portrait (see Fig. 1.18) and its construction is likely to follow that of similar surviving garments (see Fig. 1.17). Both display the scalloped flounces attached to elbow-length sleeves characteristic of sacque gowns at this date, and both are trimmed with the same golden yellow fabric of the dress itself, which is applied in a serpentine pattern down the front. Flat lead weights were sometimes sewn into the sleeve flounces to help them hang properly. In Queen Caroline's accounts of 1733 'leads in the sleeves' are itemised separately and supplied by Johan Christian Krake.[22] Pleated 'winged' sleeve cuffs of the type worn by Fredericka, Duchess of Saxe-Weissenfels (Fig. 3.14), had been replaced by scalloped sleeve flounces during the 1750s – sometimes double- or even triple-layered – but by the 1770s these had again been replaced by longer sleeves finished with small cuffs, and sleeve flounces were retained for only the most formal events.

Like a mantua, a sacque was usually worn as an open gown, most frequently with a matching petticoat supported by a hoop petticoat or hip pads, and a stomacher. The latter was a separate triangular panel of fabric filling the gap between the two front edges (robings) of a gown. It was either pinned, sewn or laced into position. This area of the body was a focal point for decoration, ornamented with lace, passementerie or embroidery, or it could be highlighted with a contrasting colour, as demonstrated by Princess Caroline (sister of George III), whose pink stomacher is worn with a white gown (Fig. 3.15). In this portrait, both princesses' stomachers are decorated with matching bows, which could be so large and profuse as to entirely conceal its surface. Often the ribbons were arranged

Fig. 3.14  Antoine Pesne (1683–1757), *Fredericka, Duchess of Saxe-Weissenfels*, c.1740–6.
Oil on canvas, 144.2 × 113.9 cm. RCIN 405657

Fig. 3.15  Francis Cotes (1726–70), *Princess Louisa and Princess Caroline*, 1767.
Oil on canvas, 265.0 × 185.9 cm. RCIN 404334

into rows (an *échelle*) across the bodice allowing a scarf to be threaded through, as in the portrait of Queen Marie Leczinska (see Fig. 1.8). Sometimes the stomacher included a pocket for holding scented herbs or a corsage of flowers. It could also be jewelled profusely, as in the coronation garments of Queen Charlotte (see Fig. 3.56). Another style of stomacher seen from the 1760s was known as a *compère front*, which gave the false appearance of a buttoned waistcoat worn beneath the dress, commonly in the same fabric, as in the portrait of Princess Elizabeth Albertina by Allan Ramsay (Fig. 3.16). These fastenings were usually decorative rather than functional.

In its earliest form the sacque, like the nightgown, started as an informal fashion, but by the 1770s a highly decorative version worn over a wide hoop was the common form of female dress at the English court. Careful analysis of the prior stitching holes on surviving garments indicates that sacques could be converted into nightgowns by sewing down the back pleats, repositioning the fabric gathered at the waist towards the centre back and creating cuffs from leftover fabric to replace unfashionable sleeve flounces.

An early type of gown popular in the 1720s and 1730s that formed a stylistic link between the mantua and the sacque was known as a *robe volante*. This had pleats at both front and back, but, unlike the mantua, was not belted at the waist and was worn with a circular hoop to create a wide bell shape (Fig. 3.17). Gowns of this type were regularly portrayed by French artists such as Jean François de Troy and Nicolas Lancret, although their rarity in English portraits is noticeable. Never popular in England, where women preferred a more structured garment, the *robe volante* was criticised by moralists for its supposed ability to invite intimacy and conceal the result of sexual indiscretions (although it was worn with stays). While most women in *St James's Park and the Mall* (see pp. 2–3) wear sacques or nightgowns, the elegantly dressed Black lady at the centre left may be wearing a cream-coloured *robe volante*, with loose pleats hanging at the front and back (Fig. 3.18). Although the figure has not yet been identified, her central position (in line with the Prince of Wales), the lighting (she is stepping out of the shadows), the directness

of her gaze towards the viewer and the pointing finger of the man behind ensure she captures our attention. The fact that she is one of the few women shown wearing this characteristically French style of fashionable dress, together with her placement directly in front of a sailor, may be intended to suggest that she is a recognisable visitor to London, perhaps having travelled from the Continent or the Caribbean. An alternative explanation is that she is intended to represent a courtesan, which would also align with the direct gaze, highly fashionable attire and position close to figures from lower down the social spectrum.[23]

A wrapping gown, sometimes described as a *robe à la lévite,* was a style of informal dress, usually worn inside the home before changing into formal attire in the afternoon. Early examples of the wrapping gown were constructed like a dressing gown, with a sash at the waist and sometimes a modesty piece at the neck – they were a comfortable and adaptable option during pregnancy. The lady of the house in Laroon's *A Musical Tea Party* (Fig. 3.19) wears a deep blue wrapping gown as she receives visitors and drinks tea in Chinese porcelain served by a maid wearing an orange mantua. The greater level of informality of her attire compared to that of her attendants is further emphasised by the fact that her hair is covered with a scarf, rather than being appropriately arranged.

In the 1770s Sir Joshua Reynolds promoted the idea of painting sitters in a form of timeless dress that would withstand the changing vagaries of taste. Many of his sitters, such as Maria, Duchess of Gloucester (see Fig. 9.7), wear drapery that follows the line of the wrapping gown. Such garments gradually became more formal and decorative, as attested by the frequent appearance of the *lévite* in fashion periodicals of the 1780s, their popularity in part driven by the interest in Eastern styles of dress established during the period (see Chapter 9). Various other styles of gown with names influenced by the East were introduced in the later decades of the eighteenth century, including the *robe à la turque,* the *circassienne* and the *robe à la polonaise.* Strictly speaking, according to periodicals of the time, a *robe à la polonaise* had a bodice cut along the lines of a male coat, without a waist

seam, the sides meeting at chest level in front then sloping away to reveal a triangular gap, with the skirt pulled up into three rounded swags, one at the back and one at each side.[24] Anecdotally, the style is said to have been inspired by the division of Poland by its three more powerful neighbours (Prussia, Russia and Austria) in 1772, as well as by Polish folk dress. However, the term has sometimes been applied inaccurately to any gown in which the skirt is arranged into puffs of fabric to reveal the petticoat beneath, a fashionable style that could be achieved in many gowns by adding a pair of ribbon loops under the skirt, each of which is then passed through a pocket slit on the side of the skirt and caught over a button at the waistline.[25]

OPPOSITE

Fig. 3.19  Marcellus Laroon the Younger (1679–1772), *A Musical Tea Party*, 1740 (detail).

Oil on canvas, 91.4 × 71.0 cm. RCIN 403544

Fig. 3.20  A.B. Duhamel (1736–*c*.1800) after Claude-Louis Desrais (1746–1816), Woman wearing a *robe en chemise*, from *Cabinet des modes*, 11ème cahier, 15 April 1786, Paris, pl. I.

RCIN 1000881

Fig. 3.21  French or English, *Robe en chemise*, 1783–90.

Cotton muslin. Manchester, Platt Hall, 1947.1714

Those at the forefront of fashion in the 1780s adopted a new dress known as a chemise gown, *robe en chemise* or *chemise à la reine*, which marked a significant departure from earlier styles (Fig. 3.20). Cut along broadly the same lines as a woman's undergarment, it was put on over the head (marking a significant change in the process of dressing), with the fit achieved through drawstrings on the bodice and a sash at the waist like a child's frock dress (see Chapter 5). Despite its name, the chemise gown was always worn with an undergarment and did not replace the chemise. One possible source of inspiration was the style of cool cotton gown (known as a *gaulle*) worn in the area of the Caribbean known as the French Antilles by wealthy women as comfortable clothing in the tropical heat, who then brought the gown to Paris where it was described as a *vêtement à la Créole*.[26]

Surviving chemise gowns are very rare: the one in the collection of Platt Hall, Manchester (Fig. 3.21),

is constructed from a fine cotton muslin known as *jamdani*, with the body decorated with *chikan* embroidery.[27] The flounced neckline is typical, as are the drawstrings at the waist and bust, features that made the chemise gown suitable as maternity wear. Although commonly made of muslin, silk and linen versions also existed. Portraits demonstrate that white was the most popular shade, but coloured examples appear in fashion plates, and others were worn with a coloured petticoat beneath the transparent fabric ('pink taffeta' for Fig. 3.20, according to the commentary in *Cabinet des modes*).[28]

Named *à la reine* after Queen Marie-Antoinette, despite other aristocratic women such as Madame du Barry having worn it earlier, the chemise gown was initially controversial for its informality and similarity to an undergarment. A portrait by Elisabeth Louise Vigée Le Brun showing the French queen in a chemise gown made of semi-transparent imported muslin was withdrawn from the Paris Académie in 1783 due to public outcry.[29] A swiftly painted replacement depicted the queen in a more conventional blue silk satin gown, a garment considered more dignified and appropriate to her role, while also serving to demonstrate support for the Lyons textile industry.[30] The chemise dress was first worn in England by the actress Mary 'Perdita' Robinson, who in 1782 was reported as having 'received a dress from *Paris*, which was introduced this Autumn by the Queen of France, and has caused no small anxiety in the fashionable circles.'[31] Although the Duchess of Devonshire has been credited as having popularised the style in England, in fact she was initially reluctant to wear her version – a gift from Marie-Antoinette in 1784 – on the grounds of immodesty.[32] Soon, however, the style became associated with the duchess's circle. By the end of the 1780s a more fitted style of chemise gown with long tight-fitting sleeves and a wide belt had become popular: this is what Russian Princess Galitzine and her younger daughter Sofia are wearing in a drawing by Richard Cosway (Fig. 3.22). Her other daughter, Ekaterina (seated on the left), wears a style known as a greatcoat dress, which the artist suggests is made of a thick material, perhaps wool, by the way it crumples around the waist.

The chemise dress was the precursor to the neo-classical gowns of the early nineteenth century, such as that worn by Princess Mary (daughter of George III) in a portrait of 1802 (Fig. 3.23), which also took inspiration from the chitons and tunics of classical antiquity.[33] By now, the waistline has risen to just under the bust – it would remain high for another decade, even longer for formal attire – while the bodice has become more fitted, often constructed with a falling bib at the front rather than a drawstring. The use of seams instead of pleats became more commonplace. Such construction techniques worked better with the newer lighter-weight fabrics, while the increased availability of cheaper fabrics made it less necessary to preserve them for the future than expensive silk. This portrait and a similar surviving dress (Fig. 3.24) demonstrate the fashion for volume at the lower back, created through the inclusion of excess fabric at the

waistline (useful in case the gown needed to be adjusted if waistlines lowered in the future) and sometimes a pad worn beneath. Both gowns include a fashionable small train, seen in day and evening wear at this date, although skirt lengths gradually grew shorter, revealing the ankles and facilitating lively dancing at fashionable assemblies. Princess Mary's gown is of plain cotton, devoid of the decorative detail that would come to characterise gowns during the Regency and reign of George IV, although this extreme simplicity is also perhaps partly artistic license. Long sleeves would have been more common for daywear than the short, puffed sleeves depicted here, and it is also unrealistic that the princess is shown without any outer garments or accessories for walking outdoors. Another variation was the addition of an overgown or tunic of a different colour, as Princess Augusta wears in her portrait by Sir William Beechey (Fig. 3.25). This dates from around 1800 and similar representations are shown in fashion periodicals of the same time (Fig. 3.26). The sheen and drape of Princess Augusta's elegant dusky pink overgown suggests it is made of a light silk, providing a contrast with the translucent cotton gown beneath. A gold sash tied under the bust matches the bandeau in her hair, setting off the jewellery and gold trim on her delicate spotted silk slippers and green parasol.

As an alternative to a gown a woman might choose to pair her petticoat with a more informal hip-length jacket, known as a *caraco*. Such a garment had long been common attire among the non-elite and, as part of the move towards fashionable styles influenced by working-class dress, became a very popular option during the last quarter of the century, especially in England. Elite versions were made of silk or cotton rather than the harder-wearing woollens. Some jackets were cut with shoulder pleats like those seen on a sacque gown (in which case it was known as a *pet-en-l'air*), while others had the tighter-fitting lines of the *robe à l'anglaise*, as seen in a fashion plate of 1786 (Fig. 3.27). This example is of puce-coloured silk taffeta. It is sharply cut away at the sides to reveal white silk smooth-covered stays worn as outerwear with the tabs outside the petticoat and decorated with knots of puce ribbons.

Fig. 3.23 Henry Edridge (1769–1821), *Princess Mary*, 1802.

Pencil and slight wash, 32.1 × 22.7 cm. RCIN 913862

Fig. 3.24 English, Gown made from Indian muslin *c*.1800.

Cotton muslin, embroidered with cotton thread. London, Victoria and Albert Museum, T.785&a–1913

Fig. 3.25 Sir William Beechey (1753–1839),
*Princess Augusta*, c.1797–1802.
Oil on canvas, 240.2 × 148.7 cm. RCIN 404556

Fig. 3.26 Nicolaus Heideloff (*fl.* 1761–1837),
Fashion plate, 1800.
Hand-coloured etching and aquatint, 28.2 × 21.3 cm (sheet).
RCIN 507094

## RIDING HABITS

A riding habit was another informal and practical alternative for women, which over the course of the eighteenth century developed from being a utilitarian garment reserved for sporting activities to a stylish form of day dress, particularly popular in England. Riding habits were comfortable and warm and could be worn at home before changing into full dress, or while visiting or travelling. Consisting of a jacket, petticoat and optional waistcoat, a riding habit was worn over a linen habit shirt and the usual underpinnings, sometimes adapted for comfort while riding. During the middle of the century jackets were hip-length and cut with generous skirts enabling them to fit over wide petticoats, as seen in Sandby's *Miss Isherwoods* (Fig. 3.28).

Requiring the same techniques of construction as a man's suit, riding habits were usually tailored by men (unlike gowns, which were made by female mantua-makers) and followed the same stylistic changes as those seen in male dress. Like men's coats they buttoned left over right and often included pockets. They were also made of similar materials: broadcloth, worsted and linen. Riding habits could be left plain or ornately trimmed with braid, and came in a range of colours. Their utility did not preclude the use of pale fabrics, but red cloth was a popular choice in the 1770s and was linked to the patriotic support of British redcoat soldiers. In 1779 Queen Charlotte and the Princess Royal were reported as wearing riding habits based on the colours of the Windsor uniform (see Chapter 11). During the 1780s muted dark shades were most fashionable (a shift also seen in male suits of the period), including a blackish green known as pitch, as well as deep blues, juxtaposed against light-coloured waistcoats beneath.[34] In *Laetitia, Lady Lade* by George Stubbs we see a riding habit in action (Fig. 3.29). A skilled horsewoman and close friend of the Prince of Wales, Lady Lade is shown side-saddle, her horse *en levade*. Her jacket is short and tight-fitting, with a double row of gold buttons and a small frill at the back, while the sweeping full petticoat has been pleated into the waistband. Both are probably made of dark blue broadcloth, which forms a striking contrast with the brilliant white linen of her cravat. Her hat is decorated with a long plume and subtle black cockade. By the last quarter

of the century full-length coat dresses (also known as a greatcoat dress, or *redingote* in France) were a very fashionable option even when not riding (Fig. 3.30). Reinira van Tuyll appears to wear a greatcoat dress in a portrait by George Romney (Fig. 3.31). It is made of a dark grey fabric and incorporates the double-caped collar also seen on men's greatcoats around the same date (see Chapter 4).[35]

Thomas Gainsborough's painting technique means the elegant riding habit worn by Lady Elizabeth Luttrell as she sketches (Fig. 3.32, on the far right) is less articulated than that of Lady Lade, although it is a very different style of dress to that worn by her sister standing nearby. The subtle variations in colour between the sea green and sandy yellow of Lady Elizabeth's jacket and skirt suggest they may be made of a changeant silk like that in the fashion plate seen here (see Fig. 3.30). The tight-fitting sleeves and jacket curving away at the front to reveal a cream waistcoat beneath are typical of this date, and are also seen in a surviving example from the 1790s (Fig. 3.33). This is made of green felted wool with a velvet collar and the sides are cut away so sharply that it fastens with only two gold buttons at mid-chest height. A riding habit was worn with a habit shirt beneath rather than a shift. The habit shirt was cut more like a male shirt, with a higher neckline and ruffles down the centre front opening, which can be seen emerging from the top of Lady Elizabeth's waistcoat (see Fig. 3.32).[36] The close link between riding habits and male dress is clearly demonstrated when the surviving garment is compared to the portrait of the Prince of Wales in the uniform of the Kentish Bowmen (Fig. 3.34).

Riding habits were accessorised with items traditionally found in the male wardrobe, such as cravats, hats, jockey caps, boots and riding crops. The full impact of the ensemble could create an androgynous appearance that was a source of criticism in some circles, with Samuel Richardson writing in 1741 'one cannot easily distinguish your Sex in it. For you neither look like a *modest Girl* in it, nor an *agreeable Boy*'.[37] A miniature painted at around the same date (Fig. 3.35) gives an idea of the type of outfit he probably had in mind: were it not for the sharply defined

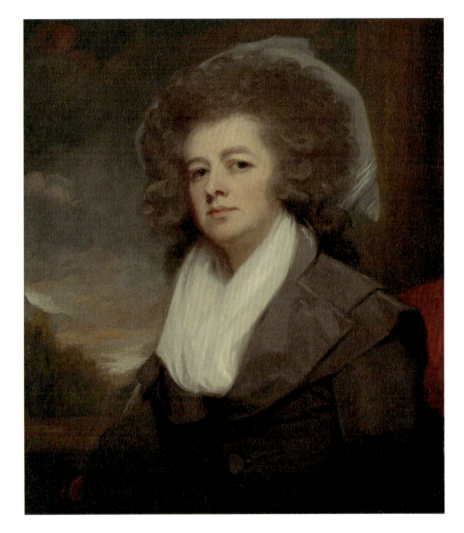

Fig. 3.31 George Romney (1734–1802), *Reinira van Tuyll*, c.1788–9.
Oil on canvas, 76.7 × 64.5 cm. RCIN 409064

Fig. 3.32 Thomas Gainsborough (1727–88), *Henry, Duke of Cumberland with the Duchess of Cumberland and Lady Elizabeth Luttrell*, c.1785–8.
Oil on canvas, 163.5 × 124.5 cm. RCIN 400675

Fig. 3.33  English, Riding habit jacket, 1790s.
Wool cloth. London, Victoria and Albert Museum, T.670–1913

Fig. 3.34  John Russell (1745–1806), *George IV when Prince of Wales*, 1791 (detail).
Oil on canvas, 250.2 × 180.3 cm. RCIN 405414

waistline, the sitter might be mistaken for a man, with the hair arranged like a male wig. An inscription on the back identifies this as the German countess Anna Sophia of Erbach (1708–59) who in 1737 had married Balthazar Frederick, Graf von Promnitz.[38]

## NECKWEAR

Although necklines were low throughout much of the eighteenth century, the chest was rarely unadorned. It was covered for informal wear and decorated with a lace tucker and jewels on formal occasions. The most common type of everyday neckwear for women (and frequently depicted in portraits) was a handkerchief or kerchief.[39] This was a large square of fabric, usually fine linen or muslin, folded diagonally or cut into a triangle (half-kerchief), which could be wrapped around the neck in a variety of configurations to provide warmth and conceal the bosom. Eva-Maria Veigel (see Fig. 1.18) wears hers with the ends twisted together in front and tucked into the stomacher, while some were large enough to cross at the front and tie at the back. For practical reasons, kerchiefs worn by the lower classes were mostly coloured or patterned, while bright white was a perennial favourite among the elite. Although portraits often show handkerchiefs as plain, surviving examples indicate that many were decorated with whitework embroidery.

During the 1780s a style known as a buffon was the most fashionable type of handkerchief, starched and puffed to add volume at the bosom. In 1786 the German novelist Sophie von La Roche was amazed to find women wearing 'neckerchiefs puffed up so high that their noses were scarce visible',[40] although Reinira van Tuyll's is more understated (see Fig. 3.31). By the end of the century women had started to wear chemisettes as modesty pieces: Princess Amelia wears one with a double ruff collar to fill the neckline of her black gown (Fig. 3.36). A similar chemisette, made of starched white organdie (cotton muslin), is shown alongside (Fig. 3.37). It fastens into position with a drawstring tape just below the bust, and the neckline can be tightened with a tassel-trimmed cord. This chemisette is finely pleated; others were elaborately embroidered. They could be made of

Fig. 3.36 Henry Edridge (1769–1821), *Princess Amelia*, 1804 (detail).
Pencil and wash, 32.0 × 22.4 cm. RCIN 913866

Fig. 3.37 Chemisette, 1800–25.
Cotton. Snowshill Wade, National Trust, 1349948

finer-quality fabric than the chemise itself, since only a small amount was needed. Such an item was an easy way to modify the appearance of an outfit without significant expense.

## OUTERWEAR

Voluminous cloaks without sleeves were the most practical type of outerwear to pair with the wide dresses of the mid-century. They came in a variety of styles: full-length cloaks of heavy wool provided protection against the weather, but for warmer days a shorter cloak was considered most stylish. Elegant short black cloaks are worn by many of the richly dressed women in *St James's Park and the Mall* (Fig. 3.38), while those from the lower classes wear plainer styles of scarlet wool with small collars. Red cloaks were considered a peculiarly English item of clothing and were popular throughout the century as country wear for all classes. Unusually for a portrait miniature, Princess Caroline (third daughter of George II and Queen Caroline) is shown here dressed for outdoors (Fig. 3.39), wearing what might have been termed a pelerine: a small mantle that covered the shoulders with extended lappets on each side, sometimes long enough to tie at the back. Princess Caroline's has a hood with a stiffened brim and is trimmed with fringing. The word pelerine is perhaps a reference to the traditional pilgrim's cloak.

In its first incarnation a pelisse had originally been a type of cloak worn by men, usually lined with fur (as indicated by the name, derived from the Latin *pellis*, pelt), with slits for armholes. By the 1790s the term was also being used to describe a long-sleeved coat dress worn by women over the slimmer-fitting neo-classical gowns of the period. The pelisse was an adaptable garment. Despite its etymology, it could be made in a wide variety of materials so was appropriate all year round, and it could range in length from knee to ankle. While ubiquitous in fashion periodicals of the early nineteenth century, pelisses are rarely depicted in formal portraiture. The painting of Princess Elizabeth in what appears to be a finely striped pelisse, with a belt made of the same fabric that fastens below the bust, is therefore interesting (Fig. 3.40). The setting is apparently indoors,

LEFT
Fig. 3.40  After Sir William Beechey (1753–1839), *Princess Elizabeth, Landgravine of Hesse-Homburg, c.*1795–1805.
Oil on canvas, 77.0 × 63.0 cm. Private collection

BELOW
Fig. 3.41  Andrew Robertson (1777–1845), *Princess Amelia*, 1811.
Watercolour on ivory, 8.4 × 6.9 cm. RCIN 420652

but the inclusion of a muff suggests she is dressed for outside. Although covered by the scarf, this pelisse would have been high-necked, supporting a separate frilled collar that is just visible. By the 1820s the pelisse had become fashionable everyday dress and examples of this date are often exuberantly trimmed, some taking military decoration as inspiration, sometimes with short, puffed sleeves (mancherons) over longer sleeves. Queen Caroline of Brunswick's wardrobe contained several pelisses, including one of 'white velvet lined with fur'.[41]

An alternative to the pelisse was a spencer, a cropped jacket that reached the bust line of the bodice worn below and had long sleeves. Like the pelisse, this had originated as a male garment. Fashion periodicals of the time attribute its development to Lord Charles Spencer (1740–1820), the result of a bet to sport a fashion 'the most useless and ridiculous that could be conceived', a coat without tails

being the absurd result.[42] Princess Amelia (youngest daughter of George III) wears a blue velvet spencer in a miniature by Andrew Robertson (Fig. 3.41). The bright colour provides a dramatic contrast to the cotton gown beneath: a spencer lent variety to the universal fashion for classical white. The artist recorded that the clothing was selected 'because the Duke of Sussex [her brother] likes the dress', although he lamented that the cap and hat did not show off her best feature, what he called the 'finest hair imaginable'.[43]

Aprons were worn throughout the century at all levels in society, from queen to scullery maid, although some were never able to overlook their humble origins, Beau Nash of Bath reprimanding the Duchess of Queensbury for wearing an apron to the Assembly.[44] While some aprons served the utilitarian purpose of protecting more expensive clothing beneath, others were

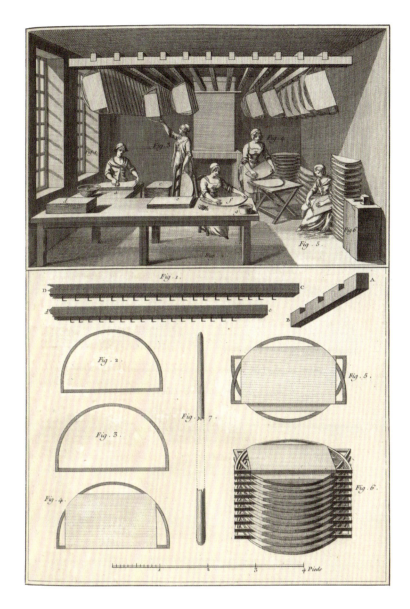

fashionable items and portraits often depict aprons decorated with valuable lace or whitework embroidery. In Benjamin West's portrait of Queen Charlotte (see Fig. 1.16), he represents her wearing a fine muslin apron of surprisingly simple design. It is covered with tiny white five-petalled flower sprigs, probably embroidered in satin stitch, with a similar frill around the hem. By this date aprons were wide, covering a broad expanse of the petticoat beneath and reaching the hemline; earlier in the century they were narrower, despite the wider skirts. Comparable examples survive in large numbers, usually constructed from a single width of fabric pleated into a waistband. Aprons tended to go out of fashion with the introduction of the narrower neo-classical gowns of the 1790s. They were a typical feature of children's dress for both boys and girls, usually with attached bibs pinned to the bodice. While such bibs were a mark of infancy, they were also worn by the lower classes into adulthood.

## FANS

Folding fans had arrived in England by the reign of Elizabeth I,[45] but in the eighteenth century their fashionable status reached its zenith. Both brisé and folding fans were popular, the former consisting of rigid sticks joined together by ribbons, the latter requiring a folded leaf of paper, vellum or textile to be attached to each stick. Portraits showing sitters holding fans usually depict them closed, with only the guards (outer sticks) on display, as in Allan Ramsay's portrait of Princess Elizabeth Albertina (see Fig. 1.12), which makes it difficult to tell how they are constructed. Guards were often a focus for rich decoration. Made of ivory, mother-of-pearl, wood, bone or tortoiseshell, they could be elaborately carved, gilded and set with jewels. Diderot's *Encyclopédie* (Fig. 3.42) illustrates the processes involved in the production of fans, which could require 20 different types of craftspeople, overseen by a fan master, to assemble the components.

Fan leaves in the seventeenth century had usually been patterned, but by the eighteenth century figural designs were common. Stories of love from mythological

sources were popular motifs, a direct reference to the fan's role during social introductions and courtship. A finely painted example (Fig. 3.43, overleaf, top) shows a romanticised depiction of the abduction of Helen from Homer's *Iliad*, with the Queen of Sparta as a willing protagonist. She accompanies Paris towards his ship bound for Troy, watched by soldiers, courtiers and simply dressed bystanders. Imagery on fans could be highly topical, relating to political events, notable figures or innovations. The invention of hot-air ballooning was a newsworthy subject in the 1780s. The fan in the centre overleaf (Fig. 3.44) references the second manned balloon flight, which departed from the Tuileries in Paris in December 1783, and successfully landed 22 miles (36 km) away two hours later. Onlookers can be seen watching and waving to Jacques Charles and Nicolas Robert in their gondola suspended below the balloon. While the most expensive

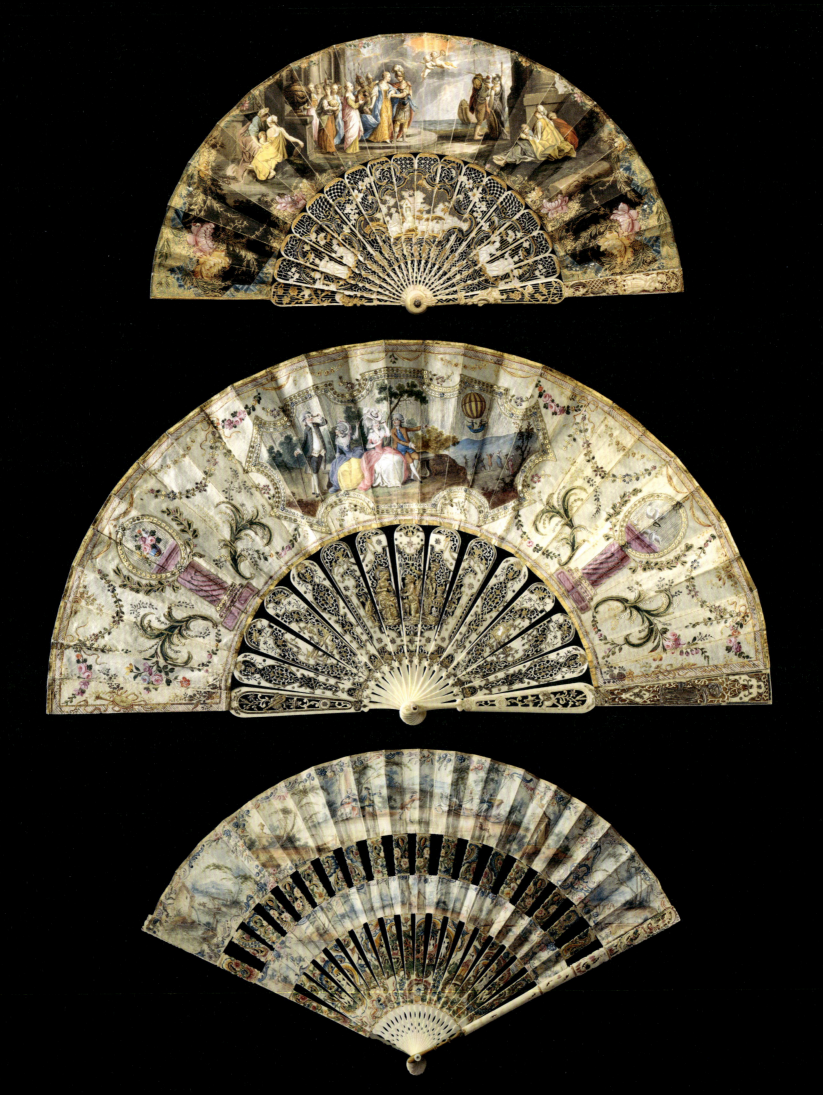

fans had unique leaves painted by hand, cheaper printed versions were widely available. These were classified as 'published objects' by the Engraving Copyright Act of 1734, requiring them to include the name of the publisher and date of issue.

Fans were adopted across the social spectrum, but elite examples could be distinguished by the quality of their materials, and the expert way they were handled. Various sources reference a formalised and elaborate 'language of the fan', although the most famous guide, by the French fan-making firm Duvelleroy, was not published until the nineteenth century, partly as an attempt to revitalise the declining fan industry.[46] There was certainly an appropriate fan etiquette in the eighteenth century: at Versailles the fan had to remain closed in the presence of the sovereign, unless being used as a tray to support a gift during a formal presentation.[47] Fans were carried both indoors and outside and could serve to shield the face from unwanted attention as well as the elements. The invention of lorgnette fans in 1759, with concealed optical devices or peep holes within the hinge or sticks, allowed the user to satisfy her curiosity while maintaining modesty.[48] In the 1750s fans designed to open *à grand vol* (to 180 degrees), like the upper two shown opposite, became highly fashionable. This was clearly an innovative decade, with cabriolet fans being introduced at around the same time (Fig. 3.45). Named after a new form of horse-drawn carriage that was widely adopted as a decorative motif, cabriolet fans were made by mounting two or three fan leaves on the same set of sticks. Both the leaf and guard sticks in this example include depictions of figures riding in cabriolet carriages.

## SHOES

While eighteenth-century women's shoes survive in significant numbers, they are rarely depicted in formal portraits, which typically show skirts to the ground (although they were often slightly raised in front). The ankle was considered the epitome of femininity, occasionally glimpsed beneath petticoat skirts and shown to best advantage by an elegantly curved heel. High heels have their origins in riding footwear, serving to provide a firmer foothold in the stirrup. Their adoption in Europe in the early seventeenth century can be linked to a diplomatic mission sent by Shah 'Abbās I of Persia. Initially considered a masculine feature and used to demonstrate military might, by the mid-seventeenth century heels were widely worn by both sexes.

Shoes can be seen in informal drawings of a body in motion, as in Sandby's depiction of an unidentified lady, which illustrates the fashionable shape of the mid-century, with the 'Louis' heel curving sharply to sit under the centre of the foot (Fig. 3.46). As this demonstrates, a well-designed heel also reduced the size of the footprint and gave the impression of a smaller foot, considered a desirable attribute in women. In fact, women may have deliberately worn shoes that were too small for this reason.[49] A slightly later pair of shoes of similar style, which include a label identifying them as having been made in London, are shown overleaf (Fig. 3.47).

Uppers could be made of silk, leather or wool and decorated with the same trimmings, such as silver lace, as seen on clothing. Silk designs were comparable to those seen in gowns, although the efficient use of tailor's offcuts meant the patterns might not match precisely and sometimes slightly different silks were employed, even within the same shoe. An ornate embroidered court mantua survives alongside a matching pair of shoes covered with the same silk (see Fig. 8.10). Like most footwear of the period, they fasten with latchet straps across the front, joined together for much of the century with buckles. Ribbons were an old-fashioned alternative that avoided the pitfall of buckles catching in the fabric of the skirt. Large square buckles are illustrated by Sandby, but by the mid-1780s these were increasingly replaced by string ties: the first shoelaces, with aglet ends for easier threading being patented in 1790. At around the same date slip-on styles also became popular.

The red heel (*talon rouge*) initially popularised for both sexes at the court of Louis XIV perpetuated for some time into the eighteenth century across Europe. As Laroon shows (see Fig. 3.19), by this date red heels were even worn by maidservants, despite them being a fashion originally restricted to those attending court, thereby indicating political and social privilege (the term *talon rouge* remains in use today

BELOW
Fig. 3.46 Paul Sandby (1731–1809), *A Lady*, *c.*1754 (detail).
Pencil on paper, 12.2 × 7.3 cm. RCIN 914413

LEFT
Fig. 3.47 Fras Poole (dates unknown), Shoes, *c.*1760.
Silk, linen, leather and silver. London, Museum of London, A12570–1

BOTTOM
Fig. 3.48 Peter Edward Stroehling (1768 – *c.*1826), *Princess Mary*, 1807 (detail).
Oil on copper, 60.7 × 48.3 cm. RCIN 404866

to describe an old-fashioned manner appropriate at the court of Versailles). In general, British women tended towards a sturdier wooden block heel, thicker and lower than the tall, slender French counterparts. Heels continued to be worn until the very last years of the eighteenth century, when the prevailing taste for classicism favoured a low 'Italian heel' or flat soles. Some of these were designed to imitate Grecian sandals: Princess Mary wears this style in her portrait of 1807 (Fig. 3.48 and see Fig. 10.14). While her outfit, with its blue fabric tied under the bust, involves a measure of artistic imagination, her footwear, with its delicate ribbon ties, does resemble surviving shoes of the time. Some were made more practical by the inclusion of an additional layer of fabric beneath the straps to imitate skin. Shoes of around this date are often decorated with a rosette or bow. Here, the hearts on the uppers are a nod to the prevailing taste for this motif. The shape of the toe was important, as this was the most visible part of the shoe. During the 1710s a needlepoint toe shape was prevalent, with a distinctively upturned sole. By the 1740s this had been replaced by a blunter toe, which later became rounded, until the pointed shape re-emerged in the 1790s with the lower heel.[50]

The making of shoes required a combination of techniques and materials. Shoemakers were represented by the Worshipful Company of Cordwainers, although cobblers operated separately and required less formal training. Shoemakers could also supply protective clogs in a coordinating fabric, which slipped over the shoe, raising it above the dirty streets, while providing arch support. Versions made of wood or metal, known as pattens, were worn by the lower classes. Not until the last decade of the eighteenth century were shoes made with a distinct left and right foot as both were built using the same wooden last. Patterns of wear indicate that so-called 'straight' shoes moulded to the foot over time, although their longevity could be improved by switching sides regularly.

The royal accounts indicate that shoes were frequent purchases. Between January and March 1733, John Reynolds (the 'shoomaker') supplied 27 pairs of shoes for George II's two youngest daughters, Princess Mary (aged 10) and

Princess Louise (aged 9), at a total cost of £9 2s 6d – approximately £1,600 in 2021.[51] All were made of silk damask or silk satin, in blue, green, pink or white. Identical descriptions indicate the two princesses were probably dressed alike and most pairs cost 6s 6d each (£57 in 2021).[52] Labels in shoes appear from around 1750, reflecting the increasing importance of advertising and consumer choice. Some proudly proclaim royal patronage, as seen inside one pair of red leather shoes dating from around 1790 whose label reads 'Sutton Shoe Maker, to Her Royal Highness the Duchess of Cumberland, Henrietta Street, Covent Garden, London'.[53]

## GLOVES

Gloves continued to symbolise a leisured lifestyle and were regarded as an indispensable component of elite dress. In 1733 Queen Caroline bought them by the dozen from the glover John Wood for herself and her children.[54] In paintings gloves are usually shown carried rather than worn. The gesture of a glove being removed, as in the portrait of Princess Augusta (Fig. 3.49), implies respect, as good etiquette required the removal of gloves in the presence of superiors or during the exchange of gifts. Long gloves were a requirement with a formal gown of this kind and could be tied above the elbow to avoid the crumpled appearance depicted by Beechey. Compared to the ornately embroidered gloves of the preceding century, those of the Georgian era were much simpler in design. One of two surviving pairs of evening gloves that belonged to Princess Charlotte is shown here (Fig. 3.50). They are made of thin, supple leather prized for its fit and comfort: this became a specialty of Limerick in Ireland, where this pair was produced. A variety of other fabrics were also used by glove-makers, sometimes with insertions of crochet, applied braid or embroidery. Knitted silk gloves were popular, with the Midlands an important centre for production, although others were imported from Italy and France.[55] Fingerless mittens were another practical option. These usually ended in a point on top of the hand, which could be turned back like a cuff.

Fig. 3.51  Thomas Rowlandson (1757–1827), *The Comforts of High Living*, 1794 (detail).
Hand-coloured etching, 15.5 × 22.3 cm (sheet). RCIN 810458

Fig. 3.52  Princess Sophia (1777–1848), Purse, 1791–1820.
Silk and metal, 10.5 × 5.2 cm. London, Museum of London, 55.19/2

## POCKETS AND PURSES

Most eighteenth-century gowns were made with inconspicuous openings in the side seams, which allowed the wearer to access separate pockets beneath, suspended from waist tapes. Rarely visible in elite portraits, they sometimes appear in prints, such as Rowlandson's etching (Fig. 3.51), where a woman is shown undressing and has removed her gown and stands in her shift and petticoat, a pocket tied around the waist. Pockets were an important item of dress, providing a secure and easily accessible means for women to carry money and possessions.[56] They were often given as gifts and could be ornately embroidered or quilted. By the end of the eighteenth century, small bags known as reticules or ridicules had become popular. Marketed in fashion periodicals as a more modern alternative to traditional tied pockets, they came in a huge variety of styles. The traditional view that tie-on pockets fell into disuse with the rise of slimmer-cut neo-classical dresses and were replaced by handbags is inaccurate. Detachable pockets continued to be worn throughout the nineteenth century – beneath the petticoat to be less noticeable – although they were considered increasingly old-fashioned.[57]

Purses could be acquired from a number of retailers, but purse-making was also a popular creative pastime for women at all levels of society, with the openwork techniques of netting and knotting becoming fashionable in the second half of the eighteenth century. Queen Charlotte and her

daughters were enthusiasts and a delicate netted reticule created by Princess Sophia survives today, made of silk twist in four colours (Fig. 3.52). Once the princess had completed her needlework it would have been taken to a professional to be trimmed with the metal opening bars. In West's portrait (see Fig. 1.16), Queen Charlotte is shown holding a knotting shuttle in her right hand, which has been used to tie a series of knots in the thread held in her left hand. The resulting knotted thread could then be employed for embroidery or as a trimming. Mary Delany was given a gold knotting shuttle ('of most exquisite workmanship and taste') by George III in 1783, which she used to make white silk fringing to decorate her work bag.[58] Perhaps it was similar to the silk bag in the queen's lap, which is decorated with white tassels comparable to surviving examples.[59] Such pastimes were considered appropriate for the leisured classes, the minimal equipment required meaning they could be undertaken anywhere and worked unobtrusively while receiving visitors or attending the theatre. Queen Charlotte was also a keen and highly skilled needlewoman, and a pocket book, probably embroidered by her, was given to Delany in 1781 (Fig. 3.53). It was described by her waiting-woman: 'the outside satin work'd with gold and ornaments with gold spangles, the inside lined with pink satin and contained a knife, sizsars, pencle, rule, compass, bodkin'.[60] In addition to these practical tools, pocket books could hold valuable documents (letters, newspaper articles) as well as pocket almanacs containing useful information such as hackney coach fares, recipes and song lyrics.[61]

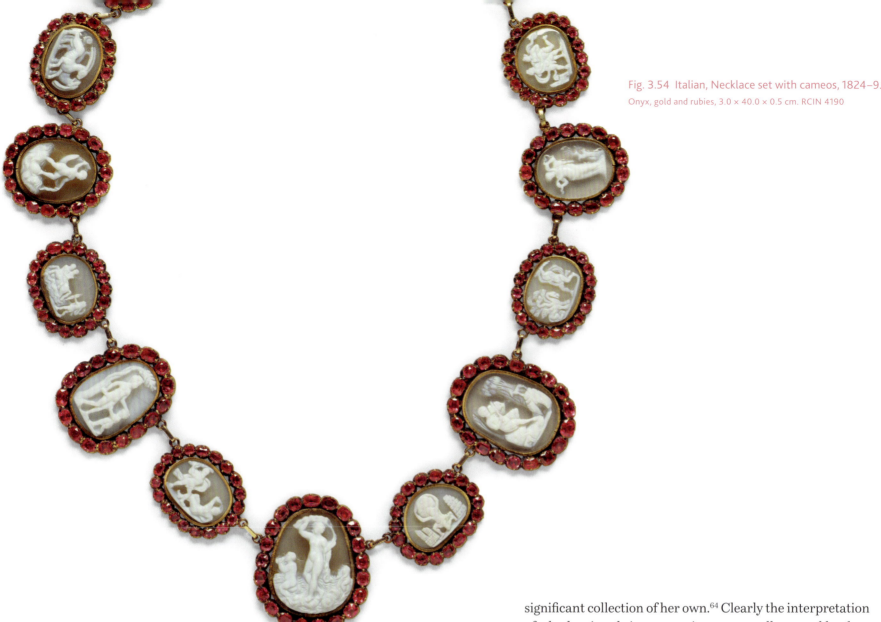

Fig. 3.54 Italian, Necklace set with cameos, 1824–9.
Onyx, gold and rubies, 3.0 × 40.0 × 0.5 cm. RCIN 4190

## JEWELLERY

The extraordinary expense of gemstones compared to the cost of the settings meant that eighteenth-century jewellery was recycled and repurposed in the same way as textiles, explaining why so few pieces survive in their original state. Important jewellery was a form of currency, portable wealth that was passed from one generation to the next and indicated dynastic connections. A bride would mark her marriage by appearing at court in the heirloom jewels of her new family, sometimes reset, although they remained part of the estate and were returned upon death or divorce. The borrowing of important jewels was a common occurrence among friends, proudly reported and used to demonstrate shifting allegiances.[62] Attending court in 1729, Delany 'borrowed my Lady Sunderland's jewels, and made a tearing show'.[63] For her coronation Queen Caroline was lent magnificent diamonds from a dealer, despite owning a

significant collection of her own.[64] Clearly the interpretation of whether jewels in a portrait were actually owned by the wearer should be subject to some scrutiny.

Throughout the eighteenth century, diamonds were the most highly prized gemstone, set off to greater effect by the development of an early version of the multifaceted brilliant cut, perfected in London by the early 1700s.[65] This was combined with foiling techniques (used to enhance reflection and create colour) and less obtrusive collet settings. Although supplies became more plentiful with the discovery of new mines in Brazil in 1725, diamonds remained expensive. Imitation alternatives of glass paste or rock crystal were popular – even among the wealthy – and a refined production technique developed in France in 1734 by the 'King's Jeweler' Georges Stras resulted in an imitation stone that could be highly polished.[66] In 1720 Christopher Pinchbeck also invented an eponymous alloy that resembled gold. The ubiquity of counterfeit items makes establishing the authenticity of jewels or settings in portraiture difficult – even Queen Charlotte had the genuineness of her jewellery questioned.[67]

Fig. 3.55 Josiah Wedgwood & Sons, Chatelaine, *c.*1770–1800.
Jasperware and cut steel, 26.3 × 2.4 × 0.7 cm. RCIN 45860

OVERLEAF
Fig. 3.56 Allan Ramsay (1713–84), *Queen Charlotte, c.*1760–1 (detail).
Oil on canvas, 249.0 × 161.6 cm. RCIN 405308

Jewellery settings of the eighteenth century were more delicate than those of previous years. Newly popular motifs during the first half of the century included ribbon bows, shells and naturalistic flowers, many illustrating the rococo taste for asymmetry. Later, with the rise of neo-classicism, the visual grammar of the antique (palmettes, honeysuckle, Greek keys) became prominent. The cameo technique – which utilised the natural bands of colour found in hardstones and shells – saw a revival in France under the influence of Empress Joséphine, with ancient, Renaissance and contemporary examples reset into parures. Queen Charlotte also owned a collection of cameo-set jewellery. The necklace shown opposite (Fig. 3.54) includes 16 oval cameos carved from onyx, representing scenes from the Labours of Hercules and other mythological stories. Each is encircled by foiled Burmese rubies in various faceted cuts. Such cameos were often made in Italy and carried back to Britain as souvenirs of a Grand Tour. Their influence can be seen in the ceramic plaques (known as jasperware) produced by Josiah Wedgwood, which were incorporated into jewellery with cut-steel mounts by the industrialist Matthew Boulton (Fig. 3.55). Intaglios, created by carving a design into the surface of a stone, were also popular, especially for smaller items like rings and seals.

Eighteenth-century jewellery was often designed with detachable components, providing flexibility in how it could be worn: a pendant could be transformed into a brooch or drop earrings into clusters. The Georgian era saw the introduction of the first clip-on earrings (known as snaps), together with mechanisms for the weight of the earring to be better distributed to alleviate discomfort, such as ribbons tied into the hair.

Queen Charlotte's magnificent collection of jewellery was widely admired and rightly famous. Foreign visitors made requests to see it. To the jewels of her own family with which she arrived in England, Queen Charlotte added those inherited by George III from his father, as well as a group bought from his uncle, the Duke of Cumberland. One of the most noteworthy pieces in the collection was a diamond stomacher, much remarked upon by spectators and valued by the Duchess of Northumberland at £60,000

(equivalent to more than £9.8 million in 2021).[68] Constructed from a fine network of small diamonds, overlaid with a foliate design of larger stones, it was worn for both the royal wedding and coronation (Fig. 3.56). On her wedding day the bride must have presented a glittering spectacle, with earrings, cap, aigrette, necklace and clasps all made of diamonds too.[69] Queen Charlotte also acquired jewels herself, and was given other important gifts, including several large diamonds presented by the Nawab of Arcot during the 1770s in recognition of English support against the French in India. Many prints depict her covered in jewellery, playing on a supposed thirst for gemstones. In one of a pair of prints (Fig. 3.57) she is portrayed as 'The Queen of Hearts Cover'd with Diamonds', the other showing George III as the 'King of Diamonds'. The bulse diamond (seen top left) was a gift to George III from the Nizam of the Deccan, presented to the king by Warren Hastings (1732–1818) on his return to Britain after serving as Governor-General of Bengal and referenced here in the handwritten inscription below. The act was interpreted by many as an attempt by Hastings to bribe the monarch in advance of his impeachment trial for high crimes and misdemeanours in India and was satirised in a number of prints of the time. In her diary, Fanny Burney, Assistant Keeper of the Robes (see Chapter 8), notes that her mistress told her 'how well she had liked at first her Jewels & Ornaments as Queen' so much so that she thought she should 'always chuse to wear them'.[70] This is clearly demonstrated in one of the earliest miniatures of Queen Charlotte, which shows her, aged 17, wearing an elaborate parure set with sapphires and diamonds (Fig. 3.58). With time, however, this enthusiasm seems to have dissipated due to 'the fatigue & trouble of putting them on, & the care they required, & the fear of losing them'.[71] In her will the hereditary jewels were bequeathed by Queen Charlotte to the 'House of Hanover', and after a protracted lawsuit they were returned during the reign of Queen Victoria to George V, King of Hanover.[72]

Bracelets with integrated portrait miniatures were especially popular as royal jewellery, adopted firstly by Augusta, Princess of Wales (see Fig. 8.27), and subsequently Queen Charlotte, who, as Princess of Mecklenburg-Strelitz in her portrait by Johann Georg Ziesenis (see Fig. 8.6), wears on her right wrist a pearl bracelet with a miniature. Soon after, she was presented with a pair of pearl bracelets by George III. One clasp was set with a miniature of the king in profile painted on ivory by Jeremiah Meyer, the other with his hair and cipher, and each surrounded by diamonds. The bracelets are shown in numerous portraits, most clearly by Johan Joseph Zoffany, whose image of the queen in blue also depicts her wearing a multi-strand pearl necklace and large pearl-drop earrings (Fig. 3.59). When boredom overcame the queen during a portrait sitting for the 20-year-old Thomas Lawrence in 1789, she asked Charlotte Papendiek (Assistant Keeper of the Robes to Queen Charlotte after Fanny Burney) to sit as her proxy wearing the bracelet, and rather incongruously it reappears in another drawing of Papendiek with her son, made by Lawrence at the same time.[73] On her wedding day Queen Charlotte was given a ring set with a reduced version of this miniature, also by Meyer, beneath a large flat-cut diamond (Fig. 3.60), which she wore on the little finger of her right hand (see Fig. 3.57), as well as a diamond keeper ring engraved with the date of the ceremony, 8 September 1761 (Fig. 3.61), to 'serve as a guard' to her wedding ring. Papendiek notes that 'On that finger the Queen never allowed herself to wear any other in addition, although fashion at times almost demanded it.'[74] Two other rings belonging to Queen Charlotte also survive, a cushion-shaped diamond (Fig. 3.62) and another set with an opal and nine large pearls (Fig. 3.63). While the queen is often shown wearing pearl bracelets and necklaces in paintings, she rarely wears rings, Gainsborough's portrait of c.1781 being an exception (see Fig. 8.11), although here it is only her simple wedding band.

A greater differentiation between day and evening wear is a feature of jewellery in the Georgian era. Girandole (triple pear-drop) earrings of the type worn by Queen Charlotte in the portrait by Ziesenis were the height of fashion for evening wear but far too grand for daywear (see Fig. 8.6). In fact, the prestigious jewels deemed appropriate for formal court occasions are infrequently

OPPOSITE
Fig. 3.59  Johan Joseph Zoffany (1733–1810),
*Queen Charlotte*, 1771 (detail).
Oil on canvas, 162.9 × 137.2 cm. RCIN 405071

BELOW, CLOCKWISE FROM TOP LEFT
Fig. 3.60  Jeremiah Meyer (1735–89), Ring with a miniature
of George III, 1761.
Gold and diamonds, miniature on ivory. RCIN 52211

Fig. 3.61  English, Queen Charlotte's keeper ring, 1761.
Gold and diamonds. RCIN 65429

Fig. 3.62  English, Queen Charlotte's finger ring, *c.*1810.
Gold and diamond. RCIN 52228

Fig. 3.63  English, Queen Charlotte's opal finger ring, *c.*1810.
Gold, opal and pearls. RCIN 52214

LEFT
Fig. 3.64  Previously attributed to Angelica Kauffmann
(1741–1807), *Queen Charlotte*, 1770–2.
Oil on canvas, 69.5 × 60.4 cm. RCIN 409388

represented in paint, and instead portraits tend to depict
the forms of jewellery more commonly worn during the
day, such as a simple string of pearls around the neck or
a fabric choker, both of which are shown in Francis Cotes's
painting of Princess Louisa and Princess Caroline (see
Fig. 3.15). Similarly, in a portrait previously attributed to
Angelica Kauffmann, Queen Charlotte's hair is decorated
with a jewelled pin, but tied around her neck is a wide
blue choker made of ruched ribbons in different shades
of blue (Fig. 3.64). Black silk ribbons were also popular,
worn by both Queen Charlotte and Lady Charlotte Finch
in Zoffany's portrait of *c.*1771–2 (see Fig. 5.8), the
colour prized for its ability to emphasise the whiteness
of the complexion.

# 4

# Dressing Men

*And there's your pretty Gentlemen,*
*All dress'd in Silk and Satin*
*That get a Spice of ev'ry Thing,*
*Excepting Sense and Latin.*

HENRY CAREY, 1730[1]

The development of the three-piece suit in the 1660s provided the blueprint for the key components of the male wardrobe worn throughout the eighteenth century: coat, waistcoat and breeches. Although all three continued to be worn during the Georgian period, both in Britain and on the Continent, as the century progressed a new style of informal coat known as the frock presented a more relaxed alternative to the tightly fitted court style, while trousers began to replace breeches in the early nineteenth century. The selection of fabric from which the garments were made, together with their trimmings, was influenced by the fashionability, status and wealth of the wearer along with the formality of the occasion. Textiles decorated or woven with metal threads supplied much of the requisite sparkle on the most formal occasions, and jewellery for men was limited to functional items such as buckles, watches and fob seals. While all of these could be ornate, set with diamonds or other gemstones, a shift towards a simpler and less ostentatious style saw the adoption of alternative metals, including cut steel and pinchbeck.

PREVIOUS PAGE
Detail of Fig. 5.8

Fig. 4.1  Pietro Longhi (c.1701–85), *The Married Couple's Breakfast*, 1744.
Oil on panel, 48.9 × 60.3 cm. RCIN 403029

## UNDERGARMENTS

In the informal setting of *The Married Couple's Breakfast*
(Fig. 4.1) Pietro Longhi depicts a husband and wife in
relaxed morning dress. The woman is wearing a wrapping
gown, open to reveal her shift (worn without stays); the
man sits in bed wearing only a shirt, undone at the neck,
his lower body concealed by a luxurious blanket. The shirt
demonstrates the typical construction features of this date
(1744): the sleeves are voluminous and finely pleated into
the cuffs and shoulder seams, while the neckline has a deep
opening trimmed with a modest frill, known as a jabot. The
man's position makes it difficult to determine whether he
is still wearing a nightshirt or has changed into a day shirt.
Although similar in construction, a nightshirt was often
longer and fuller. The style of the collar seems to suggest
a day shirt; nightshirts usually had flatter collars.

As the dress of the male servant shows, men's shirts
were almost completely concealed by the upper garments,
with only the cuffs and collar visible, although during the
first half of the eighteenth century it was fashionable to
leave the top waistcoat buttons undone to reveal the jabot,
which could be made of lace or ornately embroidered.
While the plain cuffs on the husband's shirt are probably
integral, more elaborate lace or whitework ruffles of
the type worn by Prince Frederick in a portrait formerly
attributed to George Knapton (Fig. 4.2 and see Fig. 2.1)
were usually detachable so that they could be carefully
washed separately. Such an impractical element served as
a clear indication that the wearer had no need to undertake
manual labour. After reaching their peak size around the
mid-eighteenth century, sleeve ruffles for men had fallen
from favour entirely by the end of the century.

The association of a shirt in the Historic Royal Palaces
Collection (Fig. 4.3) with George III is confirmed by a
monogram and crown embroidered in red cross stitch
above the right side vent, together with the date (1810).
The collar fastens with two Dorset thread buttons and the
jabot is plain. Shirt construction did not change dramatically
throughout the century and was based on a series of
geometric pieces of fabric that minimised wastage across

Fig. 4.2  Formerly attributed to George Knapton (1698–1778), *Frederick, Prince of Wales*, c.1745 (detail).
Oil on canvas, 127.1 × 101.3 cm. RCIN 405249

it could be tied in various ways, such as tucked through a buttonhole 'à la Steinkirk'.[3] Although cravats continued to be worn well into the eighteenth century by older men, including George I who wears one in a portrait painted when he was in his sixties (see Fig. 2.2), by the 1720s fashionable young men had begun to adopt the stock instead, especially on formal occasions. This consisted of a piece of pre-pleated fabric that fastened behind the neck, simplifying the processes of dressing and laundering. Stocks were most commonly made of white linen or cotton, although black silk versions were worn by military officers (see Fig. 11.12). A surviving stock owned by George II demonstrates its construction: a piece of finely pleated linen attached to tabs on either side (Fig. 4.4). The connection to the king is indicated by a crown and the number 46 embroidered in fine red cross stitch on the reverse. On one tab are three eyelet holes, through which would be poked a triple-pronged stock buckle. These could be highly decorative, providing an opportunity for the display of jewels and precious metal. The other tab would then be threaded through the buckle and tightened to the appropriate length. 'The Stock with Buckle made of Plate / Has put the Cravat out of date', wrote Laurence Whyte in 1742.[4]

By the 1780s the cravat had become fashionable once again, with the stock increasingly only worn by the elderly or provincial: an illustration of the peculiar circularity of fashion. The Prince of Wales was at the forefront of the return of the cravat in the 1780s among stylish young men. In a portrait of 1787 he wears his in a large bow nestled into the collar of his elegantly cut blue coat (see Fig. 4.12). French fashion periodicals described cravats of this type as a *cravat à l'anglaise*, an example of the trend for English styles, although for many the garment was simply known as a neckcloth. The manner in which it was tied allowed for individual expression, and by the Regency period the process of wearing a cravat had been elevated to an art form, requiring perfectly laundered white linen and starch to maintain the appropriate combination of understated but crisp precision. Beau Brummell was renowned for his exactitude regarding a faultlessly tied cravat, with one

the width of the roll. However, subtle changes in shirt design can be seen: the tighter-fitting coats of the latter decades necessarily required narrower shirt sleeves, and at the same time collars became higher. Like most garments worn directly next to the skin, George III's shirt is made of linen, a comfortable yet hardwearing textile that could withstand regular washing to remove sweat and dirt. Cotton was also frequently used for shirts from the 1820s. Men were advised to wear clean linen every day,[2] cleanliness being an important indicator of pride and self-worth, regardless of economic position. Shirts of a similar style and cut were worn across the social spectrum, the fineness of the linen being the key measure of quality and therefore cost. For warmth, an undershirt of fluffy wool flannel might be worn. These were particularly associated with the elderly and those suffering from illness.

For formal wear, the collar of the shirt was always fastened, and the join concealed in some manner. A cravat had been the most fashionable style of neckwear during the seventeenth century – in 1688 Randle Holme described it as 'a long Towel put about the Collar' – and

Fig. 4.3 Shirt worn by George III, 1810.

Linen. London, Historic Royal Palaces, 3502558

Fig. 4.4 Stock worn by George II, 1740–60.

Linen, 10.2 × 43.2 cm. Virginia, Colonial Williamsburg, 1993-166, A

Both these items of personal linen incorporate a crown embroidered in red cross stitch, indicating their royal connection. While the number 46 on the stock may represent an abbreviated form of the date (1746), it may alternatively be a numbering system used to track the king's linens.

biographer recounting him 'coming downstairs with a quantity of tumbled neckcloths under his arm', and Brummell's manservant stating solemnly, 'Oh, they are our failures.'[5] One loosely knotted style was known as 'à la Byron', its self-consciously relaxed appearance a reference to the Romantic poet (although portraits tend to show Lord Byron wearing conventional forms of neckwear). The multiplicity of ways in which a cravat could be tied was satirised in George Cruikshank's book *Neckclothitania or Tietania* (1818),[6] indicating that by this date the cravat had started to be referred to as a tie, an item of dress that still today can be used either to express individuality or to bind certain social groups together.

While invisible in portraits, drawers seem to have become more common for men as the eighteenth century progressed, providing a separate comfortable and washable layer between the body and the outer legwear. Usually made of linen, drawers were cut in the same manner as a pair of breeches, fastening at the waist with buttons and gathered below each knee with drawstring ties. Drawers do not appear to have been an obligatory item in the male wardrobe, however, and many men probably continued wrapping the long tails of the shirt around the legs instead.

## STOCKINGS AND GARTERS

Stockings, also known as hose, were worn by men and women and there was very little difference in style between the sexes. They were knitted from a variety of materials, and regular innovations to the stocking frame (originally invented by William Lee in 1583) meant that, by the eighteenth century, England was renowned for the quality of its knitted garments. One of the most important changes to stocking design at the end of the seventeenth century was the introduction of triangular inserts, or gores, which enabled a better fit around the ankle. These elements (at the time known as clocks) were a focus for decoration until the mid-eighteenth century, becoming taller and increasingly ornate. Clocks were often made in a contrasting colour, with motifs added through plating (knitting in an extra thread of a different colour to the ground thread) or embroidery,

sometimes using metal threads. In the early eighteenth century stockings were pulled up over the bottom of the breeches (Fig. 4.5), but this fashion was out of date by the 1730s.

While stockings are often excluded from paintings by virtue of the popular (and cheaper) half-length canvas format, in a full-length portrait like that of Johann Christian Fischer by Thomas Gainsborough (see Fig. 4.10) stockings are a prominent feature, confronting the viewer at eye level when the painting is hung above dado height, as was typical within a historical setting. Moreover, most stockings worn by men in eighteenth-century portraiture are white, creating a strong contrast against the breeches and the surroundings, projecting the calves forward as the darker colours recede. An attractive and shapely male leg had long been considered a mark of masculinity, and this remained the case in the eighteenth century. To minimise the appearance of hair and create a smoother surface, understockings could be worn, while those with less muscular calves could strap stuffed pads to the leg. Although such aids were probably quite rare, they were a favourite subject for satirists, for whom the inauthenticity of the clothed human body was a recurrent theme. Stockings could also be padded with layers of fabric or wool: a source of complaint for Richard Brinsley Sheridan's Lord Foppington, who remarks to his hosier, the appropriately named Mr Mendlegs, 'The calves of these stockings are thickened a little too much; they make my legs look like a porter's.'[7]

Although there was a shift away from the brighter colours popular earlier in the century, the ubiquity of white silk stockings in eighteenth-century portraiture is unlikely to be an accurate representation of what was worn every day. Rather, most men would have owned stockings in a variety of colours and materials for different occasions. White silk, being easily soiled and difficult to clean, was considered most appropriate for special situations. The presence of this colour therefore reflects the fact that many people chose to dress in their 'best' outfits to be recorded in paint. Plain white stockings do not survive in great number, however, presumably because the unusual decorative

Fig. 4.5 After Robert Edge Pine (c.1730–88), *George II*, 1759–60 (detail).
Oil on canvas, 128.5 × 103.0 cm. RCIN 404629

Fig. 4.6 Stocking worn by George III, 1780–1820.
Knitted silk. London, Historic Royal Palaces, 3502559

versions were regarded as more worthy of preservation, making the silk stockings worn by George III a rare example (Fig. 4.6). Knitted flat on a stocking frame then seamed at the back of the leg, these demonstrate the careful shaping required to fit around the calf. The decoration is limited to a small self-coloured geometric motif above each gore.

In 1750–1 Conrad Fulling supplied cotton hose for several of the royal children. These varied in price depending on the age of the child, with the '12 Pair of the Best Knit Cotton hose', for the one-year-old Prince Frederick, costing 1s 6d a pair, while the '24 pair of fine Cotton hose', for the thirteen-year-old Princess Augusta, cost 10s 6d a pair.[8] Stockings made of cotton were initially spun and knitted by hand, the fibres being weaker than linen or silk and unable to withstand the pressure of the mechanical process. However, by the end of the eighteenth century, improvements in technology that enabled the

machine spinning of a high-quality cotton thread strong enough to use for hosiery allowed the production of very fine cotton stockings in England, an industry centred around Nottingham. These were ultra-fashionable and much admired across Europe, including by Empress Joséphine, who ordered six pairs despite France being at war with England at the time.[9]

Stockings were held up by garters tied or clasped above or below the knee. In the foreground of *St James's Park and the Mall* (Fig. 4.7), an elegantly dressed woman wearing a wide hoop holds a bright red garter in her mouth while pulling up her white stocking. Garters were made of ribbon or braid and were usually concealed by the breeches or petticoat. In 1783 spring garters were patented in England by the surgeon-dentist Martin Van Butchell (1735–1814), incorporating fine wire springs encased within strips of fabric to add elasticity.

By virtue of being hidden during most activities, garters were considered intimate items of dress, sometimes given as gifts between lovers and woven with amorous messages. *The Morning after Marriage* (Fig. 4.8) is a drawing after a print by James Gillray that was reissued in 1788 in response to widespread speculation that the Prince of Wales, later George IV, had secretly married the Catholic Maria Fitzherbert on the Continent (in fact he had done so in London in 1785, but without the consent of his father). Both the prince and Fitzherbert are shown with loose garters, one stocking slipping down. Each garter is embroidered with words: the motto of the Order of the Garter for the prince, the name Fox (indicating a gift from Charles James Fox) for Fitzherbert. The stocking's intimate nature led to it having a symbolic role in a marriage ceremony. One account of the wedding of Frederick, Prince of Wales, to Princess Augusta in 1736 records, 'After Supper, they retired to the Prince's Apartments, where as soon as they were in bed, the stocking was thrown, by the four young Ladies that supported the Train, and all the Company passed through the room.'[10]

A fallen stocking was widely recognised as a symbol of dissolute behaviour and loose morals. In the tavern scene of William Hogarth's *A Rake's Progress* (Fig. 4.9),

the inebriated protagonist sits lopsidedly, knee buttons of his breeches undone, one stocking falling towards the ankle, unaware that his pocket watch has been purloined. Hogarth here inverts the typical gendered association of a fallen stocking with a promiscuous woman. While the prostitute at the lower right reveals her stockings to the viewer, hers have remained fully gartered for longer than the Rake's and their upcoming removal feels intentional, unlike his.[11]

## COATS AND WAISTCOATS

For most occasions men wore both a waistcoat and coat on top of the shirt. During the early years of the Hanoverian period, the coat was cut tightly at the waist and flaring out into skirts reaching the knee to create a distinctive triangular silhouette. Stiffened with materials such as buckram and horsehair, the coat skirts formed a series of side pleats, with a slit at the centre back. The waistcoat

Fig. 4.10 Thomas Gainsborough (1727–88), *Johann Christian Fischer*, 1774–80.

Oil on canvas, 229.0 × 150.8 cm. RCIN 407298

and coat were nearly the same length as each other, with muted shades of brown, grey and blue being popular, although they were usually made of different fabrics. At this date the waistcoat would often be sleeved, sometimes utilising a cheaper textile for those parts concealed by the coat.

The depiction of Henry Popple standing within a family group portrait by Hogarth demonstrates how the coat and waistcoat had changed by 1730 (see Fig. 1.11). Overall, the line has become more relaxed, the coat now falling in a natural shape without stiffening. The waistcoat and coat are made of contrasting fabrics: a rich forest green silk for the waistcoat, and a plain pale grey fabric for the coat, which also matches the breeches. The waistcoat and coat are still of a similar length, but the waistcoat is the more decorative of the two, with applied silver lace focused on the most visible areas, down the front fastening and around the pockets. The coat is now worn unbuttoned, and the top buttons of the waistcoat are undone to reveal the ruffle attached to the shirt beneath and enabling Popple to rest his hand inside the waistcoat in the fashionable manner. The cuffs of the coat have developed into deep boot cuffs reaching beyond the elbow, and stopping well before the wrist to reveal the ruffles of the shirt. Cuffs would become much smaller over the following decades.

In a portrait by Gainsborough, Johann Christian Fischer wears a style that had returned to fashion during the 1770s, a three-piece suit made of matching fabric (Fig. 4.10). Shades like this russet-coloured velvet were popular around this date, as illustrated by the number of similar suits that survive from the period, including a beautiful example shown opposite (Fig. 4.11). As a young man in his thirties, Fischer is wearing a suit that reflects the fashionable line of the 1770s: the coat is made with tight-fitting sleeves and small round cuffs, the waistcoat by now much shorter than the coat, the front cut on the diagonal rather than straight across. Fischer's suit creates a cohesive colour scheme, enhancing the warm hues of the violin and pianoforte-harpsichord while contrasting with the olive-green textiles, and ensuring the viewer's attention is focused on his face, seemingly illuminated by the light of inspiration.

Fig. 4.11 Possibly French, Court suit of coat, waistcoat and breeches, *c*.1760s.
Red and gold cut silk velvet. Bath, Fashion Museum Bath, BATMC II.24.9 to B

The similar surviving suit (see Fig. 4.11) is made of red silk velvet, woven to create a textured surface in a small-scale geometric pattern reminiscent of brickwork, and accentuated with stripes of woven gold thread.

A portrait by Alexandre-Auguste Robineau shows George, Prince of Wales, at the forefront of fashion in 1787, both in his ensemble's limited colour palette and the elegance of its fit (Fig. 4.12). One visitor to London noted in 1790, 'dark blue is the favourite colour of the English … of fifty persons whom one meets in the streets of London, at least twenty are dressed in dark-blue coats'.[12] The style of the prince's coat is inspired by riding dress, close-fitting but sloping away at the front to reveal a shorter waistcoat cut horizontally at the waist. Only the upper buttons of the coat are designed to fasten, meeting at the upper chest, then falling away in a graceful curve, thereby allowing a glimpse of the fashionable striped waistcoat. A similar surviving waistcoat from around the same date, made of cream silk woven with narrow green stripes, is shown here (Fig. 4.13). This demonstrates the new double-breasted style: often only one row of buttons is functional, the other being purely decorative. Waistcoat pockets by now are straight, horizontal and without flaps. One type of waistcoat seems to have become associated with the future George IV, being referred to by a visitor to court in 1792 as a 'waistcoat à la Prince of Wales'. Although there is no visual record of its appearance, it was described as having 'two rows of silk buttons, which stand very far apart … The neckline of the waistcoat is so low that it does not even cover the heart … The material is of yellow cotton with Windsor-blue stripes'.[13] The 1790s also saw the development of a fashion for more than one waistcoat to be worn at once, or for waistcoats designed to look like multiple layers.

One significant change in English men's dress during the eighteenth century involved the widespread adoption of the frock coat. Originally a form of working dress, the frock was adopted by fashionable English gentlemen as an informal style suitable for riding and other country pursuits, but by the 1760s it was considered appropriate for all but the most formal occasions requiring full dress. David Garrick wears a blue frock coat for his portrait

Fig. 4.14  After Sir Joshua
Reynolds (1723–92),
*Portrait of the Artist*,
c.1788–1800.

Oil on canvas, 76.2 × 63.4 cm.
RCIN 406437

by Hogarth (see Fig. 1.18), lending his attire an air of
informality that suits the domestic setting and contemplative
pose. The most distinctive feature of the frock coat is its
small turndown collar, unlike the formal coat, which
was initially collarless, then developed a standing collar.
Beneath his frock coat, Garrick wears a waistcoat, also
blue but richly decorated with broad bands of gold lace.

Sir Joshua Reynolds chose an understated frock coat
for his self-portrait, painted in c.1788 (Fig. 4.14). Frock
coats were made of plain materials, usually woollen cloth
or linen, in dark or neutral colours. They had minimal
adornment, with simple buttons and no lace or embroidery,
although the collar could be finished with velvet. Surviving
examples are rare, as they were well-used garments,
probably worn and recycled until threadbare. The frock
was unstiffened and cut with a looser fit, making it more
comfortable: 'I frequently sighed for my loose Frock', wrote
an English visitor to France, 'which I look upon as an
Emblem of our happy Constitution; for it lays a Man under
no uneasy Restraint, but leaves it in his Power to do as he
pleases.'[14] Although French men also adopted the frock coat,
and it appears regularly in fashion periodicals of the 1780s,
the French version, known as a *frac*, was more decorative
and tight-fitting, often made of silk, with one young man

in the *Cabinet des modes* described as wearing 'a dragon green frock, adorned with apple green silk embroidery'.[15] Over time, frock coats of this type were considered formal enough to wear at court. The Prince of Wales is recorded as having bought many frock coats, including 'a black Frock with silk linings and black velvet collar' in 1799.[16]

By the end of the century English men had firmly embraced a smart version of country clothing as the standard form of everyday dress, and this style remained popular throughout the Regency, suitable for riding, walking and visiting. Coats could be single or double breasted, cut horizontally across the front, as in the portrait of Robert Stewart, Viscount Castlereagh, by Sir Thomas Lawrence (Fig. 4.15), or sloping down like a traditional riding coat. Both styles revealed the full length of the wearer's legs. In a miniature painted during the sitter's extended visit to London from Vermont, Colonel John Graham demonstrates the fashion for the collars of men's coats to increase in size during the 1790s, the edges turned back to produce wide lapels that framed the neckwear (Fig. 4.16). The Prince of

Wales wears a similar coat in a watercolour by Richard Dighton (Fig. 4.17), although here it is of a particular style known as a 'Jean de Bry'. Named after the French president of the National Convention in Revolutionary France, it was characterised by bulky puffed sleeves, achieved by gathering the fabric into the shoulder seams and padding. These sleeves, which extended well over the wrist, in combination with the large collar, pinched-in waist and narrow tails, lent the coat's wearer a top-heavy appearance that was satirised regularly in prints by Gillray in the years around 1800.[17]

Allowing for subtle variations in style, by the end of the century the most fashionable men's coats were invariably made of woollen fabrics in sombre dark tones. Emphasis now lay firmly on the superiority of cut and manipulation of quality cloth by a skilful tailor, rather than ostentatious decoration. In this regard English tailors were admired across Europe. The best were able to use fabric and padding to enhance the male body towards the eighteenth-century physical ideal (accentuating the pectoral muscles,

Fig. 4.17 Richard Dighton (1795–1880), *George Prince of Wales on Horseback*, 1804.
Watercolour and touches of bodycolour on paper, 61.2 × 50.0 cm. RCIN 453262

Fig. 4.18 Thomas Rowlandson (1757–1827), *Three Principal Requisites to Form a Modern Man of Fashion*, 1814.
Hand-coloured etching, 27.1 × 38.5 cm (sheet). RCIN 810936

for instance, and slimming the waist), while concealing imperfections, a process that was always undertaken in close consultation with the customer. The dark coats were usually worn with a light or buff-coloured waistcoat of silk or cotton, which elite men would have ordered in bulk: George IV, for example, ordered '24 White Marseille Waistcoats single breasted' in 1810 from the tailor John Weston, at a total cost of £45 12s.[18] Three plain white waistcoats worn by George IV still survive in the Museum of London, each marked with the date.[19] Their increasing circumference reflects the king's changing body shape, regularly mocked by satirists.

Outerwear options to protect against inclement weather included different styles of overcoat (variously known as a greatcoat, box-coat or 'surtout' in fashion periodicals). Like the frock coat, it was inspired by functional garments of working-class men, particularly coachmen, whose overcoats incorporated one or more broad capes extending across the shoulders as protection against rain. The greatcoat made the transition from utilitarian to fashionable garment around the middle of the century, with triple collars very popular from the 1780s. The fashion can be seen within the broader context of young men adopting the mannerisms of the lower classes, resulting in a blurring of traditional class boundaries that was a source of dismay and ridicule to many. Thomas Rowlandson's *Three Principal Requisites to Form a Modern Man of Fashion* plays on this concern (Fig. 4.18), commenting that a man of fashion was required to dress like a coachman, study boxing and bull-baiting and speak in slang fluently.

The most recognisable overcoat in portraiture may be that worn by Napoleon Bonaparte, a garment that formed an important component of his iconography. In all three paintings of Napoleon by Hippolyte Paul Delaroche in the Royal Collection he wears the same grey greatcoat over military uniform, one of which still survives in the Musée de l'Armée in Paris. Painted posthumously in the 1840s, Delaroche based his likeness of the emperor on the description in Baron Norvin's *Histoire de Napoleon*, published in 1827. In one painting he is shown slumped

in a chair (see Fig. 12.23), wearing the blue and white uniform of a colonel of the *Grenadiers-à-Pied* of the Imperial Guard, the practical unadorned grey coat in contrast to the luxurious red textiles of his surroundings.

## BREECHES AND TROUSERS

Breeches reaching just below the knee were the standard lower body covering for most men throughout the eighteenth century. During the early years of the Hanoverian period, breeches were often cut from a fabric matching the coat, with the waistcoat in a different material. This remained the most formal combination and is what George II continued to wear throughout his life (see Fig. 2.3), while younger men began to adopt a more informal option, with the breeches cut from a contrasting fabric. Breeches were rarely embroidered, although the cuff at the knee could be decorated with buckles and buttons.

Given that breeches were largely concealed by the longer coats of the first half of the century, a precise fit

Fig. 4.19 George Stubbs (1724–1806), *George IV when Prince of Wales*, 1791.
Oil on canvas, 102.6 × 127.7 cm. RCIN 400142

was not a high priority: the seat was cut quite full for comfort when sitting, while laces could be used to adjust the sizing around the waist. The front opening was usually fastened with a set of buttons arranged vertically. However, the combination of the new cutaway style of coat and shorter waistcoat led to greater attention on body coverings below the waist, and there was a shift away from the baggier shapes towards a more form-fitting style. There were also changes in colour, with breeches of a pale buff or stone-coloured fabric becoming increasingly popular during the neo-classical period, as seen on the Prince of Wales in his portrait by George Stubbs (Fig. 4.19). While these paler colours provided a visual contrast against a dark coat, they also evoked a classical aesthetic ideal by echoing antique statuary, their tight fit emphasising the human form.

During the first half of the century breeches had been made of similar materials to the coat and waistcoat: woollen cloth or silk. Hardwearing breeches of thick leather had long been a functional option for working men, but the softer, more pliable skins such as doeskin and lambskin were now highly desirable among men of fashion. Nankeen, a thick washable cotton usually used in its unbleached yellow hue that gave the appearance of soft leather,

was also fashionable for breeches (Fig. 4.20). This pair illustrates the new style of front opening most typical of the second half of the eighteenth century. Known as a fall flap, it fastened with buttons at each top corner and provided a neater and more practical option. Tightness at the knee is achieved here through three cut-steel buttons and a tiny buckle on each leg; string ties are also often seen. During the 1790s bunches of ribbons below the knee were especially fashionable (as seen in Fig. 4.19), commonly believed to have originated in the clothing worn by the notorious thief and highwayman John Rann (1750–74), 'Sixteen-string Jack', to his execution.[20] In the relaxed comfort of his own home a man would undo the buttons, buckles or ties at the bottom of his breeches, although this is rarely depicted in formal portraits.

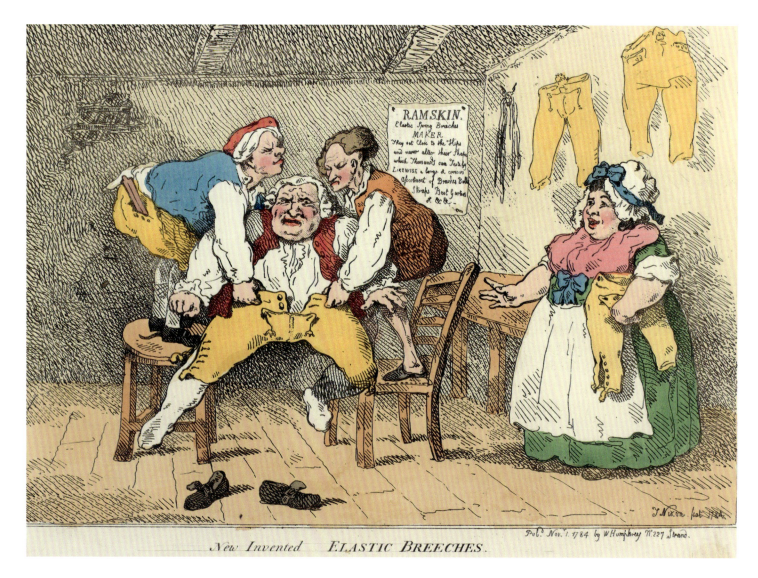

New Invented ELASTIC BREECHES.

Tightly fitting fine leather was the most expensive option for breeches towards the end of the eighteenth century, but was not without its practical difficulties, as Robert Southey recounted:

> When a gentleman was in labour of a new pair of leathern breeches, all his strength was required to force himself into them … when it was nearly accomplished, the maker put his hands between the patient's legs, closed them, and bade him sit on them like a saddle, and kick out one leg at a time, as if swimming. They could not be buttoned without the help of an instrument.[21]

Rowlandson ridicules such efforts in a print that shows a man of large girth being manhandled into an optimistically small pair of breeches by two tailors. A placard on the wall proclaims 'RAMSKIN Elastic Spring Breeches MAKER. They set close to the Hips and never alter their Shape' (Fig. 4.21).

Pantaloons were a key transitional garment in the shift from knee breeches to trousers for all but the most formal court events by the 1830s. Reaching to calf or ankle level, pantaloons (named after the *commedia dell'arte* character Pantalone) required fabrics with sufficient elasticity to pass over the foot, while also retaining the appropriate clinginess and close fit that were considered desirable. Machine-knitted silks and cottons and cloth cut on the bias were popular options, although fine leather is also regularly recorded. Pantaloons had long formed a component of the dress of Hungarian hussar regiments (two officers wearing red and blue pantaloons appear in the lower right of *St James's Park and the Mall*, dating from *c.*1745; see pp. 2–3) and the Prince of Wales had adopted them as part of his fascination with hussar uniform in the 1780s. They were also familiar to many as a form of masquerade costume. But it was not until the 1790s that pantaloons made the transition into popular and fashionable civilian dress. The wardrobe accounts of the Prince of Wales reveal that he much

Fig. 4.21 Thomas Rowlandson (1757–1827), *New Invented Elastic Breeches*, 1784.
Hand-coloured etching, 30.3 × 45.3 cm (sheet). RCIN 810113

Fig. 4.22 George Sanders (1774–1846), *George Gordon, 6th Lord Byron*, c.1807–8.
Oil on canvas, 112.5 × 89.4 cm. RCIN 402411

admired the look, although sadly we can only imagine his remarkable appearance in the 'lilack striped Callico Pantaloons' acquired in 1798 for 19 shillings.[22] We can, however, get a sense of what his 'leather pantaloons' of 'prime doeskin' might have looked like from Dighton's watercolour of the prince (see Fig. 4.17). Costing £4 14s 6d – the equivalent of more than £380 in 2021 – they were one of two pairs of leather pantaloons acquired from Joshua White (named as 'breechesmaker') in July 1801, who was also required to 'clean and alter' a third pair.[23]

Long worn as part of working-class dress, by the end of the eighteenth century trousers had been embraced as a form of children's clothing (see Chapter 5), a factor which may have played some role in encouraging adults to accept them. 'Trowsers' were looser in cut than pantaloons and more forgiving for those without muscular legs. The Prince of Wales was one of the earliest adopters of the new style, choosing trousers for his beachside walks in Brighton, which seems to have helped cement their popularity among the fashionable set. The depiction of Lord Byron (1788–1824) at the age of around 20 wearing trousers (Fig. 4.22) also puts him in the vanguard of the new fashion, which only started to appear in periodicals at around the time the portrait was being painted (*c*.1807–8). Byron's preference for boots and trousers over shoes and knee breeches has been connected to a self-consciousness about a physical disability of his right foot.[24] Suitably, he is shown at a rocky seashore, perhaps a deliberate nod to the historic popularity of trousers among sailors (see Chapter 11). Byron's outfit, however, looks nothing like a sailor's 'slops', his garment being elegantly cut from high-quality dark cloth, with a fall flap opening, and a matching waistcoat and short jacket. The second figure, probably Byron's manservant Robert Rushton (1793–1833), is dressed in a similar manner, although his trousers are in a lighter fabric, more typical of the earliest styles and linking back to the taste for pale-coloured pantaloons. Within a decade, dark-coloured trousers – usually black – which were designed to match the coat, had become standard for men's everyday wear, and this was to remain the case throughout the nineteenth century.

An exception to the trend for subdued colours can be seen in the style of dress worn by the so-called 'macaronies', originally consisting of a group of young elite men who, from 1764, gathered regularly at Almack's club, in London. Named after the Italian pasta dish (possibly derived from *maccherone*, Italian for boor) they were supposed to have popularised in England after experiencing it on their Grand Tour through Italy, macaronies were known for their exaggeratedly flamboyant and ultra-fashionable styles of dress, incorporating tight coats in bright colours, oversized buttons, nosegays, towering wigs, tiny hats and patterned stockings. 'The infection at St. James's was soon caught in the city, and we have now Macaronies of every denomination, from the colonel of the Train'd-Bands down to the errand-boy', denounced *Town and Country Magazine* in 1772.[25]

Fig. 4.23 John Vanderbank (1694–1739), *George I*, 1726. Oil on canvas, 316.0 × 240.4 cm. RCIN 404412

eighteenth century, after which they were rarely worn, other than with formal court dress. Similarly, the fashionable square toe of the seventeenth century gradually became more rounded by the 1740s, although some people (including George II) continued to wear the old-fashioned style into old age. The new shape can be seen in Pietro Longhi's *Blind-Man's Buff*, which shows shoes from a variety of angles simultaneously (see Fig. 1.15).

Most men's shoes in the eighteenth century were made with a tongue and two latchet straps, which were fastened together with a buckle. Buckles had been introduced at the Stuart court under Charles II and continued to be worn throughout the eighteenth century, providing the main focus of interest to the lower half of the body. Buckles were interchangeable between pairs of shoes and could be oblong or round, with a curved cross-sectional profile to fit the form of the foot. At court, buckles made of precious metals and decorated with diamonds were a luxury, although pinchbeck or steel set with vitreous paste stones were cheaper alternatives. Cut steel was another new technique that produced buckles with highly faceted surfaces, which were much admired in France. Buckles reached their maximum dimensions in the so-called Artois buckle, introduced in the 1770s and named after the comte d'Artois, brother of Louis XVI. Fischer wears a large pair in Gainsborough's portrait from around that date (see Fig. 4.10). This painting also demonstrates the typical low heel height for men's shoes in the second half of the century. The Prince of Wales evidently had an enthusiasm for shoe buckles. In 1789 the comtesse de Boigne was shown his dressing room, where she found 'a large table entirely covered with shoe buckles. I expressed my astonishment at the sight and Mrs Fitzherbert, with a laugh, opened a large cupboard which was also full; there were enough buckles for every day of the year.'[26] By the end of the century shoe buckles had largely been replaced by shoe strings or ribbons, traditionally a working-class style.

Although boots made of soft leather had been highly fashionable at the court of Charles I, by the early eighteenth century boots were considered utilitarian rather than fashionable. George I wears the most typical style, known

Macaronies were a dream for caricaturists, with numerous prints ridiculing their extreme fashions, which – being deemed excessively foreign – were considered both unpatriotic and effeminate.

## SHOES AND BOOTS

While boots were worn for practical activities, such as riding and travelling during the eighteenth century, it was not until the 1780s that they became fashionable items of dress. Instead men wore shoes, usually made of plain black leather (often imported from Spain), the design of which did not change significantly over the course of the century. The seventeenth-century fashion for shoes with tall red heels for both men and women, initially popularised at the court of Louis XIV, persisted into the first decades of the

Fig. 4.24  Thomas
Rowlandson (1757–1827),
*Four O'Clock in the Country*,
1788–90.

Hand-coloured etching with
aquatint, 27.4 × 34.0 cm (sheet).
RCIN 810388

as jackboots, in an equestrian portrait by John Vanderbank (Fig. 4.23). Square-toed and made of very thick, shiny leather, they have a wide top that could be turned up to protect the thigh. The name derived from the process of waterproofing or 'jacking' the leather by treating it with wax and tar or pitch. Boots were associated with military dress, as well as civilian riding and hunting, the uppers providing protection for the leg while the stacked block heel, a feature introduced to Europe from Persia, kept the foot in the stirrup. In fact, their weight and bulk did not make such boots comfortable for walking. The amount of leather required to produce a pair was significant and this material cost, together with their bespoke fit, meant boots were much more expensive than a pair of shoes. Their association with cavalry officers, meanwhile, lent them a high status; regular foot soldiers instead wore gaiters over shoes.

During the first half of the eighteenth century it would have been considered inappropriate for a man to attend an event indoors wearing boots, but attitudes began to change and by the end of the century boots were the height of fashion for men, worn for all but the most formal occasions. As the century progressed new styles of boot were introduced, lighter and less bulky than the jackboot, with a thinner and more flexible sole, which made them suitable for activities both on and off the horse, and gave an elegant, streamlined

appearance when paired with tight-fitting breeches or pantaloons. One of the most recognisable was the jockey boot (later known as a top boot), which came to be considered a national style, its popularity connected with the rising interest in horse racing in England. Top boots were characterised by a soft leather upper folded over to reveal the untreated hide, creating a brown or pale-coloured top section that contrasted with the black leather of the lower portion. The husband in Rowlandson's *Four O'Clock in the Country*, having risen before dawn to go hunting, is shown in the process of pulling on his top boots with the aid of side straps (Fig. 4.24). He has not yet fastened the buttons and ties on his breeches and one stocking is still around his ankle.

In another portrait the Prince of Wales wears a different type of boot known as a Hessian (see Fig. 4.17). Originally a military style worn by light cavalry troops from Hesse, Germany, during the American Revolutionary War, in the 1790s such boots passed into civilian dress. Dighton's detailed drawing clearly shows the characteristic features: highly polished and jet black, cut higher in front than the back, with a V-shaped notch from which hangs a decorative tassel, accessorised with spurs. Hussar boots were similar, but shorter, reaching to mid-calf and without the tassel. In June and July 1801 the Prince of Wales acquired five pairs

Fig. 4.25 Rosalba Giovanna Carriera (1673–1757), *Philip, Duke of Wharton*, c.1718–20.
Pastel on paper, 55.9 × 44.5 cm.
RCIN 406905

of 'Hussar Boots with high heels' from the bootmaker Andreas Meyer, each at a cost of £3 3s.[27] At around this date Arthur Wellesley, Duke of Wellington, was in communication with another royal bootmaker, George Hoby of St James's Street, to perfect the fit on a new style of boot, slightly shorter than the Hessian and with a flat top and no tassel, enabling it to be worn either over pantaloons or under the newly fashionable trousers. From 1819 it was known as the Wellington boot.[28] Sometimes different colour leathers were used to give the appearance of a shoe and silk stocking, without the fuss of stockings and garters: so-called 'Dress Wellingtons'.

## GOWNS

The pastel by Rosalba Giovanna Carriera above (Fig. 4.25) shows Philip, Duke of Wharton, who sports informal 'undress': his shirt is left undone, and he wears a soft cap instead of a wig. When relaxing, working or entertaining informally at home, a man might choose to swap his coat for a loose gown, worn over breeches, shirt and sometimes waistcoat. Such a garment was a comfortable and practical option, providing respite from the weight and constrictive nature of the various layers of men's dress, and enabling a more relaxed posture, while also reducing the likelihood of

best clothes becoming crumpled or stained. Popularised in Europe in the late seventeenth century, such garments were known by a variety of names: nightgown, morning gown, *robe de chambre*, Indian gown or banyan/bannian, the latter derived from a Gujarati word for a Hindu merchant.[29] They could be made of lavish textiles, with warm winter versions quilted or lined with fur or silk, and thin-layered light silks or printed cottons for summer. Presumably feeling the chill of a winter's morning, in February 1799 the Prince of Wales bought a 'Superfine White Swansdown Robe de Chambre with superfine Flannel lining' for £7 7s.[30] Some nightgowns seem to have been designed to match soft furnishings, so that a gentleman could coordinate elegantly with his surroundings.

Gowns worn by men during the eighteenth century as a form of undress can be divided into two main types. The first, worn throughout the century, was cut along the lines of a modern dressing gown, usually full length with wide sleeves, the fronts joined together using a sash or left unfastened, as seen on one of the protagonists in Longhi's *Blind-Man's Buff*, here made of changeant silk in shades of brown and blue (see Fig. 1.15). The Japanese *kosode* (an early form of the kimono), first brought to Europe by Dutch merchants in the seventeenth century, seems to have been a key source of inspiration in the early development of the European version, and the nightgown retained exotic associations even when made of European textiles.[31] Since a precise fit was not necessary, nightgowns like this could be acquired as ready-to-wear items. Although worn by both sexes, they were most commonly considered items of male dress.

The second type of informal gown seems to have developed out of this earlier *kosode* style and most surviving examples date from the second half of the eighteenth century. Instead of the loose fit of the first type, these are more structured, cut along the lines of a fashionable coat, with fitted sleeves and fastenings down the front, often decorated with frogging. Hogarth's Tom Rakewell wears a three-quarter-length version to receive visitors during 'The Levée' (Fig. 4.26), but they could also be full length. Some were designed with integrated waistcoat fronts to give the appearance of a matching waistcoat worn underneath. The Rake also illustrates the fashion of wearing a soft nightcap over his shaved head as a form of undress, like the Duke of Wharton (see Fig. 4.25).

Gowns in the looser style were a popular choice for many men sitting for a portrait, allowing the artful arrangement of fabric in the style of antique drapery, thereby creating a more timeless form of dress that would not date as quickly as everyday fashions. Unlike a man's coat, the nightgown required little cutting or piecing of the fabric, making it ideal for showing off luxurious textiles with exuberant pattern repeats, although these are less commonly depicted in painted portraits than the plainer silks. Widely worn by men from a variety of professions,

Fig. 4.27 Georg Wilhelm Lafontaine (1680–1745), *George I*, c.1720–7 (detail).
Oil on canvas, 127.7 × 101.9 cm. RCIN 405247

including scholars, scientists, composers and artists, the nightgown provided an opportunity to denote a mind dedicated to study or creative endeavour: 'Loose dresses contribute to the easy and vigorous exercise of the faculties of the mind … studious men are always painted in gowns', remarked the physician Benjamin Rush in 1790.[32] By this time it had become acceptable for gowns to be worn outside the house: 'Banyans are worn in every part of the town from Wapping to Westminster, and if a sword is occasionally put on it sticks out in the middle of the slit behind. This however is the fashion, the ton, and what can a man do? He must wear a banyan.'[33] It is interesting to note that, while aristocrats and royals certainly owned and wore banyans, they were rarely painted in the style.

## BUTTONS AND FOBS

Whereas the various elements of female dress were traditionally assembled and joined by means of laces and pins, buttons had long been used to fasten the front of a man's doublet and breeches, and they were considered primarily a masculine feature of clothing. The relationship between a button and its buttonhole was also ripe for double entendre and sexual innuendo in satirical imagery and verse of the period.[34] Similarly, the notion of being inappropriately unbuttoned – as is Hogarth's Rake (see Fig. 4.9) – carried the same sort of moralising undertones as being ungartered.

Although generally not concerned with the intricacies of dress, George III was unusually interested in buttons, with Charlotte Papendiek noting that 'in his youth one of his favourite occupations had been turning and button-making. Of a German in Long Acre he had learned how to make the loop and attach it to the button'.[35] The hobby was relished by satirists, who regularly represented the king forsaking his official duties to focus on buttons.[36] Upon being presented with a new style of mourning button the king is said to have exclaimed, 'Send me several sets of buttons, for as I am called George the button-maker, I must give a lift to our trade.'[37]

Buttons remained a feature on men's coats and waistcoats throughout the century, as the means of fastening the fronts but also appearing on cuffs and pocket flaps. Surviving examples reveal that some of these buttons were decorative rather than functional, with buttonholes absent or uncut. The buttons on George I's coat in the painting above (Fig. 4.27) are made in the traditional style: a hemispherical core of wood covered with metallic thread. In one place a visible pentimento (change by the artist) shows that the coat was extended to cover more of the sitter's left hand, and the buttons repositioned accordingly. As illustrated here, buttonholes were often accentuated with decorative braid or embroidery and the apertures excessively elongated, with the extra length sewn up. Silk thread-wrapped buttons were worn throughout the eighteenth century, with Leek and Macclesfield developing into important centres of the growing button-making trade in England. The distinctively quartered 'Death's head' style was popular during the second half of the century, seen opposite, for example, adorning Prince Karl's coat in Johan Joseph Zoffany's group portrait (Fig. 4.28).

Buttons were easily transferred from one garment to another, but valuable examples could also be reconfigured into entirely new objects, such as the set of 22 dress-coat buttons belonging to George III, later reset into a necklace, bracelet, three brooches (Fig. 4.29) and a pair of earrings, probably at the request of Queen Adelaide. Each button consists of a central pearl, set within three concentric circles of tiny pearls against a blue enamel ground with gold settings. Made in two sizes, the larger perhaps decorated the coat fronts while the smaller trimmed pockets and cuffs. Sadly, there are no images depicting the coat to which they were originally attached.

The fashion for buttons embellished with diamonds and other gemstones at the end of the seventeenth century continued for formal occasions into the eighteenth century, although a wide variety of other materials were used for everyday wear, including mother-of-pearl, glass, cut steel, brass and enamel. Portraits tend to show central gemstones in sets of buttons as being perfectly uniform in shape and size. In reality this would have been unlikely, as the overall effect was far more important than the detail.

Over the course of the century buttons became larger, sometimes reaching extreme proportions and providing sufficient surface area for the inclusion of initials or mottoes. 'Picture buttons', too, were popular in the 1770s, which incorporated painted, printed or drawn images ranging in subject matter from amorous themes to landscape views, while Josiah Wedgwood produced similar items in jasperware and brass with classical motifs (Fig. 4.30). It was

also very fashionable for buttons to be covered in the same fabric as the garment itself, rendering them almost invisible in portraits (see Fig. 4.14). Concern about the detrimental impact of such cloth-covered buttons on the livelihoods of traditional gilt metal button-makers prompted the revival of an Act of Parliament from 1721, originally designed to protect the English silk industry, which had imposed fines on 'any taylor or other person convicted of making, covering, selling, using, or setting on to a garment any buttons covered with cloth or other stuff'. The revised version of 1790 imposed a penalty of £40 (more than £5,000 in 2021) on the wearers of such buttons,[38] the result being, according to one commentator, that 'soon they had all disappeared, and are now replaced by simple gold-plated buttons for Half Dress'.[39]

The term 'fob' was applied to a variety of items that could be suspended from the clothing on a chain or ribbon and then tucked inside a pocket. They were named after the small horizontal fob pocket located just below the waistband of the breeches. Fob seals are often shown hanging below the waistcoat in portraits (Fig. 4.31), where they were easily accessible when writing letters and dealing with other paperwork. Although functional items, used to provide a tamper-evident wax seal and prove the authorship of a document, seals could also be highly decorative, made of precious metals, hardstones or glass, with a motif carved in intaglio. Two examples shown above are of quartz and amethyst set into gold mounts (Figs 4.32 and 4.33), one cut with the Brunswick-Wolfenbüttel arms of Queen Caroline.

A watch was another indispensable item, carried by both men and women. Men wore theirs as a fob watch, attached to a chain or ribbon and tucked away in a pocket within the breeches or waistcoat when not in use, necessitating the regular gesture of pulling out the watch to open its casings to read the time. Women tended to wear their watch as a pendant, suspended on a chain from the

waist or from a brooch. Watch cases were usually made of precious metals with the face either visible through glass or concealed by a front cover, and could be enamelled, engraved or set with gemstones.

The eighteenth century was a period of great technical innovation in the field of horology and both George III and Queen Charlotte took a particular interest in the latest developments. The modest surface decoration of a watch made 1802–3 by the Swiss-born clock and watchmaker Louis Recordon for George III (Fig. 4.34) conceals a clever invention within: a quarter-repeating mechanism that could inform the wearer of both the hour and quarter hour with the press of a button, a useful feature in the dark of night. George III did not see such items just as fashion accessories, however, but was also fascinated with their internal mechanisms, spending time taking them apart and reassembling them. Queen Charlotte is reported to have kept 25 watches, 'all highly adorn'd with jewels', beside her bed at Buckingham House.[40]

Robineau's portrait (see Fig. 4.12) shows the Prince of Wales wearing two different accessories at the waist in

a symmetrical manner that was fashionable in the 1780s. On the right is the fob for a watch, made of ribbon and set with an enamel disc or hardstone, while on the left is a chatelaine, probably of cut steel. The term chatelaine dates from the 1820s; at the time, such an item is likely to have been described as a chain or equipage. Worn by both men and women, chatelaines were attached by a clasp at the waist and were used to carry a variety of useful accessories, each suspended from a chain: perhaps a pocket watch along with its winding key, a perfume bottle or small box. Surviving examples range from the highly decorative, often designed as presentation items or gifts, to simpler versions more practical for everyday use. The chatelaine shown right (Fig. 4.35) includes a watch whose reverse is set with diamonds in the shape of the crowned cipher of George III, which was probably given as a token of friendship to the king's godson, James George, 3rd Earl of Courtown, or his father, who had served as Lord of the Bedchamber. Even more extravagant was the 'watch chain and trinkets' presented to Queen Charlotte in 1778, described as incorporating more than 3,800 brilliant and rose-cut diamonds.[41]

## SNUFFBOXES

The taking of snuff – an aromatic powdered tobacco sniffed through the nostrils – was a fashionable craze for both men and women throughout the eighteenth century, as demonstrated by the lady on the left of Marcellus Laroon's *A Dinner Party* and the man seated by her side who reaches for a pinch (Fig. 4.36). Queen Charlotte had started taking snuff before arriving in England and was a particular enthusiast of a blend known as Violet Strasbourg, which combined powdered rappee (dark tobacco), ambergris, bitter almonds and attar (an essential oil derived from botanicals). Among the possessions sold after her death were more than 90 snuffboxes, one of which was described as a 'Snuff box of the rare and fine root of amethyst, the lid set with flowers formed of diamonds and coloured stones'.[42] It may perhaps have been that shown opposite (Fig. 4.37), which is made of amethystine quartz, and its gold mounts set with rubies and diamonds.

Being so frequently and ostentatiously brought into public view, snuffboxes provided an opportunity to display precious decoration and an owner's fashionable taste, the best examples illustrating the extraordinary virtuosity of the goldsmith's craft in miniature. Noted snuff aficionado Viscount Petersham (1780–1851) was said to use a different snuffbox for each day of the year.[43] With snuffboxes often given as tokens of affection, designs relating to themes of love were popular, incorporating mottoes and amorous scenes.

Snuffboxes were also favoured as a diplomatic presentation gift from members of the royal family to visiting ambassadors, foreign heads of state and loyal members of the royal household. Such gifts could include portrait miniatures or monograms linking them to the donor, an indication of their intimacy and degree of personalisation. An example shown opposite (Fig. 4.38) incorporates an enamel portrait of Frederick, Prince of Wales inside the lid, by the leading miniaturist and 'Cabinet Painter to his Royal Highness', Christian Frederick Zincke. The casket-shaped snuffbox is made of gold, exceptionally finely chased with pastoral scenes and, at the top, the

Prince of Wales's feathers and initials F L (Frederick Lewis). In 1749 this snuffbox was presented by the Prince of Wales to Francis North upon his appointment as preceptor (governor) to the prince's son, the future George III. The imagery of a toiling farmer preparing the land for a rich harvest is perhaps a deliberate reference to an instructor cultivating the mind of his young charge. North had served as Gentleman of the Bedchamber to the Prince of Wales since 1731.

London, Berlin and Geneva were among the cities best known for the excellence of their production of gold boxes, although those made in Paris were the most highly sought-after of all, with the quality of craftsmanship maintained through the strict guild system. French examples often incorporated the work of specialist enamellers, with vignettes taken from contemporary prints, as in the example shown opposite (Fig. 4.39), which has domestic scenes after paintings by Jean Honoré Fragonard, each framed with enamel flowers and foliage.

An unusual style of snuffbox incorporates a hole for the thumb, providing a secure base while pinching the

Fig. 4.41  English, Ring with cameo of George IV, *c*.1820.
Gold, garnet, onyx and foil, 1.0 × 2.0 cm. RCIN 4202

Fig. 4.42  Probably Chelsea Porcelain Works, *Etui*, 1750–70.
Porcelain and gold, 8.7 × 2.3 cm. RCIN 4472

Fig. 4.43  English, Scent bottle holder, *c*.1750.
Agate, gold and diamond, 4.2 × 2.5 × 1.8 cm. RCIN 4508

snuff from one of its two compartments (Fig. 4.40). The hallmarks indicate it was made in 1796/7 by George Cowdery, described in 1817 as a 'small worker in gold' based on King Street in Holborn, London.[44] The GP cipher and coronet identify the snuffbox's first owner as George, Prince of Wales, who later presented it to Thomas Bidwell, Superintendent of St James's and Hyde Park. Another popular type of gift for George IV to give to his favourites were finger rings set with his likeness, either in cameo or intaglio, one of which he gave to the 6th Duke of Devonshire on New Year's Day 1828. These were regularly supplied by the royal goldsmiths Rundell, Bridge & Rundell, the makers of an unusual example in which a tiny, finely cut cameo is inlaid into a garnet (Fig. 4.41).

One identifying feature of a snuffbox, which can help distinguish it from other types of small boxes, is a hinged lid, freeing the second hand to take the pinch. Men tended to carry their snuffbox in the left waistcoat pocket – regularly and conspicuously removing it with a flourish – while women carried theirs in removable pockets tied around the waist or attached to a chatelaine. The 'ceremony of the snuffbox' developed into an elaborate social ritual, requiring elegance in gesture to demonstrate the snuff-taker's gentility. Some of the sellers of such objects offered lessons regarding the appropriate movements, which included the act of offering snuff to a stranger and the correct use of snuff napkins (handkerchiefs) to remove excess snuff from the face. Sneezing was absolutely frowned upon. George III

was described as having sneezed prodigiously when trying snuff for the first time early in his marriage and afterwards did not take up the habit.[45]

Other types of boxes were used to hold materials besides snuff. Bonbonnières carried breath-freshening sweetmeats and patch boxes held the fabric patches applied to the face during the toilette, while an *étui* might contain narrow items relating to writing, sewing or personal hygiene, such as tweezers, needle, toothpick, bodkin, knife or spoon (Fig. 4.42). This example is made of porcelain in imitation of a posy of lilies and roses. Small containers could also hold scent, and a scent-bottle case made of agate with scrolling gold mounts and a diamond thumb piece is also shown above (Fig. 4.43). Although agate hardstones were less expensive than some other materials used, such boxes could be luxurious, expensive objects, forming an important and coordinating element of attire. Mary Delany remarks of her cousin's dress for court, 'her watch and étuy suited to the rest'.[46]

## SWORDS AND CANES

During the seventeenth century a light sword had become established as a civilian item of dress for gentlemen, serving both as an indicator of status and as a means of protection within a society that traditionally settled disputes through duels. In portraiture often only the sword hilt is visible, the blade tucked towards the rear and projecting through the slits in the back of the coat, and the sword belt concealed by the waistcoat. Occasionally, portraits show the sword swung round to the front of the body, presumably only for the purposes of portrayal in paint as such a position would have been highly inconvenient when walking.

Over the course of the eighteenth century the fashion for gentlemen to carry a sword was gradually replaced by the cane or stick (at this date the terms were used interchangeably). By 1733 it was being reported that the Englishman leaves 'his Sword at Home, takes his Cane and goes where he pleases'.[47] A shift from swords to pistols for duelling may have played a role in the decline of the sword for everyday wear, although it is interesting that pistols are almost never depicted with civilian dress in portraiture, even though they could be just as decorative as swords (see Chapter 11). During the first half of the eighteenth century, both cane and sword could be carried simultaneously, as in a portrait of Fredrick, Prince of Wales, of c.1745 (see Fig. 2.1), although by the time of Zoffany's group portrait (c.1771–2) Queen Charlotte's brothers are depicted swordless, with elegant canes

prominently on display instead (see Fig. 5.8). Eighteenth-century canes were often made of rattan, a material derived from the stems of palm trees, as shown below (Fig. 4.44). This stick includes a silver-gilt handle hallmarked 1773/4, which is engraved with the royal insignia incorporating the Hanoverian arms, although its original owner has not yet been identified. Decorative heads could be made of precious metal as in this example, or of carved stone or porcelain, and some incorporated devices such as an eyeglass or small containers for holding perfume or other liquids (the fashion for physicians to carry canes containing phials of disinfectant was a source of satire for artists including Hogarth).[48] Tassels and ribbons could be included to attach the cane to the wrist and hang it up when not in use. The switch was a shorter, more flexible option to the cane and was generally adopted by younger people. By the late eighteenth century swords were worn in England for only the most formal court occasions, although their use continued for longer on the Continent.

# 5

# Dressing Children

*The taylor may make his clothes modish,*
*and the dancing-master give fashion to his motions;*
*yet neither of these, though they set off well,*
*make a well-bred gentleman.*

JOHN LOCKE, 1693[1]

One important strand of Enlightenment philosophical enquiry concerned the nature of childhood. First published in 1693, and influential throughout the following century, John Locke's *Some Thoughts Concerning Education* proposed the novel notion of a *tabula rasa* ('blank slate') at birth, a break with the Puritan concept that children were born innately sinful and required salvation through instruction and the strict correction of behaviour. Locke's treatise emphasised the fundamental importance of education and emulation in the development of a child's moral character and encouraged parents to identify and nurture the strengths of each individual child. Queen Charlotte took close personal interest in the education of her 15 children, and the inclusion of Locke's treatise in her portrait by Allan Ramsay with her two eldest sons must have been a conscious decision (Fig. 5.1, overleaf).

Building on Locke's ideas around the innate malleability of the childhood mind, Jean-Jacques Rousseau's *Emile, or On Education* (1762) identified childhood as a unique period of freedom and happiness that was to be cherished. It emphasised the importance of providing a child with the opportunity to learn about the world through experience rather than instruction: a child's natural

PREVIOUS PAGE
Detail of Fig. 5.8

OPPOSITE
Fig. 5.1 Allan Ramsay (1713–84), *Queen Charlotte with her Two Eldest Sons*, c.1764–9 (detail).
Oil on canvas, 247.8 × 165.0 cm. RCIN 404922

RIGHT, AND DETAIL OVERLEAF
Fig. 5.2 John Singleton Copley (1738–1815),
*The Three Youngest Daughters of George III and Queen Charlotte*, 1785.
Oil on canvas, 265.4 × 185.7 cm. RCIN 401405

instinct for play, creativity and curious exploration was to be encouraged. Moreover, such traits were to be maintained into adulthood, with the purity of a child's emotional response to be admired and cultivated, an attitude contributing to the rise of sensibility that was such a key theme in literature of the period. This fundamental shift in perceptions had a significant impact on the styles of dress worn during infancy over the course of the century.

While this change was seen across Europe, the informality of children's dress in England was noteworthy to visitors from the Continent from the 1760s onwards, and became increasingly distinctive as the century progressed. John Singleton Copley's lively portrait of the three youngest daughters of George III and Queen Charlotte (Fig. 5.2) exemplifies this new vision of childhood inspired by the writings of Locke and Rousseau. The children are outdoors and surrounded by nature: they play with jumping dogs, make noise and openly demonstrate their sisterly affection. At two years old, Princess Amelia is the youngest of the three. Barefoot, she sits in a monogrammed carriage, steadying herself by clutching the thumb and skirts of her big sister. Amelia's gown is of plain white linen or cotton, its fine translucency emphasised by the horizontal bands in the skirt, which may represent tucks in the fabric, allowing for adjustments as the child grew (the practical Charlotte Papendiek incorporated tucks and hems into her children's clothing for this purpose).[2] The colourful broad sash tied with a large bow around Amelia's waist is a common feature in children's portraits of this period, and here the blue silk provides a striking contrast to the pristine white. On the baby's head is a wide plumed hat over a frilled cap, both possibly made by Queen Charlotte's milliner, Emilia Pohl. Behind Amelia stands her eight-year-old sister Sophia, still wearing the typical back-fastening gown of childhood. In contrast, Princess Mary on the left – although only one year older than Sophia – wears clothes cut along the lines of adult female dress, which are noticeably more elaborate. The yellow silk of her petticoat has been densely pleated

into the waistband of the gown and her attire includes adult accessories such as the handkerchief crossed over the bodice and tied at the lower back. The ribbon around her waist is of striped silk, unlike the plain blue ones of her younger sisters. The informality of Copley's portrait represents a significant departure from traditional depictions of royal children and although the painting seems to have pleased its royal patrons (by 1805 it was hanging in the Ballroom at Windsor Castle) others were less complimentary when it was displayed at the Royal Academy in 1785, finding the profusion of dogs, parrots, flowers, toys and fabric an overwhelming distraction from the sitters themselves. The artist John Hoppner remarked, 'Is it, Mr Copley, because you have heard that fine feathers make fine birds that you have concluded that fine clothes will make fine princesses?'.[3]

## THE SKIRTS OF INFANCY

The practice of swaddling a newborn had long been accepted as best practice in Britain, its intended purpose being to provide warmth and ensure the limbs grew straight. The child was first dressed in a 'clout' (nappy/diaper) and shirt, before being wrapped in a rectangle of cloth known as a 'bed' and then in a series of swaddle bands (a 'roller'). This is how the young Prince George William, second son of the future George II, appears while being nursed by an unidentified wet nurse in *c.*1717 (Fig. 5.3). Initially the child's arms were also wrapped within the bands, although they were left out from about six to eight weeks old, which is probably around the age of the prince in this image, given that he died at only three months. A baby's head was typically dressed in a forehead cloth, cap and biggin, while a bib and stay band might be added on top.

From the mid-eighteenth century swaddling became increasingly unfashionable, criticised by both physicians and philosophers. Rousseau recommended that 'The limbs of a growing body ought all to have room in their garments. Nothing ought to hinder either their movement or their growth'.[4] By the 1780s swaddling was considered archaic in England, and babies were instead dressed in a long gown, which was still worn with a shirt, clout and at least one cap. This is what we see Princess Mary wearing aged around six months in Benjamin West's group portrait (Fig. 5.4). Suitably for a portrait, all the children are dressed in their best clothes including Mary, whose gown is not of the typical linen for everyday use, but silk elaborately trimmed with strips of pierced and ruched silk, similar to a surviving example worn by the future George IV (Fig. 5.5). This gown is made of cream silk satin, with a bodice and petticoat cut as one, the bodice gathered into fine vertical pleats to create the fit around the torso but left unstitched to the sleeves under the arms, enabling greater freedom of movement as recommended by Rousseau.

In the early eighteenth century the process of 'coating' marked the transition from swaddling garments to gowns. However, with the decline in the practice of swaddling as the century progressed, the shift instead represented a change from these newly introduced long garments to short ankle-length ones, and as a result the transition was increasingly known as 'short-coating'. Typically, this switch occurred at around the age of eight to nine months, avoiding the hindrance of a long gown as the child became more mobile and learnt to walk. The timing of this transition, however, depended on the child as well as on external factors, with one treatise recommending children 'be short-coated as early as the season of the year will permit'.[5] In West's group portrait (see Fig. 5.4), Prince Adolphus (aged two), wearing red shoes, has made this transition.

During the first half of the century these 'short-coats' consisted of a short-sleeved lightly stiffened bodice attached to a skirt at the waist: a combination of garments that was variously known as a frock, gown, coat, tunic or vest. Usually this fastened at the back with ties or buttons, although boys sometimes wore a front-fastening version. In Ramsay's group portrait (see Fig. 5.1) the two-year-old Prince of Wales wears an ornate frock: a blue underlayer covered with expensive lace and accessorised with a blue silk sash decorated with gold fringing. This painting illustrates the fact that at this age definitive visual clues in dress distinguishing boys from girls were rare. In fact, hairstyles and accessories served as the most helpful indicators: here the hunting bow and cropped hairstyle are more suggestive of a boy. Very low necklines were common for both boys and girls, and aprons, sometimes with attached bibs, were also worn by both, as were petticoats.

Fig. 5.4 Benjamin West (1738–1820), *Princess Augusta, Princess Elizabeth, Prince Ernest, Prince Augustus, Prince Adolphus and Princess Mary*, 1776.
Oil on canvas, 168.5 × 206.4 cm. RCIN 404574

Fig. 5.5 Baby gown worn by Prince George, later George IV, c.1762.
Silk satin. London, Historic Royal Palaces, 3501055

Throughout the eighteenth century, colour was not
an indicator of a child's sex. Gowns in shades of pink
and white are worn by the young Prince William (Fig. 5.6),
Prince Henry (Fig. 5.7) and Princess Charlotte (Fig. 5.8),
while in another portrait the infant Princess Royal wears
a white gown with blue petticoat and sash (Fig. 5.9). Here
the simplicity of the young child's gown is in stark contrast
with the formality of Queen Charlotte's dress: an elaborate
sacque of white silk brocaded with gold sprigs, trimmed
with gold lace and accessorised with triple flounced lace
sleeve ruffles. The queen's hand gesture requests silence
from the viewer so as not to disturb the peacefully sleeping
infant. The affectionate pose suggests a concerned mother
ensuring the needs of her child are met before she departs
to undertake her courtly duties.

Fig. 5.9  Francis Cotes (1726–70), *Queen Charlotte with Charlotte, Princess Royal*, 1767.

Oil on canvas, 239.7 × 150.6 cm. RCIN 404396

Fig. 5.10  After François-Hubert Drouais (1727–75), *Louis XVI and Louis XVIII when duc de Berry and comte de Provence*, c.1800–30, after an original of 1757.

Watercolour on ivory, 13.0 × 18.3 cm. RCIN 421444

The similarity in styles of dress for young boys and girls can lead to misidentifications. On the back of the double portrait shown below (Fig. 5.10) is a nineteenth-century inscription that describes the children as two daughters of George II, Princess Anne (1709–59) and Princess Mary (1723–72), painted by Alexis Simon Belle. Clearly the difference in birth dates of the two princesses casts doubt on this identification, and the miniature is now known to be a copy after a painting by François-Hubert Drouais in the São Paulo Museum of Art, depicting the grandsons of Louis XV and exhibited at the Paris Salon in 1757. On the right is Louis, duc de Berry (later Louis XVI,

1754–93), and beside him Louis, comte de Provence (later Louis XVIII, 1755–1824). The boys are three and two years old respectively and both wear gowns of ornate brocaded silk, arranged to resemble the wide panniers of female dress that were fashionable during the 1750s. The sleeve ruffles for both boys and the comte's apron are of expensive lace, undoubtedly French. Coloured shoes for children were popular and here they coordinate with the details in the silks: blue for the duc de Berry and brown for his brother.

As the century progressed white muslin frocks became increasingly fashionable for children during infancy, the bodice and skirt cut in one piece with the shaping created

Fig. 5.11  John Russell (1745–1806), *Caroline,
Princess of Wales with Princess Charlotte, c.1797.*
Pastel, 93.5 × 76.0 cm. RCIN 453658

Fig. 5.12  Baby shoes worn by Princess Charlotte, 1796–8.
Cotton, silk and linen. RCIN 72008

by vertical pleats or gathers, and the waistline covered by a brightly coloured sash. Princess Charlotte wears a frock of this type at around the age of one in a portrait by John Russell (Fig. 5.11). White was certainly a common colour for children's gowns from the 1770s onwards, although its prevalence in portraiture probably exaggerates its popularity; many surviving examples are of patterned or coloured linen or cotton. While white clothing for children might seem impractical to modern eyes, it could be washed more easily than dyed fabrics, which were prone to run or fade. Princess Charlotte appears to be wearing shoes very similar to a pair from around the same date that belonged to her (Fig. 5.12). Made of soft twill cotton with cream silk-satin rosettes, they fasten with string ties on each side. In the pastel the ribbon rosettes are pale pink to match her sash and the bow on her cap.

## DRESSING BOYS

Breeching referred to the moment a young boy switched from the skirts of childhood into adult clothing. For many centuries it had represented a significant and ceremonial rite of passage that was expected to be accompanied by changes in activities and guardianship, as a young boy moved from the protection of the nursery to the world of men. In the seventeenth century breeching had usually occurred at around the age of six or seven, but during the eighteenth century it happened earlier, at three or four. Factors such as the height of the child and his social status also played a role in the decision. The four-year-old Prince Frederick wears a smart red velvet coat with silver lace – perhaps his first – in a portrait by Jean-Etienne Liotard (Fig. 5.14, overleaf), very different in style from the red gown he wears, aged only one, in George Knapton's family group (Fig. 5.15, overleaf).

Rousseau's *Emile* stressed the importance of suitably loose clothing for boys, asserting that 'defects of body and of mind come almost all from the same cause: one wants to make them men before it is time',[6] and in fact dress for young boys in England did see an important change by the 1780s with the development of transitional styles of clothing. These provided a visual extension to the stage of childhood and were a comfortable and practical alternative to the tailcoat, breeches and knee-length stockings of adulthood. One option consisted of a loosely cut hip-length coat worn with long pantaloons. Considered an English style across Europe, one German writer linked it directly with the theories of Locke.[7] This is what three of George III's sons (Ernest, 11, Augustus, 9 and Adolphus, 8) wear in the family series by Thomas Gainsborough (Fig. 5.13). The coat was usually made of a dark fabric (here it is navy with red facings, a modified version of the Windsor uniform introduced by the king), worn over a pale waistcoat and open-necked linen shirt. The boys wear their own hair, rather than the wigs of the older males. During the first half of the century wigs were sometimes worn by young boys (see, for example, Prince George and Prince Edward in Fig. 5.7), although the practice continued for longer on

the Continent than in England, where from the 1760s a boy's hair tended to be simply styled, cut to jaw length with a straight fringe.

Turning to the other portraits in Gainsborough's family series (see pp. 10–11), we can identify two other forms of clothing for boys. The posthumous portrait of the youngest son, Alfred, shows him aged nearly two, still in the white frock of infancy. Meanwhile, Prince Octavius (aged three) wears a very different transitional style, later known as a skeleton suit. A full-length portrait by West depicts it more clearly (Fig. 5.16) and a similar surviving suit in the Victoria and Albert Museum (Fig. 5.17) shown overleaf enables us to see the construction: a pair of short, ankle-length

BELOW
Fig. 5.14 Jean-Étienne Liotard (1702–65), *Prince Frederick William*,
1754.
Pastel on vellum, 40.6 × 30.5 cm. RCIN 400898

LEFT
Fig. 5.15 George Knapton (1698–1778), *The Family of Frederick,
Prince of Wales*, 1751.
Oil on canvas, 350.9 × 461.2 cm. RCIN 405741

Fig. 5.17  English, Skeleton suit, *c*.1800–5.
Nankeen cotton. London, Victoria and Albert Museum, T.165&A–1915

Fig. 5.18  Bland & Foster, Cavalry sword, *c*.1782.
Steel, wood, silver and silver gilt. RCIN 61378

trousers with a fall front opening, attached to a matching
jacket by buttons at the waist. Prince Octavius's jacket is
cut with wide shawl lapels and is again worn over a shirt
with a frilled collar and with a sash tied around the waist.
Such sashes were common during the last decades of the
eighteenth century but became less so. Like the surviving
suit, the young prince's outfit is probably made of natural
unbleached nankeen cotton – a practical fabric that was both
hard-wearing and washable – although portraits indicate
that red and dark blue were also popular colours for this type
of ensemble. A particularly English style of dress, with its
origins in the working-class clothing of sailors and fishermen,
the skeleton suit had evidently become socially acceptable by
1782, when the portrait was displayed at the Royal Academy.
At the age of three, Prince Octavius was young to wear a
skeleton suit and his death in 1783 meant that he was never
to transition into the clothing of his older brothers, an
occasion that usually happened at around the age of ten.
Although skeleton suits were also adopted in other countries
in the 1780s, their popularity was short-lived and by the
1820s they were rarely worn. In the nineteenth century
sailor suits – with their distinctive collar inspired by sailors'
dress – became popular instead and the style continued
throughout the Victorian period.

Once breeched, a young boy might also start to carry
a sword, which for formal occasions remained an important
symbol of gentility for much of the century. The cavalry
sword being unsheathed by Octavius, however (see Fig. 5.16),
was not made for the three-year-old prince but for his
father, George III. Its distinctive serpentine knuckle
guard and quillon decorated with a beast's head enable
it to be identified as one still in the Royal Collection
(Fig. 5.18). George III's hat and sword belt are also
shown in the portrait and the child seems to relish
the opportunity to play at being king. The inclusion
of George III's personal accoutrements suggests his
presence nearby and reinforces the relationship between
father and son, which was especially close. The sword
also emphasises the child's small stature, being too long
to fit within the picture frame.

## DRESSING GIRLS

Although the transition to adult clothing was less obvious
for girls than boys, certain features were characteristic
of childhood. During the eighteenth century most styles of
gown worn by adult women fastened at the front and often
incorporated a stomacher, the main exception to this being
the formal 'grand habit' (see Chapter 8). However, the
bodices of gowns worn by younger girls were back-fastening,
as Paul Sandby shows in a drawing of a young woman seated
at a table wearing a pink striped gown over a linen shift
(Fig. 5.19). We can see that the top fastening has loosened,
with one side of the gown bending away from the body. For
a dress like this, the opening probably extended to just
below the waist. For young children such back-fastening
gowns simplified the process of dressing, although their use
in older children indicated a continued need for assistance.

Leading strings are another distinctive mark of
childhood. These strips of fabric hanging from the shoulder
served a practical purpose for very young children, acting
as reins to aid balance when learning to walk. They are
sometimes described as hanging sleeves, a vestigial feature
of dress from which they seem to have originally derived.
For boys, leading strings disappeared once they moved
on from wearing skirts, but girls continued to wear formal
gowns with leading strings for far longer, indicating a
symbolic dependence on the parents. At the age of eight
Princess Augusta wears a rose-pink gown with leading
strings of the same fabric in West's portrait of 1776
(Fig. 5.20). Leading strings do not seem to have been a
feature of more informal children's gowns made of linen
or cotton, with one customer noting in 1759 that 'they
only dirty and look trolloping'.[8] For formal wear they could
be made of very expensive fabrics, either matching or
contrasting with the gown. After a visit to the Queen's Lodge
at Windsor in 1799 to commemorate the Princess Royal's

birthday, Mary Delany noted Princess Mary (aged three)
wore a dress of 'cherry-colour'd tabby with silver leading
strings'.[9] During the first half of the century it was common
for girls to retain their leading strings into their teens,
although as the century progressed they were dropped
at a younger age and are conspicuously absent in another
portrait by West, also from 1776, that depicts Princess
Charlotte, older than Augusta by two years (Fig. 5.21).
This corroborates the evidence of the Copley portrait
(see Fig. 5.2) that the years between eight and nine
represented a key transitional moment in dress for the
royal daughters of George III and Queen Charlotte. This
is younger than was typical, with girls usually transitioning
to adult forms of dress at around the age of 12.[10]

## UNDERGARMENTS AND ACCESSORIES

Stays for children continued to be worn throughout the eighteenth century and were considered important for the development of good posture. In July 1730 the stay-maker John Christian Krabe provided two pairs of 'white lustring stays' to Queen Caroline for Princess Mary (aged seven) and Princess Louise (aged five).[11] In the same year William Haines supplied 'stays and stiffening' for the nine-year-old Prince William.[12] This stiffening could be produced using baleen (as in adult stays), although for younger children cording or quilting with additional layers of fabric was more common. George IV's baby stays still survive (Fig. 5.22). Made of red corded silk that has retained its bright colour, stiffened and interlined with cream linen, they are similar in construction to adult stays and lace up the back, although the shoulder straps are attached to a

ribbon using loops, facilitating ease of movement. At some point the tabs around the waist have been removed. In keeping with the shift towards greater freedom, by the 1770s stays for children were lighter and the bodices of their gowns less stiff.

Aprons were worn by young boys and girls, although for boys they were naturally dropped once they had moved from skirts into trousers or breeches. In Knapton's family portrait (Fig. 5.23) the three youngest daughters – Elizabeth (ten, wearing dark green), Louisa (two, in pink) and Caroline Matilda (only a few months old, in yellow) – and their youngest brother Frederick (one, in red) wear aprons in a variety of styles, while Princess Augusta (fourteen) and her mother, the Princess of Wales (seen in the full image, see Fig. 5.15), do not. Simple versions could be worn as practical items to provide protection for more expensive fabrics, but for formal wear an apron

could be highly decorative, constructed of expensive lace or embroidered. Aprons were adopted as fashionable garments by women of all ages during the eighteenth century, but an apron with an attached bib can often be interpreted as a symbol of infancy. The style later developed into the pinafore, which was worn throughout the nineteenth century.

A cap (also known as a bonnet) was considered essential protection for a baby's head. They were often worn in multiple layers, with a plainer undercap covered by a more ornate overcap decorated with ribbons and lace. Caps could be quilted or embroidered to provide additional warmth (see Fig. 1.35), and protective 'pudding' caps with a padded band around the crown were also worn, although they appear to have dropped out of fashion in England earlier than in France.[13] Boys stopped wearing caps at around the age of two, as demonstrated by Ramsay's portrait (see Fig. 5.1): Prince Frederick, aged one, wears a bonnet, while his brother George (older by one year) does not. A cockade worn on the side of the cap in this manner tends to indicate a boy. A decorative baby cap worn by Prince Edward survives as part of a group of gifts presented to his wet nurse, Anne Percy, upon her retirement (Fig. 5.24). Young girls tended

to wear some sort of head covering throughout childhood, both indoors and out. This might take the form of a cap, hat or pompon (hair ornament), and they could also be layered. Caps and hats for girls reflected the fashionable headdresses for women during the 1770s and 1780s: those with higher crowns were probably padded to imitate the towering hairstyles until a girl was old enough to have her hair dressed with pomade and powder, which for some happened at around the age of ten.[14]

Eighteenth-century children's clothing sometimes foreshadowed more informal and practical styles of adult dress that were popular later. It may even have played a role in encouraging the acceptance of such fashions that represented a break with convention, as it became more common to see them on younger people. The chemise dress, for example, which became fashionable in the 1780s (see Chapter 3), was constructed in the same manner as a child's frock, as a tube with gathers or drawstrings to produce the shaping. Meanwhile, the trousers of young boys, first adopted in the 1770s, pre-empt those worn by fashionable men from the 1790s and into the nineteenth century (see Chapter 4).

# 6

# Powder, Pomatum, Bonnets & Bicornes

*Rows above rows of fine ladies with towering tops … I could not help considering them with some astonishment, and lamenting that so absurd, inconvenient, and unbecoming a fashion should last so long, for though every year has produced some alteration, the enormity continues, and one of the most beautiful ornaments of nature, fine hair, is entirely disguised.*

MARY DELANY, 1780[1]

Headwear, in its multitude of forms, was a fundamental component of dress for both men and women throughout the eighteenth century, being highly visible during social interactions, ripe for individual expression and worn by all classes on a daily basis. While headwear served a clear practical purpose (providing warmth and protection from the elements), the manner in which the head was covered or uncovered was also linked to deeply entrenched notions of morality, status and etiquette – a fact alluded to by the numerous idioms referencing hats in some way or another, perhaps more than any other item of dress.[2] Closely linked to headwear are hairstyles, which changed just as much as those of clothing over the period in question – indeed hairstyles are one of the most helpful clues when dating a portrait, especially when an artist has deliberately attempted to elide the specific details of dress that would pinpoint the fashions of a particular year. Great time, effort and expense was spent on achieving the perfect coiffure, which then provided the appropriate setting for the hat, bonnet or ornament. Also discussed in this chapter are wigs, which form such a recognisable element of eighteenth-century visual culture, and which straddle both camps, being both a hairstyle and form of head covering.

## HAIR CARE

The use of soap and water to clean the hair did not become an established practice until the nineteenth century. Indeed, bathing in hot water was believed to increase the likelihood of infection. If it was necessary to submerge the hair, the recommendation was to use cold water.[3] Instead of using water, it was considered more hygienic to clean hair while it was dry, through regular combing and the application of pomatum and powder. Pomatum, also known as pomade, was an oily material derived from rendered animal fat, usually pig, although chicken, cow and sheep were also used. As the fat was boiled, the material that floated to the surface was scooped off and dried. The resulting pomatum (often sold as 'bear's grease') was combed through the hair, its purpose being to remove impurities and act as a softening agent. Pomatum was also advertised for its purported restorative qualities, apparently allowing the hair to grow thicker and longer.

Pomatum helped with the adhesion of powder, which was applied next. Initially adopted for its cleansing qualities (it absorbed natural grease, rather like dry shampoo today) and for its ability to counteract the shine of pomade, powder also enabled complicated hairstyles by making the hair less slippery, increasing its workability and helping it stay in position. Achieving the correct balance of pomatum to powder required skill to create the perfect consistency for manipulation, as well as a healthy degree of shine while avoiding the 'wet' look. Powder could be fragranced with perfume, and violet, rose and orris root were popular.

Powder was used in great quantities, with some of the most voluminous hairstyles requiring up to 2 pounds (about 900 g) in a single sitting.[4] By law, hair powder had to be made from starch and not mixed with other cheaper materials such as plaster of Paris. One hundred barbers were convicted and fined in 1746 for having illicit impure hair powder in their possession.[5] While usually used in its natural white form, powder could also be tinted, either to match a dark natural hair colour or to a pastel hue, although this is rarely depicted in portraits, the most frequently portrayed colours being white or slightly grey.

Powder was first applied before the hair was set, then another layer was added to the finished arrangement, serving to conceal any false hairpieces and create a harmonious effect. The powder could be blown or sprinkled onto the hair using various devices, including a set of miniature bellows, a shaker or a sieve (Fig. 6.2 and see Fig. 6.7). Bellows in action can be seen in a watercolour by John Boyne, a satirical interpretation of the theme of *Venus Attired by the Graces* (Fig. 6.1). On the right, the most elegant of the Graces applies the bellows, a bag filled with powder attached to the spout, and a cloud of powder covers the hair set in rollers. On the left a woman is using hot tongs to set the curls, while another is combing out the top hair. The physical transformation of a grotesque elderly woman into a beautiful young nymph was a popular satirical trope of the period. Here the figure's emaciated body is modulated by stays and hip pads; at her feet a masked man trims her toenails.

Powdering of the hair was often done in a separate 'powder closet' (the origin of the term used to describe a small bathroom today), the clothes protected with a powder cloak or mantle, and the face covered with a powder funnel. Excess powder on the shoulders must have been a common sight, although it is rarely depicted in portraits. One notable exception is Elisabeth Louise Vigée Le Brun's portrait of Charles-Alexandre Calonne (Fig. 6.3). Vigée Le Brun herself 'could not stand powder', noting that she managed to persuade one sitter to leave her hair in its natural ebony black.[6] When arranging the hair, combs were favoured over brushes, serving to remove tangles but also to distribute the pomade and powder through the length of the hair and achieve the appropriate degree of adhesion and workability. The best combs were made of tortoiseshell or ivory.

The introduction of the practice of shampooing from the Indian subcontinent can be credited to Sake Deen Mahomed (1759–1851),

Archbishop of Canterbury.   Lord Mansfield.   Trevor Bishop of Durham.   Dr Thomas Bishop of Salisbury.

1 Sir Rich Glynn
2 Sir Tho Rawlinson
3 Ladbroke

Wilmot

King

Lord Chatham

Queen Dutchess of Ancaster

4 Dutchess Northumb

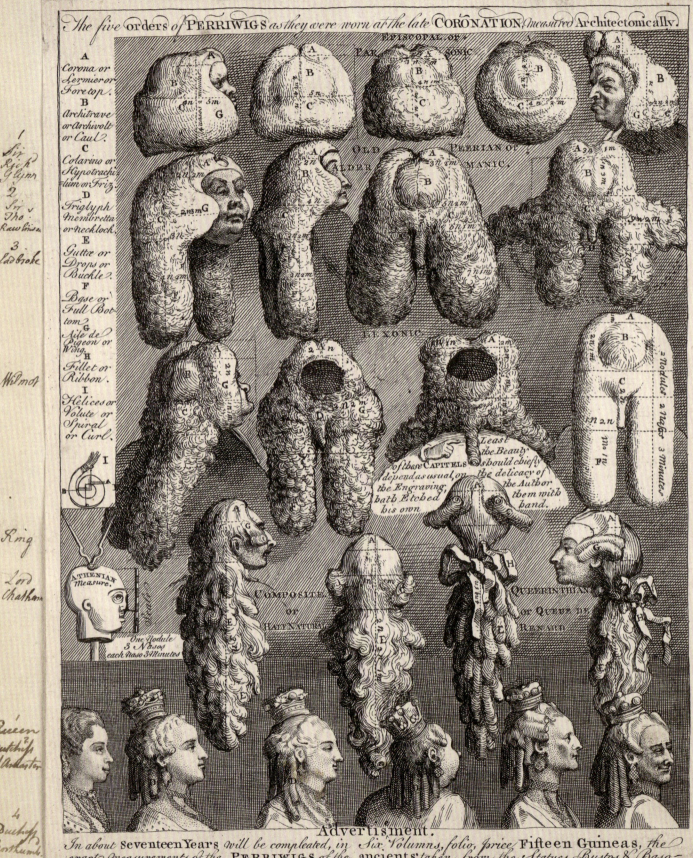

Queen   Dutchess of Ancaster   Lady Kildar   Dutchess of Northumberland   Lady Say & Scale   Lady Dudley & Ward

OPPOSITE
Fig. 6.4  William Hogarth (1697–1764), *The Five Orders of Perriwigs*, 1761.
Engraving, 29.8 × 22.0 cm (sheet). RCIN 812022

Fig. 6.5  Thomas Gainsborough (1727–88), *James Quin*, 1760–3 (detail).
Oil on canvas, 64.7 × 50.9 cm. RCIN 405949

who was born in Patna (Bihar state) and joined the East India Company at a young age before moving to Ireland and then England.[7] Shampooing originally referred to a form of massage with oils, which was a speciality at 'Mahomed's Shampooing Bath' in Brighton; only later did the process involve the use of soap. In 1822 Mahomed was appointed 'Shampoo Surgeon to the King', serving both George IV and William IV at the Royal Pavilion, where he designed the baths.

## WIGS FOR MEN

In England the convention for wealthy men to shave off their real hair and replace it with a wig (also known as a periwig, or peruke) had begun in the 1660s, and the practice was linked to contemporary ideas about health and cleanliness. Being organic, and directly integrated with the body, hair was considered a primary means by which infection could spread.[8] While this is now known not to be the case, it is true that keeping the head shaved reduced the probability of getting lice, another common problem alongside infectious disease.

The longer hairstyles that had become fashionable for men by the middle of the seventeenth century, and which continued well into the eighteenth, brought with them the need for regular styling to achieve the desirable curled look. A wig provided a far more convenient option than having to style one's own hair, as it could be removed at bedtime and regularly sent to the hairdresser to be reset. The most expensive wigs were made of human hair, which was imported into Britain from all over the world; traded through hair merchants, it was then sold on to the peruke-maker. The strength of the hair was of paramount importance, as it needed to endure high temperatures during the process of setting. Brown hair from the heads of youthful country girls was considered optimal, as it was less likely to have been treated to achieve the styles dictated by high fashion and also not subjected to the toxic fumes of urban centres. Denis Diderot recommended hair from beer- and cider-drinking countries.[9] Alternatively, a man might choose to use his natural hair for a wig, as Samuel

Pepys had done in 1663. For those unable to afford human hair, animal hair was another alternative: goat, cow and horsehair were all used, sometimes in combination with human strands.

Dating a portrait based on a wig is complicated by the fact that a variety of styles were worn throughout the century, and it was not uncommon for a man to own several wigs for different occasions. While the full-bottomed periwig so characteristic of the Restoration court continued to be worn into the first decades of the eighteenth century, it became shorter, and the curls were increasingly grouped together into separate bunches (known as tails) rather than falling as individual ringlets around the shoulders. By the 1760s full-bottomed wigs had become very outdated, and William Hogarth takes pleasure in satirising the old-fashioned styles worn for the coronation of George III and Queen Charlotte in *The Five Orders of Perriwigs* (Fig. 6.4). Here the proportions of the wigs are likened to classical architecture. This impression has been annotated with the names of those it is intended to depict, with the queen at lower left, and the Archbishop of Canterbury upper left. The latter is shown wearing a traditional form of wig known as a Physical, characterised by its short curls on top arranged to stand straight up, and the wide mass of bushy curls around the ears and back. This is also what is worn by the actor James Quin, when portrayed in his sixties (Fig. 6.5). The sharply defined hairline around his temple clearly indicates this is a wig. George Frederick Handel, too, wears a longer,

Fig. 6.6  Attributed to Thomas Hudson (1701–79),
*George Frederick Handel, c.*1756–60.
Oil on canvas, 80.6 × 72.1 cm. RCIN 405649

Fig. 6.7  Sprinkler and bag for hair powder, *c.*1750–1800.
Wood, leather and metal (modern leather drawstring), 18.0 × 8.0 × 8.0 cm (sprinkler);
25.0 × 13.0 × 13.0 cm (bag). London, School of Historical Dress, TSHD.2013.022a–b

A similar sprinkler and drawstring bag are illustrated in the lower left
of Plate II opposite.

they were attached to ribbons, and sewn onto a net caul.
The wig was built on a wooden head based on the size of the
customer's head, so precise measurements were required.
Wigs rarely survive due to the fragility of the caul, while the
hair itself was valuable enough to be repurposed into a new
wig as fashions changed.

The entry for 'Perruquier-barbier' also illustrates a
variety of tools used during the process of dressing and
powdering the hair, as well as a selection of wigs available
when this volume was published in 1771 (Fig. 6.8). As the
century progressed, the most fashionable styles were those
in which the hair was caught into a tail ('queue') at the
back (Fig. 6.9). The tail could be set into ringlets and tied
with a bow or encased within a silk bag at the nape to create
a bag-wig. This style, the most formal of all, was introduced
in the 1720s but was popular for much of the century for
special occasions. It is clearly shown in a pastel portrait
depicting George III in profile view (Fig. 6.10). A wig bag
decorated with black ribbons of a strikingly similar style,
with tiny regular picot loops along each edge, is shown
alongside (Fig. 6.11). The bag fastens with a drawstring
and serves to protect clothing from both pomatum and
powder, while also preventing the hair of the wig from
drying out. The portrait also shows that here it is being
worn *en solitaire*, with two wide black ribbons from the
bow brought to the front where they have been tied and
the ends tucked out of sight. The king's wig is set with one
frizzed horizontal side curl over each ear. These were known

old-fashioned style in a portrait painted towards the end
of the 1750s, when the composer was in his sixties (Fig. 6.6).
The curls are arranged into a rather frizzy mass on each
side. No attempt has been made to match the colour of
the heavily powdered pale grey wig with his dark eyebrows,
leading to a striking contrast and adding to the sense
of artificiality. The centre parting is strongly emphasised
and probably continues down the back of the head. A more
modern style was to have the top brushed back into a small
peak without a parting.

Diderot's *Encyclopédie* includes the most complete
description of the process of producing a wig: the hair was
first cleaned and sorted by length, then combed to remove
tangles and get the hair to lie parallel. Small sections of hair
were wound around wooden or ceramic curlers, and boiled
in water for three hours, before being dried in an oven.
Next, they were covered in flour paste and baked, and then
the individual curls were woven onto silk thread. Finally,

Fig. 6.8  Denis Diderot (1713–84), *Encyclopédie*, [*t. 25, planches M–S*], Paris, 1771,
Perruquier, barbier, baigner-etuviste, pl. II (below) and pl. VII (below right).
RCIN 1195946

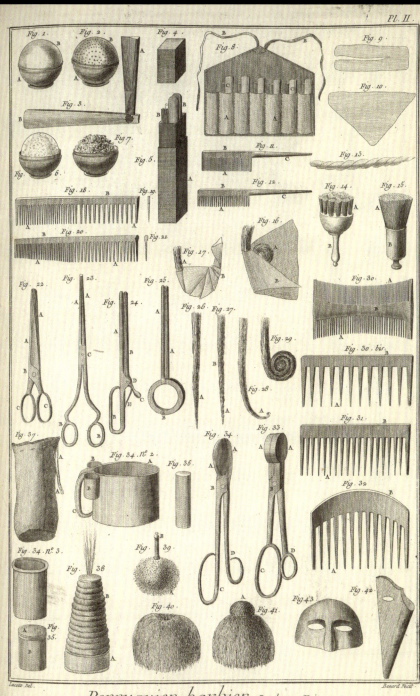

Perruquier-barbier, Barbe et Frisure.

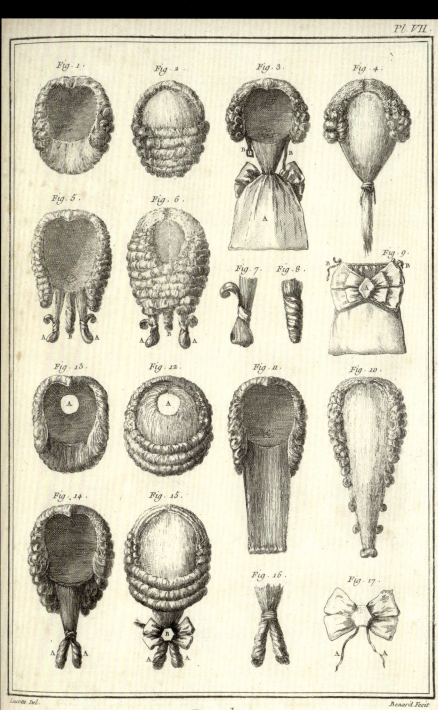

Perruquier Barbier, Perruques.

Fig. 6.12  Prince Ernst, Duke of Mecklenburg-Strelitz, in Johan Joseph Zoffany (1733–1810), *Queen Charlotte with Members of her Family*, c.1771–2 (detail).
Oil on canvas, 105.3 × 127.0 cm. RCIN 401004

as buckles, from the French *bouclé* (curl). This was a fashionable style in the 1750s, although two curls were worn in the 1760s, and sometimes even three (Fig. 6.12). The raised front portion of the wig above the forehead was known as a toupet. It increased in height during the 1770s, as did women's hair. Sometimes the tail was looped back up on itself and tied with another section of hair to form a style known as a Cadogan or club wig. This was a favourite style for the macaronies, whose exaggerated large club wigs were a common subject for satire.

Shorter styles of wig without a tail were considered more practical and informal, the most typical example being the bob-wig. This became popular among the professional classes and tradesmen, although it was also worn by upper-class men for riding and travelling. The democratic nature of the style is referenced by Charles Philips in his depiction of the members of a club known as 'La Table Ronde' within what is probably an imaginary hunting lodge (Fig. 6.13). While little else is known of the club's membership or rules, the emphasis is clearly on the men meeting under equality, with echoes of King Arthur and his knights. They all wear the matching blue and red royal hunting uniform introduced by Frederick, Prince of Wales, in 1729, and no servants are present so the men serve each other at the round table, at which there can be no head or preferential seat. At first glance their wigs also give an impression of singular uniformity. While most of the members have simple shoulder-length bob-wigs considered especially practical for hunting, the prince (seated in front of the fireplace) and four men sitting near him wear the more fashionable queue style, two with silk bags visible, one of which is worn *en solitaire*. Perhaps the queue wigs are indicative of youth, although they might also be a nod to their position at the right-hand side of the prince. Two of them also wear the blue sash of the Order of the Garter, like the prince.

Certain styles of wig were associated with military dress. These included the campaign wig, characterised by its knotted lock of hair on each side and a long curl at the back, which was worn until around the middle of the century. This is shown on the second row of the illustration in Diderot's *Encyclopédie* (see Fig. 6.8, Plate VII) and worn

Fig. 6.13 Charles Philips (1708–47), *Frederick, Prince of Wales, with the Members of the 'La Table Ronde'*, 1732.
Oil on canvas, 127.6 × 102.3 cm. RCIN 406101

Fig. 6.14 Paul Sandby (1731–1809), *A Young Officer*, c.1752–60.
Pen and ink and watercolour, 12.9 × 6.5 cm. RCIN 914465

considered an essential component of respectability. By the 1740s only the lowest classes would not have worn a wig and appearing without one was regarded as both emasculating and offensive. The removal of a wig in mixed company was particularly rude: 'to the utter consternation of the company, he took off his wig to wipe his head! which occasioned such universal horror, that all who were near the door escaped into other apartments', writes Fanny Burney in *Cecilia*.[11] While the wealthy would have their wig made-to-measure, a thriving second-hand trade also existed. Notoriously easy to steal, sometimes directly from the head of the wearer using hooked sticks or even – according to some possibly apocryphal accounts – trained monkeys, a specialist wig market on Rosemary Lane was a popular location for their resale. One option was a 'lucky dip' whereby the purchaser paid a penny and dug into a sack of old wigs. The wig-making trade in London seems to have been centred around the West End and the Strand, although many sellers also visited wealthy customers in their own homes.

## NATURAL HAIR FOR MEN

Given that the starch used to create hair powder was derived from crops such as wheat and barley, its use for this purpose generated concern and moral censure, particularly when harvests were poor. In 1795 the Tory prime minister, William Pitt the Younger, introduced a hair tax that required wearers of hair powder to acquire a licence each year, at a cost of 1 guinea (£1 1s). Those who continued to wear powder without paying the fee could be charged a fine of £20, with incentives also given to those who reported offenders.[12] The funds raised from the tax were intended to help finance Britain's costly war with France. The use of hair powder therefore became a political issue: a public demonstration of support for Pitt's foreign policy. Some Whigs on the other side of the political spectrum proudly sported an unpowdered coiffure, the 5th Duke of Bedford (1765–1802) being a notable and prominent example. The military were excluded from the powder tax, and among soldiers the use of powdered wigs continued for longer

by George II along with armour (see Fig. 11.2). Another wig originally with military connections was the Ramillies, worn by a young officer in a watercolour by Paul Sandby (Fig. 6.14). Named after the battle of 1706 fought in the Spanish Netherlands as part of the War of the Spanish Succession, the Ramillies wig can be identified by the long plait at the centre back, which, as here, could reach the waist, and was tied with a large bow at the nape and a smaller bow at the bottom. Sometimes the plait was entirely wrapped in a black ribbon. By the 1730s the Ramillies was also worn by civilians.

At the beginning of the eighteenth century even the cheapest wig cost around £3, the equivalent of over £400 today.[10] They were therefore expensive luxury items in a man's wardrobe and a clear indication of status and wealth. Over the course of the century, however, wigs became cheaper and much more widely accessible, and were

than in the civilian population. They were also worn at court for many years after they had passed out of fashion for everyday wear.

The introduction of the powder tax is often given as the reason why men swapped wigs for their natural hair at the end of the eighteenth century. However, both the wearing of wigs and the use of hair powder had been falling out of fashion in Britain long before 1795. Some young men had reverted to wearing their real hair in the 1760s: curled, greased and powdered in the manner of a wig, which can make it difficult to detect in portraiture. In that decade, wig-makers, alarmed about the impact of changing fashions on the long-term survival of their industry, petitioned the government to impose sumptuary laws making the wearing of wigs mandatory, while in 1765 George III received a delegation of wig-makers to hear their concerns. *Town and Country Magazine* wrote in 1772 that 'most gentlemen now wear their own hair'.[13] By then it was only older men who continued to wear wigs, although those who left off a full wig might still supplement their real hair as required. In 1791 the Prince of Wales acquired three pairs of 'false curls' for £3 3s.[14] Perhaps these contribute to his full and fluffy hairstyle depicted by John Russell that same year (see Fig. 2.10). Whereas the wearing of a powdered wig had once served to indicate wealth and prestige, in an Enlightenment society that increasingly favoured the simple and the natural, wigs came to represent an artificial

world, out of touch with the changing social landscape. Earlier in the century physicians had recommended the head remain covered, with a wig keeping the head warm much like a hat, but by the end of the century medical advice had altered, and instead men were advised to allow the head to breathe and sweat.[15]

Karl Anton Hickel's portrait of Richard Brinsley Sheridan (Fig. 6.15) is a preparatory study from life for a larger work depicting William Pitt the Younger addressing the House of Commons, now in the National Portrait Gallery, London.[16] Sheridan, painted here at the age of 42, was a playwright and theatre manager, committed Whig, and close friend of the Prince of Wales. In the final painting, although at first glance all the Members of Parliament appear to have similar short, powdered hairstyles, they represent a mix of those who continue to wear a wig and those who have switched to their natural hair. Comparing the portrait of Sheridan, for example, with another preparatory sketch for the same painting, this time depicting Welbore Ellis, 1st Baron Mendip (Fig. 6.16), clearly indicates the difference in appearance: Sheridan's hair is cut short and arranged into two puffs spreading over the ears, whereas Ellis, as an older man of 80, retains his wig with its defined widow's peak on the forehead and two buckles on each ear. Although discarding the wig was a symbolic political statement for some, the group portrait illustrates that this explanation is a simplification, as wigs appear on both sides of the chamber.

OPPOSITE, LEFT
Fig. 6.15  Karl Anton Hickel (1745–98), *Richard Brinsley Sheridan*, 1793.
Oil on canvas, 65.3 × 54.2 cm. RCIN 406937

OPPOSITE, RIGHT
Fig. 6.16  Karl Anton Hickel (1745–98), *Welbore Ellis, 1st Baron Mendip*, 1793.
Oil on canvas, 59.4 × 49.2 cm. London, National Portrait Gallery, 3993.

LEFT
Fig. 6.17  Paul Emil Jacobs (1802–66), *Augustus, Duke of Saxe-Gotha-Altenburg*, c.1840–4, after an original of 1807.
Oil on canvas, 66.2 × 50.5 cm. RCIN 407166

The shift towards neo-classicism also favoured the wearing of natural hair, cropped short. The echo of the antique is evident in the nomenclature of the styles: the 'Brutus' and hair worn *à la Titus*, for example. The trend for young men at the forefront of fashion to wear their hair short and artfully tousled first aroused remark in the 1780s. Associated with the lower classes, the wearing of natural hair was regarded as confrontational because of its blurring of social boundaries and connection with a violent underworld, including the increasingly popular sport of boxing. After the events of the French Revolution the symbolism of the crop became starker, with some considering it an indication of sympathy with Revolutionary ideals. Styles named *à la Victime* and *à la Guillotine* consciously connected short hair with the brutal chops imposed prior to execution. By the early nineteenth century, the fashionable style involved more height and less width, as seen in a portrait of Augustus, Duke of Saxe-Gotha-Altenburg (Fig. 6.17), after an original of 1807 by Ludwig Döll at Schloss Friedenstein.[17] The duke's hair is left longer on top and falls in perfectly windswept ringlets over the brow, while the sides are also brushed forwards and worn with longer sideburns. By this date, men who continued to wear a wig due to hair loss often selected a more natural style deliberately intended to mimic these cropped haircuts, a reversal of the fashion around the middle of the century for real hair to be dressed to look like a wig.

## FACIAL HAIR

At certain points during the seventeenth century a beard had been considered a symbol of masculinity, interpreted as an outward sign of inner virility, directly linked to male sexuality and an indicator that the wearer had made the transition through puberty.[18] This shifted, however, at the beginning of the eighteenth century, and across Europe a clean-shaven face for men quickly became the favoured mode, a convention rooted in changing ideas about polite society. With the increasing focus on the potential to 'read' a man's facial features and emotions to gain a clearer insight into his character and motivations, a beard was seen as deliberate concealment. It was also taken to suggest a lack of interest in or funds to enable the necessary routines of self-care to maintain a clean-shaven appearance and thereby meet social expectations. All of this makes Jean-Etienne Liotard's self-presentation with an enormous greying beard even more unusual (see Fig. 9.5). Despite a shift away from the medieval humoral model as an explanation for the workings of the human body, traditional interpretations of facial hair as a type of excrement perpetuated, and its removal was therefore seen as a means of disposing of bodily waste.[19] The rise of the wig may also have played a role in the decline of the beard, both in the incongruity between real and false hair presented when the two were worn together, and in the overwhelming volume of hair encompassing the facial features that resulted. The rediscovered interest in the Greek and Roman statues of antiquity provided examples of tactile smooth surfaces, even when the figures themselves were bearded.[20]

During the eighteenth century beards came to signify otherness when set against the European gentlemanly ideal, being variously bound up with notions of eccentricity, old age, barbarity and low social status, as well as perceived hierarchies and conceptions of 'cultivation' across different cultures.[21] A clean-shaven face was a fashion that would be reversed dramatically during the Victorian era.

Fig. 6.18  Louis Carrogis de Carmontelle (1717–1806),
*Madame Brissard*, c.1765.
Red and black chalk, and watercolour, 28.3 × 17.4 cm. RCIN 913117

Fig. 6.19  Jean-Baptiste Pigalle (1714–85), *Madame de Pompadour*,
1748–51.
White marble, 75.9 × 47.3 × 28.9 cm. New York, Metropolitan Museum of Art,
49.7.70

## HAIRSTYLES FOR WOMEN

It is a common misconception that full wigs were regularly worn by both sexes at this time. While it is true that for much of the century a wig was a mark of status for men, the immensely tall and wide hairstyles adopted by many women in the latter half of the eighteenth century were almost always created using the wearer's own hair raised over pads, although sometimes with the addition of pieces of false hair. Similarly, during the Regency period, hairstyles could be enhanced with the addition of individual ringlets, known as drop curls. Satirical prints showing women entirely transforming their appearance by adopting a full wig (commonly known as a *tête*) to conceal a bald head are an exaggeration of a practice generally limited to the elderly or ill.

In Britain during the first half of the century, a relaxed approach to dressing the hair was preferred, with it usually left in its natural unpowdered state, and either pinned up into a small bun perched high on the head (see Fig. 3.10), or falling in loose curls to the shoulders, as worn by many of the women in *St James's Park and the Mall* (see pp. 2–3). On the Continent a more formalised hairstyle known as the *tête de mouton* became popular during the 1740s and was worn into the 1760s. Named after its similarity to a sheep's fleece, here the hair was wrapped around rollers or papers to create tight curls, which were then pinned into position close to the head and powdered. Madame de Pompadour wears her hair dressed in this way in a portrait after François-Hubert Drouais (see Fig. 9.17). In Louis Carrogis de Carmontelle's depiction of Madame Brissard, the sitter is shown at her toilette, seated in front of a wide-open window (Fig. 6.18). Her long hair is in the process of being set. Wearing hair loose in the manner shown here would not have been appropriate in a public space. The top seems to have been arranged into *tête de mouton*

style curls, the height at the front of the head suggesting a date of c.1765. A portrait bust of Madame de Pompadour by Jean-Baptiste Pigalle showing her with a similar hairstyle reveals how the back hair could be divided into sections and plaited before being pinned up into position (Fig. 6.19). Madame Brissard's hair has perhaps been separated for this process.

Over the course of the 1760s women's hairstyles started to rise in both Britain and France, with the hair assembled into a bun on the top of the head and height introduced over the forehead: nascent indications can be seen in Francis Cotes's portrait of George III's sisters, Princess Caroline and Princess Louisa, painted in 1767 (see Fig. 3.15). The height and complexity of female hairstyles would increase during the 1770s, peaking around the middle of the decade. Two drawings attributed to the German-born artist Daniel Nikolaus Chodowiecki show an ornate example from both front and side (Figs 6.20 and 6.21). To create such volume at the crown, the hair was raised up over pads or cushions stuffed with wool, horsehair or cork ground into small pieces, and then pinned into position, while the side rolls could be created by wrapping the hair around soft banana-shaped rollers.

Fig. 6.20 Attributed to Daniel Nikolaus Chodowiecki (1726–1801), *The Head of a Woman, Full Face, with High Coiffure, c.*1770–80.
Watercolour with touches of bodycolour and pencil, 15.0 × 11.9 cm. RCIN 912164

Fig. 6.21 Attributed to Daniel Nikolaus Chodowiecki (1726–1801), *The Head of a Woman in Profile, with High Coiffure, c.*1770–80.
Watercolour with touches of bodycolour and pencil, 14.9 × 11.6 cm. RCIN 912165

Two French hairdressers, Monsieur Léonard and Madame Campan, credited the fashion for extremely tall hairstyles to their client, Marie-Antoinette, and indeed the French queen was, in her own words, 'a bit occupied by my hairstyle' (see Fig. 12.17).[22] According to some reports, Marie-Antoinette's hair measured 36 pouces (91 cm) from the roots to the top, a fact that did not impress her mother, Maria-Theresa of Austria, who recommended instead that her daughter 'should follow fashion moderately, but never carry it to excess … A simple hairstyle suits her better and is more appropriate for a queen.'[23] In 1775, however, one French courtier reassured Maria-Theresa that 'the queen is only following a fashion that has become widespread'.[24] The fashion for big hair quickly spread across the Channel and was also adopted widely by women in Britain. Although traditionally considered conservative in dress, portraits reveal that Queen Charlotte followed fashions in hairstyle closely. In Benjamin West's portrait of the queen from 1776 she has adopted the heart-shaped styles of that date, with her hair widening at the peak on both sides (see Fig. 1.16).

Such fashions provided ripe material for caricaturists, with both the effort required to achieve such a style, as well as its innate impracticality, being common themes: Michel Vincent Brandoin's hairdresser, for instance, has to climb a ladder to reach the peak of his client's towering coiffure (Fig. 6.22). The printmaking couple of Matthias and Mary Darly were enamoured with the comedic opportunities inspired by hairstyles of the 1770s and their prints ridiculed both macaroni men and fashion-forward women. In one example (Fig. 6.23), an airborne 'Miss Shuttle-Cock' is positioned midway between two men playing battledore and shuttlecock (a precursor to modern badminton), with both the height of her hair and the addition of enormous ostrich feathers serving to echo the shape of a shuttlecock, while the use of cork fillings for false rumps is referenced in the inscription, 'Ladie[s] likes [*sic*] Shuttle-Cocks are now array'd, The tail is Cork'd and feather'd is the head'.

In another topical print, published in March 1776, a woman's massive hairstyle has been dressed to commemorate the Battle of Bunker's Hill, a key moment in the American Revolutionary War, which had occurred the previous

Fig. 6.22
Michel Vincent Brandoin (1733–1807), *The Hairdresser*, c.1771.
Pen and ink and watercolour, 22.1 × 18.5 cm. RCIN 913258

Fig. 6.23 Attributed to Richard Brinsley Sheridan (1751–1816), 'Miss Shuttle-Cock', from Mary Darly (1736–91), *Darly's Comic-Prints of Characters, Caricatures, Macaronies &c.*, London, 1776, pl. [1].
RCIN 1133151

Fig. 6.24 Associated with Matthias Darly (c.1721–80) and Mary Darly (1736–91), 'Bunkers Hill, or America's Head Dress', from Mary Darly, *Darly's Comic-Prints of Characters, Caricatures, Macaronies &c.*, London, 1776, pl. [63].
RCIN 1133151

year (Fig. 6.24). Although officially considered a victory for the British, they had suffered significant casualties and the battle provided an important boost in morale for the American fighters, whose retreat was mainly due to a lack of ammunition. Atop the hairstyle we see tiny soldiers, tents and an artillery train, with a sea battle below, while instead of feathers, the top of the hair is set with huge flags, incorporating images of an ape, a goose and two women (conjectured to represent, respectively, Louis XVI, General Israel Putnam, and America and Britannia).[25] Clearly there is an intention to ridicule the British forces, who seem to be firing at each other. While it is easy to interpret such images as humorous exaggeration, too distorted to be based in reality, documentary records indicate that topical events certainly did inspire the manner in which hair was dressed, and in some instances the prints themselves seem to have influenced fashions. At a masquerade at the Pantheon in London in May 1776, one lady is reported to have attended 'dressed agreeable to Darly's caricature of a head, so enormous as actually to contain both a plan and model of Boston, and the provincial army on Bunker's hill'.[26] The widespread trend for such fashions *à l'américaine* in France is easier to understand, allied as the country was with the American colonists at the time. Similarly, headdresses that integrated models of full-rigged frigates to commemorate French victories over the English Royal Navy were popular in French fashion plates. Other contemporary events provided inspiration for such ephemeral *pouf aux circonstances*. The *pouf à l'inoculation*, for example, celebrated the inoculation of Louis XVI and his two brothers against smallpox in 1774.

During the 1780s the height was swapped for horizontal volume, and women instead wore their hair cut shorter around the face and arranged into frizzed curls. Here again the fashion was widely attributed to Marie-Antoinette and her hairdresser Léonard and was said to have been prompted by the queen experiencing hair loss after the birth of the dauphin in 1781: the style became known as the *coiffure à l'enfant*. Two portraits of Louise Augusta, Duchess of Augustenburg (one of George III's nieces), and her brother Frederik, later King of Denmark,

Fig. 6.27  Thomas Gainsborough (1727–88), *Anne, Duchess of Cumberland*, 1775–c.1784.
Oil on canvas, 241.7 × 142.6 cm. RCIN 405937

Fig. 6.28  Thomas Gainsborough (1727–88), *Anne, Duchess of Cumberland*, 1775–c.1784 (detail), before conservation in 1959.
Oil on canvas, 241.7 × 142.6 cm. RCIN 405937

clearly show the fashion in 1784 (Figs 6.25 and 6.26). While there is still volume at the crown, the height of Louise's hair is much lower and balanced by width at the sides. The back hair is now arranged into thick ringlets, which could be left hanging down or looped back up underneath into a chignon. On top of her hair the young princess (she is only around 12 years old) wears a *pouf* (hair ornament) of orange blossom, roses and striped ribbon to match the colour of her pink gown set with green and white bows. The pendant portrait of Frederik shows him wearing a bulbous wig that echoes the shape of women's hair at this date.

The rapidity with which fashions in hair changed during this period could result in a portrait quickly going 'out of date' and artists were sometimes requested to update a likeness. Thomas Gainsborough's portrait of the Duchess of Cumberland, for example, was initially painted in the mid-1770s and exhibited at the Royal Academy in 1777 (Fig. 6.27). The duchess (who had married the Duke of Cumberland in secret six years earlier) is shown with the rather triangular hairstyle of that time. However, at some point in the 1780s, probably around 1784, the hair was repainted – presumably by Gainsborough himself to whom the duchess was very loyal – to make it much wider and so bring it more in line with the newer styles.[27] This later addition was removed when the painting was conserved in 1959 but was recorded in a pre-conservation photograph (Fig. 6.28). Similarly, Johan Joseph Zoffany's portrait of Queen Charlotte (see Fig. 1.14) was reproduced as a mezzotint, initially in 1772 with hair arranged as in

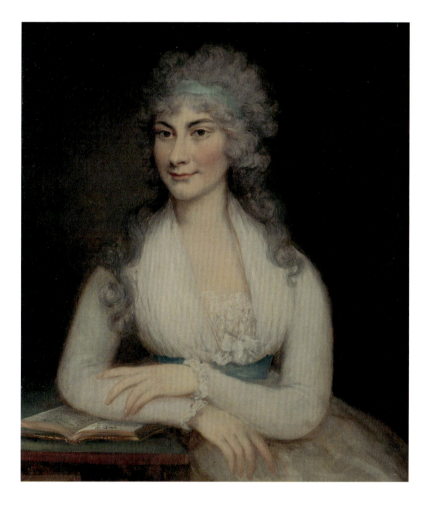

the painting, and later in 1794 with an updated hairstyle more characteristic of the 1780s.[28]

By 1800 some fashion-forward English women had started to adopt a cropped hairstyle *à la Titus*, which echoed classical styles and was analogous to the cropped natural hair also fashionable among men at around the same date. Giovanna Zanerini, known as 'La Baccelli' (1753–1801), celebrated Venetian-born ballerina and long-term mistress of the 3rd Duke of Dorset, wears a transitional style in a portrait dating from *c*.1795, the hair around her head cut short and curled but with some tendrils left long over her shoulders (Fig. 6.29). Other women arranged their hair into a knot at the nape, with the hair over the forehead trimmed into a fringe and curled. In portraits this can sometimes give the impression of short hair.

George Dawe's portrait of Princess Feodora of Leiningen illustrates the most popular hairstyle for women during the Regency period, clearly based on classical precedents (Fig. 6.30). The hair was divided into two sections: the front hair (stretching over the head from one ear to the other) was cut short and set into face-framing curls on either side of a centre parting, while the back hair was left to grow long and then arranged into a high bun, which could be ornate, incorporating braided sections and necessitating the assistance of a lady's maid. By this time powder was considered very outdated and the hair was instead worn in its natural shade, healthy and shiny, something indicated in this portrait as the light source from the right-hand side creates highlights on the princess's curls and plait. Hairpieces were sometimes used, including fake fringes.

## BARBERS AND HAIRDRESSERS

During the eighteenth century several overlapping trades were involved in the care of hair. For a long time, barbers had been regarded as part of the medical community, their work encompassing a diverse range of activities broadly related to the care of the body (for example, drawing teeth, bloodletting and draining boils), alongside the principal task of cutting or shaving the hair on the head and face. Reflective of this is the fact that from 1540 onwards surgeons and barbers working in London were regulated by the same 'Worshipful Company of Barber-Surgeons', with at least 26 other similar guilds across England, Scotland and Ireland.[29] As the eighteenth century progressed, surgeons pressed for increasing distinction between the two professions, partly in an attempt to be considered equivalent in status to physicians, and in 1745 the company formally separated. Many barbers, however, persisted to operate under the title of 'barber-surgeon' into the nineteenth century and continued to provide additional bodily services, such as nail cutting, ear syringing and tongue scraping, although the degree to which they also undertook minor surgical procedures probably depended on a number of factors, including locality, customer base and availability of other specialists.

Thomas Rowlandson's *A Barber's Shop* illustrates some of the tools of the trade (Fig. 6.31). In the centre a portly man has been encased in a protective sheet, his own hair being combed and set into curls with tongs; on the right another customer has had soapy lather applied to his face in preparation for being shaved by an elderly barber; nearby, an apprentice holds up a curved basin for a man who attends to a bleeding cut, either accidental or medicinal. On the left a looking glass provides the opportunity for two men to check their final appearance, while in the foreground two dogs have pulled a bag-wig from its stand. As Rowlandson shows, barbers also sold and dressed wigs, which needed to be reset regularly, and in this they overlapped with the activities of the 'peruke-maker'. In fact, this is a late portrayal of wig-wearing, with many men having abandoned the practice of shaving off

their head hair by this date (1811). Although only indicated here by the figure on the left reading a newspaper, a barber's shop served as a social space in which to catch up on gossip and hear the news of the day, sometimes with musical entertainment and alcoholic enticements on offer. This is a connection still visible today in France's *Le Figaro* newspaper, founded in 1826 and named after the unscrupulous barber in Pierre Beaumarchais's *The Barber of Seville* (1775). Customers were generally, although not exclusively, male, and while barbers themselves were typically men, there is some evidence to suggest that barbering was also becoming a respectable profession for women.[30]

The frequency with which men shaved is difficult to establish, given that payments to a barber were often made on a quarterly basis and visits usually went unrecorded. While the elite were probably shaved on a daily basis, for those further down the social spectrum a visit to the barber two or three times a week seems to have been more typical, with a common price for a single shave being around sixpence.[31] Some barbers offered a 'penny shave' for the poor, and for those who could only afford a weekly shave this was likely to have been undertaken on Saturdays, in preparation for attending church the following day. While eighteenth-century portraits almost exclusively depict men freshly shaven, a few days of stubble may have been a more frequent occurrence than visual sources would have us believe, at least for those lower down the social scale.

Technological innovations that enabled the development of new cast-steel razors made shaving at home a popular option from the 1770s onwards, at least for those who could afford to buy and maintain the necessary equipment. At the same time there was a growth in both advertising and instructional literature, which emphasised shaving as a fundamental gentlemanly skill. The switch from paying a barber to self-shaving was certainly not immediate however, and for most men during the eighteenth century, visiting the barber (or having a so-called 'flying barber' attend to them at home) remained an important component of their depilatory regime. This shift meant that whereas in the first half of the century a barber's clientele would probably have been drawn from across the entire social spectrum, as the century

A BARBERS SHOP.

progressed the barber's shop was increasingly associated with the working classes.

The focus on hair during the eighteenth century, together with the complicated styles that required a significant degree of expertise and substantial investment of time, led to the development of an entirely separate trade to that of the barber: the hairdresser.[32] As a profession it was deliberately distinct, with hairdressers consciously attempting to distance themselves from the barber's less appealing practices and instead laying greater emphasis on creativity and individualism. Hairdressers also styled wigs and sold hair products and perfume. Growth in demand was exponential, and by 1795 there were an estimated 50,000 hairdressers working in London alone, from only two reported at the time of George II's coronation in 1727.[33] Whereas the activities of dressing an elite woman's hair had traditionally been a female occupation, undertaken by a lady's maid as one of her many responsibilities, over the course of the century the profession became dominated by men.

The eighteenth century saw the rise of what might be considered the first celebrity hairdressers, their reputations built on the fame of their clients and the originality of their creations. Legros de Rumigny (1710–70), for example, worked for two of Louis XV's mistresses: Madame de Pompadour and Madame du Barry. Originally trained as a chef, he also sold hair products and published a five-volume treatise, *L'Art de la Coëffure des dames françoises* (1768–70), with a number of fold-out templates, which he considered would be of benefit to artists looking to depict hair in portraits with accuracy. This was one of many manuals devoted to hairdressing published around this time. De Rumigny also established a hairdressing school, the Académie de Coëffure, aimed at both professionals and servants, the ability to dress hair being an important skill for ladies' maids, valets and butlers, and frequently specified in job advertisements.[34]

While some hairdressers operated out of commercial premises, it was common practice for them to visit clients in their own homes, enabling an unusual level of access and degree of intimacy that crossed social classes and disrupted established boundaries between men and women. Brandoin's lightly satirical depiction of a hairdresser ascending a ladder to perfect the towering hairstyle of his client shows her in a private moment: at her toilette wearing her peignoir, while attended by an abbé (see Fig. 6.22). Some clients were concerned about the propensity for hairdressers to share private details about their lives with others and required them to agree to exclusivity clauses, although this was not the case for Marie-Antoinette and her hairdresser Léonard, the French queen requesting that he continue to serve other customers in order to remain up to date on the most fashionable new trends.[35]

France was undoubtedly the leader in fashions for hair. In England, French hairdressers were highly sought after and sometimes servants were sent to Paris to learn the latest styles and techniques.[36] While a hairdresser might be hired for a specific occasion, those who could afford to do so might engage one on a quarterly retainer for regular or even daily services, leading to loyal relationships lasting many years. For a number of decades Queen Charlotte employed a hairdresser named John Baptist Suardy, although the cost-conscious queen drew the line at his request for payment of £200 (the equivalent of around £27,000 today) to attend on her for the summer season of 1788, instead preferring to pay as occasions required.[37] She was unimpressed with his replacement, William Duncan, however, whom she felt had 'no taste'.[38] Besides the typical social events that might warrant particular attention to the hair, having a portrait painted was another reason to employ the services of a professional, with Charlotte Papendiek engaging the hairdresser Mr Read to 'contrive a headdress' in preparation for her portrait sitting with Zoffany.[39]

## HEADWEAR FOR MEN

The prominence of hats, which were worn by virtually all men, regardless of rank, combined with their easy mobility, made them a prime object for social manoeuvre and sartorial signal, leading to the development of a ritualised system of hat etiquette during the seventeenth century. This included removing the hat in the presence of social superiors and doffing the hat upon being introduced to a new acquaintance. In the eighteenth century such formalised behaviours were gradually relaxed, with men's headwear less frequently worn indoors, a wig often serving instead to maintain both dignity and warmth. While doffing or touching the hat remained a mark of civility, when passing a lady of high rank in the street for example, the decline of formal hat signals coincided with the rise in popularity of the more egalitarian practice of shaking hands, which did not require participants to make an immediate assessment of their relative social status to determine who should make the initial gesture of deference.[40] Despite this, the hat retained its association with authority, and the removal of a man's hat in the presence of the king was still a requirement. The practice of doffing the hat has its echoes in the military salute of today.

Men's hats were usually created from a felted material in which the fibres had been matted together through a combination of friction and water. The finest were fashioned from the soft dense underfur of the beaver, which resulted in a glossy and waterproof material. During the Georgian period most beaver pelts were imported from North America, originating from the American beaver (*Castor canadensis*), the population of the Eurasian beaver (*Castor fiber*) having been overhunted almost to extinction in the seventeenth century for their fur. Cheaper felt hats could be made from alternative furs, including rabbit and sheep. These were also used in combination with beaver to construct so-called 'demi-castors', the production of which was regulated at various points in both Britain and France.[41] In the early eighteenth century the process of felting the fibres to create a matted textile was speeded up by a new innovation that involved boiling the pelts with mercury nitrate, a dangerous practice known as carrotting (because it changed the colour of the fur to orange), but which often led to mercury poisoning and neurological damage among hatmakers, possibly the origin of the term 'mad as a hatter'.

The three-cornered (tricorne) hat, first popular in Britain from the 1690s, remained the most popular style of headwear for men for much of the eighteenth century. The characteristic shape, forming an approximate equilateral

Fig. 6.32  William Grimaldi (1751–1830), *George III*, 1804.
Watercolour on ivory, 14.0 × 10.9 cm. RCIN 421441

triangle, was created by turning up (cocking) the brim in three places, originally introduced by soldiers to funnel away rain water. Each side was held in place with a looped button. The tricorne was worn with one point to the front, often positioned over one eye rather than central. Within this broad style were subtle differences in the cocking of the hat (including the sharpness of the pinch) and its manner of wearing that could demonstrate an affiliation with a particular social group.[42] Wearing a hat uncocked was a practical but less fashionable option to protect against inclement weather, and was more frequently adopted by those lower down the social scale. For court events, the tricorne hat was always carried under one arm (as a mark of respect), leading to the development of a flat style in the 1760s specifically intended for carrying rather than wearing (*chapeau bras*). From the 1780s the bicorne hat (turned up on two sides instead of three) had started to replace the tricorne, and was easier to carry.

The hat held by the young Prince William in Zoffany's group portrait (see Fig. 5.8) reveals how hats could be lined with a contrasting fabric, here a silvery-blue silk, with a circular label inside (illegible in the painting) presumably identifying the hatmaker. Unlike many other garments, hats were generally not made-to-measure, being moulded over different-sized blocks. The requirement for a good supply of water during the production process initially encouraged the development of a concentrated hatmaking trade just south of the River Thames in Southwark, although as the century progressed other centres (especially Manchester and Stockport) became increasingly important.[43]

Many hats were dyed black during a late stage in the production process, although Richard 'Beau' Nash (1674–1761), Master of Ceremonies at the Assembly Rooms in Bath, bucked convention by wearing a signature white beaver hat, supposedly to avoid losing it among the crowd. Dark-coloured hats could be enlivened with ribbon or braid, feathers, fancy buttons and jewels, while ribbon cockades were used to indicate military allegiance. In a miniature of George III painted in 1804, the king's bicorne hat is decorated with the black cockade of the House of Hanover, trimmed with gold braid (Fig. 6.32). The bicorne was initially worn sideways (as shown in this example), but by the early nineteenth century the points were increasingly positioned from front to back, except in France where Napoleon and his armies continued to wear the hat in the traditional manner.

One alternative to the tricorne was the wideawake hat, with a low rounded crown and a slightly upturned brim on each side, generally made of woollen felt in drab colours. It originated as a rural style popular among the labouring classes: in satirical prints characterising George III as 'Farmer George' he is typically shown wearing such a hat.[44] As the century progressed, this type of headwear was increasingly adopted by the elite for informal occasions, although was never considered suitable for court, where the tricorne or bicorne remained obligatory. Wideawake hats were also associated with the Quaker community who had settled in North America.

The 1790s saw the development of the precursor to the top hat or 'topper' that was to become so ubiquitous during the nineteenth century. In his portrait by George Stubbs, the Prince of Wales wears an example of the style for riding, incorporating a tall tapering crown and round stiffened brim (see Fig. 4.19). In the same decade the first hats made of silk plush ('waterproof hats in imitation of beaver') were

OPPOSITE, LEFT
Fig. 6.33  Philippe Mercier (1689–1760), 'The Music Party':
Frederick, Prince of Wales with his Three Eldest Sisters, 1733.
Oil on canvas, 79.4 × 57.8 cm. RCIN 402414

OPPOSITE, RIGHT
Fig. 6.34  French, Lappets of Valenciennes bobbin lace, 1720s.
Linen thread, 63.5 × 9.0 cm. Durham, Bowes Museum, 2007.1.2.251

OPPOSITE, FAR RIGHT
Fig. 6.35  Flemish, Lappets of Brussels bobbin lace, 1750s.
Linen thread, 63.0 × 12.5 cm. Durham, Bowes Museum, 2007.1.2.260

patented by George Dunnage of Middlesex.[45] By 1807 even George III, who was not known for embracing changes in style, had swapped his bicorne for the newly fashionable silk top hat, again decorated with the Hanoverian cockade, which he wears with the Windsor uniform in Peter Edward Stroehling's portrait (see Fig. 11.30). A variety of hat styles appear in the scene showing the Westminster election of 1796 (see Fig. 12.15), with the majority of men having switched to top hats, some (generally older or wearing military dress) retaining the bicorne and the poorer figures in the crowd on the left sporting brown wideawake hats.

Within the home and before putting on his wig, a man might choose to wear a soft cap over his shaved head as a form of undress. These came in a variety of styles, some more structured than others, and were usually known as nightcaps, although they could be worn at any time of the day. A tailor illustrates this fashion (see Fig. 1.1) as does the Duke of Wharton (see Fig. 4.25), both of whom also wear informal banyan gowns.

## HEADWEAR FOR WOMEN

The convention for married women to cover their heads for modesty reasons has its origins in religious doctrine across a multitude of faiths and denominations. In Britain, women continued to endorse the practice throughout the eighteenth century, wearing some form of headdress for church, but also in the presence of company and when outside, as seen in *St James's Park and the Mall*, where every woman is shown with a head covering (see pp. 2–3). Hair worn loose was an indicator of youth and was considered appropriate only for unmarried women.

Caps were worn for much of the century in some form or another, both indoors and out. In Britain, during the first half of the eighteenth century, women wore their hair arranged into a neat hairstyle off the face, providing a setting for a small cap (sometimes known as a 'pinner'), which had replaced the towering and wired commode headdress characteristic of the end of the seventeenth century. In a series of drawings titled *The Exact Head Dress of British Court Ladies* (see Fig. 7.6), Bernard Lens shows how a

fashionable woman's headdress (often known as a 'head') at this date typically consisted of four components: a horseshoe-shaped cap-back, a pair of lappets and a frill.

When made of fine lace lappets could be one of the most expensive elements of female attire. They came in a variety of lengths, with some reaching all the way to the waist and others to just below the shoulders. Some women pinned them up in concertina-like pleats on top of the head, while others left their lappets hanging loose or tied them under the chin. The latter was the most informal style. All these arrangements are demonstrated by the three princesses in Philippe Mercier's *The Music Party* (Fig. 6.33). Lappets worn hanging ('pendant') was the most common style for younger unmarried women, with its echoes of hair worn loose over the shoulders. By the 1730s, the square-ended styles commonly seen in the 1720s (Fig. 6.34) had been replaced by lappets with deeply scalloped edges, which later developed into a more stylised wavy outline (Fig. 6.35). The design of the lace used for lappets reflects stylistic changes throughout the eighteenth century, so that by the 1780s a mesh ground covered most of the lappet, with small sprays of flowers and neo-classical motifs scattered across the surface and trimming the edges. While lappets had passed out of fashion by the middle of the century, they remained an obligatory component of court dress. Caps in various styles continued to be worn throughout the period, with the large hairstyles of the late eighteenth century contained within voluminous versions (one was known as a *dormeuse*) that typically incorporated face-framing gathered frills at the front.

Female headwear could be multilayered, with a hat set on top of a cap when outdoors. Straw hats originated as practical country wear, although as the century progressed more elegant versions trimmed with silk ribbons were increasingly adopted as fashionable dress in town. In a drawing by Sandby (see Fig. 3.8), over her cap each lady wears a style of hat known as a *bergère*, which is characterised by its shallow crown, the name alluding to the pastoral ideal of the shepherdess. As the height of the hair grew taller, the *bergère* was increasingly worn tilted down over the forehead, as seen for example

in Chodowiecki's watercolours (see Figs 6.20 and 6.21). Here it has become so shrunken as to no longer shield the face and is instead merely decorative.

The fashionably flat wide hairstyles of the 1780s provided a stable base to support the so-called 'picture hats' with similarly exaggerated proportions and elaborate construction. An etching of 1787 imagines a visit to a milliner's shop in Windsor by the royal family (Fig. 6.36). Seated at the counter in the centre is Queen Charlotte, while George III stands to her right, wearing the Windsor uniform. The queen herself wears an understated headdress and veil, at least in comparison to the other female shoppers, who illustrate the variety of styles available, all of which are enormous and provide a counterbalance to the rounded rump then most fashionable. Large ostrich feathers, as seen worn by the woman on the far left, had become especially popular under the influence of the Duchess of Devonshire, who was reported in 1775 to have been presented by the French ambassador with a feather four feet long (122 cm), which she wore in an arch across her head.[46] A style of

headdress known as *à la Devonshire* was named after her, incorporating 14 plumes.[47]

French periodicals of the 1780s regularly included special plates featuring headwear with a variety of names (chapeau, demi-bonnet, *pouf*) and accompanied by extensive descriptions: multilayered concoctions of fabric, frills, feathers, ribbons and straw (Fig. 6.37). Such complicated gauzy confections rarely survive intact, requiring careful storage so as not to crush the fragile three-dimensional arrangements. Queen Charlotte wears a headdress of this kind in her portrait by Gainsborough (see Fig. 8.11), here apparently created from a pleated fabric base set with flowers, foliage and spotted silk.

While the size of the hair during the 1770s and 1780s precluded the wearing of a traditional form of hooded cloak for protection outside, a new style of travelling hood known as a calash was popular, the name derived from the folding hood of a *calèche* carriage. Made of fabric sewn with a series of circular channels into which strips of cane or whalebone were inserted to create a circular hood, it folded down with a concertina-like action. The calash

rarely appears in formal portraiture, although a number are extant, most frequently made of green or black silk, sometimes lined with pink linen or cotton to enhance a rosy complexion.

For riding, women typically chose hats that followed the line of male headwear, so the Isherwood sisters sport black beaver tricorne hats (see Fig. 3.28), distinctively worn with the cock pointed to the back, while Lady Lade adopts the newly introduced tall-crowned hat (see Fig. 3.29), accessorised with a black cockade and long plume. While not shown in these examples, some riding hats for women incorporated a veil to provide protection from the sun.

During the 1790s and early 1800s turbans developed into a fashionable style of headwear. Drawing their influence from styles worn across the Ottoman Empire and further afield, the way such fashionable accessories were wrapped and tied was not formalised. In construction they ranged from a simple strip of fabric or ribbon worn as a bandeau, which could be wound and tied each time it was worn, as seen in the portrait of La Baccelli (see Fig. 6.29), to more elaborate styles in which the pleats of fabric were set over a frame and sewn into position, thereby allowing it to be removed in the manner of a hat. These were known as *toques* in the fashion periodicals. For all these styles it was important to choose a fabric with an appropriate degree of drape: gauzy silks and cottons woven with metallic stripes were highly fashionable. Augusta, Duchess of Cambridge, wears a late example of the more structured style of turban (see Fig. 9.14), here apparently made of the same red Kashmir fabric as her dress, and decorated with a similar

OPPOSITE
Fig. 6.36  Published by Samuel William Fores (1761–1838),
*A Milliner's Shop*, 1787.
Hand-coloured etching, 42.3 × 54.2 cm (sheet). RCIN 630790

BELOW
Fig. 6.37  A.B. Duhamel (1736–c.1800) after Jean Florent Defraine
(b. 1754), Variety of headdresses, from *Magasin des modes nouvelles,
françaises et anglaises*, 2de année, 25ème cahier, 20 July 1787, Paris.
RCIN 1000882

BOTTOM
Fig. 6.38  Thomas Rowlandson (1757–1827), *Light Summer Cloathing
for the Year 1801*, 1801.
Hand-coloured etching, 25.0 × 19.8 cm (sheet). RCIN 810571

braid. By the early nineteenth century, the most typical
style of hat for women was the bonnet. Fashion periodicals
illustrate that bonnets came in a huge variety of styles and
were easily customised with ribbons, flowers (both real and
artificial), draped fabric and a multitude of other trimmings
acquired from the milliner to suit the occasion and updated
as required. Some bonnets were made of a fabric 'cawl'
draped over a pasteboard brim, while more structured
examples were made of straw or a material known as chip,
created from flat strips of wood shavings plaited or woven
together. An important bonnet industry using English
straw developed in Bedfordshire, around Luton, although
the finest and most flexible straw was imported from Italy.
This was known as Leghorn after its town of origin (now
Livorno). Over time, the length of the front brim became
more pronounced, in contrast to the diminishing 'curtain'
that covered the back of the neck and sometimes
disappeared entirely. The fashion for the most extreme
of these so-called 'poke bonnets' was a subject for satire,
as seen in *Light Summer Cloathing for the Year 1801*
(Fig. 6.38): here the brim has reached such exaggerated
proportions as to impede visibility and conceal the wearer's
face entirely.

# 7
# Facing Fashion

*Let the French ladies white wash and plaister their fronts,
and lay on their colours with a trowel: but these dawbings of art
are no more to be compared to the genuine glow of
a British cheek, than the coarse streaks of the painter's brush
can resemble the native veins of the marble.*

CONNOISSEUR, 1754[1]

Historically, Western beauty ideals have tended to follow the looks of health and well-being, and by default this has favoured the wealthy and the youthful: bodies untarnished by hard physical labour, a complexion protected from sun damage, and a nutritious diet that prevented either malnutrition or obesity. While these factors persist across time, each age has its own model. Society's concept of beauty is not permanent, being both a reflection of and a contributing factor to the aesthetic of its era. For example, the pastel colours and gentle curves that characterised the rococo style found their analogy in the female body and face – for both were considered integral in eighteenth-century definitions of beauty – and were expressed perfectly in portraits like those of Madame de Pompadour by artists such as François Boucher and François-Hubert Drouais (see opposite and Fig. 9.17). Clear differences existed between countries: in England an oval face was considered admirable, along with 'a nose somewhat longish, but of a fine turn, and like the antiques', while in France a rounder or heart-shaped face was preferred.[2] Similarly, the ideal body shape varied over time and between countries, moulded by the underpinnings and supportive layers of dress. For men, over the course of the century the cut of

PREVIOUS PAGE
Detail of Fig. 9.17

clothes created a conscious shift in emphasis: from a long torso with little difference in proportion, to a more triangular physique, with broader shoulders, a narrower waist and longer legs.

The classical importance placed on symmetry and ideal ratios in both body shape and facial features was, as the eighteenth century progressed, replaced by an emphasis on individuality and a recognition of the role of personal taste. Some of the key tastemakers of the era were not regarded as conventionally attractive. Moreover, in addition to external attributes, intangible elements of character and behaviour (both learnt and innate) were deemed essential to be considered beautiful within a social sphere. Again, these varied, but deportment, modesty, manners, grace and charm were all discussed as components of attraction at one point or another. Meanwhile, the development of the concept of sensibility meant society increasingly valued a face that naturally and vivaciously expressed the emotions within: 'nothing is more seducing than looks animated by tenderness, or pain; by hope, or desire; by candour, or ingenuousness'.[3]

## TOILETTE

The term 'toilette' (anglicised to toilet) initially referred to the cloth (*toile*) covering the dressing table, and later came to describe the collection of objects and utensils required to make up the face and clean the body (a toilette service), as well as the ritualised process during which such items were used (the morning toilette or *levée*). By the eighteenth century the toilette adopted by royal and aristocratic men and women to prepare for the day had evolved into an informal but performative ceremonial event: friends, family and business acquaintances were received while cosmetics were applied, and the hair dressed or shaved. In reality, many women carried out a 'first toilette' before visitors arrived, the public event being the occasion for the final touches. Attire typically consisted of a morning gown or peignoir over a chemise and stays for women, and a banyan for men, to prevent best clothes from being tainted by powder and lotions. Queen Charlotte preferred to use the time of her toilette to read the papers or be read to.

A portrait by Johan Joseph Zoffany (Fig. 7.1 and see Fig. 1.29) depicts Queen Charlotte at her dressing table. Here, the process of getting ready has been completed and she is formally dressed for dinner in a silk gown. The dressing table is positioned in the centre room of Buckingham House, within the king's ground-floor apartments, impractically blocking a doorway, perhaps because the queen's apartments were undergoing renovation at around this date. The table is covered with a toile probably of French needlepoint lace (see Chapter 1), while on top is a toilet service of silver gilt, its forms suggesting it was produced in Germany, probably Augsburg, and possibly brought over by the queen when she arrived in England several years earlier.[4] A tray and ovoid box from another, slightly later, toilet service belonged to Queen Charlotte and incorporate her cipher (Fig. 7.2). Toilet services were often presented as betrothal or wedding gifts and were usually designed as a set en suite, with similar decoration. The boxes of various sizes were used to hold patches, curls, paste, powder and paint.

A magnificent example of a travelling toilet set acquired by the Prince Regent in 1819 for £300 and presented to his Private Secretary Sir Benjamin Bloomfield can be seen opposite (Fig. 7.3).[5] It incorporates more than 100 separate components, including various containers, razors, a shaving brush, scent bottles, combs, toothbrushes, tongue scrapers and scissors, as well as drinking utensils for tea and hot chocolate, and tools for cleaning guns, each nestled within its snugly tailored slot. A travelling service was usually made by a *tabletier* – in this case Pierre Leplain – working in collaboration with a number of other craftspeople. The range of materials includes silver gilt, tortoiseshell, ivory, ebony, mother-of-pearl and cut glass, and the objects are all set within a mahogany and brass box with leather and velvet lining.

## COSMETICS

Beauty manuals provided the amateur cosmetician with a wealth of recipes and techniques designed to improve the appearance and preserve the elixir of youth: *The Art of Beauty* (1760) and *The Toilet of Flora* (1779, republished 1784)

Fig. 7.1  Johan Joseph Zoffany (1733–1810), *Queen Charlotte with her Two Eldest Sons*, 1764 (detail).
Oil on canvas, 112.2 × 128.3 cm. RCIN 400146

Fig. 7.2  Thomas Heming (active 1745–95), Toilet tray; box, 1771/2.
Silver gilt, 3.0 × 30.0 × 20.0 cm; 11.4 × 19.0 × 11.6 cm. RCIN 100234; RCIN 48656

Fig. 7.3  Pierre Leplain (active 1803–after 1822), Travelling service, c.1788–1819.
Mahogany, brass, leather; with silver gilt, steel, ivory, glass, mother-of-pearl and silk,
15.6 × 46.0 × 29.6 cm. RCIN 50467

were notable examples. It is impossible to ignore the uncomfortable fact that beauty ideals in Britain during the eighteenth century openly favoured white skin, with a smooth pale complexion most admired, as it had been in the seventeenth century. Beauty manuals featured concoctions to enhance the whiteness of the skin, remove freckles, conceal blemishes and prevent tanning. The unusual ingredients for one tonic included melon water, bean flowers and breadcrumbs, together with 'seven or eight White Pigeons' minced small and distilled in an alembic with sugar-candy.[6]

Artists had additional tools at their disposal when creating the ideal skin tone for a sitter, through the application of the various pigments on their palette. This allowed them to enhance the appearance to whatever shade was ultimately sought, whether or not it was achieved in reality. Sometimes the skin tone in a portrait looks paler to modern eyes than originally intended by the artist, due to the fugitive nature of the organic pinkish-red glazes, which tend to fade over time, unlike the more permanent lead white, giving a false impression of what may have been considered 'ideal'.

At the beginning of the eighteenth century, beauty conventions at court in Britain and France required a self-consciously artificial face for both men and women, the skin lightened with white pigment, and cheeks and lips emphasised with red. For centuries, the main source of make-up for the face had been ceruse, produced by exposing lead plates to vinegar, which could then be combined with a pigment to create 'paint'. The dangers of such a toxic ingredient were well known by the early eighteenth century, and the hazardous side effects of lead included rotting teeth, hair loss, poisoning and miscarriage. Despite an Act of Parliament in 1724 that attempted to regulate its use, the ability of ceruse to provide a flattering and smooth coverage was too tempting for many.[7] One of the most high-profile sufferers was the noted beauty Maria, Countess of Coventry, born Mary Gunning (1733–60), whom Horace Walpole describes as having died of lead-white poisoning at the age of only 27, soon after her marriage.[8] By the end of the century various less harmful

alternatives – deliberately described in beauty manuals as 'nourishing' to distinguish them from these earlier recipes – were available, such as a powder derived from real pearls, and others from bismuth, chalk and starch.

In France, cosmetic artificiality prevailed for longer than in England. There the wearing of rouge was a privilege reserved for the nobility and it served as a recognisable symbol of high birth, the sharp contrast between white and red being known as the *manière noble*. Various colourants were available, the most dangerous being vermilion (red mercuric sulphide), or ceruse combined with red pigments including cochineal (derived from a beetle native to Mexico). Cheaper alternatives included henna and madder. Rouge came in both liquid and powdered forms, and it could also be made into crayons to apply to the lips. Aesthetically, it was considered to bring out the sparkle in the eyes, while counterbalancing the rather ghostly appearance created by the application of pale powder to both hair and face. It also held erotic connotations, reflecting the flush of sexual desire. At the French court rumours proliferated as to whether Madame de Pompadour would reduce her use of cosmetics once she publicly moved from the position of Louis XV's mistress to his chaste companion. In fact, portraits continued to depict her with pink cheeks (see Fig. 9.17) and she wore rouge until her death at the age of 42. The rouge worn by aristocratic French women at court was often not applied to imitate a natural flush, but was instead spread thickly across the whole cheek, sometimes reaching the lower eyelid, in a manner known as *en plaçage*. An indication of this is given in the profile portrait of Madame Brissard (Fig. 7.4). Louis

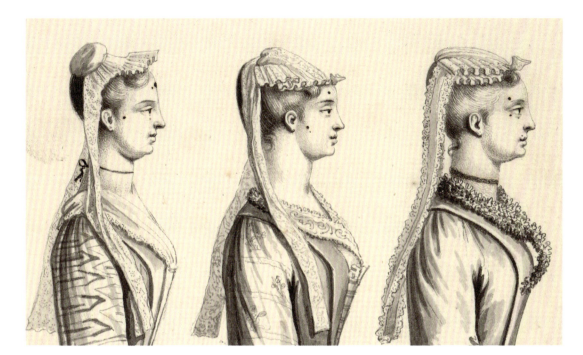

Carrogis de Carmontelle specialised in such profile portraits of members of the French court.

The exaggerated use of cosmetics in France was the focus of much comment by British visitors, with Tobias Smollett remarking in 1766 that the use of rouge 'daubed on their faces, from the chin up to the eyes, without the least art or dexterity, not only destroys all distinction of features, but renders the aspect really frightful, or at best conveys nothing but ideas of disgust and aversion.'[9] By the 1790s, the wearing of rouge in France had largely died out.

For most of the century English women favoured a more natural application of cosmetics, restricted to powder and rouge, which covered up blemishes, smoothed skin tones and gave the appearance of a wholesome blush, evocative of a brisk walk in country air. Even such understated usage, however, prompted some criticism, as it was deemed a form of deception. By this reasoning, at least the French lack of subtlety indicated an openness about the degree of pretence involved. The theme of artifice was a recurrent one in both visual caricature and literature of the period, playing on the well-worn trope of an older person (usually female) attempting to appear younger than they really are, or continuing to adopt cosmetics for longer than considered appropriate. The wearing of artificial teeth, plumpers to fill out sunken cheeks, wigs and false eyebrows was also singled out for critique.

Since the early seventeenth century both women and men had worn patches of black silk taffeta or velvet to highlight pale skin, and the fashion continued during the eighteenth century. Some were even set with diamonds.

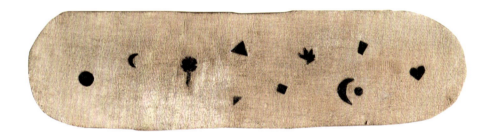

In March 1733 Queen Caroline acquired '6 papers of patches' from her milliner, Catherine Vezian, at a total cost of 6 shillings.[10] Patches were kept on the dressing table or carried on the body in a patch box, and they came in an array of sizes and shapes, including stars, moons, circles and hearts, as seen in a rare surviving set in the Science Museum, London (Fig. 7.5). A deliberate rococo asymmetry in the placing of patches was most admired, with William Hogarth writing in *The Analysis of Beauty* (1753), 'no two patches are ever chosen of the same size, or placed at the same height; nor a single one in the middle of a feature.'[11] Although unusual in portraits, Bernard Lens clearly illustrates the fashion in his collection of headdresses, showing patches worn near the ear, above and below the eye, and in the centre of the forehead (Fig. 7.6). The position of a patch could be used to draw attention to the wearer's best features or – according to some accounts – send a message of sexual invitation, perhaps the reason why they rarely appear in portraits of the period. Patches sometimes concealed scars, the most common cause of which was smallpox.

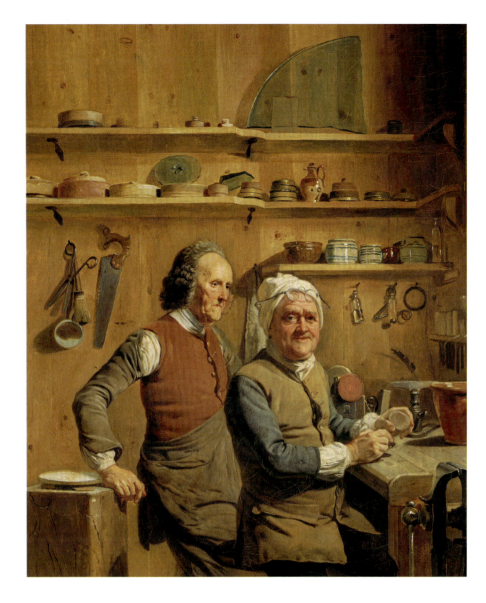

Fig. 7.7 Johan Joseph Zoffany (1733–1810), *John Cuff*, 1772 (detail). Oil on canvas, 89.8 × 70.0 cm. RCIN 404434

## SPECTACLES

The eighteenth century saw several developments in the field of wearable optical aids designed to correct defects in vision, aid magnification or protect the eyes from the sun. Although spectacles had been worn in Europe during the seventeenth century, they had been of the pince-nez type, balancing on the nose. An alternative was a single eyeglass hung around the neck on a chain. By 1727 the first spectacles with side pieces ('temple spectacles') were being advertised by the London optician Edward Scarlett (1688–1743), who had earlier served as master of the Worshipful Company of Spectacle Makers and in 1727 was appointed optician to George II. Scarlett also established a system of classifying lens strength according to focal length. A century later Robert Brettell Bate (1782–1847), whose invoice advertises his position as 'Optician to the King', supplied George IV with 13 pairs of spectacles, the frames made in a range of materials including pale gold, blued steel and tortoiseshell, with lenses of atmospheric glass or pebble.[12] The latter was a clear quartz mineral, originally from Brazil, which could be ground to produce lenses stronger than glass and less susceptible to scratches.[13] There was also a vogue for coloured lenses, with blue considered beneficial for removing glare. Glasses with bifocal lenses were introduced in England during the second half of the eighteenth century. Their invention has been attributed historically to Benjamin Franklin, who was living in London between 1757 and 1775, although a number of other contenders have been suggested, including Peter Dolland.[14] Franklin found bifocal glasses valuable while attending events in his role as United States ambassador to France, as they allowed him to see what he was eating and at the same time to read the lips of other guests across the table, enabling him to follow their conversation in French.

Despite the association of spectacles with a learned (and therefore wise) mind, portraits showing sitters wearing optical devices are rare, in part because their use tended to be interpreted as a sign of physical weakness or old age. Moreover, because spectacles left the hands free to undertake practical activities, they were linked with the professional or working classes. In a portrait by Zoffany, for example, the Fleet Street optician John Cuff sits at his workbench, in the process of polishing a lens, wearing practical working clothes with a pair of spectacles propped up on his forehead, the arms resting on the soft cloth cap worn instead of a wig (Fig. 7.7). Around him are the various tools and materials of his trade (including a sheet of rough glass on the upper shelf), while an attentive assistant stands behind.

One royal sitter unconcerned by being shown wearing glasses was Princess Sophia, fifth daughter of George III, who suffered an increasing loss of sight over the course of her life, becoming almost completely blind in old age. In a drawing that shows the princess wearing spectacles in her mid-twenties, she is depicted in an assertive frontal pose looking directly at the viewer (Fig. 7.8). Her glasses are similar in shape to a pair of silver spectacles in the Royal Collection (Fig. 7.9). According to the hallmarks they date from 1816/17 and may have been made by John Lawrence & Co. of Birmingham.

Fig. 7.8  Attributed to Henry Edridge (1769–1821), *Princess Sophia*, c.1800.
Pencil and watercolour, 10.1 × 8.0 cm. RCIN 452422

Fig. 7.9  John Lawrence & Co., Spectacles, 1816/17.
Silver and glass, 3.2 × 13.2 × 14.2 cm. RCIN 55178

Fig. 7.10  Schäffner (active 1830), *Princess Sophia*, 1830 (and detail).
Watercolour on card, 22.8 × 16.1 cm. RCIN 420237

Jean-Siméon Chardin (1775), Anna Dorothea Therbusch (1777), Francisco Goya (*c*.1800), Johan Joseph Zoffany (*c*.1800–3) and Sir Joshua Reynolds, whose self-portrait of *c*.1788 at the age of 65 is in the Royal Collection, along with a contemporary copy (Fig. 7.11). Such optical aids drew attention to the importance of sight and intellect for artists, as well as perhaps alluding to the detrimental impact of such close work on vision. In 1789 Reynolds experienced a sudden blindness in his left eye, 'like the falling of a curtain'. By 1791 he was almost completely blind, and he died the following year.

## DENTISTRY

While Horace Walpole found little to recommend in the physical appearance of Queen Charlotte, describing her as 'pale and very thin', he did note that 'her teeth are good'.[16] A full set of straight teeth was highly desirable, and dentistry became increasingly professionalised and regulated over the century. Here, France was widely acknowledged as leading the field, evidenced in the language of the profession still in use today, with *dent*, the French for tooth. The 'tooth-puller' of the seventeenth century (part surgeon, part street entertainer) was gradually replaced by the dentist, with the status of the profession accordingly raised to equal that of a physician. The eighteenth century saw several improvements in dentistry, many of which were developed by Pierre Fauchaud (1679–1761) and documented in his book *Le Chirurgien Dentiste* (The Surgeon Dentist) in 1728. These included techniques to minimise the need for extractions – long established as the standard treatment for toothache or decay – as well as new types of artificial dentures such as crowns and bridges to conceal gaps. The vogue for French dentists is referenced in a print by Thomas Rowlandson, *A French Dentist Shewing a Specimen of His Artificial Teeth and False Palates* (Fig. 7.12). The dentist, a 'Monsier [*sic*] De Charmant' (who is based on a real prosthodontic pioneer, Nicolas Dubois de Chémant), is on the left, dressed in an old-fashioned bag-wig, his own brilliantly white set of teeth on display. He holds the chin

Considered more elegant than spectacles was the hand-held single-lens 'quizzing glass', the use of which by the late eighteenth century had become a fashionable affectation, notably favoured by Beau Brummell. A later portrait of Princess Sophia shows her holding a quizzing glass on a gold chain (Fig. 7.10). The quizzing glass was later developed into the lorgnette (folding spectacles with a handle) and the monocle (a single lens that was set into the eye socket). Such modish devices were sometimes adopted purely for fashionable reasons rather than medical need, much to the dismay of physicians who warned of long-term damage: 'a single glass in a smart ring is often used by trinket fanciers merely for fashion's sake, by folks who have not the least defect in their sight and are not aware of the mischievous consequences of such irritations.'[15]

By the 1770s artists were choosing to include spectacles or monocles in their self-portraits, including

Fig. 7.12 Thomas Rowlandson (1757–1827), *A French Dentist Shewing a Specimen of his Artificial Teeth and False Palates*, 1811.
Hand-coloured etching, 25.5 × 36.0 cm (sheet). RCIN 810834

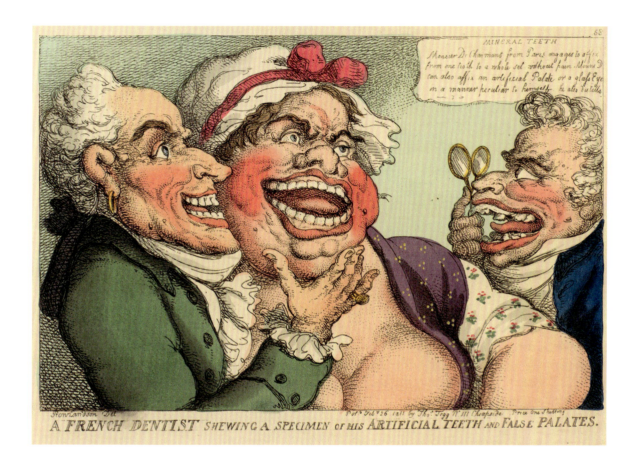

of his female patient, her mouth wide open to show off a complete set of new dentures in a terrifying grin. On the right another man inspects the result through a pince-nez, his own mouth open to reveal many rotten teeth. According to the inscription above, the dentist offers a service 'without pain' and can also fit glass eyes.

The eighteenth century saw the development of the first orthodontics used to move the position of the teeth. Known as a *bandeau*, it consisted of a piece of metal curved into shape with wires attached, a precursor to modern braces. At the age of 13, Marie-Antoinette was subjected to three months of such treatment to correct what were considered unsightly crooked teeth, as part of a series of modifications to her appearance instigated prior to her marriage.[17] Queen Charlotte and the Prince of Wales both patronised the French dentist Jacob Hemet (the first patent holder for a dentifrice, or toothpaste), while George III

was attended by Thomas Berdmore, author of the first comprehensive treatise on dental disorders in English.[18] The same manuals that provided beauty tips also gave various recipes relating to products for the mouth. *The Toilet of Flora*, for example, includes tooth powders, 'water for the gums' and 'The Duchess de la Vrilliere's Mouth Water' (to be gargled), which combined cinnamon, cloves, rose leaves and spirit of wine.

The transplanting of live teeth was another eighteenth-century development, first recommended by the surgeon-anatomist John Hunter in 1778. The operation involved fitting the donor tooth within the empty socket, then attaching it to the two neighbouring teeth with silk or seaweed. Young secondary teeth from children were preferred for their ability to fit more easily into the gap in the gum. The process was famously represented in a print by Rowlandson (Fig. 7.13). A fashionable dentist, declared in the sign as 'Dentist to her High Mightiness the Empress of Russia', is shown extracting a healthy tooth from the mouth of a grimacing young chimney sweep. The future recipient sits alongside him, a fashionably dressed woman holding a bottle of smelling salts to her nose. Is she recovering after having had her own decaying tooth removed, or is she offended by the odour and appearance of the donor? On the right another woman opens her mouth for examination by an assistant, while a gentleman examines his new visage in a mirror. Two children, their ragged clothing indicating their impoverished state, can be seen leaving the room, each clutching their cheek, and the girl looking down at a single small coin in her palm. The print can clearly be interpreted as a condemnation of the exploitative and unethical nature of the practice, irreversibly harming poor children for the vanity of rich adults. Indeed, the print seems to have contributed to a growing distaste for the (often unsuccessful) procedure, which fell from favour in Britain soon after.[19] False teeth made of bone, and later porcelain, were an alternative, and Lord Hervey was described as having teeth made from 'Egyptian pebble' (jasper) in 1735.[20] A set of dentures belonging to George Washington survives today, which incorporates teeth from horses, cows and humans within a lead and wire frame. By the time of his inauguration as president in 1789, Washington had only one real tooth left and just before the sitting for his most famous portrait by Gilbert Stuart (see Fig. 12.9), the original of which was painted in 1795, he had been provided with ill-fitting new dentures made of 'sea horse' (hippopotamus) ivory, which caused him much discomfort.[21]

In France under Louis XIV the court had developed a formalised code of civility that emphasised the importance of gravitas and dignity. The French king himself was rarely known to smile, and when he did it was with a closed mouth that tended to indicate irony rather than pleasure, and this set the pattern for his courtiers to follow. A tight-lipped smile also served the practical purpose of concealing missing teeth, an affliction that particularly affected the aristocracy, with a rise in the consumption of expensive imported sugar. Louis XIV had lost all his teeth by the age of 40, along with part of his jaw during a difficult tooth extraction. Moreover,

the heavy white *fard* make-up used to create an artificially pale complexion remained fashionable in France until the middle of the eighteenth century, and maintaining its smooth mask-like surface required the wearer to avoid exaggerated facial expressions for fear of cracks. This situation largely continued under Louis XV, with the return of the court to Versailles from Paris, accompanied by strict codes of etiquette. Again, the most appropriate facial expression for public occasions was one of solemn impassivity, indicating a person in control of their emotions.

'Each age has a deportment, a glance and a smile of its own', wrote Charles Baudelaire in 1863,[22] and indeed the eighteenth century has been described as a period during which the smile itself underwent a revolution.[23] Technological improvements in dentistry were accompanied by a cultural shift in attitudes, linked with notions of sensibility, which viewed natural emotional expression as a positive attribute, rather than something to be concealed. Historically, portraits had shown sitters with a closed mouth resting in a neutral expression, while an open mouth – whether laughing or grimacing – had tended to indicate someone either of lower social status or in a state of emotional imbalance, regularly a feature of low-level genre scenes but not acceptable for a formal portrait. In 1708 Roger de Piles had advised artists that a smiling expression should affect the full face if it was to look natural: 'when the sitter puts on a smiling air, the eyes close, the corners of the mouth draw up towards the nostrils, the cheeks swell, and the eyebrows widen.'[24] By the middle of the eighteenth century, references to smiling (*sourire* in French) were more frequent in literature (Samuel Richardson's *Clarissa* of 1748 was influential) and the act itself came to be described in positive terms rather than sardonically.[25] While portraits depicting broad grins were still rare, some artists, most notably Sir Thomas Lawrence, Maurice-Quentin de La Tour and Elisabeth Louise Vigée Le Brun, perfected the art of capturing sitters with smiles and slightly open mouths that revealed a glimpse of teeth. The shift remained challenging, however, with one contemporary critic referring to it as 'an affectation which artists, connoisseurs, and people of good taste are unanimous in condemning'.[26]

Fig. 7.13  Thomas Rowlandson (1757–1827), *Transplanting of Teeth*, 1787–90.

Hand-coloured etching with aquatint, 35.2 × 49.4 cm (sheet). RCIN 810243

# 8

# Court, Ceremony & Ritual

*So forward we mov'd, midst the ladies and lords,*
*A charming confusion; hoops, trimmings and swords,*
*As they mingled together delightfully tangled,*
*No doubt the whole floor was most tastefully spangled,*
*Lace, tissue and gauze, flowers, feathers and foil,*
*So pleasant a romp I han't had a great while.*

JOSEPH MOSER, 1794[1]

---

While 'court' can be interpreted in several ways, in its most literal sense it can be considered the physical spaces in which the activities surrounding the royal family were enacted. Tied to this were those people whose attendance 'at court' formed an important element of their position: personally, socially or professionally, whether as an official employee of the royal household or someone tangentially connected to it. In the seventeenth century the centre of both court and government in England had been focused around the Palace of Whitehall. In 1698 a fire destroyed most of the buildings within the Whitehall complex, resulting in the official seat of court transferring to St James's Palace (where it remains today), although court life itself became more fragmented and was spread across a number of smaller royal residences. The lack of a centralised court was further exacerbated in the eighteenth century by the emergence of a series of rival courts in opposition to the sovereign, in each case headed by the heir to the throne, operating out of a separate physical location, with a conflicting calendar of events and oppositional political views. Moreover, the spaces for the domestic business of monarchy were increasingly distinct from those used for entertaining. George II and Queen Caroline lived at Kensington

PREVIOUS PAGE
Detail of Fig. 8.4

Palace for much of the year, where the state apartments provided the backdrop for grand court occasions. During the reign of George III, St James's Palace was the primary location for ceremonial court events such as Birthday Balls or presentations, and most royal weddings took place in the Chapel Royal, whereas Buckingham House and Windsor Castle contained the private apartments in which the royal family slept, relaxed and raised their families. While this increased the separation between the private and public activities of monarchy, the parkland setting of these latter two royal residences ensured a certain degree of visibility for members of the public, bringing the royal family closer to the population, a fact alluded to by the inclusion of Frederick, Prince of Wales, within the crowded space depicted in *St James's Park and the Mall* (see pp. 2–3). The influence of traditional court structures was also diluted by the rising importance of commercial locations for entertainment and socialisation, notably assemblies, coffee houses, pleasure gardens and theatres. These provided another forum for fashionable display and members of the royal family were frequent attendees, making an appearance in a supper box at the pleasure gardens or in the royal box at one of the theatres with royal patronage, all spaces plainly in public view.

In the eighteenth century the London season ran from October to early June, a period dictated by both weather considerations (winters were milder in urban centres, meaning less chance of being snowed in) and business need, especially the parliamentary calendar. For a significant proportion of that time most elite families would relocate to London to participate in the social events of metropolitan life, returning to their country estates for the summer months to enjoy more clement weather and rural pursuits. George I and George II tended to move from St James's Palace to Kensington Palace after the last parliamentary session or used this time to return to Hanover.

Compared to the size of the nobility in many European nations (where younger sons and daughters were granted titles in their own right, in addition to those firstborn), the number of noble families in Britain was small, with only around 200 peers. Circles of influence were tight-knit,

and it would have been common for members of the fashionable set to run into acquaintances at gatherings, whether intentionally or not. Multiple stops on the same evening were not uncommon and certain families became known for entertaining on particular days.

## THE ROYAL HOUSEHOLD

During the reign of George I as many as 1,000 people served the sovereign and the satellite royal courts, although this figure had dropped to around 800 by the end of George IV's reign, after government legislation was instituted following enquiries into household expenditure in the early years of the Regency.[2] Of the three departments making up the royal household, the largest was the Lord Chamberlain's, also known as 'the Chamber'; transport was organised by the team reporting to the Master of the Horse (known colloquially as the 'Stables'); food and other housekeeping activities were the responsibility of the Lord Steward (the 'household below stairs'). Those involved with managing the clothing and physical appearance of the members of the royal family included tailors, brushers, furriers, embroiderers, laundresses, hairdressers, dentists and barbers, as well as a multitude of grooms, ladies, maids, clerks and keepers. Economic reform beginning in 1782 meant that royal expenditure on clothing was budgeted and controlled by the Treasury,[3] making it subject to greater scrutiny than in earlier years and providing the government with a powerful bargaining tool with which to try and influence royal behaviour and allegiance.[4]

Within the household were a number of prominent roles open only to the nobility, which brought with them accommodation, board and a salary, as well as intimate access to the royal family and invaluable opportunities to network. Many of these were involved in the handling of royal clothing, whether it be in the privacy of the royal apartments during the daily process of dressing and undressing, or for ceremonial and social events. Such positions were strictly defined in both status and level of responsibility. Of those available to women, for example,

Fig. 8.1 Thomas Rowlandson (1757–1827), *The Grand Procession to St Paul's on St George's Day, 1789*, 1789 (detail). Hand-coloured etching, 25.9 × 72.8 cm (sheet). RCIN 810341

the most prestigious was 'Lady of the Bedchamber', for which the postholder was required to be of noble birth, that is, the daughter or wife of a peer. In 1761 all six were viscountesses, countesses or duchesses. In exchange for a salary of £500 a year and an apartment within the royal palace, the Ladies of the Bedchamber provided companionship to the queen, taking on a conspicuous role at ceremonial events.[5] The most senior Lady of the Bedchamber was the 'Mistress of the Robes', the title indicating that she was ultimately responsible for looking after the queen's clothing and jewellery. In 1761 this post was occupied by the Duchess of Ancaster, shown to the right of Queen Charlotte in *The Five Orders of Perriwigs* (see Fig. 6.4). Next in rank were the 'Women of the Bedchamber', paid £300 a year. These were married women or widows, between four and six in number, who worked on a roster, and assisted the queen with daily activities such as holding a basin of water while she washed. Finally, there were the more junior 'Maids of Honour', unmarried women, usually of aristocratic birth, who were paid £200 a year during the reign of George I, rising to £300 by 1727.[6] Even within the informal British court, the process of dressing the queen was ritualised and carefully managed, with the Woman of the Bedchamber having responsibility for handing the clothes, one by one, to the Lady of the Bedchamber, who then passed them on to the queen. Similarly, at a formal event, the Woman of the Bedchamber would carry the queen's train to the anteroom, at which point she would pass it to the Lady of the Bedchamber for the final procession.

Working alongside these roles were the consort's personal servants, not necessarily of noble birth but sometimes reaching positions of great influence and long service. Juliana Elizabeth ('Madame') Schwellenbergen (1728–97) served as Keeper of the Robes for Queen Charlotte, having travelled with her from Mecklenburg-Strelitz in 1761. She remained the queen's close confidante until her death 36 years later. Madame Schwellenbergen's influence at court is indicated by her regular (often derogatory) appearance in satirical prints of the time: in one depicting the procession to St Paul's Cathedral,

London, in 1789 to commemorate the king's return to health, she is the only person to sit alongside George III and Queen Charlotte in the town state coach (Fig. 8.1). The fact that no formal portrait seems to exist of her is surprising. Madame Schwellenbergen was assisted in the role of Keeper, initially by Johanna Hagerdorn (d. 1789) and from 1786 by the novelist Fanny Burney, later Madame d'Arblay (1752–1840), whose memoirs provide a vivid depiction of life at court. These make it clear that by this date the prestige of such positions was in decline, and that the job itself involved long hours, filled with monotony and a strictly regimented routine. After much wrangling and six months of petitioning the queen, Burney was eventually permitted to leave the role in 1792 on the grounds of ill health, willingly forgoing her salary of £127 a year.[7]

Upon his accession George I had dispensed with the established position of 'Groom of the Stool', one of the most intimate roles within the Tudor and Stuart court. Although many of the other traditional bedchamber roles were filled by British courtiers, their responsibilities were in part rendered superfluous by the king continuing to employ a separate group of around 25 German servants who had originally arrived in England in his entourage and remained after the coronation. These included Mehemet von Königstreu (*c.*1660–1726; Fig. 8.2), who in Germany had occupied the position of chamber-attendant (*Kammerdiener*) and retained the responsibilities of washing and dressing the king each day, until Mehemet's death at Kensington Palace in 1726.

Fig. 8.2 Sir Godfrey Kneller (1646–1723), *Ludwig Maximilian Mehemet von Königstreu*, 1715.
Oil on canvas, 91.0 × 71.6 cm. RCIN 405430

Although the details of his early life have not been fully established, Mehemet may have been the son of a Turkish pasha ruling part of the Ottoman Empire. He is believed to have been brought to Hanover after being captured as a prisoner of war during the campaigns against Turkey in the 1680s, during which Hanover was affiliated with the Holy Roman Empire. Despite converting to Christianity and being baptised with a new name, Mehemet continued to be known by his Muslim name throughout his life. Sir Godfrey Kneller's portrait, painted just after the sitter's arrival in England in 1715 as part of George I's household, indicates that Mehemet did not adopt typical European clothing as worn by his employer (see Fig. 2.2) and instead continued to demonstrate his foreignness through dress. His waistcoat is made of luxurious green silk, perhaps imported from China, with a wide green waist sash, and over this a loose-fitting red silk gown or coat. He wears no wig, and his bald head is instead covered by a large fur tocque of a style commonly worn in parts of the Ottoman Empire.[8]

## DRESSING FOR COURT

Attending court was an essential component of the social calendar for many, particularly members of the royal household and the aristocracy, as well as their foreign equivalents during visits to London. Access to the most public spaces within the royal palaces was not restricted to these groups, however, and for those further down the social hierarchy, including the gentry and professional classes, fine clothing was the most important element in determining whether entry was granted. Dress was used to inform whether the attendee would then be allowed to progress through the sequence of rooms (guard chamber, presence chamber, privy chamber) that culminated in reaching the drawing room in the presence of the monarch, although here credentials and contacts were also key.

The most frequent type of event at court were assemblies, also known as Drawing Rooms, for which the dress code was strictly regimented. The most important and extravagant of these assemblies were those held in honour of a royal birthday, so-called Birthday Balls (Fig. 8.3). For much of the eighteenth century such events were held in the State Apartments at St James's Palace and followed a morning church service and dinner for the royal family. Convention dictated that while it was customary for everyone to attend in their finest clothes, the person whose birthday it was normally dressed in a more understated manner, as an indication of his or her humility. For her birthday in 1792 Queen Charlotte appeared 'as plainly habited as the dignity of her situation could allow'.[9] Key dates relevant to the history of the British monarchy (for example, the Restoration of Charles II in 1660) were also cause for commemoration, although these were gradually supplanted by dates personally linked to the current monarch and his family, including the date of accession. On these occasions it was common for crowds to gather at the gates of St James's Palace to catch a glimpse of finely dressed people arriving in carriages, events that also provided rich pickings for thieves. Being presented to the king or queen at court was an important occasion for the family in question, used to mark a significant change in circumstances, either personal or professional. These might include a wedding or the birth of a child, or an imminent departure on a long journey or tour of service. While such presentations took place as part of a Drawing Room, for men the *levée* also provided a

Fig. 8.3 George Noble (c.1763–1828) after Daniel Dodd (active 1761–d. 1780), *View of the Ball at St. James's on the Celebration of Her Majesty's Birth Night*, 1786.

Etching with engraving, 14.3 × 19.4 cm (sheet).
RCIN 750529

different opportunity to meet the king within an intimate setting as he dressed for the day.

Although the specific details of the type, number and formality of events at court depended on the monarch in question, there were certain consistent features of court dress throughout the century. The first focused on newness. For the most important occasions – a Birthday Ball for the monarch, for example – it was essential that an attendee's dress be new and specially made for that event. Garments or fabrics that had been worn previously or were noticeably out of date were the subject of gossip and interpreted as a mark of disrespect towards the host. Moreover, such actions could be deliberately manipulated to demonstrate allegiance to a particular faction. George II expressed dissatisfaction at the insult implicated by the 'very thin appearance' of the Drawing Room on his birthday in November 1735, the reason given to him being that attendees were saving their fine clothes for the wedding of his estranged son, Frederick, Prince of Wales, to Princess Augusta the following year.[10] At another ball in 1768 an attendee remarked that 'many people had gone to Court, on the Queen's Birthday, in Clothes they had the year before and that it was the Worst Ball that had ever been remembered'.[11] Even if someone was ultimately unable to attend an event, it was common practice for them to publicise to friends, family and even the host that new clothes had been acquired in preparation, so as to avoid reputation-damaging rumours of disloyalty or frugality.

It was important that the clothing be new, but it was less important that it be fashionable. Indeed, while court dress could incorporate the latest fabric designs, it usually represented an old-fashioned and anachronistic style of clothing rarely worn in other settings, as seen for example in John Graham's record of *The Marriage of George, Prince of Wales* in 1795 (Fig. 8.4, overleaf). Queen Charlotte is shown seated on the right, her dress according with the detailed description in the *Gentleman's Magazine*: 'a silver tissue petticoat, with the drapery embroidered with white and gold, ornamented with green and silver laurel, a gold tissue body and train'.[12] It is fascinating to compare Graham's painting with a collection of silk samples that were presumably supplied by the mercer when planning the outfits for various members of the royal family at this event: the top two relate to the clothing of the queen (Fig. 8.5, overleaf). Although not explicitly mentioned, the queen is also clearly wearing a hoop beneath her skirt, lending it great horizontal width. Queen Charlotte insisted on the use of such hoops at court until her death in 1820, although they represented an ossified form of dress that had fallen from favour by the 1770s and was no longer worn at fashionable events in town. The groom's outfit was described as 'a blue Genoa velvet coat and breeches, with a silver tissue waistcoat and coat cuffs, richly embroidered with silver and spangles. The whole suit was covered with large and small spangles'.[13] In fashionable circles most men had swapped such an elaborately embroidered *habit à la française* with its standing collar and matching breeches for a simpler, more understated frock coat with a small turn-down collar, and plain breeches, usually in a contrasting colour to the coat.

Fig. 8.4 John Graham (1754–1817),
*The Marriage of George, Prince of Wales,*
1795.

Oil on canvas, 122.6 × 160.4 cm. RCIN 409254

Fig. 8.5 English, Collection of dress
samples relating to the marriage of
George, Prince of Wales, and Princess
Caroline of Brunswick, January 1795.

Silk and metal threads. London, Historic Royal
Palaces, 3502548

While it is difficult to determine whether
these fabric samples were preserved as
potential options or final selections, they
demonstrate the richness of the textiles
and the coordinating colour scheme of
white with gold and silver metal threads
in both striped and floral patterns that
was considered appropriate for guests
attending the wedding of the heir to
the throne.

Fig. 8.6  Johann Georg Ziesenis (1716–76), *Queen Charlotte when Princess Sophia Charlotte of Mecklenburg-Strelitz with a Servant*, c.1761.
Oil on canvas, 134.9 × 96.8 cm. RCIN 403562

Fig. 8.7  Bodice worn by Lady Mary Douglas, 1761.
Cloth of gold, silver plate, purl and frieze, silk, cotton, linen and baleen. Los Angeles, Fashion Institute of Design and Merchandising Museum & Galleries, L2010.3.2AB

The prince's sword, too, is a ceremonial relic of an older time and only worn at court, it having been exchanged for a stick or cane for most other occasions.

Clothing worn at court needed to be ostentatiously expensive, and therefore provide a public demonstration of the wearer's wealth and status. The planning of such an outfit took several months, requiring special silks, sometimes woven to order, and the engagement of various skilled workers to deliver the final result. A suit worn by the Duke of Bedford in 1790 was the subject of much discussion, and rumoured to have cost in excess of £500 (the equivalent of more than £63,000 in 2021) due to the array of spangles and brilliant-cut diamonds set onto its surface, along with its ornate silver embroidery.[14] Sometimes friends and family were invited to preview a new outfit before the event itself, during which its details could be studied and explained, so that they might be communicated with accuracy. The price of raw materials could increase with demand before a significant event, and some tradesmen opened their workshops to the public to publicise their involvement in an outfit and therefore showcase their skill.

Another factor to consider was to what extent court dress should reflect the wearer's patronage of domestic craftsmanship. In 1765 Queen Charlotte had specifically requested all ladies of the court wear only Spitalfields silk as a sign of support to the domestic textile industries, given that imports had resumed after the Seven Years' War, and later in the eighteenth century similar protocols were introduced stipulating the wearing of English silks at court. Some who continued to 'buy French' were thwarted by observant customs officers acting to seize goods at Dover. In 1792 those affected included a number of supporters of the Whig opposition whose collective intention to wear court dress of foreign manufacture had been a deliberate attempt to undermine the Crown's instructions.[15]

## THE COMPONENTS OF COURT DRESS

The most formal style of court dress for women in the eighteenth century was the 'grand habit', an archaic form of clothing based on fashions introduced in France during the 1670s under Louis XIV. This became the established mode in most courts across the Continent, as seen worn by Queen Charlotte when Princess Sophia Charlotte of Mecklenburg-Strelitz, for example, in her portrait painted by Johann Georg Ziesenis before her arrival in England (Fig. 8.6). The grand habit was remarkably similar across geographical regions and remained largely unchanged for most of the century. It consisted of three components: a boned bodice (sometimes described as smooth-covered stays in contemporary accounts); a petticoat worn over a hoop; and a separate train, which hooked onto the bodice. The bodice had a low round neckline that left the shoulders bare and short capped sleeves, below which additional sleeves (*manchettes*) were attached, made of multiple tiers of pleated lace or silk gauze. This type of bodice, laced tightly up the back and heavily stiffened, served as the stays, so did not require an additional supportive undergarment for the torso. A very rare court bodice survives (Fig. 8.7), made of cloth of gold, boned with baleen and decorated with silver embroidery and silver paillettes. The wearer was Lady Mary Douglas, one of the six peeresses chosen to assist Princess Augusta in her role as train-bearer during the coronation of Queen Charlotte in 1761.[16]

In England the grand habit was known by a variety of other names, including a *robe de cour*, stiff-bodied gown

and royal robe, the latter indicative of the fact that it was only worn by members of the royal family or their closest attendants, and even then, only on the most formal occasions, notably royal weddings and coronations. Mary Delany first records seeing the style worn by the royal princesses at the coronation of George II in 1727, writing that Princess Anne and her two sisters wore 'stiff-bodied gowns of silver tissue, embroidered or quite covered with silver trimming, with diadems upon their head, and purple mantles edged with ermine, and vast long trains'.[17] A group of family portraits commissioned by George II from the miniaturist Christian Zincke at around the time of the coronation includes a depiction of the Princess Royal that closely matches this description (Fig. 8.8), while Princess Amelia and Princess Caroline wear similar stiffened bodices made of different silks.[18] Delany again remarks on the dress worn by the Princess Royal at her wedding to the Prince of Orange in 1734, describing it as 'the prettiest thing that ever was seen – *a corps de robe*, that is, in *plain English*, a stiff-bodied gown'.[19]

An attempt by Queen Charlotte to try and encourage the grand habit to be adopted more widely at the English court in the 1760s seems to have been quickly abandoned by the majority, with only the queen herself continuing to appear in such a gown regularly. Instead, most English women chose to wear either the mantua or the sacque, both of which were less formal. A beautiful surviving mantua in the Fashion Museum Bath is recorded as having been worn at court in the 1760s, although no further information about its wearer is currently known and the style of the fabric suggests it might have been made in the 1740s and altered later. In construction, it shows the characteristic features of a mantua, which are also clearly depicted in a print of a ball at St James's on the queen's birthday in 1786 (Fig. 8.9). The gown is tightly fitted at the waist, with the front openings pulled round to the back and arranged into stylised pleats before falling in a long train over a broad petticoat worn over a wide hoop. The Bath mantua is made of cream silk and the surface of both gown and petticoat are covered with embroidery of the very highest quality, representing an abundance of floral motifs. The petals

Fig. 8.9  George Noble (c.1763–1828) after Daniel Dodd (active 1761–d. 1780), *View of the Ball at St James's on the Celebration of Her Majesty's Birth Night*, 1786 (detail).
Etching with engraving, 14.3 × 19.4 cm (sheet). RCIN 750529

and leaves are picked out in a spectrum of coloured silks to create naturalistic shading, while metallic threads represent serpentine stems and three-dimensional ears of corn (Fig. 8.10). Contemporary accounts go some way to demonstrating the visual impact of such gowns worn en masse. Delany describes in detail the clothing worn by visitors to the Prince of Wales's court at Norfolk House in 1741. The dress she found most pleasing was worn by the Duchess of Queensbury, embroidered with tree stumps 'round which twined nastersians, ivy, honeysuckles, periwinkles, convolvuluses and all sorts of twining flowers which spread and covered the petticoat'.[20]

The archaic grand habit is rarely shown in formal portraiture in Britain during the second half of the eighteenth century, with even Queen Charlotte choosing instead a sacque for her magnificent full-length portrait by Thomas Gainsborough exhibited at the Royal Academy in 1781 (Fig. 8.11), a diaphanous confection of silk gauze, its surface covered with gold spangles and tassels. Unlike the back-fastening bodice of the grand habit, the queen's gown opens at the front, the gap filled by a matching stomacher decorated with a silver-grey bow. Both the large hoop over which the gown is worn and the multiple flounced sleeve ruffles had long passed from fashionable dress by this date. According to a contemporary account 'The drapery was done in one night by Gainsborough and his nephew, Gainsborough Dupont; they sat up all night, and painted it by lamp-light'.[21] In France the grand habit remained obligatory formal wear at court until the 1780s, as seen worn by Marie-Antoinette in a portrait derived from a full-length version at Versailles dating from 1778 (see Fig. 12.17). In a typical year, the French queen acquired 36 new grand habits, as well as more than 70 less formal gowns.[22] In fact, the French queen disliked the constrictive style of the grand habit, preferring instead the more informal sacque (usually known in France as a *robe parée*), which was adopted for most events from around 1783.

The continued requirement, at the insistence of Queen Charlotte, for women to wear hoops at court, even with the fashionably high-waisted gowns of the early nineteenth century, resulted in a rather absurd silhouette (all hoop and

Fig. 8.10  British, Court dress (gown, petticoat, stomacher and shoes), c.1740–60.
Silk with metal thread. Bath, Fashion Museum Bath, BATMC I.09.1406 to B

Fig. 8.11 Thomas Gainsborough (1727–88), *Queen Charlotte*, *c*.1781. Oil on canvas, 238.8 × 158.7 cm. RCIN 401407

no torso), which – perhaps unsurprisingly – never seems to have been represented in paint and only occasionally appears in prints (Fig. 8.12). One commentator remarked that 'the ladies who go to court on the birth-day are dressed in the fashion of fifty years ago, as more suitable, I suppose, to the age of their majesties'.[23] The key sartorial change introduced by George IV upon his accession in 1820 was to announce that hoops were no longer obligatory at court and, in a rare instance of a fashion changing almost overnight, women left them off, enthusiastically embracing the more elongated silhouette, further accentuated by enormous feathered headdresses (Fig. 8.13). Both of the prints opposite illustrate another essential feature of court dress: a pair of lappets, often made of lace and worn hanging on each side of the face. Those of the finest lace could be one of the most expensive components of an outfit.

For men, the fundamental garments of court dress were the same as for fashionable wear, that is, coat, breeches and waistcoat, although differentiated from the everyday by the expense of the materials used and the abundance of decoration. While men's clothing became more understated and monochromatic over the course of the eighteenth century, attendance at court still required brilliant clothing with an appropriate degree of formality, newly made for the occasion and incorporating archaic accessories: powdered wigs, shoe buckles and hats carried under the arm. Whereas in everyday dress a mismatched look became more popular as the century progressed, for court dress coats and waistcoats were usually designed en suite with the breeches, as seen in the court suit dating from *c*.1780 (Fig. 8.14). Here the same ivory silk fabric is used for all three garments, woven with fine horizontal stripes of silver thread and blue silk, and a tiny rosebud pattern. Both coat and waistcoat are heavily embroidered with metal thread, while the breeches have matching embroidery around the leg openings, incorporating spangles of silver, gold and blue, with a pattern of stylised tulips and roses infilled with green and red foil. Suits of this type (known as the *habit à la française* or *habit habillé*) still survive in some number in museum collections, preserved

Fig. 8.12  Anonymous, 'A Lady in a Court Dress', from Charles Lamb, *The Book of Ranks and Dignitaries of British Society*, 4 June 1805, Tabart & Co., London, pl. 23.
Private collection

Fig. 8.13  Anonymous, 'Court Dress', from *R. Ackermann's Repository of Arts*, XIII, 1 October 1821,  London, pl. 23.
RCIN 1069880

Fig. 8.14  Court suit, *c.*1780.
Silk, silver thread, linen and foil. London, Historic Royal Palaces, 3501323

Fig. 8.15  Possibly French, Wedding robe worn by Sophia
Magdalena of Denmark (bodice, petticoat and train), 1766.
Silver and white damask brocaded silk, metal threads, silver lace and linen.
Stockholm, Livrustkammaren, 3502 (25915–7)

Fig. 8.16 French, Wedding suit worn by Prince Gustav of Sweden (coat, waistcoat and breeches), 1766.
Silver cloth, embroidery of metal foil, sequins and gold thread.
Stockholm, Livrustkammaren, 3485 (31255–7)

for the quality of their workmanship, the shaping necessary for a tight fit rendering them difficult to repurpose as fashions changed. Such court suits are rarely represented in British portraiture, however, with royal and aristocratic men choosing instead to be depicted in uniform (either civilian or military), fashionably understated attire influenced by sporting dress, or heavy ceremonial dress such as Parliament, Garter or coronation robes, which, although infrequently worn, made explicit their status in society while reinforcing concepts of continuity and tradition.

## MARRIAGE

The convention for brides in Britain to wear white is well established today, yet this was not the fashion until the end of the eighteenth century. For most brides during the Georgian period there was no set colour and they simply wore their best clothing for the occasion. Weddings were generally intimate events, with only close members of the family and friends in attendance. The majority of ceremonies took place in church in the morning, so morning dress was considered appropriate. However, for those who could afford it, a specific type of marriage licence provided flexibility on both venue and time of day for the ceremony, and royal marriages served as occasions generating great spectacle and commentary.

Across most European courts royal brides wore a silver *robe de cour*. That worn by Sophia Magdalena of Denmark for her wedding to Prince Gustav of Sweden in November 1766 is a rare surviving example of a complete outfit and it provides some indication of the extraordinary impact such attire must have had on those present (Fig. 8.15). The bodice, petticoat and train are all made of rich cloth of silver, its shimmering metallic threads remarkably unaffected by tarnishing. At almost 3 metres long, the train, which hooks into the bodice at the waist, is further enriched with silver filé bobbin lace and silver spangles.[24] Also extant is the marriage suit of Prince Gustav: a *habit à la française* sewn from cloth of silver with an unusual mother-of-pearl effect, both coat and waistcoat embroidered with a dazzling

pattern of gold sunbursts and blue clouds created from blue metallic foil (Fig. 8.16).

When marrying the future Louis XVI in 1770, Marie-Antoinette also wore a gown of cloth of silver, the train trimmed with gold filigree lace, while the dauphin wore a suit made of cloth of gold. In contrast, when Louis XVI's grandmother, Marie Leczinska, had married the reigning king Louis XV in 1725 – at the same time becoming Queen of France – she had been

Fig. 8.17 Gainsborough Dupont (1754–97), *Caroline of Brunswick when Princess of Wales*, 1795–6 (and detail opposite).
Oil on canvas, 239.3 × 148.0 cm. RCIN 404550

entitled to wear the royal cloak of purple velvet, decorated with gold fleurs-de-lis and trimmed with ermine.

Princess Charlotte also became queen upon her marriage to George III on 8 September 1761, although the coronation ceremony itself took place two weeks later. For the wedding, Horace Walpole reports that the queen wore white and silver and 'an endless mantle of violet-coloured velvet – lined with ermine and attempted to be fastened on her shoulder by a bunch of huge pearls – dragged itself, and almost the rest of her clothes, half-way down her waist'.[25] No indication of this purple mantle (nor its awkward fit) is given in Sir Joshua Reynolds's sketch of the ceremony (see Fig. 8.20), which depicts the queen in a white *robe de cour*, its petticoat of modest dimensions, attended by her bridesmaids (ten in number) who are similarly attired in robes of white and silver.

In Gainsborough Dupont's portrait of Caroline of Brunswick (Fig. 8.17) the princess is shown in her nuptial robes, which in this instance do correlate with the contemporary description: 'A royal robe; silver tissue petticoat, covered with silver Venetian net and silver tassels; body and train of silver tissue, festooned on each side with large cord and tassels'.[26] The same dress appears in the painting of the wedding ceremony itself (see Fig. 8.4), providing a rare opportunity to see the same outfit depicted by different artists. Tassels were a practical feature of the court train, the cords allowing it to be pulled up, making it more manageable for the wearer. While Princess Caroline's bodice is typical for the grand habit (its short sleeves trimmed with tiers of separate lace sleeves below), the waistline is higher than in the bodice worn by Lady Mary Douglas more than 30 years earlier (see Fig. 8.7), reflecting the contemporary silhouette of 1795. Another modern feature is the width of the skirt, much smaller than that worn by Sophia Magdalena (see Fig. 8.15). Indeed, Princess Caroline's hoop was noted by the press for being 'very small, such as is used for morning dress; and so were the hoops of the Bridemaids [*sic*], that they might be unincumbered as possible in the procession'.[27]

The only royal wedding dress that still survives from the Georgian period (and the earliest British royal bridal

**RIGHT**
Fig. 8.18  Mrs Triaud (active 1816), Wedding dress worn by
Princess Charlotte, 1816.
Silk satin, silk net and metal thread. RCIN 71997

**BELOW**
Fig. 8.19  Anonymous, *The Princess Charlotte of Wales &
Prince Leopold of Cobourg*, 1816 (detail).
Stipple engraving, 25.2 × 16.2 cm (sheet). RCIN 605455

Fig. 8.20  Sir Joshua Reynolds (1723–92), *The Marriage of George III*, 1761.
Oil on canvas, 96.0 × 124.8 cm. RCIN 404353

Fig. 8.21  Ede & Ravenscroft, Coronation robe worn by George III, *c*.1760.
Silk, ermine and gold thread. RCIN 75083

dress in existence) is that worn by Princess Charlotte of Wales for her marriage to Prince Leopold in 1816 (Fig. 8.18). While taking inspiration from the silver *robe de cour* worn by royal brides in the previous century, this gown is quite different in construction. In fact, it appears to have been significantly altered from its original form, which was depicted in an engraving reproduced in *La Belle Assemblée* a month after the wedding (Fig. 8.19). Only a small number of components, most notably the shell-ornamented borders of silver thread (which were described as a principal motif of the dress in publications at the time), may be from the wedding dress itself.[28] These seem to have been incorporated into a different court dress at a later date.

The combination of silver and white favoured by brides for their wedding was not exclusively reserved for royalty and was also a popular choice for aristocratic women during the second half of the eighteenth century. By the last decade of the century white had become the most fashionable colour for women's everyday dress, which is when it also became established as the colour worn most often by brides. Veils were not commonly worn at weddings until the 1820s, and even then they did not conceal the face, being derived from a fashionable feature of evening dress and hanging down the back along the line of lappets. For aristocratic and royal weddings, a mantle was worn rather than a veil, as seen in Reynolds's marriage portrait of George III and Queen Charlotte, where the mantle hangs from the queen's shoulders (Fig. 8.20).

## CORONATION

The coronation outfits worn by George III (Fig. 8.21) and Queen Charlotte were meticulously recorded in paint by Allan Ramsay in what were to become the formal state portraits of the royal couple (Figs 8.22 and 8.23, overleaf). The production of these portraits illustrates the practice for clothing to be lent to an artist once the initial sitting had been completed in order to capture a likeness, so as to avoid the subject being required to sit for lengthy periods: on 19 December 1761 Ramsay reported that he had 'the Royal robes set up upon my figure'.[29] One visitor to Ramsay's studio in Soho Square described it as being 'crowded with portraits of His Majesty in every stage of their operation'.[30] Catering to the demand for additional versions was a task that would occupy the artist for the rest of his life: more than 150 orders for copies of the pair were recorded, along with numerous other single copies. Some were sent overseas as gifts (for example to the Governor of The Bahamas), while others were acquired by aristocratic families and corporations.

During the coronation ceremony itself, George III wore two different robes, both made by the firm of Ede & Ravenscroft. The first, worn by the king as he entered Westminster Abbey, was the red coronation robe that survives today and is made of silk velvet, trimmed with ermine and gold passementerie.

Fig. 8.22  Allan Ramsay (1713–84),
*George III*, *c*.1761–2.

Oil on canvas, 249.5 × 163.2 cm.
RCIN 405307

Fig. 8.23 Allan Ramsay (1713–84)
*Queen Charlotte, c.*1760–1.
Oil on canvas, 249.0 × 161.6 cm.
RCIN 405308

Fig. 8.24 Sir Thomas Lawrence (1769–1830), *George IV*, 1821.
Oil on canvas, 295.4 × 205.4 cm. RCIN 405918

After the coronation ceremony the red robe was exchanged for the purple velvet state robe, worn at the coronation banquet at Westminster Hall. Beneath both the king wore a coat and breeches of cloth of gold and cut in the fashionable line of the 1760s, although these no longer survive; those depicted here (see Fig. 8.21) are a modern recreation. It is the purple state robe that Ramsay depicts in the portrait, although over the course of time the painted garment has become much bluer in tone, due to the disintegration of organic and fugitive red lake glazes, which were laid over blue pigments to create a purple hue. Purple was a traditional colour of mourning for royalty, and the purple robes worn for a coronation – which naturally demarcated the death of one monarch and the beginning of a new reign – may have originated as a result of this transition.

Perhaps understandably, given that she had arrived in England only two weeks earlier, Queen Charlotte wore the same gown for the coronation as for her wedding (see Fig. 8.23): the skirt made of cloth of silver and heavily embroidered with gold thread, the diamond stomacher, and the purple velvet mantle, which also appears bluer in the painted version, as in the pendant portrait of George III. The peers and peeresses in attendance wore crimson velvet robes edged with white miniver fur, which incorporated a short ermine cape across the shoulders. For the men, the number of rows of powderings (black spots) indicated the wearer's rank – from four rows for a duke down to two for a baron – while for the peeresses, the wearer's rank was signalled by the length of the train and the number of centimetres of ermine trimming the cape. Given that the opportunity to wear coronation robes was such a rare and historic occasion, it is unsurprising that many attendees chose to be painted in their outfits.

The coronation of George IV on 19 July 1821 was the most lavish and expensive coronation ever held in Britain. In part paid for by funds from France as one element of the country's financial indemnity after the Battle of Waterloo, the new king (who had been serving as Regent since 1811) was determined that the event should be appropriately spectacular. He was personally involved in planning the details of his own clothing and that of the processional attendants. Taking inspiration from Elizabethan dress, the king's outfit, depicted in a dramatic and highly flattering portrait by Sir Thomas Lawrence, painted over an earlier image of the king in Garter robes (Fig. 8.24), consisted of a silver tissue doublet and matching trunk hose, each trimmed with gold braid, worn beneath a surcoat of crimson velvet, with a lace-trimmed ruff at the neck. The king wore the curled wig that was now an established feature of his appearance. An enormously heavy coronation mantle of red velvet, ornately embroidered and lined with ermine, was so weighty it required eight train-bearers, the whole ensemble almost causing the king to faint. Around his neck are four collars representing the Golden Fleece, the Guelphic Order, the Order of the Bath and the Order of the Garter. As in earlier coronations, after the event the crimson robes were exchanged for a purple velvet mantle for the banquet. The dress of the procession was also inspired by the sixteenth century, the overall colour scheme being red, blue, white and gold.

Since 1220, St Edward's Crown, named after its connection to Edward the Confessor, had been used during the coronation ceremony. While the medieval crown had been melted down in 1649 after the Civil War, it was replaced by a new version for the coronation of Charles II in 1661. After each coronation ceremony, St Edward's Crown was traditionally exchanged for a second crown (known as the state crown), which was worn by the monarch on other ceremonial occasions throughout the year. Prior to his coronation in 1714, George I commissioned a replacement state crown from the royal goldsmith Samuel Smithin. Broadly similar in design to the previous state crown and reusing many of the same gemstones, in a break with tradition it was this state crown that was employed at the crowning ceremony rather than St Edward's Crown, which was instead carried in the procession.[31] George I's state crown also featured in the coronations of George II in 1727 (although the coloured stones were replaced with more fashionable diamonds, hired temporarily for the occasion) and of George III in 1761. It appears in state portraits of all three monarchs.[32] For George IV's coronation in 1821, however, a new crown was commissioned from

Rundell, Bridge & Rundell, consisting of a more open lattice-work frame, into which were set more than 12,000 diamonds, again hired for the event. Whereas Queen Caroline had used the state crown created for Mary of Modena in 1685 for her coronation, Queen Charlotte wore the small nuptial crown that had formed part of the Hanoverian hereditary jewels presented to her by George III upon her arrival in England.[33] The nuptial crown is depicted in Ramsay's portrait, alongside the Queen Consort's Sceptre with Cross and the Queen Consort's Ivory Rod with Dove (see Figs 3.56 and 8.23).

All crowns worn by a monarch incorporate a double arch, while that worn by the heir to the throne has only a single arch, as shown in a portrait of George III when Prince of Wales (see Fig. 2.6). The wearing of a crown was specifically reserved for members of the royal family, while peers and peeresses in attendance wore a coronet, similar in appearance to a crown but differentiated by its absence of arches. The details of decoration on a coronet varied by rank, with different combinations and arrangements of pearls and strawberry leaves. All levels are depicted in William Hogarth's *The Five Orders of Perriwigs*, with the bottom row representing (in decreasing rank from left to right) the queen, shown here without a crown, a duchess, a marquess, a countess, a viscountess and a baroness (see Fig. 6.4).

## MOURNING

The practice of adopting a particular style and colour of dress as a public symbol of mourning has its origins in royal and aristocratic convention, although mourning dress had become more widespread during the seventeenth century, something that continued throughout the next century. While mourning dress served as a demonstration of affection for the deceased and helped the wearer feel they were responding appropriately, it also reinforced social status and wealth, indicating a knowledge of etiquette and an ability to afford special clothing acquired for the occasion.

For court mourning, adherence to the specific protocols could also be interpreted as a public demonstration of patriotism and loyalty to the sovereign, while honouring the death of a foreign ruler had an important diplomatic function, being a conspicuous gesture of allegiance and familial ties between different countries. Court mourning of this kind was a frequent occurrence: between 1750 and 1767 there were 44 separate periods of mourning observed at the British court for foreign royalty.[34] Unlike full public mourning, such occasions required only those attending court to change their style of dress, rather than the entire population.

During the eighteenth century the rising wealth of the middle classes, coupled with a desire to emulate fashionable trends, enabled a broader section of society to adopt mourning dress for occasions other than private family mourning. This situation was greeted with displeasure among some commentators, who viewed it as 'a meer Affectation of the Mode at St James's.'[35]

In some countries, including France, prosecutions were brought against people deemed to be wearing elements of mourning dress that were restricted by sumptuary law to the nobility, although such laws had long been abandoned in Britain.[36] Mourning rules remained complex, however, and would become ever more so in the nineteenth century.

As in the seventeenth century, mourning dress was cut along the same lines as clothing for other occasions, the main differences being in the colour and type of fabric used. The most important element was that dress and accessories were to be matt, with no reflective surfaces, and ornamentation was to be limited. Specific textiles were prescribed depending on the period of mourning in question, so after the death of George II in 1760, for first mourning (lasting three months) women were required to wear 'Black Bombazines, Plain Muslin or Long Lawn Linnen, Crape Hoods, Shamoy Shoes and Gloves, and Crape Fans', while for second mourning (lasting six weeks) linen could be fringed instead of plain, and shoes, gloves, necklaces and earrings could be white.[37] For third mourning (one month) black silks and velvets could be introduced, along with coloured ribbons.[38] A separate form of 'undress' for less formal occasions was also specified. Bombazine (by this date usually a silk/worsted mix, named after the *bombyx* silkworm) and its cheaper relation bombazet (cotton/worsted mix) were both twill fabrics, while mourning crape had a distinctive crimped surface produced by incorporating extra twists into the thread before weaving.[39] All had an appropriately dull appearance. For second mourning, lustring in either black or white could be worn. This was a silk with a characteristic glossy sheen ('lustre'). The great quantity of mourning fabrics required throughout the eighteenth century, together with the increased prices that could be charged for them after a royal death, made such textiles a focus for experimentation, with various patents being introduced over the course of the Georgian era. Norwich was a particular centre for mourning fabrics, so much so that court mourning protocols from the 1720s specified the wearing of 'Norwich crape': a conscious attempt to encourage the purchase of domestic goods by the royal household.[40]

During first mourning all accessories were required to be matt black, as seen in a sword acquired by the Prince of Wales from Thomas Gray of Sackville Street (a dealer in 'fancy articles') for the funeral of Princess Amelia in November 1810 (Fig. 8.25), which incorporates a blackened-steel hilt and black fish-skin scabbard.[41] The same bill also records the prince buying two black sword belts, two pairs of black stone shoe buckles, and a diamond locket containing a miniature of his late sister. Half-mourning swords could be more elaborate: that shown opposite (Fig. 8.26) incorporates a blade of blued steel and a copper-alloy hilt inset with sparkling diamond-faceted beads of deep blue glass.

As in many countries across Europe during the eighteenth century, the death of the British sovereign or a close member of their family prompted a period of public mourning. The duration and depth of mourning varied depending on the proximity of the deceased to the monarch and also from one reign to the next, becoming shorter as the century progressed. The specifics of timing were set out by the Lord Chamberlain's office of the royal household and published in newspapers. Unsurprisingly, the death of the monarch prompted the deepest form of mourning for the whole population, lasting for a minimum of a year in the first half of the century, but reduced to six months from 1760. After the death of George I in 1727 the mourning period was divided into three degrees (first, second and third), each characterised by subtle differences in the clothing required.[42] For his Birthday Ball at St James's Palace in 1738 the widowed George II requested that no finery be worn, despite more than a year having passed since the death of his wife, Queen Caroline – a period that covered the public order for six months of deep mourning and six months of second mourning.[43]

The death of the heir was another significant occasion. Upon the death of Frederick, Prince of Wales, in March 1751, George II announced a total mourning period of six months, with first mourning observed from the date of death, and second mourning from 7 July until 6 October. The family portrait painted by George Knapton in the year of the prince's death provides an insight into mourning

convention at the time (Fig. 8.27 and see Fig. 5.15). Frederick's widow, Princess Augusta, is shown with all nine of their children, while the Prince of Wales himself is included by virtue of a painted portrait hanging on the left. Augusta's fashionably cut dress is of white silk, accessorised with simple linen cuffs rather than expensive lace, and she wears no jewellery except a miniature of her husband on her wrist. Although black clothing had long been established as the colour most associated with mourning dress, for female members of the royal family white was another option with historical precedent, and this is what Augusta wears – her gown is possibly of white lustring – accessorised with a long black diaphanous veil, perhaps of silk crape. The inclusion of the youngest daughter, Caroline Matilda, on her mother's lap suggests that this was painted during second mourning, the child having been born in July, four months after her father's death. Notably, all the children are dressed in bright colours, their clothing decorated with metallic thread

Fig. 8.28  English, Memorial snuffbox for Frederick, Prince of
Wales, 1751.
Tortoiseshell and gold, 3.1 × 6.4 × 4.8 cm. RCIN 22170

Fig. 8.29  John Opie (1761–1807), *Mary Delany, née Granville*, 1782.
Oil on canvas, 76.5 × 63.6 cm. RCIN 400965

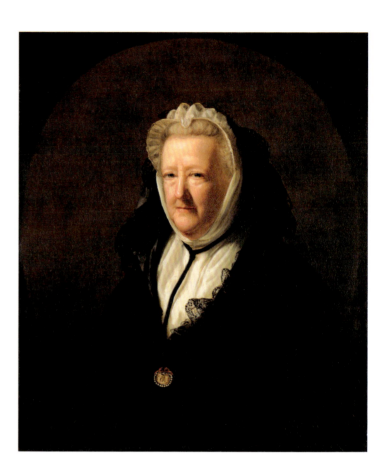

and expensive lace. It is surprising that there is no
acknowledgement of their father's death in their dress,
given that children were regularly put into mourning dress
(often white) and followed the same timescales as adults.
The memorial snuffbox shown below (Fig. 8.28) was also
made in 1751 following the death of the Prince of Wales.
The lid of the tortoiseshell box is inlaid with gold using
a technique known as *piqué coulé* to create a design
incorporating the Prince of Wales's feathers and motto
together with the date of death and age (45).

Private mourning was observed for the death of a
family member, with the deepest mourning reserved for
the death of a spouse. John Opie's portrait of Mary Delany,
née Granville (1700–88; Fig. 8.29), was painted in 1782,
14 years after the death of her second husband, Dr Patrick
Delany. The 25-year marriage had been happy, with the
couple sharing a love of botany, a passion reflected in Mary's
famous flower paper-cuttings. Like many widows – and
especially royal women – the sitter has chosen to retain
her widow's weeds (derived from *waed*, a historical term
for garments) long after convention would have allowed
her to remove them. The plain black dress, possibly
made of bombazine, is worn with a white cap with 'falls'
on either side of her face that reach her chest. Over this
is another black hood, trimmed with black lace: a small
concession to fashionability that would not have been
appropriate during first mourning. Covering the hair was
an essential feature of dress for widows. Around her neck

is a locket set with pearls and the crowned cipher CR,
almost certainly a gift from Queen Charlotte. The two
women were close friends, and this portrait was hung in
the queen's bedchamber at Buckingham House. Delany
was a prodigious letter writer, and her correspondence
regularly recounts her own preparations for mourning
dress. After the death of her mother in 1747 she discusses
the appropriateness of 'black bombazeen' cut in a sacque
style for full dress, and describes a gown in 'dark grey
unwatered tabby' worn for informal occasions.[44] At the
same time Delany provided her housekeeper and personal
maid with mourning dress, as was customary for servants
after the death of a member of their employer's family.

Mourning dress is infrequently depicted in formal
portraits, the process of sitting for an artist after a
bereavement perhaps appearing inimical with an ability
to mourn appropriately. As these examples show, however,

exceptions were made for members of the royal family and for those women who continued to wear mourning dress long after the death of their husband. A portrait of the Duchess of Kent wearing a black velvet evening gown cut with a fashionably short bodice and capped sleeves provides another case in point (Fig. 8.30). Given that the duchess granted sittings to the artist George Dawe in July and August 1818, she cannot yet be in mourning for her mother-in-law, Queen Charlotte, who died in November of that year. In addition, the sparkling diamond-set tiara, earrings and brooch would not have been worn during the

first stage of deep mourning. Instead, the duchess's dress may represent the second mourning stage for her niece, Princess Charlotte, who had died in childbirth in November of the previous year. Within two years the duchess would again be in mourning, this time for her husband who died in 1820, after only two years of marriage and before his daughter (the future Queen Victoria) had reached her first birthday. In a second portrait (Fig. 8.31), painted in 1821 and more overtly commemorative by virtue of the inclusion of a miniature of the duke clutched in his daughter's hands, the duchess

wears only pearl jewellery, and the short sleeves of her gown have long silk gauze oversleeves encircled with ribbon: a fashionable feature of evening dress at the time, but perhaps also considered a more appropriate style for a widow than the bare arms of the earlier portrait.

In France a royal ordinance of 1716 had reformed the archaic styles of mourning stipulated in the reign of Louis XIV, reducing the overall duration and distinguishing between *grand deuil* and *petit deuil* (the latter was also known as *demi-deuil*, literally half mourning). Despite this, for most of the eighteenth century, mourning etiquette in France continued to be more strictly observed than in Britain, with some form of court mourning (*deuil de cour*) a regular instruction for the whole population. Occasions warranting the observance of *grand deuil*, however, were infrequent and short in length, requiring plain matt black fabrics to be worn, with no additional ornamentation. As in Britain, accessories were to be made of black steel rather than silver or gold. The austerity of such dress meant it was largely unchanged from year to year, or person to person, and seldom portrayed in fashion periodicals. The man shown in the first stage of mourning dress for the *grand deuil de cour* after the death of the King of Portugal in 1786 is a rare depiction from the *Cabinet des modes* (Fig. 8.32). His coat is described as being of black cloth, made without buttons on the pockets (a similar requirement was in place in Britain during first mourning), the shoe buckles are of bronzed steel and the black hat is trimmed with black crape. During later stages of mourning grey and white fabrics could be incorporated gradually, along with reflective jewellery and diamonds. These stages provided greater opportunity for imaginative and individualised interpretations of the mourning regulations, which were frequently included in fashion periodicals such as the *Magasin des modes nouvelles, françaises et anglaises* (Fig. 8.33). The example included opposite shows second stage options for both men and

women, with the trend for stripes, enormous muffs, double watch chains and the newly introduced short 'pierrot' jacket dramatically evoked in black and white. The blue-hilted sword carried by the man is perhaps similar to the half-mourning sword in the Royal Collection (see Fig. 8.26), and his shoe buckles are now silver rather than bronzed steel.

Deprived of the requirement to supply new clothing during long periods of court mourning, with balls and other social events suspended and theatres closed, the impact of mourning conventions on the textile industry was significant, with reduced income for workers and a surplus of colourful seasonal stock unable to be sold. With the death of Louis XV in May 1774, Louis XVI was successfully convinced to reduce the length of time of court mourning to seven months, so that the usual season of court events between Christmas and New Year could proceed with full splendour.[45] Similar petitions were presented to Parliament in Britain, citing the detrimental impact on domestic silk manufacture and related industries, and public demonstrations were staged by silk weavers to express their concerns. In response, a royal order from George III in 1768 shortened court mourning by half, and the king was presented with an address signed by more than 500 manufacturers to convey their thanks.[46] In 1816 the Prince Regent indicated his support for further measures, requiring court mourning only be worn at court on Sundays.[47]

Although illustrations in French periodicals encouraged people to buy new mourning clothing that reflected fashionable trends (thereby supporting the domestic textile industry), for others mourning provided an opportunity for thrift, excusing the requirement for new clothing. Some chose to have their existing clothing dyed black with Indian logwood rather than acquiring new for the occasion. The frequency with which mourning dress had to be worn in France probably played a role in the rise of black as a fashionable colour for everyday dress unconnected to mourning. During the 1780s French mourning etiquette became more relaxed, with a black ribbon sufficient to indicate *demi-deuil*. By 1789 the sartorial symbolism of black clothing was further

complicated by the events of the French Revolution, with a public demonstration of mourning for those executed by guillotine a dangerous act in itself.

In the eighteenth century there was a rise in the market for mourning jewellery, often made of inexpensive materials but closely connected to the deceased through inscriptions and imbued with a language of symbolism. Willow and cypress trees were popular, along with broken columns, urns and landscape scenes. Memorial jewellery incorporating human hair had been in use since the seventeenth century, the earliest examples displaying the hair in its natural form, as a lock of hair within an enclosed compartment or beneath a rock crystal or glass cover. The eighteenth century saw the development of new techniques and by the early nineteenth century hair was increasingly used as a raw material, detached from its natural appearance by being laid over card, glazed and cut into shapes that were arranged to create a picture, sometimes in three dimensions. Hair could also be plaited or woven to produce a decorative background, or to form

Fig. 8.35  English, Bracelet with nine lockets, one with a miniature
of the left eye of Charlotte, Princess of Wales, c.1800–20.
Silver gilt, enamel, gold, diamond, ruby, pearl and human hair; watercolour
on ivory, 20.0 × 3.9 × 1.7 cm. RCIN 10919

a structural component of the jewellery itself. A mourning
ring (Fig. 8.34) made in honour of Georgiana Cavendish,
Duchess of Devonshire, has the date of her death
(30 March 1806) inscribed into the bloodstone, along
with the ducal coronet. The use of a swivelling bezel was
a typical feature of mourning jewellery, allowing the
reverse to be displayed. Here, the back is set with plaited
hair, presumably the duchess's own. Although the owner
of the ring is not recorded, the marks of wear on the
black enamel indicate that it was much worn. Hair was
also incorporated into sentimental jewellery as a symbol
of friendship. The bracelet shown below (Fig. 8.35) has
six lockets containing hair, while another holds a painted
miniature of the left eye of Charlotte, Princess of Wales.
It does not appear to be an item intended for mourning,
instead illustrating a practice of intimate and personalised
gift exchange, although the recipient in this instance is so
far unknown.

# 9

# Influences from Afar

*The single Dress of a Woman of Quality is often the Product
of a hundred Climates. The Muff and the Fan come together
from the different Ends of the Earth. The Scarf is sent
from the Torrid Zone, and the Tippet from beneath the Pole.
The Brocade Petticoat rises out of the Mines of Peru,
and the Diamond Necklace out of the Bowels of Indostan.*

JOSEPH ADDISON, 1711[1]

Written towards the very end of the Stuart era, Joseph Addison's comments on the disparate regions from which the elements of fashionable clothing were sourced feels prophetic, given that in the eighteenth century Britain expanded its global reach far beyond anything achieved at Addison's time of writing, via the combined arms of trade, travel and empire. British people looked overseas for innovative consumer goods and novel styles of dress, although the influence of clothing from afar often saw its earliest incarnation during those moments when a form of 'fancy dress' was required, most notably while sitting for a portrait or attending a masquerade. However, elements of clothing sourced from different places gradually slipped into everyday styles, where they were combined with established fashions of the era (sometimes in an incongruous or inauthentic manner), initially as informal dress but later more formal. This chapter examines the ways in which such components from outside Europe were transmitted and transmuted into a form of 'dressing up' that was considered appropriate for these various audiences and occasions, focusing specifically on three regions of notable influence: the Ottoman Empire, India and China.

## 'TURKISH' DRESS

The Ottoman Empire (which in the eighteenth century encompassed modern-day Turkey and Greece as well as parts of northern Africa and the Middle East) was a source of great fascination for Europeans, evoking a world of luxury and exoticism that had gradually become disassociated from historical notions of 'barbarity' which had developed during earlier periods of warfare. The influence of what came to be known as 'turquerie' was felt across the arts, inspiring theatrical productions, musical compositions and carnivals. Similarly, Turkish motifs and scenes were integrated into the vocabulary of European decorative arts, appearing on porcelain, tapestry and interior architectural schemes. In such representations, the clothing incorporates elements that had come to be thought of as stereotypically 'Turkish', a form of sartorial shorthand that made it immediately recognisable, including luxurious textiles, fur trims, long flowing gowns, jewelled girdles, baggy trousers (for both men and women), turbans, striped fabrics and tassels. Distinctions between regions were often ill-defined or misunderstood, with the result that terms such as Turkish, Persian, Eastern and Oriental were used interchangeably or conflated, making the original intentions of writers difficult for modern readers to interpret. Moreover, when European sources describe clothing as being of a certain style or derived from a specific part of the world, it is rarely an accurate depiction of what was actually worn in that region. Instead, it is a Eurocentric interpretation, modulated by different ideals of beauty and body image, assimilating and appropriating aspects of non-European dress into current fashions and combining components from a number of regions to create an inauthentic result.

Long established as an important producer of fine textiles, the geographical location of the Levant (as this area was frequently described) ensured its importance as a key trading link between East and West for a wide variety of luxury goods. The name Levant is derived from medieval French, translating as 'the rising', reflecting the fact that Europeans viewed it as the land where the sun rises. Many expatriate merchants of European citizenship were based in this area – particularly the main port cities – some adopting Turkish clothing and conveying its details to relatives living in Europe. Over the course of the eighteenth century the balance shifted, as more consumer goods (including European textiles) were imported into the region, and direct trade between Europe and China and India via ship superseded the need for goods to travel overground via the Near East. The Levant also became more accessible to European travellers, and from the 1740s onwards Turkey was a fashionable place for aristocrats to visit after Italy as part of a Grand Tour. Founded in 1744 by John Montagu, 4th Earl of Sandwich (1718–92), the short-lived 'Divan Club' (*divan* was used to mean both a council and council chamber under the Ottoman Empire) offered its attendees the opportunity to relive their experiences or plan forthcoming jaunts. Meeting fortnightly in St James's, London, members dressed in Turkish-inspired regalia, including a turban.[2]

A key figure responsible for encouraging an interest in Turkish dress in Britain was Lady Mary Wortley Montagu (1689–1762), who lived in Turkey with her husband while he served as ambassador to the Sublime Porte between 1717 and 1718. A prolific letter writer, Montagu's correspondence recounts her experiences in vivid detail, making clear her concern to correct established misconceptions about the customs of the region. While living in Turkey, Montagu adopted the local style of dress, which she continued to wear on occasion after returning to Britain. So associated was she with the style that it became common for unidentified portraits of women dressed in a vaguely Turkish manner to be described as being of her. The woman opposite (Fig. 9.1), tentatively identified as Montagu in the nineteenth century, may be an example of this practice. While most other portraits speculatively identified as Montagu tended to show her in a fanciful interpretation of Turkish dress with Western modifications, the clothing here appears to represent an accurate depiction of styles worn by Turkish women. It consists of a blue silk *entari* (long gown) with small gold buttons, tightly fitted over the chest and held in position by a belt – Montagu describes this as a 'girdle of

about 4 fingers broad' – which could be set with precious stones or embroidered. The half-length format of this painting does not allow us to see whether the sitter has chosen to wear one side of the *entari* tucked into the belt to reveal the layers beneath, as was popular. Under the *entari* the sitter wears a white smock with large sleeves folded back to the elbow. Her elaborate headdress resembles Montagu's description of a style of cap known as a *talpock*:

> which is in winter of fine velvet embroidered with pearls or diamonds, and in summer of a light, shining silver stuff. This is fixed on one side of the head, hanging a little way down with a gold tassel … On the other side of the head, the hair is laid flat; and here the ladies are at liberty to shew their fancies; some putting flowers,

others a plume of herons' feathers … The hair hangs at its full length behind, divided into tresses braided with pearl or riband, which is always in great quantity.[3]

Unlike many other portraits of British women dressed '*à la turque*' in which modesty pieces are incorporated to conceal the cleavage and the figure adapted to create the idealised eighteenth-century silhouette – an indication that the sitter is wearing stays – neither is evident here. Invisible in this half-length portrait are the loose trousers (*şalvar*) that many Turkish women wore beneath their other layers.

Diplomatic embassies sent from the Ottoman Empire to European courts were an increasingly common sight after the Peace of Karlowitz (1699), their large entourages providing an opportunity to see authentic and magnificent

Turkish dress in person (albeit only that worn by men) rather than transmuted via images and hearsay. In return, European ambassadors were similarly welcomed to Constantinople. An unusual pair of watercolours illustrates the protocol during one of these visits. They were painted by Francis Smith, an artist invited to accompany Frederick Calvert, 6th Baron Baltimore, on his tour of the region. The first picture (Fig. 9.2) shows the British ambassador to the Ottoman Empire, Henry Grenville (1717–84), being introduced to the Grand Vizier (Chief Minister), Köse Bahir Mustafa Pasa, in Topkapi Palace. Grenville wears

formal English court dress typical of the 1760s, a white silk suit with gold braid, and his entourage are similarly dressed, all with powdered bag-wigs and tricorne hats. In contrast, the Turkish men wear long gowns and a variety of turbans, the difference in height of headdress an indicator of status. That worn by the Vizier is a *kallâvi kavuk*, identifiable by its gold stripe. In the foreground we see the Turkish robes with which Grenville is to be presented before being granted an audience with Sultan Mustafa III (r. 1757–74), an event depicted in a second watercolour (Fig. 9.3). Here Grenville has changed into

a yellow fur-lined robe, along with other members of his
entourage, although incongruously they have retained their
bag-wigs and black hats. The sultan's turban is differentiated
from the others in incorporating the *sorguç* at the front,
an expensive decoration made of feathers and jewels.
A reciprocal event is portrayed in an engraving (Fig. 9.4),
which shows George III formally receiving Yusuf Agâh
Efendi at St James's Palace in 1795, the first Turkish
ambassador to be dispatched to Britain, sent by Sultan
Selim III. Yusuf Agâh bows before the king as he is
introduced by the Foreign Secretary, William Grenville
(nephew of Henry), and presents his credentials. According
to one account, 'He was himself dressed, as in the manner
of his country, in his simplest dress.'[4]

The Levant was a popular area for foreign artists
to settle, including the Swiss-born Jean-Etienne Liotard
(Fig. 9.5) who found a ready market for portraits and
picturesque depictions of the sights and customs of the
region, and illustrated dress with great precision. Liotard
had travelled to Constantinople at the invitation of

Sir William Ponsonby, 2nd Earl of Bessborough (1704–93):
as the official artist for the trip, part of his role involved
drawing 'the dresses of every country they should go into'.[5]
He ended up staying for five years, and adopted a style of
dress for which he became known as 'le Peintre Turc'. The
artist signed his self-portraits with this nickname, which
seems to have become part of his visual identity, retaining
it even after returning to London (although he did concede
to shave off his enormous beard in 1756, apparently on the
request of his wife). The distinctive red felt fes, traditionally
used as a base around which a turban could be wrapped,
reappears in a number of Liotard's self-portraits, often
worn beneath a large sable cap.[6] In fact, this fur cap
was Moldavian, not Turkish, and was probably acquired
by Liotard during his time as court artist to the Prince
of Moldavia in 1742–3. While Liotard praised his
characteristic style of Turkish dress for its comfort,
it also seems to have been a helpful commercial selling
point, differentiating him from the various other
European artists working in the region.

Turkish dress was a favoured choice for the
fashionable masquerades of this period. In October 1768
King Christian VII of Denmark hosted a masquerade
at the Haymarket in London, said to have been attended
by more than 2,500 people. Although the theme was not

Fig. 9.6  Prince Frederick in Johan Joseph Zoffany (1733–1810), *Queen Charlotte with her Two Eldest Sons*, 1764 (detail). Oil on canvas, 112.2 × 128.3 cm. RCIN 400146

explicitly Turkish, the Duchess of Ancaster appeared as a sultana: 'her robe was purple sattin bordered with ermine, and flutter'd on the ground so much in the stile of eastern magnificence, that we were transported in fancy to the palaces of Constantinople from the borders of the Thames'.[7] Mary Delany reported that at the same event the Duchess of Richmond had been dressed 'as the Fatima; described in Lady Mary W. Montague's letters'.[8] According to Montagu, the beautiful Fatima wore 'a *caftan* of gold brocade, flowered with silver … Her drawers were pale pink, her waistcoat green and silver, her slippers white satin, finely embroidered: her lovely arms adorned with bracelets of diamonds, and her broad girdle set round with diamonds'.[9] Several years earlier, Prince Henry, Duke of Cumberland, had attended a ball at Somerset House, London, 'in a Turkish dress with a large bunch of diamonds in his turbant'.[10] In Johan Joseph Zoffany's portrait of Queen Charlotte with her two eldest sons (Fig. 9.6 and see Fig. 1.29), the one-year-old Prince Frederick wears Turkish fancy dress (including a turban and fur-lined gold kaftan complete with leading strings), which is recorded as having been ordered by the boys' governess in 1764, along with 'a Telemachus Dress' for Prince George (aged two).

Lady Mary Wortley Montagu's letters, which were officially published after her death in 1763 but circulated among a select group after her return to England in 1718, together with Liotard's stay in London from 1753 to 1755, probably contributed to the trend for women to dress in a Turkish manner for portraits, noticeable in England from the 1750s onwards. This was not the case for English men, however, who, while happy to wear Turkish fancy dress at masquerades, rarely wore it for their portraits. The artists Sir Joshua Reynolds and Angelica Kauffmann were later proponents of the Turkish style, although both tended to interpret it in a more stylised and neo-classical manner that simultaneously evoked the drapery of antique sculpture. Reynolds's portrait of the Duchess of Gloucester is an example of this hybrid. Her informal wrapping gown with loose sleeves is arranged to resemble a kaftan with a decorative waist sash (Fig. 9.7), while her hair is styled in the high fashion of the 1770s, with one long plait

falling to one side in the manner described by Montagu decades earlier.

In the popular imagination the Ottoman Empire had long been associated with sensuality and sexual freedom, the harem and the bathhouse forming leitmotifs in literature of the time. While Montagu's letters make clear that she was astounded by the magnificence and beauty of Turkish dress, she remarked on its comfortable nature, being worn without stays, and the sense of liberation for women, especially compared to the restrictive and regulated garments in England. It was this looseness of dress that lent the style an indecorous air and contributed to a continued erotic undercurrent, as John Arbuthnot makes explicit in a comedic poem from 1724: 'That you thus sweep along a Turkish Tail / And let that Robe o'er Modesty prevail / … / Why in this naughty Vestment are you seen? / Dress'd up for Love, with such an Air and Mien, / As if you would commence a Sultana Queen.'[11] Initially considered appropriate only as a costume within the permissive setting of the masquerade and later as a form of fancy dress for a portrait, Turkish styles gradually became acceptable as fashionable informal dress for women, with the *Magazine à la Mode* writing in 1777 that 'the dresses of our ladies have inclined very much to the Persian and

Turkish since the taste for masquerades as a fashion amusement prevailed'.[12] Of the 325 fashion plates published between 1778 and 1787, 72 demonstrate some form of 'turquerie', an illustration of how much the aesthetic had been integrated into European fashions of the time.[13] The broad range of terms used to describe such garments includes *à la sultane*, *Circassienne*, *à la lévite*, *Levantine*, *à la turque* and *à la Musulmanei*. In contrast, only three of the plates indicate a Chinese inspiration and four reference India, but then only in relation to the types of fabric used.

Absent from the portrait perhaps representing Lady Mary Wortley Montagu (see Fig. 9.1) is the kaftan, a long loose gown worn by both men and women. While multiple kaftans could be worn at the same time, the outermost was often lined with fur and cut with short sleeves that revealed those of the layer beneath. These distinctive double-sleeve layers are probably the key feature identifying a dress described as a *robe à la turque* in the *Cabinet des modes* of November 1786 (Fig. 9.8). Striped fabrics had also been associated with the Levant since the seventeenth century and the direction of the stripe on the sleeve here, running around the arm rather than down it as in European gown construction, is also characteristic of Turkish garments. However, this is very much a hybrid style: the petticoat and kerchief around the neck are both of white satin, and the silhouette is typical of English styles at this date, indicating the figure is wearing stays, which was not the norm for Turkish women.

A series of miniatures of the four daughters of Tsar Paul I of Russia indicates that the *robe à la turque* had also become popular among the Russian aristocracy by the 1790s. A dress worn by Princess Maria, later Grand Duchess Maria Pavlovna (1786–1859), is made of a comparable purple and green striped silk as in the fashion plate, and is similarly worn over a white petticoat and bodice (Fig. 9.9). The miniatures are thought to be copies after portraits painted by Dmitry Levitsky in 1796, when Maria would have been ten years old. Her two older sisters, Alexandra (13) and Helena (12), are also dressed in striped gowns of pink/blue and red/green, while the younger sister, Catherine (8), wears the simpler frock of childhood and her

Fig. 9.10 Henry Bone (1755–1834) after Sir Thomas Lawrence (1769–1830), *Sarah Siddons*, 1798.
Enamel, 11.7 × 9.7 cm. RCIN 421507

the eighteenth century, which can be traced back to an admiration of the hussar regiments responsible for successfully defending the Holy Roman Empire from Turkish invading troops at the siege of Vienna in 1683. The interest in the hussars was revived in the 1740s, when Britain found itself an ally of Maria Theresa, Empress of Austria and Queen of Hungary, during the War of the Austrian Succession. The flamboyant dress of the hussar regiments was notably different to that worn by other regiments, being an elaborate and picturesque interpretation of traditional Hungarian peasant dress. Its distinctive features included tight pantaloons, a tunic with an abundance of looped cord decoration, the pelisse worn over one shoulder, a waist sash, fur-trimmed hat (*kalpak*) and boots. It was further popularised by David Garrick, who wore hussar dress as Tancred in James Thomson's *Tancred and Sigismunda* at Drury Lane Theatre in 1745 (and was later painted in character), rather incongruously given that Tancred was King of Sicily in the twelfth century. Hussar dress was another common form of fancy dress for masquerades. The influence of hussar clothing rapidly spread well beyond the realm of dressing up, however, being incorporated in servants' livery, children's dress, military uniforms (see Fig. 11.1) and, by the 1770s, fashionable men's dress.

## FOREIGN TEXTILES

In general, the clothing worn further east did not influence the design of eighteenth-century European dress to the same degree as that of the Ottoman Empire. This can probably be explained by the closer geographical proximity of the Levant, together with the dress worn there being deemed sufficiently different from European dress to be 'exotic' but not entirely so, making it straightforward to integrate within an established sartorial system. One key exception to this is the banyan gown, popular throughout the eighteenth century (discussed in Chapter 4), which appears to have been influenced by the construction of the Japanese *kosode*, being made without a shoulder seam and frequently incorporating silk wadding interlining. In Europe these were often called Indian gowns.

hair is loose rather than styled with a matching ribbon like the other three girls.[14]

The bonnet in the *Cabinet des modes* fashion plate (see Fig. 9.8) is also described as being *à la turque*: a broad band of blue crepe with an upper component of puffy English gauze, the left side set with feathers and a bouquet of flowers. It is probably this asymmetry that lends the bonnet its name. An interest in Eastern forms of headwear was embodied in the fashion for women to wear turbans from the end of the eighteenth century. These came in a multitude of styles, one of which was secured with a chin strap, as shown in the portrait of Sarah Siddons (Fig. 9.10). It may have its origins in the ribbon straps of linen bonnets, although the veils worn in desert regions, which protected the lower half of the face against the inhalation of airborne sand, may also have been an influence as part of the broader interest in and adoption of clothing styles from other regions.

The Ottoman Empire also had an indirect impact on the popularity of Hungarian hussar dress in England in

Unlike Turkish styles, Chinese and Indian 'fancy dress' was a rare form of masquerade costume and only a handful of sitters were painted wearing what might be interpreted as specifically Chinese or Indian outfits, as opposed to generically 'Eastern'. Portraits of British expatriates living in India while in the service of the Crown or the East India Company indicate that they tended to retain European styles of clothing, relying on friends and family back home to keep them updated on the latest fashions, and enthusiastically welcoming the regular shipments of imported European goods, rather than adopting traditional Indian forms of dress.[15] It was common, however, for garments to be made from lighter-weight textiles better suited to the warmer climate.

China remained largely inaccessible to European travellers, while few Chinese people travelled to Europe and Chinese garments were not imported into Europe in any great number until the mid-nineteenth century. First-hand knowledge of the clothing worn in the region was therefore limited. Although a taste for 'chinoiserie' can be seen across the decorative arts during the eighteenth century – the motifs and colours finding a natural affinity with the rococo style – the clothing worn by the figures is often an imaginary conflation of 'Eastern' dress that rarely differentiates between Chinese, Japanese and Indian.

In the late 1740s, at the peak of the craze for chinoiserie in Britain, Frederick, Prince of Wales, acquired a new royal barge, 'after the Venetian Manner and the Watermen all dressed in Chinese Habits'.[16] Sadly, there is no record of their appearance. In the few eighteenth-century fashion plates described as being *à la chinoise*, there is little to distinguish the dress from other styles, its most consistent feature tending to be textiles with brightly contrasting stripes, although this was not in fact a Chinese element.[17] Similarly, while the term *en pagode* was used to refer to anything of flared design (sleeves, hats, skirts), it served as a non-specific description derived from Chinese architecture rather than Chinese garments.

Chinese and Indian textiles, however, had a significant impact on European dress. Fabric from both regions was imported in great quantity, and also influenced the design and manufacturing techniques of domestically made goods. Such textiles were not limited to garments intended for fancy dress. Although initially used for informal clothing worn within the home, they were gradually incorporated into high fashion items considered suitable for even the most formal occasions.

Sericulture (the practice of cultivating silkworms to make silk) appears to have been first established in China around 2700 BC,[18] and for many years it remained a closely kept secret, with textiles exported via a complex network of trade routes historically known as the 'Silk Road'. Knowledge of sericulture itself gradually spread west to India, Istanbul and into Italy by the twelfth century. Given this long association with the production of silk, China was renowned for the quality of its silk textiles, and a wide variety of different types, patterns and weights were imported to Britain during the eighteenth century. Painted silks were particularly fashionable and greatly admired in Europe, despite Chinese consumers considering them inferior to woven designs, which, taking more time to manufacture, were more expensive. Guangdong was the province best known for producing silks for export (as well as an array of other luxury goods), its coastal position on the South China Sea providing access to the key trading routes with Europe, the capital Guangzhou (Canton) being the official trading port throughout the eighteenth century.[19] The characteristic silk designs of the Qianlong period (1736–95) that were made for export incorporated trailing stems and colourful flowers against a pale ground of silk taffeta (see Fig. 9.16). First the silk was painted with alum size to prevent colours from spreading and ensure adherence of the paint; the outline of the design was then drawn or printed in black ink or silverpoint. Vivid colours for the motifs were achieved by painting the design with opaque lead white before applying thick layers of colour on top. Pigments were derived from similar sources to those used for easel painting: orpiment for yellow, malachite for green and vermilion for red, for example. Sometimes touches of silver were added to emphasise the outlines of the motifs and highlight other details.

The trip from London to Guangzhou and back took around 14 months. Such a delay between placing an order and receipt of goods meant that Chinese silks for export were not subject to the same seasonal variations in design as those made in Europe. As with other consumer goods produced in China for export, over time designs were adapted to suit the tastes of European customers, with East India Company employees supplying Chinese artisans with patterns for them to interpret within a Chinese visual repertoire. Similarly, European manufacturers, in response to the increasing competition from foreign goods, incorporated elements of Chinese design into their own textiles. This exchange of visual vocabulary can make identifying the country of origin of a silk difficult, although Chinese silks were woven on a wider loom than those in Europe, producing finished bolts of fabric around 20 cm wider.[20] They also tended to incorporate contrasting colour threads within the selvedges, but such details are invisible in painted portraits.

While China was the source for some of the finest silks, India was best known for the quality of its cottons, which were highly prized throughout the eighteenth century. Although produced in a range of qualities and weights, some of the most exceptional were the gossamer-fine white muslins woven in Bengal, an industry centred around the city of Dhaka (formerly known as Dacca). The area had long been renowned for its cottons, which were described by the Romans as 'woven air'.[21] A 20-yard (18 m) length of such fabric could take six months to weave, a task exclusively undertaken by men and requiring a sufficiently high humidity to avoid breaking the delicate cotton threads. Intricate patterns could be created using supplementary cotton wefts, a process known as *jamdani*. A formal sacque in the Historic Royal Palaces collection (Fig. 9.11) is unusual in combining a highly desirable and new fabric (Indian cotton muslin) with a style of dress that by this date (*c*.1780) had passed out of high fashion. The symmetrical box pleats at the upper back create an elegant fall of semi-transparent fabric, while the neckline is emphasised with silver lace. The delicate silver thread botanical embroidery was probably undertaken in India and uses

very pure silver. This element might have justified its suitability for an event at court, although wearing an imported fabric of this type is likely to have prompted disapproval from some, given that British-made silks were considered an important public demonstration of patriotism.[22] India was also known for its painted and printed chintzes, which were imported into Europe in great number.

Originating as a commercial enterprise set up to rival the trading companies of Portugal and the Netherlands, the British East India Company established its first factories in the Indian subcontinent during the seventeenth century. Within a century the Company had grown into an enormous organisation with its own armies that were deployed at the Battle of Plassey in 1757, after which the Company effectively seized control of textile production in Bengal as part of its system of colonial governance.[23] In the eighteenth century the term *Nawab* (often *Nabob* in Britain) was used to refer to the ruler of a princely state within the Indian subcontinent. In 1774 Queen Charlotte was presented with a variety of presents from the Nawab of Arcot, Mohammad Ali Khan Wallajah (1717–95), who worked closely with representatives from the British East India Company. Among the gifts were three chests containing 900 pieces of cloth.[24] Twenty years later, she recorded in her diary unpacking 'the Muslins sent by the Nabob of Arcot'.[25]

The Kashmir region of the Indian subcontinent had long been renowned for the quality of its fine woollen textiles intricately woven from Himalayan goat hair (*pashmina*), widely worn by both men and women and exported extensively throughout Asia, Russia and the Ottoman Empire for many centuries.[26] Expensive due to the labour-intensive weaving process (the finest could take 18 months to weave), such Kashmiri (anglicised to cashmere) scarves first arrived in Europe during the 1760s, with the trade monopolised by the British East India Company. By the early nineteenth century, they were considered a luxurious and versatile item of female dress, one of a woman's most valuable possessions. They were also a favoured wedding gift from husband to wife: Napoleon, for example, presented his second wife Marie Louise with 17 shawls upon their

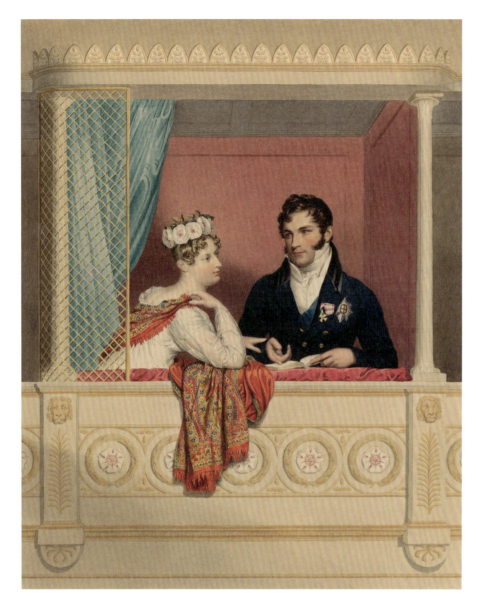

Fig. 9.12 William Thomas Fry (c.1787–1843) after George Dawe (1781–1829), *Princess Charlotte & Prince Leopold of Saxe Coburg*, 1818. Stipple with hand-colouring, 59.8 × 43.1 cm (sheet). RCIN 605459

Fig. 9.13 Indian, Shawl, *c*.1820s. Red woven cashmere embroidered with black wool and silver metal thread. Bath, Fashion Museum Bath, BATMC I.18.10

marriage in 1810. Valued for their lightweight warmth and extraordinary softness, the shawls were made in bright colours with characteristic border designs incorporating the teardrop-shaped Indian pine (*buta* or *boteh*). Such shawls provided an attractive contrast with the white neo-classical dresses fashionable at that time, as seen in a hand-coloured print of Princess Charlotte of Wales and her husband, Leopold I, in their box at Covent Garden Theatre, published in 1818, a year after her untimely death (Fig. 9.12). Perhaps the shawl was a gift from Leopold? The popularity of Kashmiri shawls in France increased after the French campaigns in Egypt (1798–1802), when officers brought them back to France. They were a favoured accessory of Empress Joséphine, who 'possessed three to four hundred shawls; she sometimes had them made into gowns, or bed-quilts, or cushions for her dog'.[27] The most expensive were made using a time-consuming process known as twill-tapestry

weave (*kani*), with the whole design created on the loom with a separate spool (*tojli*) for each colour.[28] Such shawls were often woven in pairs so that the two pieces could be sewn back-to-back, thereby concealing the construction. A later method (known as *amlikar*), which was quicker, involved embroidering the pattern onto a plain ground with a needle.[29] This is the style shown in a shawl in the Fashion Museum Bath (Fig. 9.13): the red wool ground is embroidered with metal threads, incorporating the *boteh* border at each end.

Melchior Gommar Tieleman's portrait of the Duchess of Cambridge with her two children (Fig. 9.14) demonstrates how such items could be adapted into Western styles. Here the duchess's red dress has been constructed from a shawl very similar to that in Figure 9.13, and she has another in a contrasting white draped around her. While this may be an original Indian import, it could just as well be a European version, as by this date both British and French

Fig. 9.14  Melchior Gommar Tieleman (1784–1864), *Augusta, Duchess of Cambridge with Prince George and Princess Augusta of Cambridge*, 1823. Oil on canvas, 177.9 × 126.0 cm. RCIN 407128

manufacturers had begun to capitalise on the popularity of Kashmiri scarves by producing imitation versions, which were machine-woven and used different fibres. The Scottish city of Paisley, long established as a centre for woollen textiles, became so associated with the style during the nineteenth century that the traditional *boteh* is widely known as paisley today, as are the scarves themselves.

Textiles from China were imported to Europe via the Indian depots of the East India Trading Companies, which also sold Indian textiles into China. Given the overlapping nature of such trade networks and the combined practices of sharing patterns and imitation, a similarity in design from disparate geographical regions is evident. Moreover, 'India silk' was a term used to refer to all silks traded by the East India Company, including those originally made in China.[30] In Britain, protectionist policies designed to safeguard the livelihoods of domestic textile manufacturers put limitations on the importation of foreign cottons and silks, requiring all textiles from Eastern ports be re-exported to other countries in Europe and North America rather than sold in Britain, with punishments such as fines and the seizure of goods for those found distributing or selling. Although legislation on selling imported printed cottons was repealed in 1774, policies relating to foreign silks remained in place until the 1820s. To get around this, smuggling increased and a significant trade in illicit goods developed, with contraband sold 'under the counter' rather than through public display.[31] However, although a large volume of such goods was seized (particularly 'Indian handkerchiefs', which were cheap and therefore available to a broad section of society), it was only the sellers who were prosecuted, with the people actually wearing foreign silks exempt.

The prevalence of foreign silks in British museum and private collections today attests to their widespread popularity in the eighteenth century. Eva-Maria Veigel, for example, wife of David Garrick (see Fig. 1.18), owned a hand-painted Chinese silk sacque dating from the early 1760s (Fig. 9.15). Designed to be worn over a square hoop, it would have been appropriate for formal daywear, retaining the triple-sleeve ruffle of the previous decade but incorporating the buttoned stomacher fashionable in the

1760s. The Garricks also owned a set of Indian chintz bed hangings made in the early 1770s, sent to thank Garrick for supplying plays to be performed in Calcutta (Kolkata). Although initially confiscated by customs, they were subsequently released after a protracted correspondence between Garrick and the government officials, and ended up hanging in the Garricks' villa in Hampton.[32]

A reduced version after François-Hubert Drouais's well-known portrait of Madame de Pompadour shows her wearing a beautiful gown made of a floral material (Figs 9.16 and 9.17).[33] Although by this date it was common practice for European designers to copy imported textiles, the sitter's position as patron of the French East India Company (*La Compagnie des Indes Orientales*) might suggest the fabric was imported and made up into a sacque in France. Opinions vary, however, as to whether this is a painted silk from China or a printed chintz from India.[34] Among the possessions recorded in Madame de Pompadour's posthumous inventory are '*une autre robbe et son jupon de satin des Indes, fond blanc à bouquets peints*' ('another dress with a skirt of Indian satin, white background with painted bouquets').[35] Indian here is likely to refer to it having been imported via the East India Company rather than necessarily being made in the country.

In the eighteenth century, the reasons why people from one culture adopted and integrated elements of dress from another were multifaceted and complex. Interpretations range from it being a demonstration of power or deliberate subjugation to a form of fetishised 'othering'. Some may have worn such styles to indicate their worldliness and education, others as a form of self-expression, maybe as an illustration of an artistic or unconventional mind, or an unwillingness to conform to European expectations. Explanations related to physical comfort and pure aesthetic appeal when contrasted with established cultural practices within the wearer's own country must also be considered. Some – perhaps all – of these factors may have played a part in the widespread adoption of garments and textiles from outside Britain during a period of increasing globalisation that saw the exchange of ideas and goods becoming ever more complex and multilayered.

# 10
# Walking Pictures

*… the description I promised you of the Russian masquerade …*
*Lady Betty Spencer, like Rubens's wife (not the common one*
*with the hat), had all the bloom and bashfulness and*
*wildness of youth … Lord Delawar was an excellent mask,*
*from a picture at Kensington of Queen Elizabeth's porter.*

HORACE WALPOLE, 1755[1]

Masquerades were a popular form of entertainment throughout the eighteenth century, presenting attendees with an opportunity to diverge from fashionable dress and sometimes conceal their true identity in the process. Whereas borrowing elements of dress from other countries provided one source of inspiration, another was found by looking back at the historical clothing worn in Britain. Appearing as a character from history was one option, with English and Scottish royalty a popular choice, best known through William Shakespeare's plays. At a masquerade hosted by the Duchess of Norfolk in February 1742, Horace Walpole recounted seeing:

> five hundred persons, in the greatest variety of handsome and rich dresses I ever saw … There were dozens of ugly Queens of Scots … The Princess of Wales [Augusta] was one, covered with diamonds, but did not take off her mask: none of the Royalties did … But the two finest and most charming masks were their Graces of Richmond, like Harry the Eighth and Jane Seymour: excessively rich, and both so handsome![2]

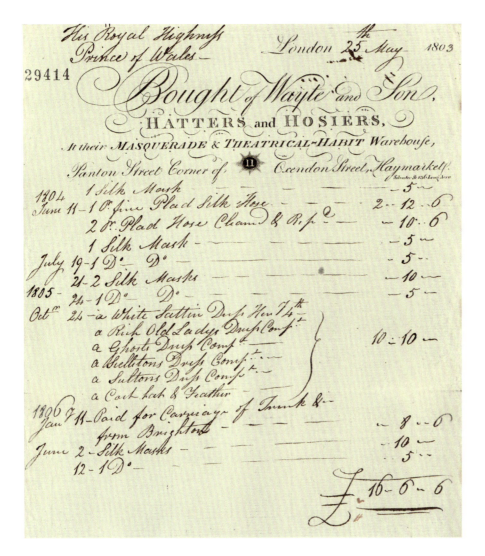

PREVIOUS PAGE
Detail of Fig. 10.3

Fig. 10.1 Bill from Wayte and Son for supplying masks and masquerade dress to George, Prince of Wales, 25 May 1803.
RA GEO/MAIN/29414

Mary, Queen of Scots was considered a tragic heroine, which, combined with a distinctive iconography incorporating the 'Marie Stuart' cap (a lace-edged heart-shaped headdress, flattering to eighteenth-century eyes), explains her continued popularity as a masquerade dress character. Sometimes the choice of person inferred a deeper meaning. In 1770 Maria Waldegrave and the Duke of Gloucester (younger brother of George III) attended a masquerade as Elizabeth Woodville and Edward IV. This must have been intended as a reference to their clandestine and unauthorised marriage four years earlier, Edward IV and Elizabeth having also married in secret, in 1464.

While many people would have had their masquerade dress created especially for the event, hiring an outfit from one of the theatrical costume shops was another option. In London these were based around the Covent Garden area. Henry Wayte owned a 'masquerade and theatrical-habit warehouse' in Panton Street and regularly supplied the Prince of Wales (a great enthusiast of fancy dress) with black silk masks, 'character masks' and 'noses', as

well as full fancy-dress outfits. In February 1802 the prince acquired a black friar's outfit complete with rosary and cross, as well as two 'rich old ladys dresses' and ten pairs of fine silk hose ('extra long').[3] In 1803 his choices were eclectic, including 'a white sattin dress Henry 4th', 'a ghosts dress', 'a scellitons dress' and 'a sultons dress' (Fig. 10.1).[4]

In his account of the masquerade in 1742, Walpole notes, 'There were quantities of pretty Vandykes, and all kinds of old pictures walked out of their frames.'[5] To eighteenth-century eyes Sir Anthony van Dyck's portraits painted at the court of Charles I during the 1630s evoked a nostalgic and romanticised vision of Britain, making them a significant source of inspiration. By the mid-eighteenth century sufficient time had passed for the dress of this period to seem beautiful rather than simply outdated. Moreover, Van Dyck's tendency to distil the essence of the fashion of his time into a simplified and generalised version of contemporary clothing probably helped make it more palatable to later audiences. While this so-called 'Vandyke dress' (the anglicised spelling is used to differentiate the eighteenth-century version from its seventeenth-century prototype) was popular for masquerades, its impact can be seen most clearly in portraiture.

In Sir Joshua Reynolds's 1768 portrait of David Garrick (Fig. 10.2) the actor is depicted as the jealous Kitely in Ben Jonson's *Every Man in His Humour*, first published in 1601 but performed throughout the seventeenth century and revived by Garrick in 1751. Garrick was considered something of a fashion authority, providing advice to members of the aristocracy on what dress might be most suitable for important occasions. Here his clothing is based on that worn by Van Dyck's English sitters during the 1630s: a brown silk satin doublet with paned sleeves, trimmed with silver braid and worn with a matching brown cloak. The spiky lace collar, although broadly similar to seventeenth-century styles and incorporating authentic details such as the tiny tassels on the drawstrings, is much smaller than the expansive falling bands most frequently painted by Van Dyck, which covered the shoulders. The convention for actors to be depicted in historical fancy dress

is logical: the portrait can be read on two levels, as a record of both the actor and his character. However, the practice of dressing up in historical dress for a portrait was not limited to those whose profession it was to impersonate others.

Johan Joseph Zoffany's group portrait of George III and Queen Charlotte with their six eldest children (Fig.10.3) is clearly intended to draw parallels with Van Dyck, most obviously through the use of Vandyke dress. The two older sons wear red and gold suits (consisting of doublet, breeches and cloak) closely modelled on those worn by George Villiers, 2nd Duke of Buckingham, and his brother, Lord Francis Villiers, in a double portrait by Van Dyck (Fig. 10.4). By 1770, this portrait (painted for Charles I in 1635, and subsequently recovered at the Restoration) was hanging in Queen Charlotte's apartments at Buckingham House. Zoffany's attention to the details of historical dress even stretches to the aglets around the waist of each doublet and the elaborate ribbon shoe roses. However, the colourful hose have been exchanged for white silk stockings. In keeping with eighteenth-century notions of sensibility, Princes George and Frederick link arms and their facial expressions are less solemn than those of the Villiers brothers.

A preparatory oil sketch by Zoffany (Fig. 10.5) reveals that the clothing worn by the king and queen was originally modelled on that of Charles I and Henrietta Maria in Van Dyck's celebrated family portrait, painted in 1632 and known at the time as 'The Greate Peece' (Fig. 10.6). There are also similarities in pose (both queens hold their youngest child on their laps) and setting (column, swagged curtain, table set with crown to one side). In Zoffany's sketch George III's outfit is almost identical to that of his ancestor: the doublet and breeches of black silk with touches of silver, the cloak lined with pink silk, pale-coloured stockings and shoes. Charlotte wears a yellow gown with a white collar similar to that worn by Henrietta Maria. However, in the final portrait the colours of each outfit have been transformed, the queen's from yellow to white, the king's from black to sapphire blue. This particular shade of blue was more frequently seen in Van Dyck's portraits of female sitters, but it was a

fashionable shade for all during the second half of the eighteenth century, in part due to the development of new blue dyes (see Chapter 1).[6]

The outfits worn by the female figures in Zoffany's finished portrait, who are grouped together on the right, are less historically accurate than those worn by the males. While Queen Charlotte's white dress does incorporate the same style of bulbous sleeves seen in Henrietta Maria's gown, the ruff encircling Charlotte's neck is an imaginative addition, replacing Henrietta Maria's falling collar of fine lace. Stiffly pleated ruffs of this kind had long passed out of fashion by the time Van Dyck was working in England,

OPPOSITE
Fig. 10.3  Johan Joseph Zoffany (1733–1810),
*George III and Queen Charlotte and their Six
Eldest Children*, 1770.
Oil on canvas, 104.9 × 127.4 cm. RCIN 400501

BOTTOM
Fig. 10.5  Johan Joseph Zoffany (1733–1810),
*George III and Queen Charlotte and their Six
Eldest Children*, c.1769–70.
Oil on canvas, 27.9 × 41.2 cm. RCIN 400669

BELOW, RIGHT
Fig. 10.4  Sir Anthony van Dyck (1599–1641),
*George Villiers, 2nd Duke of Buckingham and
Lord Francis Villiers*, 1635.
Oil on canvas, 137.2 × 127.7 cm. RCIN 404401

BELOW, LEFT
Fig. 10.6  Sir Anthony van Dyck (1599–1641), *Charles I
and Henrietta Maria with their Two Eldest Children*, 1632.
Oil on canvas, 303.8 × 256.5 cm. RCIN 405353

there was rarely a requirement for it be copied exactly and instead an artist was expected to adjust elements as required to fit with a more modern aesthetic. When commissioning a portrait of her granddaughter from the artist Isaac Whood in 1734, the Duchess of Marlborough wrote:

> I desire that Mr. Whood will condescend to copy that picture that was done by Vandyke for that charming Countess of Bedford in the Gallery. The white satin clothes and the posture I would have just the same for you … And if you think Vandyke's dress too old-fashioned for this age, he may imitate the Countess of Bedford's as to the white satin and alter the sleeve and waist and make the hair as you like to have it.[7]

Wide skirts for women were fashionable during both the mid-seventeenth and mid-eighteenth centuries. However, when taking inspiration from portraits of the Caroline court the natural waistline of that era was lowered to fit with a mid-eighteenth-century silhouette, which incorporated a longer torso. The end result was sometimes an uncomfortable marriage of styles, as demonstrated in a portrait of Mary, Duchess of Ancaster, after Thomas Hudson (Fig. 10.7). Here the ankle-length bell-shaped skirt of the 1750s when paired with the voluminous sleeves of the 1630s appears unbalanced, and the clothing is not helped by the sitter's awkward pose.

While it is tempting to suggest that Zoffany's group portrait may have had an influence on George III's sons maintaining an interest in Vandyke dress into adulthood, in reality this was probably more a reflection of how integrated it had become into contemporary fashion. In 1781 Prince Frederick wrote to his older brother from Hanover (where he was studying at the University of Göttingen), asking that Prince George order him a 'Vandyke dress of white sattin waistcoat and breeches with a pink cloak; the hat must be white sattin with a fine plume of feathers', a request that was dutifully fulfilled.[8] A few years later Prince George acquired from Davies,

although they were revived as part of high fashion in the mid-eighteenth century, explaining its inclusion here. The light blue dress worn by the young Princess Charlotte has again been altered from that in the original sketch, which is much more characteristic of the Stuart era in both design and fabric. In the final painting the elbow-length paned sleeves have been shortened and the plain dark silk swapped for one woven with a floral design more typical of the rococo. Similarly, the frock and cap worn by the infant Princess Augusta (carried by the queen) are entirely eighteenth-century in conception, the gown made with short, capped sleeves and coloured underlayer; in the sketch she is shown in a simple white swathe of fabric.

Such mixing of old and new was not uncommon. In instances where a portrait was to be based on another,

simply intended to depict the prince in standard Vandyke dress rather than as a character from literature. Although perhaps representing a real masquerade outfit, it may just be a nod to what had become, by this date, an established artistic convention.

The historical portrait that had the most influence on women's fancy dress was Peter Paul Rubens's portrait of his second wife Helena Fourment (Fig. 10.10), which provided the inspiration for numerous masquerade costumes and portraits from the 1730s to the 1780s. In the eighteenth century it had been in the collection of Sir Robert Walpole (who attributed the painting to Van Dyck) and hung at Houghton Hall in Norfolk. Cosway's portrait of Elizabeth Milbanke, Viscountess Melbourne, is a late example of this homage to Rubens (Fig. 10.11). In both portraits the women wear gowns of black silk, the square neckline decorated with a central jewelled brooch, multilayered sleeves, a standing collar and a large black

Son and Co. a 'Vandyke white silk waistcoat embroidered in pink ribbon & silver spangles' as well as another 'Superfine short green Vandyke waistcoat'.[9] Whether these were intended as masquerade dress or evening wear is impossible to tell. However, an image of the Prince of Wales in Vandyke dress was circulated in a print by Louis Sailliar from *c*.1787 onwards, the pattern derived from a full-length drawing by Richard Cosway. A number of copies of the same portrait type also exist in miniature (Fig. 10.8). In slightly later versions, the prince wears a standing collar and high-necked doublet more characteristic of the Jacobean reign (Fig. 10.9). From the late nineteenth century, portraits of the Prince of Wales dressed in this way are described as depicting him as Florizel from Shakespeare's *A Winter's Tale*, an association based on his affair with the actress Mary Robinson, best known for playing Perdita, Florizel's love interest. However, it is likely that in his original drawing Cosway

hat, worn tilted at an angle. In Cosway's interpretation the arrangement of the hands, and specifically the fingers of the left hand, is very similar. The book she is holding appears to have been an afterthought of the artist, having been painted over the layers beneath; without it, the reference to the earlier portrait would be even more striking.[10]

Although Vandyke dress was a fashionable mode across the board, for the Hanoverians, creating a visual link with the Stuart court through clothing was also a means of demonstrating their ancestry and right to rule, George I's mother, Sophia of Hanover, being the niece of Charles I. Similarly, for the aristocracy, allusions to portraits within their own collections (as requested by the aforementioned Duchess of Marlborough, for example) would have emphasised the length of their dynasty. Such visual quotations also suggested an educated and accomplished mind, while simultaneously offering an opportunity to break away from the conventions of everyday attire, escaping – albeit temporarily – into a world of dressing up and fantasy.

By the early nineteenth century, the clothing of the Elizabethan era had begun to displace that of the Caroline court as the historical influence of choice, a situation propagated by the novels of Sir Walter Scott, which encouraged a fascination with knightly chivalry. George IV's coronation in 1821 was the grandest demonstration of this (see Fig. 8.24), the clothing sixteenth-century in conception and the spectators reminding one commentator of 'the days of jousts and tournaments'.[11]

The inspiration for the clothing of processional attendees at the coronation was also drawn from abroad, with pages wearing 'Henri Quatre coats of scarlet, with gold lace, blue sashes, white silk hose, and white rosettes'.[12] In France, clothing from the reign of Henri IV (1589–1610) had long been the overriding historical influence at court. Widely considered an enlightened monarch, comparisons with Henri IV were made upon Louis XVI's accession in 1774. A series of court balls during the 1770s and 1780s saw attendees dressed in clothing of the late sixteenth century. For one ball held in honour of the Grand Duke of Russia, Marie-Antoinette dressed as Henri IV's mistress,

*PL. CXL.*

*Dresses of the 16.ᵗʰ & 17.ᵗʰ Centuries.*

Fig. 10.12 Joseph Strutt (1749–1802), 'Dresses of the 16th and 17th Centuries', from Strutt, *A Complete View of the Dress and Habits of the People of England*, vol. II, London, 1798, pl. CXL. RCIN 1075690

transmuted via books that documented the history of costume. The eighteenth century saw the first of such publications in England, the most influential being Thomas Jefferys's *A Collection of the Dresses of Different Nations Both Ancient and Modern, and More Particularly Old English Dresses after the Design of Holbein, Vandyck, Hollar*, published in four volumes between 1757 and 1772, with 480 plates and text in both English and French. Queen Charlotte owned a copy, which was sold after her death. More comprehensive surveys of the history of dress in England were compiled by Joseph Strutt, including *A Complete View of the Dress and Habits of the People of England*, published between 1796 and 1799 (Fig. 10.12). The author, who had worked as a painter of history subjects himself, gathered information from a wide range of sources and strove to represent a much broader section of society than just the nobility.

Not everyone considered Vandyke dress a good choice for portraiture. Upon seeing Zoffany's depiction of the royal family at the Royal Academy (see Fig. 10.6), Horace Walpole pronounced it 'ridiculous'. Thomas Gainsborough, favoured artist of George III and Queen Charlotte, similarly was not a fan of what he termed in 1771 'the ridiculous use of fancy dresses in portraits'.[15] After Gainsborough's portrait of Frances Catherine Legge, Countess of Dartmouth, in fancy dress was criticised for its lack of likeness, the artist wrote to Lord Dartmouth requesting the opportunity to repaint it, suggesting that had he been allowed to represent the sitter 'dressed as her ladyship goes, no fault … would have been found with it'.[16] In a subsequent letter he describes fancy dress as 'a fictitious bundle of trumpery of the foolish painter's own inventing', warning of its tendency to overwhelm a handsome face, and remarks that 'Nothing can be more absurd than the foolish custom of painters dressing people like scaramouches and expecting the likeness to appear'.[17] As is often the case, Gainsborough's most successful portraits are those that reference historical precedents in a subtle way, modulated through the lens of contemporary fashion.

Sir Joshua Reynolds's attitude to portraying his sitters in fanciful attire changed over the course of his career.

Gabrielle d'Estrées, for whom the king had secured a divorce from his first wife, although d'Estrées was to die before the couple could marry. Marie-Antoinette's white dress had suitably historical puffed and slashed sleeves, while her black hat was adorned with the famous 141-carat Regent diamond.[13] Perhaps it is surprising that this fashion so associated with the French monarchy, and later called *le style troubadour*, was maintained after the Revolution in France, with Empress Joséphine being an influential proponent. Her coronation gown, memorably recorded in Jacques-Louis David's enormous painting in the Musée du Louvre, Paris,[14] incorporated paned upper sleeves and a standing collar of spiky lace, based on a style popularised in France by Henri IV's second wife, Marie de' Medici, and sometimes termed a Medici collar.

While portraits – both painted and printed – provided the primary source material for historical dress, an understanding about the clothing of the past was also

Fig. 10.13 Tommaso Piroli (1752–1824) after Friedrich Rehberg (1758–1835), *Emma, Lady Hamilton's Attitudes, Plate III*, 1794. Engraving and etching on ochre prepared paper, 26.3 × 20.1 cm (sheet). RCIN 655736

Despite having painted a number of sitters in a form of Vandyke dress, by the late 1770s Reynolds had started to distance himself from the style, probably because of its prevalence, considering it an easy shortcut employed by artists that deceived the viewer into thinking a painting better than it really was. By 1776 Reynolds was recommending, as President of the Royal Academy, that an artist 'dresses his figure something with the general air of the antique for the sake of dignity, and preserves something of the modern for the sake of likeness', remarking that the familiarity of modern dress 'is sufficient to destroy all dignity'.[18] His later portraits tend to encapsulate this vision, with a generalised arrangement of drapery that evokes classical statuary but also conforms to the ideal contemporary silhouette, paired with fashionable hairstyles and cosmetics.

One of the people most associated with encouraging the popularity of the neo-classical aesthetic in England was Emma Hart, an actress from humble birth who later became Lady Hamilton through her marriage to the diplomat and antiquarian Sir William Hamilton. The couple lived together in Naples during the 1780s and it was there she became famous for her dramatic performances (known as 'Attitudes'), which recreated poses seen on Greek vases in Sir William's collection. Her clothing included loose-fitting but revealing garments and shawls, and the performances were staged in front of selected guests both in Italy and after the couple returned to London. A set of engravings by Tommaso Piroli depicting Hamilton's Attitudes was acquired by the Prince Regent in 1816 (Fig. 10.13), having purchased a set of satirical prints by James Gillray mocking the performances nine years earlier.

Outside the theatrical setting, classical dress was not typically worn as a form of fancy dress, the unstructured design making it difficult to keep in a decorous arrangement while dancing at a masquerade. Moreover, it was considered to lack the specificity required to allow the immediate identification of the intended character, aside from the obvious moon headdress to represent Diana. Antique-style clothing was incorporated into portraits, however, the result being more harmonious from the end of the eighteenth century onwards, as neo-classicism exerted its influence on everyday dress. In Peter Stroehling's portrait of Princess Mary (Fig. 10.14) the sitter's fashionable white chemise dress is stripped of almost all ornament, and the air of the antique exaggerated by including an unstructured piece of fabric tied under the bust. The design of the shoes also evokes Roman sandals, while her hair is knotted up in the antique manner. The end result is a figure that fits within the other neo-classical decorative elements on display, including a low relief of the princess's father, George III, crowned with a laurel wreath in the style of a Roman emperor. The fashion to dress *à la grecque* was more popular in France, particularly after the Revolution.

Even when historicised clothing was depicted by artists with accuracy, sitters rarely modified their hairstyle to match. Thus, George III wears his powdered wig with his 'Vandyke dress' (see Fig. 10.3) and Garrick does not wear

Fig. 10.14  Peter Edward Stroehling (1768–c.1826),
*Princess Mary*, 1807.
Oil on copper, 60.7 × 48.3 cm. RCIN 404866

OPPOSITE
Fig. 10.15  Frédéric Millet (1786–1859), *Maria Amalia,
later Queen Marie-Amélie of France*, 1828.
Watercolour on ivory, 8.1 × 6.9 cm. RCIN 420349

It seems likely that some sitters are wearing garments they owned or hired, perhaps for the explicit purpose of having a portrait painted. The similarity or repetition of certain garments, even across different artists, suggests the use of pattern books or shared drawings, with only the face painted from life, and the dress created in the artist's studio.

Originally conceived as a form of costume for a masque or portrait, over time details from historical dress were gradually integrated within fashionable clothing in the same way as fashions from overseas, with 'fancy dress' elements such as ribbons, feathers, spiky lace collars and pleated ruffs appearing in fashion plates and becoming part of everyday wear. It was a trend that would continue well into the nineteenth century.

A miniature dated 1828 serves as an illuminating demonstration of the manner in which various elements of dress from across different geographies and time periods were being imaginatively combined within one fashionable outfit by the end of our period. The sitter is Maria Amalia and the artist Frédéric Millet (Fig. 10.15). Born in Italy, the daughter of the King of Sicily, Maria had married the duc d'Orléans in 1809. After spending time in exile in London during Napoleon's return to power, she was permitted to go back to France and from 1830 ruled as the last Queen of the French. In this miniature (which shows no indication of being intended as fancy dress) she wears a black pelisse, the silk probably woven in France but likely to have been dyed with logwood imported from South America. The front of the garment is decorated with military frogging originally inspired by hussar dress, while the puffed upper sleeves are derived from so-called 'shoulder wheels' fashionable at the courts of Henri IV in France and Elizabeth I in England. The exaggeratedly tall ruff and matching lace cuffs are also fashions influenced by styles of the late sixteenth century. Around the sitter's neck is a cameo set with pearls, hung on a geometric gold chain, both inspired by antique designs, while on her head is a turban of gold striped silk, derived from Turkish dress. Finally, her body is encircled by a green cashmere scarf, its *boteh* design just visible at the bottom. Possibly of Indian origin, this may instead have been made in France in imitation of imported versions.

his hair longer on one side in a lovelock (see Fig. 10.2), as would have been fashionable at the Caroline court. Instead, it is curled over the ears in the manner of a wig, here left unpowdered. Neither Lady Milbanke (see Fig. 10.11) nor Queen Charlotte (see Fig. 10.3) wear their hair in the ringlets fashionable during the 1630s: rather, each has her hair arranged in an up-to-the-minute style consistent with the date of the portrait. Modifying hair and cosmetic conventions to match historical dress was one step too far for most people. Similarly, when playing specific characters from history on stage, actors often wore their hair in a contemporary style, although this practice was gradually reformed as theatre managers and costume designers strove for greater authenticity.

Although historical dress was actually worn in a masquerade setting, the question around whether the outfits depicted in paint existed in reality or were instead concoctions created entirely by the artist is hard to answer.

# 11

# Dressed for Battle

———————————

U niforms are not usually considered as fashion, yet their ubiquity in Britain during the eighteenth century, in both everyday life and portraits (Fig. 11.1), makes them impossible to ignore in a book covering Georgian dress, particularly given that many members of the royal family took a great interest in military clothing. Although uniforms – by definition – are designed to create uniformity rather than display individual taste, nevertheless those of the eighteenth century reflect many aspects of fashionable dress. Moreover, each officer was responsible for having his uniform made up and would have had the opportunity to express his own sense of fashionability through subtle differences in fabric and cut. Military dress also exerted an influence on fashionable dress for both men and women.

## UNIFORMS

On the smoke-filled battlefield a uniformly attired regiment had the obvious practical advantage of being able to differentiate between friend and foe. Uniforms also served a psychological purpose, contributing to the sense of a military family

PREVIOUS PAGE
Fig. 11.1  Henry Bone (1755–1834), *George IV when Prince of Wales*, 1805 (detail).
Enamel, 25.2 × 20.4 cm. RCIN 405173

Fig. 11.2  German School, *George II*, c.1740–50.
Oil on canvas, 76.3 × 64.0 cm. RCIN 403402

fashionable regiments were sometimes sold at auction to the highest bidder, while an officer could 'cash in' their commission on retirement. The high social status of the officer class meant that uniforms were considered a suitable alternative to court dress. For Queen Charlotte's Birthday Ball in January 1794, the Dutch fashion periodical *Kabinet van Mode en Smaak* (Cabinet of Fashion and Taste) reported that 'The Princes of Wales and York wore their Generals and the Duke of York his Admirals uniform'.[3] Visiting Bologna in 1745, the Italian traveller and author Giacomo Casanova (1725–98) wore a uniform of his own invention, 'white, the vest blue, a gold and silver shoulder knot … with my cockade and wearing a long false pigtail, I sallied forth'.[4]

## ARMOUR

Plate armour was rarely worn for battle in the eighteenth century. While it had historically provided protection against the sword or pistol, much greater thickness was required to defend against musket or cannon and the resulting weight hindered mobility, particularly for infantry, rendering it largely ineffective. Where armour was retained, usually only by the king or high-ranking officers, it served a ceremonial rather than defensive purpose. Consistent with this, armour continued to be represented in portraiture during the first half of the century: often only a breastplate, sometimes with pauldrons and vambraces for the shoulders and arms, as in the portrait of George II by an unknown artist (Fig. 11.2). George II welcomed his reputation of soldier-monarch, and as the last British monarch to lead his troops into battle (at Dettingen in 1743), he has greater credibility than most to be depicted in martial dress, although the fine lace cuffs worn here are more fashionable than practical. His wig, with its knotted ends, is in the campaign style associated with soldiers.

The one piece of armour that did continue to be widely worn by officers across Europe was the gorget. Originally a neck defence that could be attached to the close helmet, this gradually diminished in size until it became a crescent-shaped piece of metal, made of brass or silver, worn

with a common goal, while creating an intimidating sight for the enemy or an impressive view for spectators. With the spread of uniforms from military to civilian settings, and the increasingly refined tailoring techniques that mimicked fashionable styles, they became symbols of heroic masculinity, encapsulating a sense of glamour far removed from the practicalities of warfare.

The eighteenth century saw an explosion in the popularity of uniforms across Europe, reflected in increasingly systematised attire for military regiments, as well as the rise of civilian uniforms for courtiers. Throughout the Georgian period, the position of a military officer held significant social prestige. The exchange of a commission for money rather than merit was standard practice in Britain until the Cardwell Reforms of 1871,[2] with senior military positions up to the rank of colonel available to gentlemen of sufficient wealth and suitable social connection. Commissions for particularly

ROYAL, Regiment of HORSE GUARDS

suspended from a chain or ribbon and sometimes engraved. It served no practical purpose other than to distinguish rank and regiment.

## ROYALS AND UNIFORMS

A form of military uniform had first been worn by Parliamentarian forces in the 1640s, with the style of clothing for each regiment being dictated by the colonel responsible for recruiting and equipping the unit, after whom it was often named, with the colours of the coat's turnbacks and cuffs borrowed from the coat of arms of the colonel in question. Styles of uniform and the degree to which they were enforced therefore varied widely. It was not until the reign of George II that the first official pattern uniforms were introduced for the British army under royal authority. While his interest in fashion was limited, George II was fascinated by the intricacies of military dress and took personal responsibility for creating a codified system of clothing across the various regiments. Most took as their basis a red coat made of wool, with different regiments identified by the colour of the 'facings' – originally the lining of the coat revealed by turned-back lapel, skirt tails and cuffs – and 'lacings' – the military braid (often made of worsted) used to reinforce the edges of buttonholes, lapels and cuffs. A book produced in 1742, known as 'The Cloathing Book', is the earliest visual representation of what each regiment looked like. One of the rare copies is in the Royal Collection, this version depicting only the mounted (cavalry) regiments (Fig. 11.3). It gives an impression of the richness of the arms and horse accoutrements for all ranks, including saddle cloths decorated with the royal arms for the royal regiments. The uniforms were officially sanctioned in the first set of clothing regulations released in 1747 and formalised into the Royal Clothing Warrant issued on 1 July 1751.[5]

George II's third son William Augustus, Duke of Cumberland, who at the age of 19 had been appointed colonel of the regiment of Coldstream Guards, was similarly interested in military clothing. He is thought to be the patron responsible for instigating 'The Cloathing Book' and for commissioning the Swiss artist David Morier to record

the appearance of various Guards troops in a group of paintings still in the Royal Collection. The series is notable for its breadth of uniforms (grenadiers and cavalry, privates and officers, British and foreign allies), the accuracy with which the tiny differences in attire are recorded, and for showing soldiers from different angles so details of dress are visible. One example depicts Grenadiers of the 1st Royal, 2nd Queen's and 3rd Regiments of Foot, with facings of blue, sea green and buff respectively (Fig. 11.4). A number of regiments were given nicknames linked to their clothing, the 3rd Regiment being known as 'the Buffs', for example. As this painting records, breeches were red, except those of the royal regiments (here seen on the left), which were blue to match the blue facings. They were partially covered by protective gaiters of heavy linen, white for parades, darker for everyday use, which buttoned up the outer leg and were gartered below the knee. Morier takes care to show how coats could be worn in different ways: the soldier on the left has his open to reveal the matching red wool waistcoat and waistbelt worn beneath, whereas the other two are in 'marching order' with their waistbelts over the closed coat.[6] Orders of dress varied according to the weather and season. All three

ROYAL REGᵗ    QUEEN'S REGᵗ    3 REGIMENT

soldiers have hooked the fronts of the coat back to the tails to reveal the facing, which was more convenient for marching. Buttons of brass or pewter were not sewn directly to the coat or waistcoat but held in position by leather cords threaded through button loops on the inside, allowing them to be replaced easily or polished as necessary.

Grenadiers formed a company of elite infantry forces within a regiment: they were chosen from the tallest, bravest and most experienced troops. They stored their grenades in the larger leather side pouch, while the smaller pouch in front contained cartridges for the musket. Throwing grenades required an overarm movement, which was hampered by the traditional tricorne hat worn by soldiers, hence the development of the tall mitre caps seen here, with backgrounds to match the facings of the coat. The choice of embroidered mottoes and personal crests was at the discretion of the

commanding colonel until this was forbidden by the 1751 Royal Warrant, which required them to reflect instead the authority of the monarch. The special status of the three regiments illustrated above (see Fig. 11.4) granted them permission for distinctive badges on their caps: the king's cipher for the 1st Royal, Queen Caroline's cipher for the 2nd Queen's, and for the 3rd Regiment a green dragon associated with the royal arms of Elizabeth I.[7] The grenadier caps for officers could be even more ornately embroidered with metal threads and sequins (Fig. 11.5). The example here is from the 65th Regiment of Foot, raised in 1758. It also includes the white horse of Hanover and traces of the motto 'NEC ASPERA TERRENT' (Not even difficulties deter us), which appeared soon after the arrival of George I in England and is just visible above the white horse on each of the caps in Morier's painting. By the 1770s these distinctive embroidered grenadier caps had been replaced by black bearskins with metal plates in front, a forerunner of the familiar bearskin caps worn by the Foot Guards of the Household Division today.

Soldiers joining the lower ranks were provided with
uniforms annually on the accession date of the king,
although delays in delivery meant they often arrived late.
To cover the cost of clothing and other provisions, 25 per
cent of a soldier's daily pay was deducted.[8] Regimental
tailors (many of whom had previously worked in the
profession) were responsible for ensuring clothing fitted
appropriately and for recycling fabric efficiently, for
example remodelling the previous year's coats into
waistcoats. For the average foot soldier, the coat would be
made of livery cloth, most of which was sourced from south-
west England and dyed with madder. This produced a dull
brick red, the shade of which would have varied more than
paintings suggest. By contrast, uniforms for officers were
tailor-made to fit and paid for by the wearer, requiring a
separate private income. Officers would usually have both
full-dress and undress uniform; the former was worn
for formal or ceremonial occasions and much more richly
trimmed. In both cases the coat would have been made
of a finer-quality wool than those of other ranks, dyed in
the grain with imported cochineal instead of madder,
often multiple times, to produce an intense bright scarlet.
Whereas breeches and waistcoats for most soldiers were
made of wool, those for officers could be silk.

Charles Fitzroy, later 1st Baron Southampton, wears
the full-dress regimental coat of the 1st Foot Guards in his
portrait by Sir Joshua Reynolds (Fig. 11.6). It is heavily
decorated with gold braid, and the gold rope ('aiguillette')
on the right shoulder indicates his status as lieutenant
colonel. Looking closely at the painting reveals that at this
date the blue-coloured lapels were separately applied on
top of the red wool and not formed by folding back the
lining fabric. In a portrait by Morier (Fig. 11.7), the Duke
of Cumberland wears the same style of coat in recognition

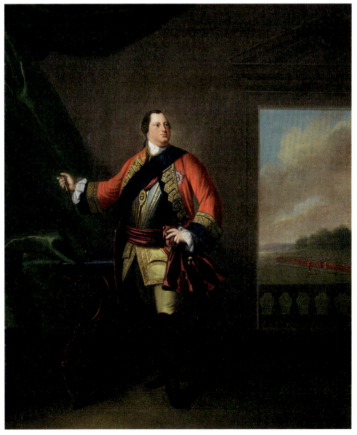

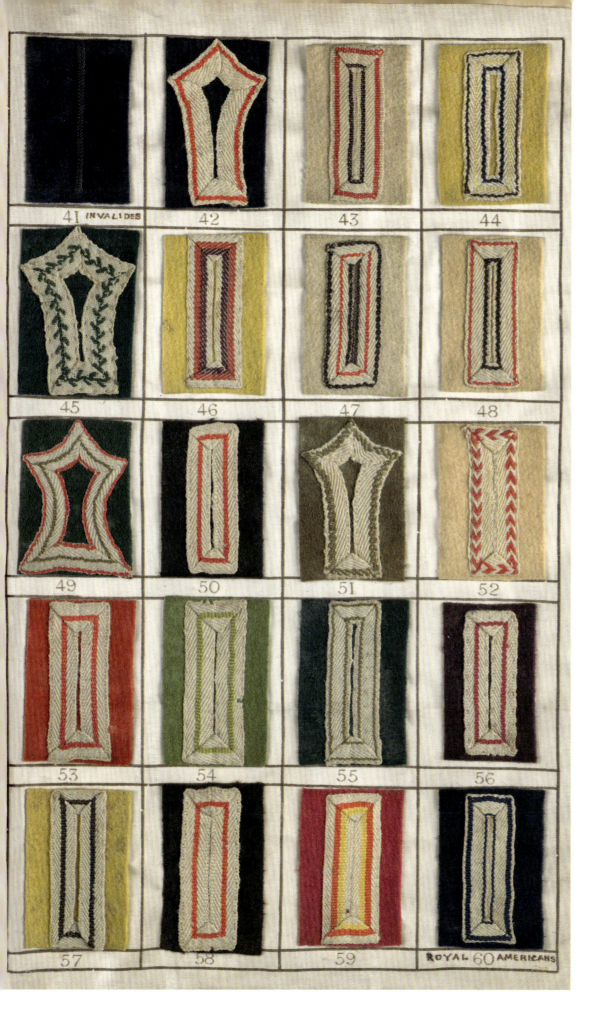

of his position as colonel of the 1st Foot Guards regiment, further emphasising his difference in rank by including chivalric orders (the riband and star of the Order of the Garter, and the badge of the Order of the Bath), and the crimson silk sash originally worn across the chest and later around the waist, which was a sign of command. Probably painted *c*.1750 to commemorate the duke's victory over the Jacobite rising at Culloden, this portrait was attacked at some point in its history (the date is unknown) with slashes in the shape of a St Andrew's Cross meeting at the sitter's heart.

Inheriting his grandfather's interest in uniforms, George III issued a more comprehensive warrant in 1768, which for the first time also regulated officers' dress. In December of that year the new system of 'facings and lacings' was recorded in a unique book for the king, with numbered buttonhole swatches for the 70 infantry regiments, each decorated with braid (Fig. 11.8).[9] The king is reported to have spent many hours memorising the different uniforms. Perhaps this is one of the books to which he referred.[10] The new coats, introduced in 1768, showed the influence of fashionable dress: more tightly cut, with turned-down collars (like the frock coat) and narrower lapels. This is the style of uniform in the portrait by Reynolds of Francis Rawdon-Hastings, 1st Marquess of Hastings, who had seen action in America between 1774 and 1779 (Fig. 11.9). He is shown in the undress uniform of a colonel and aide-de-camp to George III, although at this time (the painting was begun in 1789, the year of the first Regency crisis) he was a vocal champion of the Prince of Wales. By this date military breeches and waistcoats were white or buff, a fashion also seen in civilian clothing. The red coat is partially buttoned, with lapels turned back at the top and bottom to reveal blue facings. On his right shoulder is a gold-fringed epaulette, a new introduction in the 1768 warrant as a signal of rank for officers, replacing the previous shoulder knot.

George III took particular interest in the Royal Horse Guards regiment ('The Blues') for which he served as general and chose to relocate to newly built barracks near Windsor. The king's coat survives in the Historisches

Fig. 11.9 Sir Joshua Reynolds (1723–92), *Francis Rawdon-Hastings, Second Earl of Moira and First Marquess of Hastings*, 1789–90. Oil on canvas, 240.3 × 148.3 cm. RCIN 407508

Museum, Hanover: being a royal regiment, the uniform is blue rather than red.[11] In 1820 George IV elevated the Royal Horse Guards to the status of Household Cavalry, and the regiment still forms part of the monarch's personal troops today, having both a protective and ceremonial role. In 1969 they were merged with The Royal Dragoons to form The Blues and Royals, and in 1992 were united with The Life Guards to form the Household Cavalry.

The Prince of Wales, later George IV, adored the glamour of military dress and did not let the lack of an official role prevent him from appearing in uniform, or ordering uniforms to which he had no formal affiliation.[12] A portrait by the American artist Mather Byles Brown (Fig. 11.10) depicts the heir to the throne wearing a composite outfit probably designed by the prince himself, perhaps specifically for the portrait. The coat, similar to that of the Marquess of Hastings (see Fig. 11.9), in standard military scarlet with blue lapels, includes the buttons of a general officer showing a crossed sword and cannon within a wreath, although with non-standard gold lace decoration on the sleeves and buttonholes. The white sword belt is embroidered with the Prince of Wales's arms and feathers. He wears epaulettes on both shoulders, indicating an officer (despite no official title as such), and an elaborately fringed military sash of command around his waist.

Dragoons had originally been conceived as mounted soldiers who carried full-length muskets and fought on foot, combining the agility and speed of cavalry with the fire power of infantry. They were often issued with so-called 'dragon' firearms whose muzzle decoration created the impression of a fire-breathing dragon when fired. In 1783 the 10th Light Dragoons were renamed 'The Prince of Wales's Own' by George III and along with several other dragoon units were converted from Heavy to Light, with smaller horses and lighter weapons, which enabled greater mobility and speed. Soon after, the colour of their coat was changed from the standard red to a distinctive shade of blue. Prince George took great personal interest in the attire of his unit, which was known for its glamorous appearance and attracted fashionable young gentlemen to its ranks, notably Beau Brummell. Although George III would not

permit the heir to serve in campaigns himself, in 1793 the prince was appointed colonel of the regiment, something that caused him to feel 'boundless joy'.[13] In the same year he commissioned George Stubbs to record the uniform (Fig. 11.11). In this, the artist's only military painting, he depicts, from left to right, the ranks of mounted sergeant, trumpeter, sergeant and trooper. The sergeants can be identified by the chevrons on their right arm, although such marks of rank were not officially sanctioned for another decade. The trumpeter follows the tradition for musicians to be dressed in the facing colour of their regiment, so-called 'reversed colours'. Cut quite differently to the standard military dress, the new coat reached to the waist and concealed a flannel waistcoat beneath. The mounted officer and trumpeter illustrate how it was layered with a sleeveless 'shell' jacket on top, which was sharply cut away at the sides and made of the same fabric, similarly

Fig. 11.12  Sir William Beechey (1753–1839), *George IV when Prince of Wales*, 1803.
Oil on canvas, 128.4 × 101.7 cm. RCIN 400511

decorated with white cord loopings and buttons.[14] All ranks wear the new style of Tarleton helmet (unique to the British army, see below and Fig. 11.14), with a silver-plated peak, black bearskin crest and feather in the same mustard colour as the jacket facings. The trumpeter has a version with a white cap-line, which prevents it from being lost if knocked off. All four soldiers have breeches of white leather with white stockings, and the officer on horseback is in boots, while the others wear black leather shoes with short black gaiters and white stockings.

For some time, the uniform of the Light Dragoons had been influenced by hussar dress and in 1805 new uniforms were officially approved by the prince, with the unit renamed a year later as the 10th Royal Hussars, the first British hussar regiment.[15] The prince was evidently very

pleased with the style and was painted wearing it several times, including in a windswept and moody portrait by Sir William Beechey (Fig. 11.12) and an enamel miniature by Henry Bone after a portrait painted for the prince's lover, Maria Fitzherbert, by Elisabeth Louise Vigée Le Brun, which shows the complete outfit (see Fig. 11.1). The jacket, a version of which still survives today although without the Garter star, was made by J.C. Frank and is probably that acquired in February 1804 at a cost of £28 18s 6d (Fig. 11.13).[16] In the bill it is described as 'richly trim'd and ornamented with silver Russia Braid 5 rows of best Plated Buttons'. The braid is arranged to resemble the Prince of Wales's feathers at the wrist. The 'Yellow cassimere Collar & Cuffs' changed to royal red in 1811 with the start of the Regency, and in the same year the prince promoted himself to field marshal, the highest rank in the British army. In summer the fur-lined pelisse cloak was worn over the left shoulder (see Fig. 11.1): it is embroidered with the Garter star and heavily decorated with tassels and silver or white cord. Around the waist is a 'barrelled' sash made of red cords with tubular gold barrels and gold tassels, very characteristic of hussar dress. On a table alongside is the tall mirliton cap decorated with a white-over-red feather, which was an exotic alternative to the cylindrical fur 'busby', a style possibly named after the hatmaker supplying them (W. Busby on the Strand, London).[17] Another type of headdress worn during this period was the Tarleton cap (Fig. 11.14), characterised by its leather skull cap incorporating a peaked front, here wrapped with black silk and silver chain. Tight-fitting white pantaloons – leather or cotton depending on the season – had replaced breeches, and they were worn with tasselled Hessian boots. Just visible in both paintings is the hilt of the military sabre of the 10th Light Dragoons contained within its black steel scabbard. A surviving example intended as the pattern for the regiment is illustrated opposite (Fig. 11.15). Below the hilt is a blued-steel panel with military trophies and 'PW 10 LD' for Prince of Wales, 10th Light Dragoons.

In both portraits the prince is clean-shaven apart from his side whiskers. Officers in hussar regiments were the only British soldiers entitled to have moustaches (indeed it was

Fig. 11.13  J.C. Frank, Uniform jacket worn by George, Prince of Wales, 1804.

Wool, silk, silver lace and wooden buttons. RCIN 67195

Fig. 11.14  Mr Hanks, Tarleton cap worn by George, Prince of Wales, 1797.

Leather, silver, feather and bearskin. RCIN 67185

Fig. 11.15  James Woolley (active 1795), Stirrup-hilted military sabre and scabbard of the 10th Light Dragoons, c.1796.

Ferrous, iron, steel, blued steel, gold, copper alloy brass, wood and fish skin. RCIN 67186

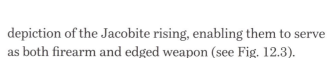

ordered by Ernest, Duke of Cumberland, in January 1807), which were worn fashionably drooping.[18] A flat pouch known as a sabretache, used to carry dispatches, was worn suspended from the sword waistbelt: a practical concession as the tight jackets and pelisses had no pockets. The sabretache also doubled as a convenient hard surface when writing correspondence. For officers these were elaborately embroidered with regimental devices in an array of stitches and metal threads: the example shown here includes the 'GP' cipher surrounded by military trophies and the Prince of Wales's feathers above (Fig. 11.16).

The eighteenth century saw advances in the technical capability of firearms, particularly the introduction of a helical groove inside the barrel: a practice known as rifling, hence the name rifle. This groove caused the bullet to spin as it was fired, making rifles more accurate than traditional smoothbore muskets such as the so-called 'Brown Bess' used by the British army for much of the eighteenth century. For close combat, weapons could be fitted with a socket bayonet attached to the end, as seen in Morier's

depiction of the Jacobite rising, enabling them to serve as both firearm and edged weapon (see Fig. 12.3).

While pistols employed during periods of warfare were utilitarian in appearance, others could be incredibly ornate, as demonstrated by the pair given to George IV by Louis XVIII in 1814 (Fig. 11.17). Described as 'very handsome' in an early inventory, they are an example of the rich presentation pieces produced in the Versailles factory under the directorship of Nicolas Noël Boutet (1761–1833). They incorporate a wide variety of neo-classical ornaments: the butt caps are cast from gold in the shape of a mask, the stock is made of ebony inlaid with rose-gold angels and centurions, while the double barrels are decorated with gold stars and palmettes. They come within a cased set that also includes matching ramrods and a powder flask.

Although scarlet remained the most popular colour for British infantry, and blue was generally adopted by cavalry units, rifle companies usually wore green uniforms, a tradition linked to 'Jäger' huntsmen raised in German-speaking states, which was imported to England as part of Hanoverian custom. Riflemen were increasingly used by the British army from 1800 onwards with the foundation of the 95th Rifle Regiment in that year. They fought separately from the main formation of red-coated soldiers, undertaking skirmishes and reconnaissance,

Fig. 11.18 Thomas Beach (1738–1806), *George Hanger, 4th Lord Coleraine*, c.1795–7. Oil on canvas, 76.3 × 63.7cm. RCIN 400554

Fig. 11.19 American, Flintlock rifle, c.1775–1803. Maple, steel, brass and silver. RCIN 61069

their green uniforms better enabling them to hide in undergrowth. The association of rifle regiments with the colour green continued, with the 95th Regiment (later renamed the Rifle Brigade) becoming the Royal Green Jackets in 1966.

George Hanger, 4th Lord Coleraine (1751–1824; Fig. 11.18), started his career in the Hessian Jäger company and with them sailed to North America. It was Hanger who presented the flintlock rifle above to George IV (Fig. 11.19). Constructed from maple wood and inlaid with a 13-point star engraved with the inscription 'UNITED STATES WE ARE ONE', it was originally made in c.1775 for Colonel John Thomas, a rifleman in command of the Spartan regiment of militia in South Carolina. Such so-called 'Pennsylvanian long rifles', developed by immigrant German and Austrian gunsmiths in the American colonies, were innovative for the length of the rifled barrel and the small calibre of the ball, which improved both the accuracy and velocity of the shot. They were, however, slower to load, making them more effective for precision shooting than traditional battlefield lines.

During the American Revolutionary War, Hanger fought in another green-coated regiment, the British Legion, which was raised in New York and was loyal to the Crown. He was responsible for leading the light dragoons within the unit, under the overall command of Lieutenant Colonel Banastre Tarleton (1754–1833), after whom this distinctive style of plumed and low-crowned helmet was named (see Fig. 11.14). The portrait of Hanger (see Fig. 11.18) shows him in the uniform of the British Legion: a short, tight-fitting dark green coat, with turn-down black collar and cuffs, trimmed with narrow gold braid for officers, with a plain broad sword-belt across the right shoulder. The gilt buttons and buttonholes were purely ornamental as the coat fastened with hooks and eyes. Although not shown here, the coat was worn with breeches of white buckskin or nankeen. After leaving the army, Hanger returned to a dissipated life in London as part of the Prince of Wales's set, from 1791 serving as his equerry, much caricatured for his affected manners, dissolute behaviour and financial straits. A macaroni in his youth (see Chapter 4), Hanger prided himself on being 'extremely extravagant' in his clothing and 'always handsomely dressed', claiming (inaccurately) to have worn, at a cost of £180, 'the first satin coat that had ever made its appearance in this country' to a Birthday Ball for the king.[19]

## NAVAL UNIFORMS

Despite important naval reforms led by Samuel Pepys in the late seventeenth century, and notwithstanding the fact that as an island Britain was more dependent on naval power than its Continental neighbours, at the beginning of the Georgian era the navy was not held in such high regard as the army. Sailors were frequently characterised as coarse and vulgar, their service driven by the prospect of bounty from captured ships rather than patriotism, and the social composition of naval officers tended to be less aristocratic than in the army, being more often drawn from professional or merchant backgrounds. In the 1740s, during the reign of George II, these attitudes started to change, leading to greater equivalence between the two

forces. Key to this was the development of naval uniforms for officers, which were introduced in 1748, late in comparison with other countries, including France. It had taken two years of discussion to agree on the final appearance of the uniform, with one (probably apocryphal) account attributing the eventual decision to George II, who is said to have been inspired by seeing the Duchess of Bedford in the park wearing a riding habit of blue faced with white.[20] The new uniforms were intended as a clear demonstration of an officer's rank, achieved through slight differences in the amount of gold lace and white cloth, and the arrangement of buttons. Regulations were frequently reissued, with notable revisions introduced during the reign of George III in 1787 and 1795, and then by the Prince Regent in 1812. Uniforms followed the broad lines of fashion, becoming more closely fitted towards the end of the eighteenth century like the coats of the army, with tighter sleeves. The shade of blue also darkened, becoming closer to the colour we recognise as navy today. This reflected a broader preference for more sombre shades in men's fashion. The wool fabric was given a felted finish, which increased its resistance to water, although the use of imported (thereby unpatriotic) superfine wool from Spain was criticised.[21]

Naval officers were issued with two forms of uniform, one for full-dress occasions, the other for undress (except between 1767 and 1774, when the dress coat was temporarily abolished). Undress was based on the frock coat, comfortable and practical to wear daily onboard ship, while full-dress was more like court dress, its splendour designed to represent the magnificence of the monarch when serving overseas and reflect individual status. Uniforms were intended to emphasise the clear distinction between junior officers (lieutenant, captain, commander) and the more senior flag officers (rear admiral, vice admiral and admiral). Subtle differences were also linked to experience. Modifications introduced in 1787, for example, indicated whether a captain had more than three years' service: white lapels on the undress frock instead of blue and buttons grouped into sets of three. Warrant officers were a separate category of sailors with specialisms such

as surgeon or carpenter. In recognition of their importance they were granted a blue uniform in 1787, although their lower status was clearly indicated by its plain appearance and the lack of distinction between full-dress and undress.

Unlike in the army, official uniforms were not defined for lower ranks of seamen until 1857, although a system of selling ready-made clothing ('slops') on board was in operation, to provide sailors with appropriate garments at a reasonable price. These were acquired by the purser from a contractor ('slopseller') and issued from the slop chest. This resulted in a recognisable style of dress frequently represented in prints of the period, such as *The Welch Sailor's Mistake, or Tars in Conversation* by Thomas Rowlandson, which plays on the established stereotype of the coarse and weather-beaten sailor (Fig. 11.20). All five sailors are clothed in the style of wide-legged trousers worn by seamen, quite different from traditional breeches or the new pantaloons introduced at around this date. Here they reach the ankle, although knee-length versions were also popular. The fact that most seamen went barefoot – to ensure greater grip when climbing rigging or on a slippery wet deck – may have influenced their adoption of trousers. The short single-breasted jacket in blue, red or brown is typical, as is the brightly coloured patterned neck scarf and round hat. Checked and striped fabrics were popular for trousers and shirts, usually of linen or, later, cotton. Many sailors would have made their own clothes on board, sewing being a necessary skill to repair canvas sails in order that the ship be self-sufficient on long voyages away from port. Textiles would have been important assets seized from defeated ships.

The rank of midshipman provided early training for life at sea and was the first step on the ladder to a commission. Midshipmen were usually young gentlemen who started their naval careers between the ages of 12 and 14. They ranked above the positions of rating and petty officer and were the most junior rank to be covered by the 1748 regulations. The midshipman's uniform consisted of a long single-breasted plain frock coat of blue wool, with brass buttons but none of the gold lace that marked an officer, worn with white trousers or breeches,

white waistcoat and neckcloth. This is what Prince William (later William IV) wears in his portrait by Thomas Gainsborough, produced as part of the family series (Fig. 11.21), which was painted in 1782 *in absentia* while the prince was at sea: he had joined the Royal Navy three years earlier, at the age of 13. Clearly depicted is the distinctive white patch on the collar, originally part of the white velvet lining visible when the collar was worn down. This was known as the 'weekly account' for its ability to indicate a wearer's cleanliness during uniform inspections.[22] A more complete representation of the prince's midshipman uniform is shown in an engraving by Francesco Bartolozzi after a painting by Benjamin West, which portrays him on board HMS *Prince George* en route to the Caribbean (Fig. 11.22). The prominence of the large sword is deliberate, it being the mark of a gentleman and an important symbol to distinguish the junior officer from the other ratings. In reality, a dagger known as a dirk was usually carried instead. Not visible in either picture are the three brass buttons trimming each cuff, supposedly

Fig. 11.21 Thomas Gainsborough (1727–88), *Prince William, later Duke of Clarence*, 1782.
Oil on canvas, 59.3 × 44.1 cm. RCIN 401010

Fig. 11.22 Francesco Bartolozzi (1727–1815) and Paul Sandby (1731–1809) after Benjamin West (1738–1820), *Prince William, later William IV*, 1782.
Engraving with stipple, etching and aquatint, 63.9 × 49.3 cm (sheet). RCIN 605494

to stop the wiping of noses on sleeves.[23] Both George III and the young prince were keen that he not receive special treatment, and he appears to have dressed exactly like any other midshipman, one early biography remarking that he 'never [wore] any other dress than his uniform, and his star and garter only when receiving addresses, or on any other public occasion'.[24]

While keen to follow convention at the start of his military career, Prince William developed a concern that the navy keep pace with other fashionable military units. When commanding HMS *Andromeda* in 1788 he established his own specific regulations for his crew,[25] and in 1814 attempted to introduce fashionable components such as pantaloons and gold-topped Hessian boots into the official naval uniform.[26] These plans, which

would have brought it into line with some of the more glamorous army regiments, were rejected by the Admiralty. In general, the dress for naval officers was rather old-fashioned compared with that of the army, which was known for the elegant appearance and social lifestyle of its 'regimentals' when not fighting abroad.

Edward, Duke of York, brother of George III, wears naval uniform in his portrait by Pompeo Batoni (Fig. 11.23), painted in 1764 while the sitter was visiting Rome. He was the first member of the royal family to undertake a Grand Tour to Italy. The duke had joined the navy at the age of 19, commanding HMS *Phoenix* in the Bay of Biscay during the Seven Years' War, being promoted to rear admiral (1761), then vice admiral (1762), although by the time of this portrait he had resigned from active command with the

BELOW, AND DETAIL RIGHT
Fig. 11.23 Pompeo Girolamo Batoni (1708–87), *Edward, Duke of York*, 1764.
Oil on canvas, 137.9 × 100.2 cm. RCIN 405034

Fig. 11.24 Buttons, Royal Naval uniform pattern, *c*.1748–87.
Ivory faced with brass, 2.1 cm and 1.5 cm (diameter). London, National Maritime Museum, NMM UNI5901

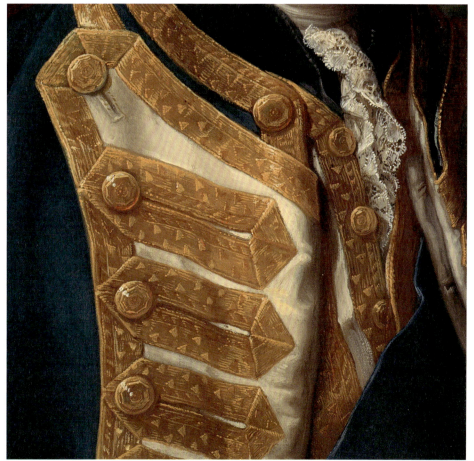

end of the war. He is, however, still shown in the undress uniform of a flag officer, according to the first pattern in use from 1748 to 1767. The blue coat has broad white facings at the lapels and cuffs, each decorated with heavily laced buttonholes. Batoni includes tiny details such as the pattern stamped on the buttons: an octagon surrounding a stylised Tudor rose (Fig. 11.24). The white waistcoat also has two rows of gold lace down the front and around the pocket flaps. The duke wears a wig arranged in a black silk bag, with the ribbon brought round to the front. A tricorne hat rests on the table nearby, with the black Hanoverian cockade on the left side. Full-dress uniform for flag officers at this date was even more richly laced than that shown here. This is one of three versions of this portrait in the Royal Collection, the other two showing slight variations in the arrangement of the finely painted lace at the neck and cuffs.[27]

John Bentinck was promoted to captain during the Seven Years' War, when he oversaw the successful capture of several French ships loaded with cargo, including the dye pigment indigo. In a portrait by Mason Chamberlin (Fig. 11.25) a diagram on the unrolled paper in front of him is a reference to Bentinck's important nautical innovations. In 1773 he collaborated with Benjamin Franklin on scientific experiments at sea (such as testing the ability of oil to calm waves) and was responsible for inventing a new style

Fig. 11.25 Mason Chamberlin (1727–87), *Captain John Albert Bentinck*, 1775.
Oil on canvas, 90.8 × 70.5 cm. RCIN 409065

of pump that was introduced on board all Royal Navy ships. Here, Bentinck wears the full-dress uniform of a captain with over three years' service, in the new pattern brought in by the 1774 regulations, which was in use until 1787. The coat has much narrower cuffs than those in the Batoni portrait, and they are cut in the scalloped 'mariners' style. While not shown in this painting, the new regulations also stipulated the original blue breeches be replaced with white, although many officers had adopted white breeches before this date, a shift also seen in fashionable dress. Breeches were worn with white stockings and black shoes with buckles, boots being rare on board. The use of white for lapels, waistcoats and breeches distinguished the British navy officers from those of the Continental navy raised in North America in 1775, who also wore dark blue coats but lined with red, with red waistcoats and blue breeches. Bentinck is wearing a wig, which is powdered and probably worn in the clubbed style dictated by regulation, although such a neat wig must have been hard to maintain at sea.

Great care was taken by artists to ensure details indicating hierarchy were represented correctly. During a long and distinguished naval career, George Keith Elphinstone (Fig. 11.26) saw significant action in North America and the Mediterranean. In the 1780s he served as comptroller for the household of Prince William, whom he had known as a midshipman. Returning to active service in 1793 with the outbreak of war against France, he was soon promoted to vice admiral. John Hoppner's portrait of Elphinstone was probably painted in 1799 and shows him in the full-dress uniform of a flag officer. In this new pattern (in use from 1795 to 1812), white lapels and cuffs have been changed to blue, and the style reflects the curved cutaway line and lean silhouette of fashionable dress. Initially Elphinstone's cuffs were painted with two bands of gold lace to represent the rank of vice admiral, but these were later repainted to include a third band, the sitter having been promoted to full admiral in 1801 (see Fig. 11.26, detail). The difference between the original gold braid and the additions is clear to the naked eye, and an early mezzotint records the initial appearance.[28] A comparable dress coat from the same period belonging to Admiral

BELOW, AND DETAIL RIGHT
Fig. 11.26  John Hoppner (1758–1810), *George Keith Elphinstone, later Viscount Keith*, 1799–1801.
Oil on canvas, 128.4 × 102.7 cm. RCIN 400990

Sir William Cornwallis shows the position of the three bands of lace on the cuffs (Fig. 11.27). Elphinstone wears the red sash of command, and his seals are prominently suspended on a chain at his waist: these were an important means by which official communications to the Admiralty were authenticated. He has retained the traditional white stock as neckwear, although more fashion-forward officers had started to adopt the black version, and wears his own hair rather than a wig. Hoppner does not depict Elphinstone's hat, but by this date the bicorne had replaced the tricorne.

The shoulders of Elphinstone's coat are decorated with epaulettes, introduced into naval uniforms with the 1795 regulations, although they had been worn by army officers since 1768, and unofficially by some in the navy. It is notable that, while the gold lace was updated to reflect Elphinstone's new rank, the epaulettes display the two silver stars of a vice admiral rather than the three for full admirals, presumably because the change would have required too much modification to the original composition. In the new naval regulations of 1812, the wearing of

Fig. 11.27 Firmin and Sons Ltd, Full-dress uniform worn by Admiral Sir William Cornwallis, pattern 1795–1812.
Wool, silk, linen, brass and gold alloy. London, National Maritime Museum, NMM UNI0027

epaulettes was extended to junior officers, with lieutenants entitled to wear a single plain epaulette on the right shoulder, and experienced captains having epaulettes with a silver crown and anchor instead of stars.

## THE WINDSOR UNIFORM

Alongside the development of martial uniforms, the eighteenth century also saw the rise of civilian court uniforms in Britain, designed to serve as a badge of loyalty and emphasise personal connections to royalty. Louis XIV had introduced such a garment at the French court in 1665, known as the *justaucorps à brevet* or warrant coat, with its use limited to only 50 men selected by the king himself.[29] The much-coveted coat was of blue fabric lined with red and granted the wearer the right to join excursions to royal residences without invitation. This seems to have been the inspiration for the hunting uniform introduced by Frederick, Prince of Wales, worn by the prince and his friends in John Wootton's painting of 1737 (Fig. 11.28). Their blue coats, decorated with gold braid, are worn with short riding waistcoats (more comfortable for riding than the longer everyday version), plain buff breeches and sturdy jockey boots. They can be distinguished from the servants who wear red livery (see below), and from the rangers, whose coats are of plain blue with no gold braid: standing next to the prince and holding a rifle is John Spencer, ranger of Windsor Great Park. In creating such a uniform, the prince also disassociated his supporters from those of his father, who wore green and gold when hunting with the king.[30]

In turn, Frederick's son George III appears to have been inspired by his father's hunting attire when he conceived the idea for what would become the Windsor uniform in July 1777, which was initially called a 'Windsor Hunt Suit' in the accounts of the Master of the Robes.[31] The main item was a dark blue coat, with red collar and cuffs. Blue lined with red had long been a favoured colour combination for men's coats, and dark blue was to become one of the most popular colours for male dress during the late eighteenth century. The inclusion of red cuffs is the distinctive feature of the uniform that enables it to be

Fig. 11.28 John Wootton (c.1682–1764), *The Death of the Stag*, 1737 (detail).

Oil on canvas, 198.1 × 200.8 cm. RCIN 407815

identified in portraits and prints. The Windsor uniform came in two styles: a full-dress coat and a more informal 'undress' frock coat, the former being distinguished by its gold lace decorating the buttonholes, collar and cuffs. The Windsor uniform became George III's favoured style of dress for the last 30 years of his life. He ordered up to 14 new coats each year, presumably appreciating their comfort and familiarity, and the uniform appears in numerous portraits of the king.[32] The introduction of the Windsor uniform coincided with the decision of the royal family to transfer its main family home from Kew to Windsor, although the move was not finalised for some years.[33]

Gainsborough's full-length portrait of 1780–1 shows the full-dress coat, which George III always wore with the Garter star and sash (Fig. 11.29). At this date a full-dress coat cost the king £3, a modest sum in comparison to one of embroidered silk that could easily cost 30 times as much.[34] The coat curves sharply away at the front in keeping with fashions of the period, and here is worn open to reveal the white waistcoat beneath: cotton for undress occasions and twilled wool for full-dress. Breeches were white or buff. In a painting of 1807 (Fig. 11.30) the coat is buttoned to the mid-chest and accompanied by a different style of straight-cut waistcoat that was fashionable by this time. The king and his companions wear the simpler undress coat with jockey caps and plain linen in James Pollard's *George III, Returning from Hunting* (Fig. 11.31). This is the style still used by members of the royal family today for some formal occasions at Windsor Castle.

Initially, the Windsor uniform was worn only by royalty, and this included children, as demonstrated by Gainsborough's series of portraits (Fig. 11.32 and see pp. 10–11). Here, the king and five of his eight sons wear the uniform, the three between the ages of eight and eleven sporting an undress version with the wide-collared shirts and natural hair of childhood. In 1779 Queen Charlotte and the Princess Royal are reported to have worn a female version of the Windsor uniform: 'All the King's suite now wear blue coats, with a small red cape and cuff, as does the Queen, the Princess Royal and her attendants the same coloured riding habit, which is their usual morning dress'.[35]

Sadly, there is no known visual record of the latter's appearance. The uniform gradually became more widely adopted by senior attendants in the royal household and members of the aristocracy with close connections to the king, who were required to seek permission first. It also increasingly appeared away from Windsor. By the time of the Thanksgiving procession at St Paul's Cathedral, London, in 1797 to celebrate victories at sea, the uniform was worn by the king, the peers, the House of Commons and all the main participants of the ceremony.[36] Although military uniforms had become a common sight at court by the 1790s, this was not the case for the Windsor uniform, which was not considered formal enough, although it was permitted at the king's Birthday Ball in 1799, when it would have been accessorised with expensive lace like that in the Gainsborough portrait. By the late 1780s the uniform had become a politically charged form of dress, worn as a public demonstration of support for both the king during his illness and Regency crisis, and for his first minister, William Pitt the Younger, in the face of rising Whig opposition. George III and Pitt are often portrayed in the distinctive blue and red coat in caricatures of the period, while their opponents – which included the Prince of Wales – were shown in Whig buff and blue (see Chapter 12). Despite his appreciation of many other uniforms, the Prince of Wales was not fond of the Windsor uniform.

KING GEORGE III

GEORGE, PRINCE of WALES

EDWARD, DUKE of KENT

ADOLPHUS, DUKE of CAMBRIDGE

## LIVERY

The Windsor uniform can be considered a type of livery: non-military uniform indicating membership of a particular household. Many European courts developed specific forms of livery, and it was also used by aristocratic households to identify servants in their employ. The smartness of livery demonstrated that its wearer was exempt from the demands of manual labour, while its richness served as an indication of their employer's wealth: livery was often extravagantly decorated, with details such as gold lace. Some liveries incorporated Ottoman or hussar elements of dress (see Chapter 9). A retinue of people in livery was also a clear sign of a household's ability to employ numerous servants to cater to its needs. The cut of livery uniform was old-fashioned, creating a deliberately archaic

effect intended to emphasise both its official nature and the long lineage of the family in question.

The man attending Princess Charlotte in the portrait by Johann Georg Ziesenis (Fig. 11.33) is dressed in livery of a red coat with blue facings and gold braid, with a turban used to signal his 'exotic' status to European eyes. Here, though, he is also shown wearing a silver collar, probably indicating that he is enslaved rather than in paid service. Such silver collars were engraved with the name of the person who had bought the wearer's life, a disturbing representation of how enslaved people were treated as property rather than as human beings.

Different members of a royal family might have separate forms of livery, that of William Augustus, Duke of Cumberland, for example, being a crimson coat faced with green and a green waistcoat, as worn by the footman depicted

in a drawing by Paul Sandby (Fig. 11.34). While this figure has not yet been identified, he appears in several other watercolours by the artist. He may perhaps be of Indian or North African descent, something alluded to by the vaguely Eastern headdress, which is not seen in Sandby's other depictions of the duke's servants.[37]

Another example of a civilian uniform can be seen in *St James's Park and the Mall* (see Fig. 3.18), where the pointing man wears a red suit decorated with a large silver badge on his left arm, indicating membership of a private fire insurance company – an eighteenth-century firefighter.

## MILITARY AND CIVILIAN DRESS

Throughout the eighteenth century the boundaries between military and civilian dress became increasingly blurred, with uniforms redesigned to fit with fashionable styles, and military details introduced into everyday clothing. Jet black Hessian boots, for example, named after German mercenary troops fighting in the American Revolutionary War, had become the most fashionable footwear for men by the 1790s, and when polished to a high shine were considered just as appropriate for the drawing room as the battlefield (see Chapter 4). Similarly, pantaloons had originally started out as an element of hussar military dress, but by the late eighteenth century were being worn as fashionable attire.

Military influence on civilian dress was not confined to men's fashion. Some women adopted riding habits tailored in the colours of their husbands' regiments, which could include military epaulettes. In 1781 the *Gentleman's Magazine* published the disapproving 'Remarks on the Rage of the Ladies for the Military Dress', which covered attire, hair and deportment. 'Miss Dorothy' is described as pulling out a watch from 'a pair of tight leathern breeches' and

returning it with a 'most officer-like air', the unwelcome result being that 'Female delicacy is changed into masculine courage'.[38] By the early nineteenth century the prevalence of martial details in fashion plates illustrates the glamour with which military dress had come to be associated. One French fashion plate dating from October 1818 represents a typical example (Fig. 11.35), the abundance of white military-style braid on the purple pelisse echoing the decoration of the 10th Light Dragoons jacket belonging to George, Prince of Wales (see Fig. 11.13). The reticule also mimics the shape of a sabretache, and the large ostrich feathers are arranged in a similar manner to those on a military helmet. Gold anchors on neck ribbons for women were included in the *Gallery of Fashion* in July 1794, while the mariner's cuff was another military detail that infiltrated civilian dress for both men and women.[39]

# 12

# Rebellion & Revolution

*Dress is the most powerful of symbols,
the Revolution was also a question of fashion,
a debate between silk and cloth*

HONORÉ DE BALZAC, 1830[1]

The Georgian monarchs were faced with the challenge of simultaneously running the kingdom of Great Britain and the Electorate of Hanover (the former being more than ten times the size of the latter, in both area and population), each with shifting allegiances, which were sometimes at odds with one another. The relationship with France was a fundamental concern, with intermittent periods of fragile peace overshadowed by the threat of invasion, protectionist foreign policy and the predictable rivalry between neighbouring territories. Added to this were complexities inherent in the establishment and rule of overseas colonies across an expansive geographical area, opposition to the Acts of Union between England and Scotland, and various altercations with Spain, Holland and Denmark. It was a delicate balancing act. This chapter looks beyond the borders of England, to highlight the role of dress in three episodes of turbulence: the Jacobite Risings, the American Revolutionary War and the French Revolution. Each is necessarily a short and much simplified introduction to events with complex and nuanced political and social factors at play. Similarly, this was a century that saw much warfare across the world and these three case studies have been selected based on their variety and the range of imagery found in the Royal Collection.

## THE JACOBITE RISINGS

Within a year of his accession, George I was faced with a challenge to his legitimacy from supporters of James Francis Edward Stuart, the son of James II, deposed in 1688 on the grounds of his Roman Catholic faith. Raised in exile in France, 'The Old Pretender', as James Stuart was known, commanded the support of his cousin Louis XIV, and was a regular visitor to Versailles, where he was treated as the rightful heir to the throne based on the notion of a divine right to rule. James enjoyed sympathy among Catholic people in Ireland and Scotland, as well as from those who opposed the Acts of Union of 1707 that had brought the kingdoms of England and Scotland under the same rule with the creation of Great Britain. Despite their various and complex political and social motivations, these groups can be collectively combined under the ideology of Jacobitism (named after the Latin for James, *Jacobus*), which had as its aim the restoration of the Stuart bloodline to the throne. After James's death, support turned to his son, Charles Edward Stuart, nicknamed 'Bonnie Prince Charlie' (Fig. 12.1). In this painting the 19-year-old prince is portrayed as a warrior, wearing breastplate and pauldron, one ungloved hand resting on a helmet, the other on his sword hilt. The gloves are made of fashionable buff-coloured leather, with elegantly pointed fingertips and three carefully stitched draws on the back of the hand. Following a convention set by his father, he wears both the Order of the Thistle (on a green riband) and the blue sash of the Order of the Garter. Although noticeably absent here, it was through Charles Stuart that the Jacobite cause became inextricably linked with the wearing of tartan.

Tartan can refer to both a fabric and a pattern. As a hardy woollen fabric, it derives from the traditional style of dress worn by farmers and hunters in Scotland. The term plaid, which is now used synonymously with tartan to describe the multicoloured checked pattern familiar to us today, originally referred to an untailored, unisex, blanket-like garment common in both the Highlands and Lowlands. It could be worn in various ways. One option was to pass the plaid over the left shoulder, then wrap it around the waist to form a skirt, which was held in place with a belt. Most plaids were made of wool, although more expensive silk versions were available. In the early eighteenth century the plaid developed into two separate garments, a short hip-length jacket and a philibeg, an early version of the kilt, which was sometimes drawn together between the legs giving the impression of breeches. For riding, the nobility favoured the addition of tight-fitting 'trews', a form of footed trouser combining breeches and stockings. The women's plaid, also known as an arisaid, continued to be worn in the eighteenth century, but was gradually replaced by a cloak.

As a locally produced fabric unique to the region and with a long history, tartan had a particular status among patriotic Scots, 'prized by them above all velvets, brocades and tissues of Europe and Asia'.[2] Despite the romanticised view of tartan being coloured with locally sourced vegetable dyes that camouflaged well with the Scottish landscape ('from the herbs and lichens of the hills', according to Sir Walter Scott[3]), in fact imported dye pigments were often employed.[4] During the early eighteenth century tartan was increasingly exported abroad, including to North America, and by the 1730s had become a clear symbol of Scotland. From 1750 export was accelerated further by the Scottish diaspora displaced by the Highland clearances. Contrary to popular conception, a 'tartan taxonomy' – the historical association of specific tartan patterns (or 'setts') with particular clans – is a nineteenth-century invention, although certain types may have been used to denote regions or regiments during the eighteenth century.

The use of emblematic symbols was fundamental to the Jacobite cause. Charles Stuart understood the value of wearing Highland dress to demonstrate his Scottish heritage and to inspire loyalty among his Scottish supporters. Even before arriving in Edinburgh, the prince and his brother Henry wore tartan to a ball in 1741 at the Palazzo Pamphili in Rome. Their clothes were possibly donated by the Duke of Perth, who was in attendance to the prince and often wore Highland dress.[5] During the 1740s Highland dress became a self-conscious component of the Jacobite iconographical identity, embraced by both supporters and opponents in images of the prince. In fact, it became his most defining

LEFT
Fig. 12.1  Louis Gabriel Blanchet (1705–72),
*Prince Charles Edward Stuart*, 1739.
Oil on canvas, 97.8 × 72.5 cm. RCIN 401208

BELOW
Fig. 12.2  After Sir Robert Strange (1721–92),
*Prince Charles Edward Stuart*, c.1745.
Watercolour on ivory, mounted with onyx, 4.3 × 3.3 cm.
RCIN 29018

feature, added to copies of earlier portraits and prints, as the facial likeness became increasingly generalised.[6] After landing in the Outer Hebrides in 1745, Charles quickly attired himself appropriately and entered Edinburgh wearing a short tartan coat, red velvet trews, a green velvet bonnet trimmed with gold lace and the white rose cockade of the Jacobites.[7] This description fits with his appearance in a miniature based on a well-known prototype by the prince's own miniature painter, Robert Strange, who is believed to have fought alongside the prince (Fig. 12.2). Portraits of Charles show him wearing a range of different tartans, sometimes within the same painting. Although some artists were highly skilled at depicting the accurate sett of a tartan, in many of the more naïve prints it was reduced to a simple check or diamond pattern more akin to a patchwork Harlequin costume.

Tartan became a conspicuous feature of the prince's dress during his early military campaigns, and he also encouraged its widespread use among his army, even for non-Highland regiments. The contrast between the British redcoats and the Jacobite troops is exaggerated in *An Incident in the Rebellion of 1745*, which was probably

painted for the Duke of Cumberland and plays on the stereotypical view of Highlanders as muscular, unshaven and barbaric, inaccurately shown wielding only axes and swords against modern firearms with bayonets attached (Fig. 12.3). Although one apocryphal account records that the figures in this famous painting were based on captured Highlanders, details of dress suggest it was actually made some years later in London.[8] Charles Stuart's decisive defeat at the Battle of Culloden in April 1746 destroyed the hopes of a Jacobite restoration, and the prince was forced to flee, evading apprehension for five months and at one point disguising himself as a lady's maid. One printed image of Charles, which advertises the enormous reward of £30,000 for his secure capture, shows him dressed entirely in tartan, while acknowledging in the inscription that it was 'a likeness notwithstanding the Disguise'.[9] The echoes of Charles II's similarly dramatic escape from the Battle of Worcester a century earlier did not go unnoticed.

The powerful link between clothing and Jacobite ideology is indicated by the 1746 Act of Parliament banning the wearing of Highland dress. Known as the Disarming Act, it identified 'the Plaid, Philebeg, or little kilt, Trowse, Shoulder Belts' as being proscribed, and specified that 'no Tartan, or party-coloured Plaid or Stuff shall be used for Great Coats, or for Upper Coats'.[10] By assimilating in dress, it was anticipated that the Scots would also be integrated within a shared political state. Threatened punishment was severe: six months' imprisonment for initial transgressions, while repeat offenders were sent abroad to live in North America for seven years. What is often misunderstood is that the Act restricted the wearing of Highland dress to Scotland only, and Highland regiments were exempt from the proscription, as were women, who capitalised on the loophole to demonstrate their loyalty to the Jacobite cause. In reality the law often went unheeded, with prosecutions having abated by the 1760s.[11]

With its emotive connections, the tartan outfit worn by the future George III in Barthélemy du Pan's enormous portrait of the children of Frederick, Prince of Wales, is perhaps surprising, given that it was completed two

Fig. 12.3 Attributed to David Morier (?1705–70), *An Incident in the Rebellion of 1745*, c.1753.
Oil on canvas, 60.5 × 99.5 cm. RCIN 401243

Fig. 12.4 Prince George and Prince Edward in Barthélemy du Pan (1712–63), *The Children of Frederick, Prince of Wales*, 1746 (detail).
Oil on canvas, 245.0 × 368.8 cm. RCIN 403400

months after the Battle of Culloden (Fig. 12.4). In fact, the young prince wears the attire of the Edinburgh-based Royal Company of Archers, which had adopted a red tartan uniform in 1713, archaic in cut with slashed sleeves.[12] Raised in the seventeenth century as a private club designed to promote the practice of archery, it was granted a Royal Charter by Queen Anne, and was presumably considered exempt from the ban on tartan clothing, in a similar way to military units. However, by the 1740s its members included a number of well-known Jacobites who fought for Charles Stuart, and the painting may have acquired additional meaning. Upon seeing it in 1761, Horace Walpole noted how remarkable it was that Prince George had a St Andrew's Cross in his cap.[13] The tartan may simply be intended to represent the heroic aspects of Scottish identity deemed desirable in a future king. Alternatively, the commission may add credence to the argument that Frederick, Prince of Wales, was keen to position himself as an alternative 'patriotic prince' with some Jacobite sympathies.[14] In 1822 the Royal Company of Archers was appointed the sovereign's personal bodyguard in Scotland, and remains so today.

Portraits showing sitters wearing tartan continued to be produced after the Disarming Act came into force, with tartan worn by sitters on both sides of the political spectrum. Interpreting the wearing of tartan in portraits post-1746 as a deliberate symbol of Jacobite defiance overlooks the subtleties inherent in the wording of the law, which allowed tartan for Highland regiments serving the Crown. For some sitters, adopting this form of military dress was a sign of loyalty and tartan gradually became a different kind of political symbol: that of the British Empire, united against a common enemy.[15] The ability for the plaid to be arranged into toga-like folds was emphasised by artists including Pompeo Batoni, adding to the notion of it being the dress of enlightened thinkers. Tartan and Highland dress were also increasingly popular for masquerades from the late 1740s.[16] The repeal of the Disarming Act by George III in 1782 was accompanied by the announcement that men were 'no longer bound down to the unmanly dress of the Lowlander', marking

the full rehabilitation of Highland dress. Forty years later, George III's four-year-old grandson would be depicted wearing a kilt dress made from so-called 'Prince Charles Edward' tartan (see Fig. 9.14), reflecting a broader fascination with the lost Jacobite cause.

The Romantic period saw a revival of interest in Scotland, with the idealisation of the Highland landscape and its people. The resulting rise of tartan as a fashionable material was increasingly based not only on the traditional functional qualities of the woollen cloth, but also on the aesthetics of the pattern, as well as its historical associations. The introduction of tartan to the London court was credited to Jane Maxwell, Duchess of Gordon, who in 1792 commissioned silk woven in China for a gown to the design of the Black Watch tartan.[17] For women's dress, tartan was most frequently used for accessories: ribbons, scarfs, parasols and caps, often made of silk instead of the traditional wool. These are regularly depicted in fashion periodicals of the time, where they add a touch of colour to the popular white gowns.

One of the key events that solidified a specific form of
Scottish 'national' dress was George IV's visit to Edinburgh
in August 1822, an occasion of huge pageantry choreographed
by the novelist Sir Walter Scott. As the first Hanoverian
monarch to visit Scotland, clothing played a key role in
presenting the king as a worthy successor to Bonnie Prince
Charlie, with costumes designed by the actor and theatre
manager William Murray, and the crowd briefed accordingly
on what to wear for each event to create a suitably splendid
spectacle. For the *levée* at Holyroodhouse, during which time

George IV was individually introduced to 1,200 people
in just over an hour, the king wore an outfit supplied
in advance by George Hunter of Princes Street – 'His
Majesty's clothier and mercer' – at a cost of £1,354 18s
(the equivalent of more than £130,000 in 2021).[18] It
was recorded in a portrait by Sir David Wilkie (Fig. 12.5).
The doublet, of Royal Stewart tartan lined with red silk
and inscribed with Hunter's name, still survives today,
along with a coordinating waistcoat of red silk velvet
(Fig. 12.6).[19] Both are embroidered with thistles in twisted

Fig. 12.7 George Hunter & Co., Edinburgh, Highland dress accoutrements consisting of belt, powder flask, dirk (with scabbard), fork, knife and sword (with scabbard), 1822.
Boxwood, steel, gold, silver, Cairngorm quartz, aquamarine, amethyst, garnet, silk velvet, leather and horn. RCIN 29023–7

gold thread and sequins: the pattern is just visible in the portrait on the standing collar and cuffs. Most of the buttons have been removed, although the small number that survive on the rear tails indicate these were set with gemstones including moonstone. The accoutrements depicted in Wilkie's portrait also survive (Fig. 12.7). Rather than a fashionable hat, the king wears a flat bonnet decorated with a black cockade and three eagle feathers, representing his position as Chief of Chiefs.[20] He also wears a kilt made of the same tartan, and although the portrait shows him bare-legged, he had been provided with 'buff coloured trowsers like *flesh* to *imitate* his *Royal knees*', for warmth and to conceal his legs, which by this date were grossly bloated.[21] The kilt still aroused comment, including the famous remark from Lady Hamilton-Dalrymple: 'Since he is to be among us for so short a time, the more we see of him the better'.[22]

For a grand ball hosted in the Assembly Rooms by the peers of Scotland, all were encouraged by Scott to wear 'ancient Highland costume' and many dutifully sought to claim a familial link to specific tartans. Not everyone was impressed with the pageantry: 'Hundreds who had never seen Heather had the folly to array themselves in tartan', wrote one Lowland-born lord.[23] The king chose the uniform of a field marshal, presumably not convinced by his first experience of the kilt six days earlier. He also wore riding boots, which was a cause for much comment.[24] In fact, the Holyroodhouse *levée* was the only occasion during his 21-day visit to Scotland when George IV wore a kilt, preferring instead the various military uniforms to which he was more accustomed.

## THE AMERICAN REVOLUTIONARY WAR

Although the early years of George III's reign were marked by the resolution of the Seven Years' War in 1763, it was not long before Britain found itself fighting to retain control over the 'Thirteen Colonies' in North America, which only a decade earlier had been allies against the French. Inspired by Enlightenment ideals of freedom and the values of self-rule rather than monarchy, the colonists envisioned a new America, free from the imposition of British taxation, an unfavourable balance of trade and interference in governance without representation in British Parliament.

Before the American Revolution, clothing in colonial America was very similar to that worn in Britain. The majority was imported as textiles, then made up into garments locally, although the wealthy sometimes ordered the most fashionable made-to-measure suits and gowns directly from London. American visitors to England also sent textiles home: Benjamin Franklin, himself trained as a printer, was impressed by the newly invented copperplate-printed cottons he saw in London in 1758. British woollens made up the majority of textiles imported by North American colonies. Linens also arrived in great quantities and a range of qualities. The coarser examples such as osnaburg (named after the German city of Osnabrück) were used to clothe the enormous enslaved population of African people who had been removed from their homes as part of the transatlantic slave trade, and forced to work on plantations. In the United States in 1810 this numbered nearly 1.2 million people, approximately 16.5 per cent of the total population.[25] Silks were a rare luxury and those found in America were usually woven in England, often in Spitalfields, although the British East India Company also imported silks from China alongside cottons from India. Ironically, these were legal in America while prohibited in Britain and France.[26]

The 'Navigation Acts' – a series of laws ratified under Charles II in the 1660s – had only allowed direct trade (both imports and exports) with the American colonies using English-owned ships. The Staple Act of 1663, for example, stipulated that nearly all goods imported by the American colonies should travel via English ports. Such regulations provided the mother nation with both a captive market and the currency raised from taxes imposed on products made abroad. This represented a large proportion of the linen textiles imported by North America, transported from England but made outside the British Isles. Similarly restrictive regulations applied to exports meant that English merchants were granted a monopoly on the rich resources exported from North America, giving them the ability to set their purchase price and then sell on to third parties. Such 'enumerated' goods included cotton, indigo and beaver-fur pelts for the textile trade. Colonists were also discouraged from manufacturing certain goods themselves, increasing their dependence on British imports: textiles, for instance, were often cheaper to import than weave domestically.

In reality, many of these regulations had only been casually enforced for much of the eighteenth century in line with the principle of salutary neglect: illegal trade and smuggling were a significant additional source of profit to American merchants alongside official trade with British ships. However, during the 1760s the trade laws were re-examined as a means to subsidise Britain's war debt arising from the Seven Years' War. Such rules imposed from afar, combined with a series of new taxes on goods, were fundamental concerns for discontented colonists supporting a revolution. Non-importation agreements were instituted that saw the boycott of British goods in many colonies. To replace textile imports, American-made alternatives were developed. Spinning and weaving were revived as domestic activities, even among the inexperienced urban elite, with spinning bees organised and prizes awarded.[27] The wearing of such homespun textiles became a conspicuous way to demonstrate resistance: a ball held in Williamsburg, Virginia, in December 1769 was attended by nearly 100 women in homespun gowns.[28] When visiting the French court of Louis XVI, American diplomats took care to dress with the humble simplicity considered fitting to the Republican ideal. Of Franklin, who wore plain wool suits without embroidery, spectacles and a fur cap on his natural receding hair, Elisabeth Louise Vigée Le Brun remarked in 1779, 'I should

Fig. 12.8  Henry Gardiner (1744–1839), Printed cotton depicting the Apotheosis of Washington, c.1785.
Cotton, 243.8 × 97.8 cm. New York, Metropolitan Museum of Art, 46.106.1

Fig. 12.9  After Gilbert Stuart (1755–1828), *George Washington*, c.1801.
Oil on canvas, 89.7 × 71.8 cm. RCIN 404356

have taken him for a big farmer, so great was his contrast with the other diplomats, who were all powdered, in full dress, and splashed all over with gold and ribbons'.[29] Similarly, at Versailles in 1788 Franklin's successor Thomas Jefferson was 'the plainest man in the room'.[30] The American presence in Paris sparked a number of fashion trends including minimalist hats for men and women *à la Pennsylvanie*.[31]

After the signing of the Treaty of Paris in 1783, American merchants were able to trade directly with other countries, and ships were soon returning from distant lands laden with exotic goods. The first American ship to trade directly with China, the *Empress of China*, had reached the port of Guangzhou (Canton) by 1784 and Americans found themselves exchanging furs and sandalwood for silks, spices and nankeen cotton. In the same year, the first American ship sailed to India, although by the 1830s America's domestic cotton industry had reached such a scale that it was largely able to serve the home market without the

need for imports. The wearing of French textiles was another way to demonstrate solidarity with the new ally. Christophe-Philippe Oberkampf's toile de Jouy cottons were especially popular, and Jefferson was an important patron while living in Paris in the 1780s. Despite these new trading partners, America's commercial interests with Britain did not cease after the Treaty of Paris, and like their counterparts in France, commercially minded cotton manufacturers in England adapted designs to feature patriotic scenes appealing to the newly founded nation. Subjects included the Apotheosis of Washington (Fig. 12.8) made in Surrey, *c*.1785, and the 'Altar of Liberty'.[32] Such designs, however, were generally used for furnishing fabrics rather than for clothing.

The Continental Army had been founded in 1775, and became increasingly professionalised under the command of George Washington (Fig. 12.9), whose experience working as an aide to General Braddock during the Seven Years' War had exposed him to British military

protocols and uniform regulations. Washington himself was well known for his immaculate appearance: 'There is not a king in Europe that would not look like a valet de chambre by his side', wrote Benjamin Rush in 1775.[33] As a member of the independent militia of Fairfax County in Virginia before the Revolution, Washington had worn a uniform of blue and buff, and this colour scheme formed the basis for the uniform introduced in many states for both officers and troops of the Continental Army fighting against Britain in the Revolutionary War. A composite version of Washington's uniform survives (Fig. 12.10). The blue wool coat, with buff-coloured lapels and cuffs, and plain copper-alloy buttons, is notable for its simplicity, without the gold lace or embroidery worn by senior officers in Britain and France. Washington continued to wear uniform during peacetime: the same coat is depicted in Edward Savage's portrait of the Washington family at Mount Vernon, an image widely known through a successful engraving

produced while the artist visited London (Fig. 12.11).[34] Alongside America's first president are his wife Martha, who gestures to a map of the city of Washington with her fan, two of her grandchildren, and a man whose identity has been debated but may be William Lee, an enslaved servant who held the position of Washington's valet.[35] Washington's coat is worn with epaulettes, which were introduced in America in 1780 to identify rank, as in Britain.

The uniform of the Continental Army was the inspiration for the clothing worn by supporters of the Whig party in Britain, which opposed the policies of George III and the Tories. Charles James Fox, the leading Whig politician (Fig. 12.12), had adopted plain buff and blue in the late 1770s in solidarity with American soldiers. During the closely fought election of 1784 the distinctive buff and blue became (for both sexes) a highly visual demonstration of political allegiance: Georgiana, Duchess of Devonshire, led the female canvassers dressed in the colours, and the

Prince of Wales supplied his household with an expensive buff and blue livery in that year. Milliners offered fox-skin muffs, while Mr Carbery, 'plume master to the Prince of Wales', provided feathers imitating a fox's brush.[36]

Fox did not share Washington's fastidiousness in dress, however, being renowned for his dishevelled, unwashed and unshaven appearance.[37] Fox's perpetual 'five o'clock shadow' is a feature in caricatures of the period, he being 'Charley Blackbeard' to the youthful William Pitt's 'Billy Lackbeard' in Thomas Rowlandson's portrayal of them playing football with East India House (Fig. 12.13).

These depictions of Charles James Fox stand in dramatic contrast to his appearance a decade earlier, when he had been one of the founding macaronies. This is the version of Fox we see ridiculed in Michel Vincent Brandoin's caricature *The Young Politician*, which links an excessive interest in fashion to political corruption (Fig. 12.14). Attended by a trio of hairdressers who

Fig. 12.13 Thomas Rowlandson (1757–1827), *Billy Lackbeard and Charley Blackbeard Playing at Football*, 1784.
Hand-coloured etching, 26.3 × 37.3 cm (sheet). RCIN 810033

Fig. 12.14 Michel Vincent Brandoin (1733–1807),
*The Young Politician*, c.1771.
Pen and ink and watercolour over pencil, 22.0 × 18.6 cm. RCIN 913259

use pages from the 'Magna Charta' as curlpapers, the zoomorphic Fox considers his reflection in the mirror. Jars of scent and rouge sit on the dressing table, while on the floor lie a bag of hair powder along with 'A New Essay on Politick By C - F- Esq'. On the far right is a bust inscribed with the words 'Cato bewailing the loss of liberty': Fox is thus simultaneously presented as the enemy of both liberty and taste.

A hand-coloured drypoint after Richard Dighton depicts the hustings raised in front of St Paul's Church in Covent Garden during the Westminster election of 1796 and demonstrates that blue and buff retained their popularity (Fig. 12.15). The various candidates stand on the raised platform: Fox in the centre flanked by identically dressed supporters, with Admiral Alan Gardner on the left wearing naval uniform (epaulettes and bicorne hat, differentiating him from others wearing blue), and the independent radical John Horne Took in a plain brown coat. The lively crowd includes people from all walks of life: a sailor clambering up the side of the platform, a woman in a green quilted petticoat distributing printed copies of Fox's speeches and numerous Foxite supporters in blue and buff.

## THE FRENCH REVOLUTION

The history of dress is tightly woven into the politics of the French Revolution, although interpretation is made more complicated by the scarcity of visual material from the period, with the production of portraits during the early 1790s limited, fashion magazines silent from 1793 to 1797 and surviving garments rare. To many, the French court had come to represent only surface grandeur, concealing decay and moral bankruptcy beneath, led by an indecisive king in the figure of Louis XVI (Fig. 12.16) at the mercy of corrupt advisers. Obvious inequalities in wealth, when combined with the development of ideas around social and political reform associated with Enlightenment philosophies, encouraged a broad questioning of established systems of authority and heightened political awareness across classes.

The reputation of the Austrian-born Queen Marie-Antoinette (Fig. 12.17), which had never flourished in her adopted country, reached a nadir during the 1780s and she was often vilified in the popular press for profligate spending, gambling and alleged extramarital relationships. Criticism of the queen's expenditure on clothing was not without validity. She regularly exceeded a generous annual wardrobe allowance, acquiring more than 100 new gowns each year, with half the sum in 1783 going to her favoured *marchande de modes*, Rose Bertin.[38] Ironically, however, while Marie-Antoinette was characterised as 'Madame Déficit', at around this time she was helping to popularise a simpler, less expensive style of everyday dress (see Chapter 3). Such a relaxed approach to traditional court etiquette also had its vocal detractors, however, being deemed unbecoming for a queen of France.

As chief finance minister to Louis XVI, Charles-Alexandre de Calonne (1734–1802; Fig. 12.18) was also the focus of scrutiny. A fiscal strategy of increased borrowing in an attempt to drive the French economy

while maintaining the appearance of solvency had resulted in huge debts (the interest payments alone took up 50 per cent of the budget each year). Calonne's recovery plan, which involved introducing taxes for the nobility, was rejected by an 'Assembly of Notables'. In 1787 he was dismissed from his post and emigrated to England. Vigée Le Brun's portrait, which was painted three years before the dismissal, gives no indication of the uncertainties ahead. Instead, Calonne's charter outlining his plan for financial recovery sits proudly on the table in front of him, and he holds a letter addressed to the king ('Au Roi'). The sitter is similarly unperturbed by the powder from his wig sprinkling the shoulders of his black silk satin suit (see Fig. 6.3), the customary dress for that section of the nobility known as the *noblesse du robe*, who occupied the most senior posts in the French government. The wig is that of a lawyer, heavily curled and powdered, while his shirt is trimmed with French needlepoint lace decorated with a pattern of scattered sprigs and a narrow cartouche border.

OPPOSITE, LEFT
Fig. 12.16  After Joseph Siffred Duplessis (1725–1802), *Louis XVI, King of France*, c.1775–1800.
Oil on canvas, 100.5 × 83.2 cm. RCIN 406514

OPPOSITE, RIGHT
Fig. 12.17  After Elisabeth Louise Vigée Le Brun (1755–1842), *Marie-Antoinette, Queen of France*, c.1775–1830.
Oil on canvas, 100.2 × 83.2 cm. RCIN 406515

RIGHT
Fig. 12.18  Elisabeth Louise Vigée Le Brun (1755–1842), *Charles-Alexandre de Calonne*, 1784.
Oil on canvas, 155.5 × 130.3 cm. RCIN 406988

In response to the growing crisis, and as an attempt to achieve consensus around reforms, in May 1789 Louis XVI summoned the Estates-General, an assembly established in the fourteenth century that included representatives from the three estates (that is, defined population classes). This was the first time the group had been called for more than 150 years. At the event dress was intended to provide a clear demarcation of rank for the delegates, a revival of an ancient system of sumptuary laws that had long been repealed. The clergy of the First Estate wore ecclesiastical robes, some scarlet with ornate lace. The aristocracy making up the Second Estate were entitled to wear suits of black silk decorated with gold braid, white stockings, feathered hats and swords. Meanwhile, members of the Third Estate – everyone else (97 per cent of the population) – were directed to wear suits of plain black cloth, cravats made of muslin instead of lace, and black stockings.[39] The regulations were a source of great discontent. Many protested that their clothing choices were being dictated and the rules were soon abolished. Without the agreement to equal political representation for delegates, no consensus could be reached during the discussions. The Third Estate re-formed itself into a new National Assembly, convening in a covered tennis court near the Palace of Versailles to swear the Tennis Court Oath, vowing to meet until a new constitution had been established. This was one of the key episodes of the Revolution, and a dramatic demonstration of opposition to the king. With the storming of the Bastille prison in July 1789 came political reform, including the abolition of hereditary titles and the introduction of the term *citoyen* (citizen) for all classes. In October the royal family was removed from Versailles to Paris, initially under house arrest in the Tuileries Palace.

Cockades had long been used as a symbol of military allegiance and the new tricolour ribbon cockade adopted by the National Guard was an early symbol of loyalty to the new Republic, combining Bourbon royal white (indicating loyalty to the sovereign), with the blue and red traditionally associated with the city of Paris (the preferred colours of the Revolutionary militia). Worn on the hat or in the buttonhole, the cockades depicted in fashion plates could reach enormous sizes (Fig. 12.19) and by September 1793 the wearing of a tricolour cockade was obligatory for both women and men. Despite a personal dislike of the cockade, Marie-Antoinette recognised the political expediency of wearing such a '*ribbon à la nation*' and included it in her attire.[40] Outfits incorporating this patriotic colour scheme appear regularly in fashion plates at around this date, with striped fabrics for coats, gowns and waistcoats being popular, as well as tailored garments for women, that evoked the military uniform of the National Guard (Fig. 12.20). Red, white and blue were also the colours of the king's cousin Philippe, duc d'Orléans (a close friend of the Prince of Wales), who was known for his Republican sympathies and renamed himself 'Philippe Égalité'. By contrast, absolutist supporters courted controversy by wearing pure white cockades and lilies to reference the

Fig. 12.19 Anonymous, Man wearing 'la cocarde de la Nation', from M. le Brun, *Journal de la Mode et du gout, ou Amusemens du salon et de la toilette*, 9ème cahier, 15 May 1790, Paris, pl. I.
RCIN 1000885

Fig. 12.20 Anonymous, 'Femme patriote', from M. le Brun, *Journal de la Mode et du gout, ou Amusemens du salon et de la toilette*, 19ème cahier, 25 August 1790, Paris, pl. II.
RCIN 1000885

royal fleur-de-lis. During the Terror years of 1793–4 this was a dangerous provocation, although an excuse could be made that white was the colour of the Roman Republic. An early attempt to instate green ribbons to symbolise the Revolution – it being considered the colour of hope – was reversed, due to its connection with the livery of the king's brother, the comte d'Artois.

Famously characterised by the novelist Honoré de Balzac as representing 'a debate between silk and cloth',[41] in fact the tumultuous events of 1789–93 hastened changes in dress for both men and women that were already well underway in France during the 1780s. For men this included the adoption of plainer styles of clothing, influenced by working-class dress and sporting fashions that had long been popular in England. Similarly, for women the classically inspired garments of the Directoire period (1795–9) saw their precursor in the chemise gown of the 1780s, with its evocations of pastoral simplicity, which ironically had been popularised by Marie-Antoinette. Both were increasingly associated by philosophers with the ideals of a more democratic society,

lacking such obvious symbols of rank as the elaborate and expensive dress worn at the French court.

In France during the early years of the 1790s, traditional distinctions in dress became intentionally blurred and it was increasingly dangerous for aristocrats to wear the *Ancien Régime* style of clothing to which they were accustomed, it being interpreted as a demonstration of anti-Revolutionary sympathies and a disregard for the new ideology of democratic égalité. One style of dress directly associated with the Revolution was that worn by the aggressive *sans-culottes* (translated as 'without breeches'), who modelled their clothing on that of peasants and labourers. They were named after their legwear, which consisted of wide trousers (*pantalons*) rather than the knee-length breeches (*culottes*) seen at court. Ardent Revolutionaries also rejected other elements of dress associated with the court, opting for laces instead of shoe buckles, and natural unpowdered hair. Many sported the short *carmagnole* jacket (named after the Italian city of Carmagnola), traditionally worn by labourers from Marseilles. Another symbolic item was the *bonnet rouge*, derived from the Phrygian cap of antiquity awarded to enslaved people on achieving emancipation, a symbol of liberty. As a less extreme measure, wearing the closer-fitting pantaloons could show support for the *sans-culottes'* cause and Republican sympathies without the need to adopt full working-class dress, although a slightly unkempt appearance was favoured to mark a complete divergence from the highly manicured court dress of the *Ancien Régime*.

Materials taken from the ruins of the Bastille prison were modelled into fashionable items of dress: shoe buckles and medals made from the metal bars and locks, jewellery from its bricks, polished and sometimes set with precious gems. More macabre were the pieces inspired by the guillotine, with earrings and brooches depicting the instrument itself, and red ribbon chokers (*ceinture à la Victime*) reportedly worn to imitate the lethal cut. Like that of other prisoners, Marie-Antoinette's hair was cut short on the morning of her execution to facilitate the clean action of the blade. On her way to the scaffold in 1793, she wore a pleated linen cap and an unadorned simple white everyday dress rather than the black mourning she had customarily adopted while imprisoned, in memory of her executed husband.[42] Lord Ronald Sutherland Gower depicted the last moments of the French queen's life in a bronze bust cast in *c.*1875 (Fig. 12.21). The figure of Marie-Antoinette held a particular fascination for Gower, whose grandmother (the Duchess of Sutherland) had been living in Paris during the Revolution and had known her personally. Gower's interest extended to compiling a collection of relics associated with the queen and undertaking numerous research visits to Paris. He noted that on the morning of her execution the queen removed the black crape bands she usually wore around her cap to indicate widowhood, and fastened them in a loose knot over her chest, in recognition of the fact that she was to shake off her headdress prior to the executioner's blow.[43]

As a reaction against the working-class styles favoured by ardent Jacobins (the collective term for various anti-royalist factions), a distinctive manner of dress developed among some fashionable young men during the Directoire period. This group, who named themselves the *jeunesse*

*dorée* and were subsequently nicknamed the 'Incroyables', wore an exaggerated form of English masculine dress, with close-fitting breeches, double-layered waistcoats, huge lapels and heavily starched cravats. Green was a favoured hue, in honour of the ultra-royalist comte d'Artois, who by this date was living between London and the Palace of Holyroodhouse in Edinburgh, with an allowance paid by George III. Some Incroyables also adopted an unusual, dishevelled hairstyle, long at the sides and short at the back, in imitation of the cut of the executioner, and reintroduced hair powder as an expression of respect for the exiled monarchy. Their female sartorial equivalent were the 'Merveilleuses': young women who courted controversy for their revealing styles of dress (described as '*à la sauvage*'), which borrowed directly from antique statuary. Sleeveless muslin gowns of such transparency that they revealed the figure beneath were paired with sandals, elegantly draped shawls and hairstyles arranged with ribbon bandeaux and cropped *à la Titus* (dubbed '*à la guillotine*' by *The Times*).[44] In reality, the most extreme styles were worn by only a select group of influential fashionable society women whose dress and behaviour were the subject of much reportage, contributing to the popular perception in England that post-Revolutionary France was a centre of immodesty and scandal. Such styles never seem to have caught on in Britain, whether for reasons of morality or practicality.

The appointment of Napoleon Bonaparte as first consul in 1799 ushered in a new era, and with it came the re-establishment of an embryonic court and associated social calendar, providing a legitimate opportunity for the display of fashionable and magnificent dress once again. Napoleon's own preference in clothing was for military attire and he instituted various styles of civilian uniform for governmental officers during the Consulate period (1799–1804). This included the *habit dégagé* for the three consuls, which for formal occasions

Fig. 12.22  French, Chasseur colonel uniform worn by Napoleon, *c.*1810–15.

Wool, silk, brass and gold thread, cannetille and silver sequins. Paris, Musées de Sens

consisted of a double-breasted coat of red silk velvet woven in Lyons, with gold embroidery in the form of honeysuckle, worn with embroidered white breeches and Hessian boots. For less formal occasions and for many of his military operations Napoleon favoured the uniform of a colonel of the mounted regiment, *chasseurs à cheval*: a dark green coat with red collar, cuffs and pipings. The coat worn in exile on St Helena still survives in the Musées de Sens and has undergone recent conservation, although fading of the yellow dye means it now appears blue (Fig. 12.22). It is embroidered with the star of the Légion d'Honneur, an order of merit established by Napoleon in 1802 that broke with tradition by being open to all professions and ranks, awarded on the basis of achievement or bravery rather than birth. Napoleon's personal insignia, the grand eagle, appears in the centre of the star, and a badge was also worn on a red ribbon. For the most important occasions Napoleon adopted the uniform of colonel of the infantry regiment, the *Grenadiers à Pied de la Garde*, comprising a blue coat with scarlet cuffs and broad white facings, sharply cut away from the chest to reveal a white waistcoat beneath, and white knee breeches of fine wool. This is what he wears in Hippolyte Delaroche's posthumous depiction of Napoleon at Fontainebleau (Fig. 12.23), although here his slumped body is enveloped by the practical grey greatcoat that became so associated with his winter campaigns. Although fastidious about personal hygiene, Napoleon's partiality for taking tobacco resulted, according to one observer, in most of the snuff falling back 'on the white lapel of his uniform until it was quite dusted with it', although naturally this is never portrayed in his portraits, which instead show his attire as spotless, perfectly fitted to his frame.[45]

Napoleon was a popular subject for British satirical printmakers including James Gillray and Thomas Rowlandson, in whose cartoons he is usually recognisable by his diminutive stature, being shown, for example, as a soldier overwhelmed by the size of his hat, or as a swaddled baby or doll. In fact, at around 5 feet 6 inches (167 cm) Napoleon was only 1 or 2 inches (2.5–5 cm) shorter than average for the time. In Rowlandson's *The Progress of*

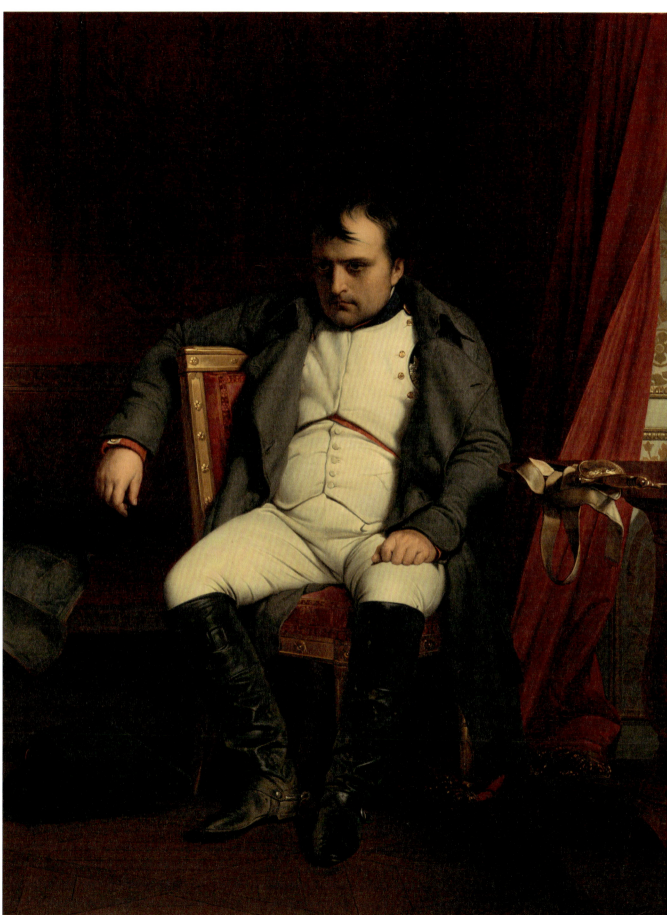

Fig. 12.23 Hippolyte Paul Delaroche (1797–1856),
*Napoleon at Fontainebleau, 31 March 1814*, 1846.
Oil on canvas, 69.2 × 53.2 cm. RCIN 405838

Fig. 12.24 Manufacture de Versailles, Robe sword
and scabbard, 1802–3.
Silver gilt, enamel, ivory, gold, steel, wood and mother-of-pearl.
RCIN 61171

*the Emperor Napoleon* the various stages of his life are demarcated by clothing (Fig. 12.25): he moves from being described as a 'Ragged Headed Corsican Peasant' in a tattered brown coat, to industrious student at the Royal Military Academy in Paris in the fashionably plain clothing of the 1780s. In several scenes he wears the standard blue military coat of a general of the French army, with enormous bicorne hat, feather and sword. Campaigns in Cairo are represented by him adopting Turkish dress, while in the final depiction he is portrayed as 'an Emperor on a Throne of iniquities'.

Napoleon was crowned emperor in 1804, a carefully choreographed event that deliberately combined elements from recent royal history with the classical past. The costumes were designed by Jean-Baptiste Isabey (1767–1855), working alongside Jacques-Louis David (1748–1825), who in the same year was appointed to the position of first painter. In Rowlandson's print the imperial mantle is shown as purple (an interpretation of *pourpre*), although in reality it was of reddish-burgundy velvet, lined with Russian ermine and embroidered with olive, laurel and oak leaves and the letter N, as well as Napoleon's personal emblem, the gold bee, selected for its diligence working on behalf of the hive (Fig. 12.26). With the mantle the emperor wore a tunic of white satin, embroidered and trimmed with gold fringing, along with white slippers with straps to imitate Roman sandals and a diadem of gold laurel leaves. The latter was supplied by the jeweller Martin Guillaume Biennais (1764–1843), who also provided the regalia: the hand of justice, the sceptre and a sword. Into the pommel of the sword was set the 141-carat Regent diamond, a jewel imbued with significance given that it had been acquired by the French regent, Philippe II, duc d'Orléans, in 1717 from Thomas Pitt (nicknamed 'Diamond Pitt', grandfather and great-grandfather of two British prime ministers). It had subsequently been incorporated into the crowns of Louis XV and Louis XVI, and was also worn by Marie-Antoinette. Despite his personal preference for uniforms, Napoleon was keen to reinstate the feeling of luxury seen in pre-Revolutionary France and to re-establish a sense of national pride in dress at the imperial court, encouraging

attendees to adopt rich textiles made in France instead of English muslins. Empress Joséphine usually exceeded her annual allowance for clothing and personal expenses, and her inventory from 1809 included more than 900 dresses.[46] She favoured the dressmaker Louis Hippolyte Leroy (1763–1829) and the historicising style of dress known as *le style troubadour* inspired by the fashions of the late sixteenth century (see Chapter 10).

Perhaps paradoxically, George IV was fascinated by the emperor and in 1827 acquired a sword that previously belonged to him (Fig. 12.24). Swords of this pattern were produced by the Versailles Manufactory for each of the three consuls installed under the new system of French government. The elaborate decoration incorporates a variety of classically inspired motifs including lions' heads, trophies of war and serpents, as well as a shield with a gorgon's head and a medallion with the figure of Mercury in profile, which was entirely appropriate for someone who had awarded himself the same title as the ruler of imperial Rome.

With the defeat of Napoleon at the Battle of Waterloo in June 1815, the French monarchy was restored, initially under Louis XVIII, and, after his death in 1824, Charles X. Both were younger brothers of the executed French king Louis XVI, and both had spent time in Britain during the intervening years, where they were provided with generous allowances by the British royal family and formed part of the Prince of Wales's social set. Once on the throne, Charles X (Fig. 12.27) embraced the royal traditions of pre-Revolutionary France, choosing Reims Cathedral for his lavish Catholic coronation and presiding over a magnificent court. In Sir Thomas Lawrence's portrait he is seen in his favoured uniform as Colonel General of the Garde Royale and for evening receptions he wore diamonds in his badge of the Order of the Holy Spirit, epaulettes, shoe buckles and sword, as well as a wig 'which suited him very well'.[47] Although nominally operating under constitutional rule rather than the absolutist *Ancien Régime*, Charles X's conservative ideals and radical royalism put him in opposition to much of the population, and he was forced to abdicate in 1830 under the July Revolution, making

63    a Ragged Headed            Studying mischief at the        An humble Ensign in a        a determined Atheistical Republican
      Corsican Peasant.          Royal Military Academy         Republican Corps. requesting   General ordering his men to fire on the Parisians
                                 at Paris                       a situation in the British     Vollies of grape shot.
                                                                Army

      A Turk at Grand            A Runaway from Egypt           A Devout Catholic              An Emperor on a
      Cairo                                                                                    Throne of iniquities
                                                                                              O Tempora O Mores

                                                                                              MURDERS
                                                                                              Duke D'Enghein
                                                                                              Prisoners at
                                                                                              Jaffa
                                                                                              Palm
                                                                                              Capt.ⁿ Williams
                                                                                              Pichegrue
                                                                                              Cabon
                                                                                              Toussaint
                                                                                              &c &c
                                                                                              Robberies
                                                                                              innumerable

Pubᵈ Novʳ 9 1808 by Thoˢ Tegg Nₒ111 Cheapside.

## THE PROGRESS OF THE EMPEROR NAPOLEON.

him the last Bourbon king to rule France. He spent the next two years of his life in exile at the Palace of Holyroodhouse, although he was never again to see his friend George IV, who had died only a month before the July Revolution.

Ten years later, the Duke of Wellington remarked of a group of portraits in the dining room at Apsley House, 'How much better … these two look with their *fleurs-de-lis* and *Saint-Esprits*, than the two corporals behind, or the fancy dress between!'[48] The 'fancy dress' was a version of Wilkie's portrait of George IV in Highland dress (see Fig. 12.5), the two 'corporals' were Alexander I of Russia and Frederick William III, King of Prussia, each dressed in the uniform of a field marshal. The two portraits that

the Duke of Wellington preferred depicted Louis XVIII and Charles X in regal robes clearly inspired by Hyacinthe Rigaud's portrait of the 'Sun King' Louis XIV: an abundance of gold, blue velvet and ermine, with the traditional symbols of French monarchy on prominent display.[49] As a group they provide a fitting example of the 'timeless' options available for men to wear in their portraits: robes, uniforms and so-called 'fancy dress'. It is perhaps ironic that in a century encompassing the 'age of revolution' that saw fundamental and distinctive changes in fashionable dress for both men and women, the clothing worn by the rulers in these formal portraits might give the impression that nothing had really changed at all.

Fig. 12.26  J.F. Cazenave (c.1770–c.1843) after Philip Vanderwal (1774–after 1810), *Napoléon Premier, Empereur des Français et Roi d'Italie*, c.1805–10.

Stipple printed in colours with hand-colouring, 71.5 × 52.0 cm (sheet). RCIN 617719

Fig. 12.27  Sir Thomas Lawrence (1769–1830), *Charles X, King of France*, 1825.

Oil on canvas, 269.7 × 178.3 cm. RCIN 405138

# NOTES

*Note: Measuringworth.com calculates the relative worth over time and here represents the value in 2021. The calculator multiplies the historical amount by the percentage increased in the RPI each year.*

## INTRODUCTION

1　North 2008, pp. 97–100.
2　See Reynolds 2013, p. 187.
3　Moreau 1822, II, p. 345: 'et ce sont eux qui donnent le ton à l'Europe entière, soit en spectacles, soit en decorations, en habillemens, en parure, en bijouterie, en coiffure'.
4　Macky 1722, I, p. 238.

## 1　SETTING THE SCENE

1　De Saussure 1902, p. 48.
2　The use of the tape measure did not become widespread until the 1830s. See Waugh 2018, p. 130.
3　North 2020a, p. 186.
4　For more detail, see Dowdell 2015.
5　Riello 2013, p. 246.
6　North 2020a, p. 171.
7　Ibid., p. 172.
8　Deane 1957, p. 213.
9　Muldrew 2012, p. 520.
10　Measuringworth.com calculation: £22,120 in 2021.
11　Walker 1813–14, p. 53.
12　For example, V&A: T.128–1921 and V&A: 656–1898.
13　The wearing of flannel for health reasons was controversial among physicians during the eighteenth century. See North 2020a, pp. 67–73.
14　Mansel 2005, p. 50.
15　Lister 2003, p. 56.
16　Riello 2013, p. 39.
17　This species had long threads and was used to produce the most highly prized cotton fabric in the eighteenth century, which became known as Sea Island cotton.
18　Riello 2013, p. 191.
19　O'Brien *et al.* 1991, p. 403.
20　Ibid., p. 409.
21　Montgomery 1970, p. 17.
22　Riello 2013, p. 154.
23　RCIN 1100579, p. 13.
24　For a full discussion, see Lemire 1991, pp. 311–28.
25　Riello 2013, pp. 212, 227.
26　North 2008, p. 97.
27　Ribeiro 2002, p. 161.
28　Thornton 1965, pp. 127–8.
29　RA GEO/ADD/17/75, p. 70. Measuringworth.com calculation: £4,665 in 2021.
30　Earnshaw 1985, p. 61.
31　RA GEO/MAIN/29284.
32　Ewing 1981, p. 80.
33　Matthäi *et al.* 2018, p. 64.
34　Ewing 1981, pp. 72–3.
35　See, for example, a fabric panel in the V&A woven to imitate leopard print (T.107–1962) and a court mantua in the V&A with silk that imitates ermine (T.252&A–1959).
36　Kay-Williams 2013, p. 11.
37　North 2020a, pp. 219–22.
38　Pastoureau 2000, p. 125.
39　Kay-Williams 2013, p. 110.
40　Ibid., p. 113.
41　Lovell 2005, p. 64.
42　RCIN 402466.
43　D'Amato *et al.* 2016, p. 5.
44　Peck 2013, p. 127.
45　Nenadic and Tuckett 2022.
46　Ehrman 2011, p. 34.
47　Levey 1983, p. 55.
48　St Clair 2016, p. 122.
49　*Cabinet des modes*, 15 September 1786, p. 166.
50　For example, a woman's gown of orange damask (Colonial Williamsburg collection, 1941-257,1) has been completely turned inside out, probably because of wear. The fabric dates from 1747–50 and the gown from 1760–75.
51　Ashelford 1996, p. 154.
52　Lee-Whitman 1982, pp. 23–4.
53　Harris 2006, p. 180.
54　Watt 2013, p. 99.
55　Oberkampf was later given the Légion d'Honneur by Napoleon.
56　The Gordon riots of 1780 were in response to the Papists Act of 1778, which had granted greater freedoms to British Catholics, including the ability to serve in the British army. Lord George Gordon (head of the Protestant Association) led the march to Parliament, which descended into several days of rioting, loss of life and the destruction of Catholic chapels.
57　From the milliner, Katherine Vezran. Levey 1983, p. 47. Measuringworth.com calculation: £2,960 in 2021.
58　The finest version of this portrait was given by the king to his prime minister, Horace Walpole, and hangs at Houghton Hall, Norfolk.
59　Levey 1983, p. 50.
60　Alençon lace has a hexagonal looped and twisted mesh ground, while Argentan is also hexagonal but the bars are made using buttonhole stitches.
61　Levey 1983, fig. 331.
62　Parmal 1997, p. 77, note 11.
63　Measuringworth.com calculation: £171,400 in 2021. The table itself only cost £5 5s (equivalent to £833). See Walton 1975, p. 113.
64　Levey 1983, p. 71.
65　Honiton lace would rise to much greater prominence during the nineteenth century.
66　Levey 1983, p. 58.
67　Ibid.
68　For a full discussion, see Birt 2021.
69　Fordyce 1766, I, p. 69.
70　Quoted in Roche 1999, p. 373.
71　North 2020a, pp. 210–11.
72　Bailey 1736, n.p.
73　RA GEO/ADD/17/75, p. 85. Two laundresses named Hetling (Katherine and Sophia) are recorded as Laundress to Princesses Amelia and Caroline until 1760 in Bucholz 2019.
74　Bucholz 2019.
75　For example, Tate, N01402 and N01403.
76　Pyne 1808, n.p.
77　Lemire 1992, p. 54.
78　Wendeborn 1791, I, pp. 265–6.
79　'Jusqu'au cordonnier, chacun est mis de même.' Morand 1964, p. 82.
80　Defoe 1725, p. 2.
81　Goldsmith 1762, pp. 31–3.
82　Archenholz 1790, p. 70.
83　Greig 2013, pp. 77–8.
84　La Roche 1933, p. 87.
85　Rothstein 1990, pp. 307–8.
86　Ribeiro 1995, p. 111, referencing Johnstone 1817, pp. 366–72.
87　For more on non-elite dress, see Styles 2007.
88　Smiles 2002, p. 26.
89　Quoted in Robinson and Calvey 2015, p. 92.
90　Quoted in Arnold 2021, p. 5.
91　*Morning Post*, 19 January 1810.
92　*Gentleman's Magazine*, 17 January 1810.
93　Quoted in Anon. 1822, p. 241.

## 2　ROYAL FASHION

1　RA GEO/ADD/9/119.
2　Macky 1722, I, p. 238.
3　Meyer 1995, pp. 45–63.
4　Wildeblood 1965, pp. 266–7. If the hat was to be carried, it would be placed under the left arm. See ibid., p. 214 and pl. IX a, b, c.
5　De Saussure 1902, pp. 45–6.
6　RCIN 406073 and RCIN 405246.
7　Quoted in Millar 1963, p. 188.
8　Home 1889–96, I (1889), p. lxxx. Quoted in Worsley 2010, p. 304.
9　Marschner 1997, p. 30.
10　Ibid., pp. 31–2.
11　Ibid., p. 29. Measuringworth.com calculation: £18,550 in 2021.
12　Rorschach 1989, p. 43.
13　Quoted in Brooke 1972, p. 278.
14　Broughton 1887, I, p. 12.
15　Museum of London, Acc. 38.294/3 (125 cm waist, dated 1817), Acc. 38.294/4 (102 cm waist, not dated), Acc. 38.294/5 (118 cm waist, dated 1816 or 1818).
16　Quoted in Foreman 2008, p. 79.
17　RA GEO/MAIN/43058–43105. Measuringworth. com calculation: equivalent to dropping from £42,950 to £23,160 in 2021.
18　RA GEO/MAIN/43058.
19　Measuringworth.com calculation: £4,377 in 2021.
20　Dunkin 1844, p. 359.
21　Hansard 1840, p. 90.
22　Quoted in Cumming 1989, p. 90.
23　Ibid.
24　Harris 1844, III, p. 211.
25　Laqueur 1982, p. 427.
26　Ibid., p. 452.
27　Ribeiro 1995, p. 240, note 96. Measuringworth.com calculation: £88,150 in 2021.
28　Cumming 1989, p. 100. Measuringworth.com calculation: 50 shillings in 1830 is equivalent to £238.10 in 2021; £6 6s is equivalent to £600.10 in 2021.

### 3 DRESSING WOMEN

1 Pöllnitz 1737, II, p. 460.
2 North 2020a, p. 194.
3 TNA, TS 11/98/308/1/75.
4 Quoted in Cunnington and Cunnington 1951, p. 110.
5 Quoted in North 2020a, p. 132.
6 Platt Hall, Museum of Costume. Illustrated in Cunnington and Cunnington 1951, p. 113.
7 The corset was originally a softer, less stiffened garment than stays, although from the early nineteenth century the two garments began to converge in design and the terms became used interchangeably.
8 M. Reisser, *Avis Important au Sexe ou Essai sur les Corps Baleinés*, Lyon 1770, p. 130. Quoted in Arnold *et al.* 2018, p. 7.
9 Fielding 1926, III, p. 129.
10 Anon. 1811, p. 96.
11 Bury 1839, I, p. 281.
12 Llanover 1861–2, Series 1, II (1861), p. 113.
13 *Tatler*, 29 December 1709.
14 Patent 560, Hoops for Petticoats, 8 February 1737, British Library. Quoted in Arnold *et al.* 2018, p. 25.
15 Letter to the *Guardian* in 1713. Quoted in Chrisman 1996, p. 12.
16 Quoted in ibid., p. 15.
17 Richardson 1985, letter 74.
18 RA GEO/ADD/17/75, p. 5.
19 RA GEO/ADD/17/75, p. 2.
20 Using V&A: T.254–1981 (dated 1739–42) as a typical example – this petticoat is made of five widths of fabric, each of which is 21 inches (*c.*55 cm) wide, with a drop from waist to hem of 40 inches (*c.*100 cm). This means 5½ yards (5 m) of fabric is required, with some additional allowance for seams.
21 Ribeiro 2002, p. 222.
22 RA GEO/ADD/17/75, fol. 84.
23 The author would like to thank Montaz Marché for her thoughts on this painting.
24 Cleave and Welborn 2013, p. 2.
25 This was known at the time as a *robe à l'anglaise retroussée*.
26 Ashelford 2018, pp. 224–7.
27 Goodman 2017, p. 53.
28 *Cabinet des modes*, 15 April 1786, p. 82.
29 1783; Hessische Hausstiftung, Kronberg.
30 Private collection.
31 *Morning Herald*, 30 October 1782. Quoted in Byrne 2005, p. 203.
32 Byrne 2005, p. 204.
33 For more, see Rauser 2020.
34 Blackman 2001, p. 52.
35 Reinira van Tuyll was the wife of Captain John Albert Bentinck who is shown in Figure 11.25.
36 Later habit shirts were made without sleeves or side seams and were also known as chemisettes.
37 Richardson 1741, p. 125. This book serves as a form of conduct manual, and contains 173 letters as templates to be adapted when dealing with particular social occasions. This example is from a concerned uncle to his niece, Betsey.
38 The inscription reads 'La Comtesse de Promnitz nèe Comtesse d'Erbach'.
39 The term 'fichu' was not in general use in the eighteenth century in England, although it was used in France to refer to such handkerchiefs but was also a generic term for a much broader range of female neckwear, including lace mantles.
40 Quoted in Ribeiro 1983, p. 125.
41 Brandenburgh House and Brunswick 1822, pp. 85–6. We might imagine a garment similar to that worn in *Portrait of a Russian Lady* (date unknown) by François-Joseph Kinsoen in the Bowes Museum (B.M.291).
42 Quoted in Davidson 2019, p. 103. Fashion histories have traditionally attributed its development to Charles Spencer's brother, George, 4th Duke of Marlborough, catching his coat tails on fire, although contemporary periodicals suggest this is an inaccuracy.
43 Quoted in Walker 1992, p. 393.
44 Spencer 2018, p. 164.
45 Roberts *et al.* 2005, p. 13.
46 Ibid., p. 17.
47 Delpierre 1997, p. 45.
48 Ibid.
49 See Fairhurst 2019, p. 29.
50 Fairhurst 2017, p. 27.
51 RA GEO/ADD/17/75, fol. 61. Measuringworth.com calculation: £1,612 in 2021.
52 Measuringworth.com calculation: £57.42 in 2021.
53 National Trust, Killerton, Acc. 1360795.
54 RA GEO/ADD/17/75, fol. 47 and fol. 60.
55 Cumming 1982, pp. 49–50.
56 See Beechey's *Portrait of Sir Francis Ford's Children Giving a Coin to a Beggar Boy* (1793; Tate, T06734) for an illustration of a pocket in elite dress.
57 Burman and Fennetaux 2019, p. 38.
58 10 October 1783. Delany 1820, p. 33.
59 See, for example, V&A: T.353B–1965.
60 Quoted in Hayden 1992, p. 155.
61 Foster 1982, p. 29.
62 Greig 2013, p. 60.
63 Llanover 1861–2, Series 1, I (1861), p. 191.
64 Pointon 2007, p. 22.
65 Ogden 2018, p. 172.
66 Collings and Redington Dawes 2007, p. 95.
67 Scarisbrick *et al.* 2008, p. 160.
68 Measuringworth.com calculation: £9,836,000 in 2021.
69 Greig 1926, p. 31.
70 Sabor 2011–19, I (2011), pp. 233–4.
71 Ibid.
72 Bury 1988, p. 15.
73 See Pointon 2016, p. 47.
74 Broughton 1887, I, p. 12.

### 4 DRESSING MEN

1 Carey 1730, p. 11.
2 North 2020a, p. 143.
3 Holme 1688, p. 17.
4 Griffin 2016, p. 103.
5 Jesse 1844, I, p. 61.
6 G. Cruikshank, *Neckclothitania or Tietania, Being an Essay on Starchers, by One of the Cloth*, London 1818.
7 Sheridan 1781, p. 13.
8 RA GEO/MAIN/55279b; RA GEO/MAIN/55301b. Measuringworth.com calculation: equivalent to £12.55 and £87.87 in 2021.
9 Farrell 1992, p. 37.
10 RA GEO/MAIN/54173–54174.
11 Gernerd 2015, p. 18.
12 Quoted in Karamzin 1803, III, pp. 217–18.
13 Quoted in Du Mortier 1988, p. 57.
14 *Gray's Inn Journal*, 13, 13 January 1752, p. 11.
15 *Cabinet des modes*, 1 October 1786, p. 172: 'Un jeune Homme en frac vert *Dragon*, orné d'une broderie en soie vert *pomme*'.
16 RA GEO/MAIN/29251.
17 See, for example, BM 1868,0808.12549 (dated 1799) and BM 1851,0901.1082 (dated 1802).
18 RA GEO/MAIN/29520. Marseille was a type of fabric woven to imitate quilting. Measuringworth.com calculation: £3,442 in 2021.
19 Museum of London, Acc. 38.294/3; Acc. 38.294/4; Acc. 38.294/5.
20 Du Mortier 1988, p. 54.
21 Quoted in Bolton 2016, p. 272.
22 RA GEO/MAIN/29248. Measuringworth.com calculation: £106.40 in 2021.
23 RA GEO/MAIN/29303. Measuringworth.com calculation: £383 in 2021.
24 Langley Moore 1971, pp. 1–13.
25 *Town and Country Magazine*, May 1772, p. 243.
26 Quoted in Muhlstein 2003, I, p. 10.
27 RA GEO/MAIN/29300. Measuringworth.com calculation: £255.30 in 2021.
28 McCormack 2017, p. 475.
29 Dr Johnson describes a 'Bannian' as 'A man's undress, or morning-gown'. See Johnson 1755, n.p.
30 RA GEO/MAIN/29251. Measuringworth.com calculation: £768.30 in 2021.
31 For more, see North 2020b.
32 Rush 1972, p. 96.
33 *Town and Country Magazine*, 1785. Quoted in Cunnington and Cunnington 1972, p. 220.
34 See Pointon 2010.
35 Broughton 1887, I, p. 213.
36 See, for example, *The Button Makers Adjusting their Differences*, *c.*1770 (BM Y,4.571), which portrays George III more interested in showing the King of Spain his buttons than in discussing the disputed Falkland Islands.
37 Broughton 1887, I, p. 213.
38 Measuringworth.com calculation: £5,085 in 2021.
39 *Kabinet van mode en smaak*, Haarlem 1791–4, I (1791), p. 4. Quoted in Du Mortier 1988, p. 54.
40 Climenson 1899, p. 117.
41 Quoted in Cummin and Taunton 1994, p. 44.
42 Sold Christie's, London, 18 May 1819 (lot 9).
43 Snowman 1990, p. 31.
44 Johnstone 1817, p. 278.
45 Greig 1926, p. 33.
46 Llanover 1861–2, Series 1, III (1861), p. 400.
47 Pöllnitz 1737, II, p. 462.
48 RCIN 811603.

### 5 DRESSING CHILDREN

1 Locke 1693, p. 78.
2 Buck 1996, p. 60.
3 John Hoppner, 'Royal Academy exhibition', *Morning Post*, 5 May 1785.
4 Rousseau 2009, p. 265.
5 M. Underwood, *A Treatise on the Diseases of Children*, London 1784, pp. 235–6. Quoted in North 2020a, p. 89.
6 Rousseau 2009, p. 265.
7 *Journal des Luxus und der Moden*, 1787, n.p. Quoted in Rose 1989, p. 50.
8 Quoted in Manning 1954, p. 42.
9 Llanover 1861–2, Series 2, II (1862), p. 473.
10 Buck 1996, p. 207.

11 RA GEO/ADD/17/75, p. 15.
12 Ibid., p. 14.
13 See, for example, V&A: B.81–1995, dated 1775–1800.
14 Buck 1996, p. 208.

### 6  POWDER, POMATUM, BONNETS & BICORNES

1 Llanover 1861–2, Series 2, II (1862), p. 524.
2 For more on language of the hat, see Corfield 1989.
3 Markiewicz 2014, p. 97.
4 Mundy 1885, p. 36.
5 *Gentleman's Magazine,* 16, 1746, p. 611.
6 Vigée Le Brun 1835, I, p. 53: 'je ne pouvais souffrir la poudre'.
7 Cameron and Hicks 1996, pp. 1495–6.
8 Markiewicz 2014, p. 40.
9 Diderot and d'Alembert 2021, XII, p. 402.
10 In 1710, for example, Jonathan Swift described buying a wig for 3 guineas (£3 3s). Measuringworth.com calculation: equivalent to £438 in 2021.
11 Burney 1820, II, p. 5.
12 Measuringworth.com calculation: 1 guinea was equivalent to £115 in 2021. The fine of £20 in 1795 was equivalent to £2,198 in 2021.
13 *Town and Country Magazine,* 4, 1772, p. 376.
14 RA GEO/MAIN/29239. Measuringworth.com calculation: equivalent to £403 in 2021.
15 Markiewicz 2014, p. 259.
16 1793–4; NPG 745.
17 1807; Schlossmuseum Friedenstein Gotha, SG 157.
18 For more, see Withey 2021, p. 24.
19 Ibid., p. 21.
20 Beards had been favoured in Ancient Greece but passed out of popularity under Alexander the Great and men remained clean-shaven during the Roman Republic, by which point a beard had become indicative of mental distraction.
21 For more, see Withey 2021, pp. 35–7.
22 Geffroy and Von Arneth 1874, II, p. 308. Translation given in Hosford 2004, p. 189.
23 Hosford 2004, p. 189.
24 Ibid., p. 188.
25 Vail 1958, p. 43.
26 Quoted in Jones 2014, p. 1.
27 The author would like to thank Kimberly Chrisman-Campbell for her comments on this portrait. Modern conservation practice would retain Gainsborough's changes.
28 1794; BM 1902,1011.2605.
29 Withey 2021, p. 85.
30 Vincent 2018, pp. 72–5.
31 Withey 2021, p. 114. Measuringworth.com calculation: sixpence in 1714 was equivalent to £3.85 in 2021.
32 In fact, the term hairdresser was rarely used until the 1780s, hair-cutter being more commonly found in directories of tradesmen.
33 Vincent 2018, p. 64.
34 Markiewicz 2014, p. 164.
35 Chrisman-Campbell 2015, p. 25.
36 Greig 2013, p. 24.
37 Measuringworth.com calculation: equivalent to £26,850 in 2021.
38 Vincent 2018, p. 67.
39 Broughton 1887, I, p. 173. Mr Read was misinterpreted as Mr Kead in this edition.
40 Corfield 1989, p. 75.
41 For more on the felt-hatting trade, see Corner 1991.
42 Corfield 1989, p. 70.

43 Corner 1991, pp. 157, 164.
44 See, for example, RCIN 630059.
45 English Patents of Inventions, No. 2022.
46 *Morning Post,* 7 April 1775.
47 Le Bourhis 1989, p. 33.

### 7  FACING FASHION

1 *Connoisseur,* 1, 1754, p. 274.
2 Rouquet 1755, p. 46.
3 *Lady's Magazine,* 3, 1772, p. 259.
4 Roberts 2004, p. 26.
5 Measuringworth.com calculation: £24,210 in 2021.
6 Buc'hoz 1784, p. 78.
7 Recent experiments to recreate historic cosmetic recipes have indicated that the effects of lead-based cosmetics were more subtle and less artificial than has traditionally been assumed, with the pigment serving to scatter light rather than reflect it. See McNeill 2022.
8 Cunningham 1861–6, V (1866), p. 30.
9 Quoted in Festa 2005, p. 29.
10 RA GEO/ADD/17/75, fol. 53. Measuringworth.com calculation: £53 in 2021.
11 Paulson 1997, p. 34.
12 RA GEO/MAIN/29209.
13 Rosenthal 1996, p. 22.
14 Elborough 2021, pp. 94–7.
15 Ibid., p. 102.
16 Lewis 1937–83, XXI (1960), p. 529.
17 Fraser 2002, p. 30.
18 Berdmore 1768.
19 Haslam 1996, pp. 252–3.
20 Llanover 1861–2, Series 1, I (1861), p. 544.
21 Van Horn 2016, pp. 8–9.
22 Baudelaire 1970, p. 13.
23 Jones 2014.
24 De Piles 1743, p. 162.
25 Jones 2014, p. 63.
26 Quoted in Jones 2014, p. 1.

### 8  COURT, CEREMONY & RITUAL

1 Moser 1794, II, p. 16.
2 Bucholz 2019, Introduction, pp. xxi–xxii.
3 Ibid., p. lxxx.
4 Staniland 1997, p. 12.
5 Measuringworth.com calculation: £500 in 1761 was equivalent to £81,970 in 2021.
6 For a detailed list of the various roles within the royal household, together with their occupants and salaries, see Bucholz 2019. Measuringworth.com calculation: £200 in 1716 was equivalent to £31,800 in 2021, and £300 in 1727 was equivalent to £47,470.
7 Barrett 1904–5. Measuringworth.com calculation: £127 in 1792 was equivalent to £16,450 in 2021.
8 For more on the dress worn in this portrait, see Behrendt 2019.
9 *The Times,* 19 January 1792.
10 RA GEO/MAIN/53585–53586.
11 Home 1889–96, II (1889), p. 177.
12 'The Prince's Wedding', *Gentleman's Magazine,* 77, 1795, p. 430.
13 *Northampton Mercury,* 11 April 1795.
14 Measuringworth.com calculation: £500 in 1790 was equivalent to £63,560 in 2021.
15 Greig 2015, para. 30.
16 For a full discussion of this bodice, see Chrisman-Campbell 2013.

17 Llanover 1861–2, Series 1, I (1861), p. 138.
18 RCIN 421798 and RCIN 421821.
19 Llanover 1861–2, Series 1, I (1861), p. 436.
20 Llanover 1861–2, Series 1, II (1861), p. 147.
21 Fletcher 1901, pp. 160–1.
22 Barrière 1823, I, p. 286.
23 Simond 1817, I, p. 208.
24 The train is 117 inches (297 cm), the equivalent of 2½ aunes, the unit of measure commonly used in France at the time. For full details and pattern, see Arnold et al. 2018, pp. 92–8.
25 Jesse 1867, II, p. 648.
26 *Gentleman's Magazine,* 65, 1795, p. 430.
27 *Northampton Mercury,* 11 April 1795.
28 Staniland 2000, p. 78.
29 Letter from Ramsay to Lord Bute, dated 19 December 1761, in the Bute MSS collection. Quoted in Russell 2004, pp. 230–1.
30 *European Magazine,* 64, 1813, p. 516.
31 Keay 2012, p. 117.
32 RCIN 405247 (c.1720–7), RCIN 405246 (before 1757) and RCIN 405307 (c.1761–2).
33 Mary of Modena's state crown is in the Royal Collection (RCIN 31707) whereas the nuptial crown is now in Hanover, and still used as the Hanoverian royal wedding crown.
34 Fritz 1982, p. 307.
35 *Universal Spectator,* 1731. Quoted in Taylor 1983, p. 108.
36 Taylor 1983, p. 119.
37 *London Gazette,* 26–28 October 1760; *London Gazette,* 13–17 January 1761.
38 *London Gazette,* 28 February–3 March 1761.
39 For an explanation of the different types of mourning crape, see Priestley 1993, p. 48.
40 Ibid., p. 51.
41 RA GEO/MAIN/25821. A.V.B. Norman first identified this sword as the one supplied by Gray in 1810.
42 Fritz 1982, pp. 306–7.
43 Chrisman-Campbell 2005, p. 68.
44 Llanover 1861–2, Series 1, III (1861), p. 34.
45 Chrisman-Campbell 2005, p. 70.
46 Fritz 1982, pp. 310–11.
47 Ibid., p. 314.

### 9  INFLUENCES FROM AFAR

1 Joseph Addison, *Spectator,* 1 (69), 19 May 1711, p. 213.
2 Williams 2014, pp. 56–8.
3 Wortley Montagu 1835, p. 68.
4 *Kentish Gazette,* 3 February 1795.
5 Cooke 1799, p. iii.
6 The fes can be distinguished from the stiffer, more cylindrical fez worn during the nineteenth century. See Jirousek 2019, p. 159.
7 *Gentleman's Magazine,* 38, October 1768, p. 450.
8 Llanover 1861–2, Series 2, I (1862), p. 180.
9 Wortley Montagu 1835, p. 89.
10 *Gentleman's Magazine,* 25, February 1755, p. 89.
11 Arbuthnot 1724. Quoted in Ribeiro 1984, p. 383.
12 *Magazine à la Mode,* 1777, p. 367.
13 Plates compiled by Paul Cornu between 1911 and 1914. For analysis, see Jirousek 2019, pp. 171–6.
14 The other miniatures are RCIN 420710, RCIN 420712 and RCIN 420714.
15 Blum 1983, pp. 55–6.
16 *Remembrancer,* 27 May 1749. Quoted in Rorschach 1989, p. 37.

17 Jirousek 2019, p. 177.
18 Harris 2006, p. 133.
19 After 1757, China instituted a 'one port policy', which required that all foreign trade be carried out through Guangzhou. See Hung 2001, p. 476.
20 Lee-Whitman 1982, p. 24.
21 Crill *et al.* 1990, p. 22.
22 Lister 2003, p. 56.
23 Skelton and Francis 1979, pp. 64–5.
24 British Library, IOR/H/114, pp. 329–30, 'The Contents of Three Chests etc. for Their Most Sacred Majesties the King and Queen of Great Britain by Their Faithful and Steady Friend and Ally the Nabob of the Carnatic'.
25 RA GEO/ADD/43/3a & 3d. Given that the queen specifically references the 'Nabob of Arcot', she is here referring to Mohammad Ali Khan Wallajah, although by this date the term nabob was also being used as a colloquial term of disparagement to refer to British merchants who had returned to Britain after becoming wealthy in India.
26 See Maskiell 2002, pp. 30–5.
27 De Rémusat 1880, II, p. 345.
28 Crill 2015, pp. 27–8.
29 Das 1992, p. 38.
30 Farrell 2016, p. 283.
31 For a full account, see ibid.
32 They are today in the V&A: 17–1906; 18–1906; 19–1906; W.70a-k–1916.
33 1763–4; NG 6440.
34 Wine *et al.* 2018, p. 198.
35 Quoted in ibid., pp. 192–4.

## 10 WALKING PICTURES

1 See Cunningham 1861–6, II (1861), pp. 422–3.
2 Cunningham 1861–6, I (1861), p. 132.
3 RA GEO/MAIN/29315.
4 RA GEO/MAIN/29414.
5 Cunningham 1861–6, I (1861), p. 132.
6 This shade of blue is seen in the suit worn by Lord Bernard Stuart (c.1638; NG6518), however. It is interesting that Gainsborough's *'The Blue Boy'* (1770; Huntington Art Museum, San Marino, California) was also painted around the same time as Zoffany's sketch. Representing another homage to the portrait of the Villiers brothers in both dress and pose, the colour of the Blue Boy's clothes appears to have been similarly adapted to appeal to an eighteenth-century audience.
7 Quoted in Scott Thomson 1943, p. 120.
8 Quoted in Aspinall 1963–71, I (1963), p. 51.
9 RA GEO/MAIN/29228.
10 This was a popular pose for women, also seen in Gainsborough's portrait of Queen Charlotte (see Fig. 8.11).
11 Anon. 1821, p. 13.
12 Lockhart 1837–8, V (1837), p. 96.
13 Mackrell 1998, p. 36.
14 *Coronation of Emperor Napoleon 1st and Coronation of Empress Joséphine in Notre-Dame Cathedral in Paris, December 2, 1804*, 1805–7, Musée du Louvre, 3699.
15 Quoted in Whitley 1915, p. 74.
16 Quoted in ibid.
17 Quoted in ibid., p. 75.
18 Reynolds 1842, p. 138.

## 11 DRESSED FOR BATTLE

1 RCIN 1085534, [p. 65].
2 A range of reforms to the organisation of the British army introduced between 1868 and 1874 by Edward Cardwell (1813–86), Secretary of State for War, including abolishing the practice of granting commissions and promotions in exchange for a fee.
3 Quoted in Du Mortier 1988, p. 58.
4 Quoted in Ribeiro 2002, p. 188.
5 These match with the images in the 1742 Cloathing Book, although with some changes to the lace patterns. See Barthorp 1982, p. 144.
6 Ibid., p. 28.
7 Ibid., p. 37. The clothing warrant indicates that the CR cipher for Queen Caroline continued to be worn even after her death in 1737.
8 2 pence out of the daily rate of 8 pence. Measuringworth.com calculation: assuming these figures for 1765, this was equivalent to £1.16 out of £4.80 in 2021. See Gale 2007, p. 47.
9 Between 1751 (the date of the Morier painting, Fig. 11.4) and 1768 (the date of Fig. 11.8), the colour of the facings for the 2nd Regiment changed from sea green to blue.
10 Cumming 1989, p. 69.
11 VM 001575a. Depicted in Lembke 2014, p. 339.
12 Mansel 2005, p. 29.
13 Ibid.
14 Barthorp 1984, p. 58.
15 Carman 1967, p. 193.
16 RA GEO/MAIN/29380. Measuringworth.com calculation: £2,497 in 2021.
17 Ewing 1981, p. 74.
18 Carman 1967, p. 195.
19 Combe 1801, p. 6. Measuringworth.com calculation: equivalent to £14,590 in 2021.
20 Annis 1969, p. 21.
21 Miller 2007, p. 45.
22 Cavell 2012, p. 31.
23 Ibid.
24 Quoted in ibid., p. 68.
25 Annis 1971, p. 30.
26 Miller 2007, p. 59.
27 RCIN 400503 and RCIN 400212.
28 The original appearance of the cuffs can be seen in a print after the painting, before the changes (RCIN 654148), which was published in 1800.
29 De Marly 1987, pp. 61–2.
30 Mansel 2005, p. 58.
31 Llewellyn 1996, pp. 12–13.
32 Mansel 2005, p. 58.
33 Llewellyn 1996, p. 12.
34 Ibid., p. 14. Measuringworth.com calculation: £3 was equivalent to £423.60 in 2021.
35 *Reading Mercury*, 1779. Quoted in Cumming 1989, p. 72.
36 Llewellyn 1996, p. 14.
37 For example, RCIN 913551.
38 *Gentleman's Magazine*, 51, 1781, pp. 57–8.
39 *Gallery of Fashion*, I (4), July 1794, figs XVI and XVIII.

## 12 REBELLION & REVOLUTION

1 'Le costume étant le plus énergique de tous les symbols, la Révolution fut aussi une question de mode, un débat entre la soie et le drap'. See Lévy 1869–76, XX (1870), p. 492.

2 Quoted in Ribeiro 2002, p. 108.
3 Scott 1853–4, I (1853), p. 177.
4 Tuckett 2016, pp. 184–5.
5 Nicholson 1998, p. 146.
6 An interesting example is RCIN 400963. Recent investigation has revealed the tartan plaid, socks and sporran to be nineteenth-century additions applied to a portrait of Louis XV in antique dress.
7 Nicholson 1998, p. 148.
8 Reid 2012, p. 40.
9 Illustrated in Forsyth 2017, p. 98. Measuringworth. com calculation: £5.27 million in 2021.
10 Quoted in Coltman 2010, p. 182.
11 Tuckett 2016, p. 187.
12 For a surviving example, see National Museums Scotland, A.1993.62.
13 Walpole 1927–8, p. 39.
14 Frederick also employed the sister of Charles Stuart's mistress as a maid of honour for his wife Augusta. See Gerrard 1994, pp. 194–5.
15 Coltman 2019, pp. 23–4.
16 Ribeiro 1984, p. 295.
17 Watt and Waine 2019, p. 40.
18 Measuringworth.com calculation: £131,400 in 2021.
19 Sold Sotheby's, Munich, 5–15 October 2005 (lot 3918).
20 Prebble 1988, p. 268.
21 Recorded by Hugh Scott of Harden. Quoted in Prebble 1988, p. 269.
22 Prebble 1988, p. 269.
23 Cockburn 1932, p. 103.
24 Prebble 1988, p. 306.
25 The 1810 United States census recorded a total population of 7,239,814, of whom 1,191,364 were enslaved. See DeBow 1854, pp. 39, 82.
26 Baumgarten 2002, pp. 79–82.
27 Thatcher Ulrich 2009, p. 177.
28 *Virginia Gazette*, 14 December 1769.
29 Vigée Le Brun, 23 March 1779, in Vigée Le Brun 1835, I, p. 251: 'je l'aurais pris pour un gros fermier, tant il faisait contraste avec les autres diplomates, qui tous étaient pourdrés, en grande tenue, et chamarrés d'or et des cordons'.
30 Boyd *et al.* 1950–2022, XII (1955), p. 504.
31 Chrisman-Campbell 2015, pp. 169–70.
32 Standen 1964, p. 121.
33 Butterfield 1951, I, p. 92.
34 1789–96; National Gallery, Washington, DC, NGA 940.1.2.
35 Miles 1995, pp. 151–2.
36 *Morning Herald*, 1 May 1784.
37 Foreman 2008, p. 80.
38 Chrisman-Campbell 2015, p. 27.
39 For more on the role of dress during the French Revolution, see Ribeiro 1988.
40 Chrisman-Campbell 2015, p. 282.
41 Lévy 1869–76, XX (1870), p. 492.
42 Fraser 2002, pp. 438–9.
43 Gower 1885, pp. 146–7.
44 *The Times*, 9 September 1796, p. 2.
45 Quoted in Noailles and Chambers 1923, p. 84.
46 Squire 1970, pp. 13–14.
47 Mansel 2005, p. 93.
48 Quoted in Stanhope 1889, p. 218.
49 1701; Musée du Louvre, 7492.

Published by William Miller, Albemarle Street, Jan.y 1, 1805.

# GLOSSARY

**AIGRETTE** A hair ornament often adorned with a tufted plume of feathers, sometimes with flowers and jewels. Name derived from the egret bird (heron).

**BALEEN (BALEINE, WHALEBONE)** Flexible material derived from keratinous plates found in the upper jaw of the baleen whale (*Mysticeti*). Used to stiffen garments and create structure. Cut into strips and sewn into channels, it moulds with the warmth of the body.

**BANYAN (BANIAN, NIGHTGOWN, INDIAN GOWN, *ROBE DE CHAMBRE*)** Informal loose morning gown for men, modelled on Eastern dress. Derived from the Gujarati word for a Hindu merchant, *vāṇiyo*.

***BERGÈRE* (BERGER)** Wide-brimmed, shallow-crowned hat. Derived from the French word for shepherdess.

**BICORNE** Cocked hat with the brim turned up in two places. Corners could be worn on either side, or to the front and back.

**BLONDE LACE** Bobbin lace made from silk thread. Usually the cream colour of raw silk, but could be made in other colours.

**BOBBIN LACE (PILLOW LACE, BONE LACE)** Lace made using multiple threads wound round bobbins, which are crossed and twisted together to create the pattern. Worked over a design marked with pins on a pillow or cushion.

**BOB WIG** Wig set with curls all over, reaching either just below the ears or to the shoulders. Increasingly associated with professional and middle classes during the eighteenth century.

**BODICE (BODIES)** The upper part of a woman's dress (from bust to waist), either a separate garment or the upper part of a gown.

**BOMBAZINE (BOMBAZEEN)** Twill fabric usually made from a silk warp and worsted weft. Black versions were popular for mourning garments due to the matt finish.

**BREECHES** Lower body garment for men, covering the hips and thighs and reaching to just below the knee. Worn with stockings on the lower leg.

**BROADCLOTH** Plain or twill-woven fabric made of fine wool yarn. Fulled, napped and sheared after weaving to create a smooth surface.

**BROCADE** Fabric woven with additional weft threads of coloured silk or metal to create a slightly raised pattern above the woven ground.

**BUCKRAM** Strong plain-woven linen fabric, stiffened with flour paste or glue. Used for lining and creating structure in clothing.

**BUFFON** Voluminous handkerchief worn around the neck, often starched and puffed up over the bosom.

**BUSK** Stiff strip inserted into the centre front of a pair of stays or corset to create a smooth line, and most often made of wood. Could be highly decorative, sometimes inscribed with amorous messages.

**CALAMANCO (CALAMANCA, CALIMANCO)** Plain or twill-woven woollen fabric with a highly glazed surface.

**CALASH** Large folding hood worn by women to protect tall hairstyles. Made of fabric supported by hoops of cane or whalebone, which folded down in concertina-like action. Name derived from the folding hood of a *calèche* carriage.

**CALICO (CALLICO, CALICOT)** Originally used to describe plain-woven cottons imported from India. Later applied to all cotton fabrics including those made in Europe, and those with mixed fibres such as linen/cotton. Name derived from the port of Calicut (now Kozhikode), India.

**CAMBRIC (FRENCH LAWN)** Fine lightweight plain-woven linen made in Europe, and known as French lawn in Britain. Named after Cambrai in France.

**CAMPAIGN WIG** Style of wig with one lock of hair tied on each side and a long curl at the back, associated with military dress.

**CAP** Broad term for any form of close-fitting headwear.

***CARACO*** Informal women's jacket that reached the hips.

**CASHMERE (KASHMIR)** Fine woollen fabric made from the soft under-hair of the Himalayan goat.

**CERUSE** Lead-based white pigment (probably lead carbonate hydroxide) used as a face cosmetic. Created by exposing lead plates to vinegar.

**CHANGEANT SILK (SHOT SILK)** Silk fabric woven with contrasting colours in the weft and warp, creating a two-tone effect in different lights.

**CHATELAINE** Chain worn at the waist to which could be attached small accessories such as scissors, keys, watch, etc.

**CHEMISE GOWN** Type of women's gown made of light cotton, named for its apparent similarity to the chemise. Shaped with a drawstring at the neckline and below the bust.

***CHIKAN*** Embroidery on muslin using white cotton thread.

**CHINTZ** Cotton or linen cloth produced in India, printed or painted with coloured patterns. Derived from the Hindi word *chint*, meaning to sprinkle, a reference to the speckled background seen on some early examples.

**CLOAK** Protective outer garment, loose and sleeveless, worn by both men and women. Derived from the Old French word *cloke*, meaning bell.

**CLOCKS** Shaping inserts added to stockings to create a better fit around the ankle, often decorative.

**COCHINEAL** Vibrant scarlet dye made from the dried bodies of the female cochineal scale insect (*Dactylopius coccus*) native to South America and Mexico.

**COCKADE** Ribbon rosette, usually circular, typically attached to headwear. Worn as a symbol of office or affiliation.

**CORSET** Undergarment providing support and shape for the torso. Originally softer, shorter and less heavily boned than stays, although from the early nineteenth century the two garments converge in style and the terms are used synonymously.

**COTTON** Fibres extracted from the soft seed hair of the cotton plant (*Gossypium*). Can be spun into threads and used to make cotton fabrics.

**CRAPE (CRÊPE)** Plain-woven fabric, usually woven from silk or silk and worsted, with a distinctive crimped matt surface created by adding extra twists to the thread before weaving.

**CRAVAT (NECKCLOTH)** Type of neckwear, formed of a folded piece of fabric tied in a knot or bow at the front, often starched.

**DAMASK** Self-coloured reversible patterned fabric, with the design created through variations in the weave structure so that the pattern on one side of the fabric appears in reverse on the other. Named after the city of Damascus, but first produced in China.

**DORSET THREAD BUTTONS** Buttons created by binding thread around a ring or disc, named after the county of Dorset, England, from where they originated.

**DOUBLET** Close-fitting men's upper body garment, worn over the shirt. Replaced with the coat by the eighteenth century.

**DRAWERS** Undergarment for legs, worn beneath breeches or petticoat. Knee-length for men, but could be longer for women.

**EPAULETTE** Ornamental trimming on the shoulder of military uniform to distinguish rank, originally used to hold a sash or belt in position. From the French word *épaulette*, diminutive of *épaule*, meaning shoulder.

**ERMINE** Soft white fur dotted with black spots, derived from the winter coat of a species of stoat (*Mustela erminea*). Typically reserved for royalty and the nobility.

**FACING** Turned-back section of a garment revealing the lining, for example at collar and cuffs.

**FARTHINGALE** Sixteenth/seventeenth-century name for a hooped petticoat worn beneath the skirt to add width and shape. Various styles included the French 'drum' farthingale and the Spanish conical farthingale. A precursor to the eighteenth-century 'hoop'.

**FILÉ** Thread made by wrapping a strip of metal round a silk or linen core.

**FLANNEL** Woollen fabric with a fluffy raised surface.

**FOB** Originally a name for a small pocket at the waist. Later the name for an ornament suspended from a chain or ribbon and tucked inside the pocket, such as a watch or seal.

**FROCK** (a) Back-fastening gown with bodice and skirt attached to each other, initially worn by children but later also by women.

**(b)** Originally an informal style of coat worn by men, with a turndown collar and no cutaway front or stiffening, which became more acceptable for formal occasions over the course of the eighteenth century. Known in France as a *frac*.

**FROGGING** Ornamental looped fastening made of braid or cord, most frequently seen on men's coats. Derived from hussar military dress.

**FULLING** Process applied to woollen fabric after weaving, involving washing, scouring and raising the nap, which causes the fibres to become more compacted. Fulled cloth is more waterproof and durable.

**FUSTIAN** Originally used to describe a fabric made with a linen warp and cotton weft. Often twill-woven and used for linings due to its softness. Later applied to any coarse cotton.

**GAITER (SPATTERDASH)** Protective covering for the lower leg, made of fabric or leather. Buttoned along the outer side.

**GARTER** Used to secure stockings, typically consisting of a sash or ribbon tied just below the knee.

**GIRDLE** Narrow band, chain or cord worn at the waist to encircle, or 'gird'. Usually decorative, and could be used to support small items such as a fan or pendant.

**GORE** Triangular-shaped piece of fabric inserted into a garment to add fullness.

**GOWN (ROBE)** Broad term used to describe the main full-length garment worn by women. Used interchangeably with robe.

**GRAND HABIT (*ROBE DE COUR*, STIFF-BODIED GOWN, ROYAL ROBE)** The most formal style of dress for women, consisting of a boned bodice with a low neckline and short-capped sleeves, hooped petticoat and a train hooked to the bodice.

**GREATCOAT (OVERCOAT, SURTOUT)** Protective outer garment worn by men, knee- or ankle-length and made of a thick, heavy material, often incorporating a cape over the shoulders.

**GREATCOAT DRESS** Style of women's gown, in imitation of a greatcoat, with tight wrist-length sleeves. Fully buttoned to the hem or to the waist, and sometimes incorporating a caped collar.

**HABIT À LA FRANÇAISE (*HABIT HABILLÉ*)** Formal style of suit for men consisting of coordinating coat, waistcoat and breeches.

**HANDKERCHIEF (KERCHIEF, MUCKINDER)** Large square of fabric folded diagonally and worn as an item of everyday neckwear. A smaller version, usually carried, was called a pocket handkerchief.

**HEAD** Style of lace headdress, consisting of a semicircular cap-back, frill and pair of lappets, which were pinned or sewn together and could be styled in a variety of ways.

**HESSIANS** Black riding boots worn by men, cut higher in the front than the back, decorated with a tassel at the front-centre. First worn by troops from Hesse, Germany.

**HOOP** Stiffened supportive undergarment worn beneath the skirt to expand its width.

**HUSSAR BOOT** Similar to the Hessian boot but reaching only to mid-calf and without the tassel.

**INDIGO** Deep blue dye extracted from the plant *Indigofera tinctoria* (found in India) and *Indigofera suffruticosa* (found in Africa and the Americas).

**JABOT** Ornamental frill or ruffle at the front of a man's shirt.

**JACKBOOTS** Heavy square-toed riding boots made of thick leather, reaching above the knee, generally worn by cavalry.

**JUMPS** Comfortable unboned women's garment worn over the torso instead of stays, usually only worn at home or during pregnancy.

**KAFTAN (CAFTAN)** Full-length outer robe worn by men and women in a variety of countries, with either long or short sleeves. From the Persian, *khaftan*.

**KOSODE** A Japanese garment that formed the main item of dress for both men and women. Originally worn as an undergarment, it later developed into outerwear. The precursor to the kimono.

**LAMÉ** Silk gauze woven with silver or gilt threads, often used for court dress.

**LAPEL** Front part of a coat or jacket opening, folded back below the collar.

**LAPPETS** Strips of fabric attached to a woman's headdress, designed to hang down either side of the head. Often made of lace.

**LATCHET** Pair of tabs on shoe uppers through which shoelaces could be threaded or buckles attached.

**LAWN** Very soft and fine plain-woven linen or cotton fabric. Named after its place of origin, Laon in France.

**LEADING STRINGS** Strips of fabric attached to the back of a child's frock. Originally used as reins but later ornamental.

**LEGHORN STRAW** Type of fine supple wheat straw, plaited and used to make hats or bonnets. Named after the Italian port of Leghorn (Livorno) from where it was exported.

**LINEN** Fabric woven from thread derived from the fibres of the flax plant (*Linum usitatissimum*). Varieties range from coarse buckram to delicate lawn.

**LINSEY-WOOLSEY** Cheap, coarse fabric woven with a linen warp and wool weft.

**LIVERY** Form of civilian uniform for men used to identify the wearer as being employed by a certain household.

**LOGWOOD** Dye derived from the logwood tree in Central America (*Haematoxylum campechianum*). Most commonly used to create a deep black, but different mordants could produce a range of hues.

**LUSTRING (LUTESTRING, LUTSTRING)** Plain-woven silk fabric with a lustrous surface.

**MACARONI** Nickname for men known for their extravagant style of dressing. Named after the pasta dish they supposedly introduced to England from Italy after returning from a Grand Tour.

**MADDER** Dye derived from roots of plants in the *Rubiaceae* family, including *Rubia tinctorum*. Produces a range of orange/purple/red hues, depending on the mordant used.

**MANCHESTER CLOTH** Hard-wearing cotton fabric, produced in Lancashire.

**MANTLE** Long sleeveless outer garment. Derived from the Latin word *mantellum*, meaning cloak.

**MANTUA** Woman's gown worn open at the front to reveal the petticoat, the sides of the trained skirt pulled back into an arrangement of stylised drapery. Later developed into a formal style of dress worn at court.

**MANTUA-MAKER** Dressmaker (usually female) producing garments for women.

**MERCER** Textile merchant. Derived from the Old French word *mercier*, meaning shopkeeper or tradesman.

**MILLINER** Supplier of accessories such as hats, gloves and ribbons.

**MORDANT** Substance used to help dye bond to a fabric or yarn. Types included alum (that is, potassium alum).

**MUFF** Tubular accessory providing warmth for the hands.

**MUSLIN** Fine plain-woven cotton fabric, originating in India but later made in Europe. Comes in a variety of weights, but is often semi-transparent. Usually white but could be patterned or embroidered.

**NANKEEN (NANKIN)** Plain-woven and closely woven cotton fabric. Made from a type of yellow cotton left in its undyed hue. Name derived from Nanjing, China, where it was originally produced.

**NAP** Raised fibres on the surface of a fabric.

**NEEDLEPOINT LACE (NEEDLE LACE)** Lace made by hand with a needle and thread, rather than bobbins, typically incorporating various types of buttonhole stitch.

**OPEN ROBE** Gown with a skirt that opens at the front to reveal a petticoat.

**PAILLETTE** Small ornaments cut from shiny flat metal and sewn onto fabric as a form of decoration. Could come in a variety of shapes.

**PANTALOONS** Tight-fitting men's legwear, worn instead of breeches and hose. Could be made with or without feet. Named after the *commedia dell'arte* character Pantalone.

**PARASOL** Accessory designed to protect the complexion from the sun.

**PARFILAGE (DRIZZLING)** Fashionable pastime of unravelling metallic threads from fabric.

**PASSEMENTERIE** Collective term for a range of ornamental trimmings including fringing, tassels and cord. Usually made from silk, cotton or metal threads, often used to add detail to interior soft furnishings. Derived from the French word *passement*, to braid.

**PATCHES** Small fabric shapes applied to the face, usually cut from black silk taffeta or velvet.

**PEIGNOIR** Informal women's upper body garment, particularly worn as morning dress.

**PELERINE** Small mantle covering the shoulders with long pendants at the front.

**PELISSE** Initially a style of men's cloak lined with fur. Later a style of women's long-sleeved coat dress.

**PERIWIG (PERUKE, PERRUQUE)** Full-bodied curled men's wig, shoulder-length or longer.

**PETTICOAT** Contemporary term for a skirt. Used to refer to both visible outer garments or skirts worn beneath a gown or another petticoat. It could also describe the skirt of a gown with an attached bodice.

**PHILABEG (PHILIBEG, FÈILEADH BEAG)** An early version of the kilt, developed from the belted plaid. The Gaelic translates as 'little wrap'.

**PLAID** Originally a component of Highland dress, consisting of a length of woollen cloth worn wrapped around the body. Derived from the Gaelic for blanket. Later used to describe a checked pattern.

**PLAIN WEAVE (TABBY)** Simplest form of weave structure in which the weft runs over one warp thread then under the next.

**POCKET BOOK** Small purse used to hold valuable documents or instruments, for example letters or tweezers.

**POMATUM (POMADE)** Scented ointment used to soften and dress the hair. Derived from rendered animal fat.

**POMPON (*POUF*)** Small head ornament for women made of ribbons, flowers, etc.

**POWDERINGS** Black pieces of fur, derived either from the tails of a species of weasel (*Mustela erminea*) or black lambskin, set into white fur to create a spotted effect.

**PURL** Coil made from a very fine pulled metal wire (often silver or silver gilt), used as a form of decorative embroidery.

**RATTAN** Strong material derived from stems of the common rattan plant (*Calamus rotang*) native to India. Used to stiffen hoops, and for walking sticks and canes.

**RETICULE (REDICULE, RIDICULE)** Small bag carried by women, often knitted or netted.

**RIDING HABIT (HABIT)** Set of women's garments based on male riding dress, consisting of a hip-length jacket, petticoat and optional waistcoat. Made by a male tailor.

**ROBE À L'ANGLAISE (NIGHTGOWN, TIGHT-BODIED GOWN)** Style of women's gown with a tight bodice fitted into the waistline. Particularly popular in England, and later in France.

**ROBE À LA FRANÇAISE (SACQUE, SACK-BACK GOWN, SACK)** Style of women's open gown characterised by pleats of fabric at the back neckline, which create a loose cascade of fabric to the ground. Originally an informal gown but later considered suitable for formal dress.

**ROBE À LA POLONAISE** Women's open gown made without a waist seam, the skirt pulled up into three rounded swags, one at the back and one on each side.

**ROBE VOLANTE** Style of women's unstructured loose-fitting gown, with pleats at the front and back and worn with a wide hoop to create a voluminous bell shape.

**ROBINGS** Fabric folded back down the front edges of an open-fronted gown, initially reaching to the waist and later to the hem. Often decorated with trimmings.

**ROUND GOWN** Style of gown in which the skirt does not open at the centre front to reveal the petticoat.

**RUFF** Form of neckwear worn in the late sixteenth and early seventeenth century. Made from pleats of stiffened linen, set into shape using a heated poking stick.

**RUFFLES (ENGAGEANTES)** Scalloped flounces of lace or linen attached to the elbow-length sleeves of a gown, worn singly or layered in multiples.

**RUMP** Padded support worn beneath the skirt to add volume at the back or sides.

**SABRETACHE** Flat stiffened pouch, forming part of military dress for cavalry. Used to carry dispatches, and employed as a hard writing surface in the field.

**SATIN** A glossy smooth-surfaced fabric with a dull reverse created using a warp-heavy weaving technique.

**SHIFT (CHEMISE, SMOCK)** Undergarment for women worn next to the skin. Usually made from linen, later cotton. Often with a drawstring neckline and short full sleeves.

**SHIRT** Upper body undergarment for men worn next to the skin. Usually made from linen, later cotton.

**SILK** A fine lustrous thread spun from the long protein fibres derived from the secretion of various types of caterpillar, including the Asian silkworm (*Bombyx mori*).

**SKELETON SUIT** Transitional style of dress worn by young boys, consisting of a short jacket and trousers buttoned together at the waist.

**SPANGLES** Small, thin, shiny discs of metal, usually round in shape, made by flattening tiny circles of wire. Used to ornament fabric in the manner of modern sequins.

**SPENCER** Short tight-fitting jacket with long sleeves. Originally worn by men and later fashionable for women.

**STAYS** Undergarment providing support and shape for the torso. Stiffened by inserting thin strips of whalebone or grass into narrow pockets stitched into the fabric. Originally longer and more heavily boned than a corset, although from the early nineteenth century the two garments converge in style and the terms are used synonymously.

**STOCK** Item of men's neckwear, consisting of a piece of pleated fabric that fastens behind the neck.

**STOCKINGS (HOSE)** Covering for the lower legs, usually knitted from wool or silk. Worn by men and women.

**STOMACHER** Triangular panel used to fill the gap between the front edges of an open gown or bodice. Could be pinned, sewn or laced into position, often highly decorative.

**SWADDLE BANDS** Strips of fabric wound round a young infant in a process known as swaddling.

**TAFFETA** Stiff medium-weight plain-woven silk, made with tightly twisted threads that create a glossy surface. Possibly from the Persian word *tāftan*, meaning to shine.

**TARLETON HELMET** Leather helmet with fur crest and peaked front. Named after Sir Banastre Tarleton.

**TISSUE** Brocaded silk fabric usually woven with silver, gold or gilt-metal threads. Popular for court dress.

**TOP BOOT (JOCKEY BOOT)** Style of leather boot for men reaching just below the knee, with the upper part folded over to reveal a lighter colour. Originally worn for riding before becoming a fashionable style.

**TREWS** Component of traditional Highland dress consisting of close-fitting footed trousers.

**TRICORNE** Cocked hat with the brim turned up in three places to create a triangular shape.

**TUCKER** Separate piece of fine fabric, often frilled or decorated with lace, worn around the neckline. Could be attached to the shift or tucked inside the bodice.

**TWILL** Weave structure in which the weft passes over one warp then under two or more in an offset manner so as to produce a distinctive pattern of diagonal ribs.

**VELVET** Weave structure in which weft threads are raised above the fabric surface as loops, which can be left uncut or cut to create a soft pile.

**WAISTCOAT (VEST)** Upper body garment worn by men and women beneath the coat. Often, but not exclusively, sleeveless.

**WARP** Structural threads running vertically (lengthways) along the fabric between which the weft is woven.

**WEFT** Threads running transversely across the warp threads, which form the pattern.

**WHITEWORK** Form of embroidery using white thread to produce designs on semi-transparent white fabrics, often using cutwork or drawn threads.

**WOAD** Blue dye derived from the leaves of the flowering plant *Isatis tinctoria*. Less intense in hue than indigo.

**WOOL** Fibre derived from the fleece of animals (usually sheep) that is spun before being knitted or woven.

**WORSTED (STUFF)** Term used to describe a lightweight woollen cloth, as well as the fine long-staple, combed wool fibres from which it is made. Named after Worstead, a village in Norfolk central to its manufacture.

**WRAPPING GOWN** Informal dress for women, similar to a dressing gown, with a sash tied around the waist. Often worn in the home and during pregnancy.

# BIBLIOGRAPHY

**Abbreviations**

BM    British Museum, London
NG    National Gallery, London
NPG   National Portrait Gallery, London
QG    The Queen's Gallery, Buckingham Palace, London
RA    Royal Archives, Windsor
RCIN  Royal Collection Inventory Number
TNA   The National Archives, Kew
V&A   Victoria and Albert Museum, London

**Royal Archives, Windsor Castle**

RA GEO/ADD/17/75, fols 47, 53, 60, 61, 84
Wardrobe and Nursery Accounts of Caroline, Queen Consort to George II, 1730–4

RA GEO/MAIN/53585–53586
John Hervey, 2nd Baron Hervey, Manuscript of 'Memoirs of the Reign of George II' for the years 1735–6

RA GEO/MAIN/54173–54174
Prince of Wales's Marriage Procession, 10 March 1736

RA GEO/MAIN/55279B
Bill Issued by Conrad Fulling for cotton hose, 10 June 1750

RA GEO/MAIN/55301B
Bill Issued by Conrad Fulling for 24 pairs of cotton hose for the use of Princess Augusta, 14 December 1750

RA GEO/MAIN/29228–29229
Bill from Davies, Son and Co., 10 April–16 June 1786

RA GEO/ADD/9/119
Letter from Princess Augusta to her brother Augustus, 22 January 1791

RA GEO/MAIN/29239
Bill from L. Santhaque, with receipt, November 1791–October 1793

RA GEO/ADD/43/3A
Diary for 'Month of January & part of February 1794', 1 January–19 February 1794

RA GEO/ADD/43/3D
Diary for 'Part of the Month of June The Month of July & part of the Month of August 1794', 11 June–7 August 1794

RA GEO/MAIN/29248
Bill from John Williams, 3 September 1798–21 January 1799

RA GEO/MAIN/29250–29251A
Bill from Schweitzer and Davidson, with receipt, 10 January 1799–9 June 1800

RA GEO/MAIN/43058–43105
Wardrobe Account Book for George, Prince of Wales, 1800–12

RA GEO/MAIN/29284
Bill and receipt from Major and Ballhorn, 10 October 1800–5 January 1801

RA GEO/MAIN/29300–29300A
Bill from Andreas Meyer, with receipt, 15 April 1801–20 July 1802

RA GEO/MAIN/29303–29303A
Bill from Joseph White, with receipt, 27 July–10 October 1801

RA GEO/MAIN/29315–29315A
Bill from H. Wayte, with receipt, 8 February 1802–27 April 1803

RA GEO/MAIN/29414–29414A
Bill from Wayte and Son, with receipt, 25 May 1803–29 January 1808

RA GEO/MAIN/29380
Bill from J.C. Frank, 4 February 1804–30 July 1805

RA GEO/MAIN/25821
Bill from Thomas Gray, 15 October–22 December 1810

RA GEO/MAIN/29520–29521
Bill from John Weston, 9 October 1810–5 January 1811

RA GEO/MAIN/29209
Bill issued by R.B. Bate for supplying spectacles, eyeglasses, pebble lenses, cases etc. with receipt, 7 July 1825–24 August 1830

**Royal Collection**

RCIN 1085534
H. Hawley, *Chaos, or Rude Collection of Crude Conceptions, without Connection, Useful Ingredients for a Noble Composition*, manuscript, 1726

RCIN 1100579
L. Kennedy, *Mrs Kennedy's Diary 1793–1816*, 1793–1816

**Newspapers and Magazines**

*Cabinet des modes*
*Connoisseur*
*European Magazine*
*Gallery of Fashion*
*Gentleman's Magazine*
*Gray's Inn Journal*
*Ipswich Journal*
*Journal de la Mode et du Gout*
*Kentish Gazette*
*Lady's Magazine*
*London Gazette*
*Magasin des modes nouvelles, françaises et anglaises*
*Magazine à la Mode*
*Mémoires Secrets*
*Morning Herald*
*Morning Post*
*Northampton Mercury*
*Reading Mercury*
*Tatler*
*The Times*
*Town and Country Magazine*
*Universal Spectator*
*Virginia Gazette*

**Exhibition Catalogues**

CRILL *ET AL.* 1990
R. Crill, J. Guy and D. Swallow, *Arts of India, 1550–1900*, Victoria and Albert Museum, London

FORSYTH 2017
D. Forsyth (ed.), *Bonnie Prince Charlie and the Jacobites*, National Museums Scotland, Edinburgh

LE BOURHIS 1989
K. Le Bourhis (ed.), *The Age of Napoleon: Costume from Revolution to Empire 1789–1815*, Metropolitan Museum of Art, New York

LEMBKE 2014
K. Lembke (ed.), *The Hanoverians on Britain's Throne 1714–1837*, Landesmuseum, Dresden

MATTHÄI *ET AL.* 2018
C.G. Matthäi, C. Hug, F. Lentzsch and K. Verlag (eds), *Fashion Drive: Extreme Clothing in the Visual Arts*, Kunsthaus Zurich, Zurich

MILLER 2007
A. Miller, *Dressed to Kill: British Naval Uniform, Masculinity and Contemporary Fashions: 1748–1857*, National Maritime Museum, Greenwich

PECK 2013
A. Peck (ed.), *Interwoven Globe: The Worldwide Textile Trade, 1500–1800*, Metropolitan Museum of Art, New York

QUEEN'S GALLERY 1994
*Gainsborough & Reynolds: Contrasts in Royal Patronage*, Queen's Gallery, Buckingham Palace, London

REYNOLDS 2013
A. Reynolds, *In Fine Style: The Art of Tudor and Stuart Fashion*, Royal Collection Trust, London

ROBERTS 2004
J. Roberts (ed.), *George III & Queen Charlotte: Patronage, Collecting and Court Taste*, Royal Collection Trust, London

ROBERTS *ET AL.* 2005
J. Roberts, P. Sutcliffe and S. Mayor, *Unfolding Pictures: Fans in the Royal Collection*, Royal Collection Trust, London

SCARISBRICK *ET AL.* 2008
D. Scarisbrick, C. Vachaudez and J. Walgrave (eds), *Brilliant Europe: Jewels from European Courts*, ING Cultural Centre, Brussels

SKELTON AND FRANCIS 1979
R. Skelton and M. Francis (eds), *Arts of Bengal: The Heritage of Bangladesh and Eastern India: An Exhibition*, Whitechapel Art Gallery and Victoria and Albert Museum, London, and Manchester City Art Gallery

STANILAND 1997
K. Staniland (ed.), *In Royal Fashion: The Clothes of Princess Charlotte of Wales & Queen Victoria 1796–1901*, Museum of London, London

WATT AND WAINE 2019
P. Watt and R. Waine, *Wild and Majestic: Romantic Visions of Scotland*, National Museums Scotland, Edinburgh

**Published Sources**

ADAMS 1848
C.F. Adams (ed.), *Letters of Mrs. Adams, the Wife of John Adams. With an Introductory Memoir by Her Grandson, Charles Francis Adams*, Boston, MA

ANNIS 1969
P.G.W. Annis, 'The first British naval uniform', *Costume*, 3 (1), pp. 19–26

ANNIS 1971
P.G.W. Annis, 'The Royal Navy', *Costume*, 4 (1), pp. 29–35

ANON. 1811
Anon., *The Mirror of the Graces, or The English Lady's Costume*, London

ANON. 1821
Anon., *A Brief Account of the Coronation of His Majesty George IV*, London

ANON. 1822
Anon., *The Recreative Review, or Eccentricities of Literature and Life*, London

ARBUTHNOT 1724
J. Arbuthnot, *The Ball. Stated in a Dialogue betwixt a Prude and Coquet, Last Masquerade Night, the 11th of May*, London

ARCH AND MARSCHNER 1987
N. Arch and J. Marschner, *Splendour at Court: Dressing for Royal Occasions since 1700*, London

ARCHENHOLZ 1790
J.W. Archenholz, *A Picture of England: Containing a Description of the Laws, Customs and Manners of England*, J. Trapp (trans.), London

ARNOLD 2021
J. Arnold, *Patterns of Fashion 1: The Content, Cut, Construction & Context of Englishwomen's Dress c.1720–1860*, London

ARNOLD *ET AL.* 2018
J. Arnold, J. Tiramani, L. Costigliolo, S. Passot, A. Lucas and J. Pietsch, *Patterns of Fashion 5: The Content, Cut, Construction and Context of Bodies, Stays, Hoops and Rumps, c.1595–1795*, London

ASHELFORD 1996
J. Ashelford, *The Art of Dress*, London

ASHELFORD 2018
J. Ashelford, '"Colonial livery" and the chemise à la reine, 1779–1784', *Costume*, 52 (2), pp. 217–39

ASPINALL 1963–71
A. Aspinall (ed.), *The Correspondence of George, Prince of Wales 1770–1812*, 8 vols, London

BAILEY 1736
N. Bailey, *Dictionarium Domesticum, Being a New and Compleat Household Dictionary, for the Use of City and Country*, London

BARRETT 1904–5
C. Barrett (ed.), *Diary & Letters of Madame D'Arblay (1778–1840)*, 6 vols, London

BARRIÈRE 1823
F. Barrière (ed.), *Memoirs of the Court of Marie Antoinette, Queen of France, Complete Being the Historic Memoirs of Madam Campan, First Lady in Waiting to the Queen*, 2 vols, London

BARTHORP 1982
M. Barthorp, *British Infantry Uniforms since 1660*, Poole

BARTHORP 1984
M. Barthorp, *British Cavalry Uniforms since 1660*, Poole

BATCHELOR AND KAPLAN 2007
J. Batchelor and C. Kaplan, *Women and Material Culture, 1660–1830*, Basingstoke

BAUDELAIRE 1970
C. Baudelaire, *The Painter of Modern Life and Other Essays*, J. Mayne (trans.), London

BAUMGARTEN 2002
L. Baumgarten, *What Clothes Reveal: The Language of Clothing in Colonial and Federal America: The Colonial Williamsburg Collection*, New Haven and London

BEHRENDT 2019
G.M. Behrendt, 'Ernst August Mustapha – a man in the second row', *Hanoverian Historical Gazettes* (NF), 73, pp. 25–45

BERDMORE 1768
T. Berdmore, *A Treatise on the Disorders and Deformities of the Teeth and Gums*, London

BIRT 2021
S. Birt, 'Women, guilds and the tailoring trades: the occupational training of Merchant Taylors' Company apprentices in early modern London', *London Journal*, 46 (2), pp. 146–64

BLACKMAN 2001
C. Blackman, 'Walking Amazons: the development of the riding habit in England during the eighteenth century', *Costume*, 35 (1), pp. 47–58

BLUM 1983
D.E. Blum, 'Englishwomen's dress in eighteenth-century India: the Margaret Fowke Correspondence (1776–1786)', *Costume*, 17 (1), pp. 47–58

BOLTON 2016
C. Bolton (ed.), *Letters from England by Don Manuel Alvarez Espriella*, London and New York

BOYD *ET AL.* 1950–2022
J.P. Boyd, M. Bryan, L.H. Butterfield, C.T. Cullen, J. Catanzariti, T. Downey, B. Oberg, J.P. McClure and M.J. King (eds), *The Papers of Thomas Jefferson*, 45 vols, Princeton, NJ

BRANDENBURGH HOUSE AND BRUNSWICK 1822
Brandenburgh House and Q.C. Brunswick, *A Catalogue of the Magnificent Furniture, Beautiful China and Glass … and Effects Removed from Brandenburgh House, Which by Order of Her Late Majesty, Queen Caroline, Will be Sold at Auction by Mr. Robins*, London

BROOKE 1972
J. Brooke, *King George III*, London

BROUGHTON 1887
V.D. Broughton (ed.), *Court and Private Life in the Time of Queen Charlotte: Being the Journals of Mrs Papendiek, Assistant Keeper of the Wardrobe and Reader to Her Majesty*, 2 vols, London

BROWNE 2009
C. Browne, 'Silk damask bed furnishings in the early eighteenth century: influences on choice in colour and design', in Jolly 2009, pp. 47–58

BUCHOLZ 2019
R.O. Bucholz (ed.), *The Database of Court Officers: 1660–1837*, <https://courtofficers. ctsdh.luc.edu/> (visited 7 January 2022)

BUC'HOZ 1784
P.J. Buc'hoz, *The Toilet of Flora: Or, A Collection of the Most Simple and Approved Methods of Preparing Baths, Essences, Pomatums, Powders, Perfumes, and Sweet-Scented Waters: With Receipts for Cosmetics of Every Kind … for the Use of Ladies*, London

BUCK 1979
A. Buck, *Dress in Eighteenth-Century England*, London

BUCK 1996
A. Buck, *Clothes and the Child: A Handbook of Children's Dress in England 1500–1900*, Bedford

BURMAN AND FENNETAUX 2019
B. Burman and A. Fennetaux, *The Pocket: A Hidden History of Women's Lives, 1660–1900*, New Haven and London

BURNEY 1820
F. Burney, *Cecilia; or, Memoirs of an Heiress, by the Author of Evelina*, 3 vols, London

BURY 1839
C. Bury, *Diary Illustrative of the Times of George the Fourth*, 4 vols, London

BURY 1988
S. Bury, 'Queen Victoria and the Hanoverian claim to the crown jewels', *International Silver and Jewellery Fair and Seminar Handbook*, London, pp. 9–16

BUTTERFIELD 1951
L.H. Butterfield (ed.), *Letters of Benjamin Rush: Volume 1: 1761–1792*, 2 vols, Princeton, NJ

BYRNE 2005
P. Byrne, *Perdita: The Life of Mary Robinson*, London

CAMERON AND HICKS 1996
J.S. Cameron and J. Hicks, 'Frederick Akbar Mahomed and his role in the description of hypertension at Guy's Hospital', *Kidney International*, 49, pp. 1488–506

CAREY 1730
H. Carey, *Blundrella or the Impertinent, a Tale to Which is Added the Beau Monde or the Pleasures of St. James's, a New Ballad*, London

CARMAN 1967
W.Y. Carman, 'Nicholas Brown, 10th Hussars, c.1809', *Journal of the Society for Army Historical Research*, 45 (184), pp. 193–5

CAVELL 2012
S.A. Cavell, *Midshipmen and Quarterdeck Boys in the British Navy, 1771–1831*, Woodbridge, Suffolk

CHRISMAN 1996
K. Chrisman, 'Unhoop the fair sex: the campaign against the hoop petticoat in eighteenth-century England', *Eighteenth-Century Studies*, 30 (1), pp. 5–23

CHRISMAN-CAMPBELL 2005
K. Chrisman-Campbell, 'Mourning and *La Mode* at the court of Louis XVI', *Costume*, 39 (1), pp. 64–78

CHRISMAN-CAMPBELL 2013
K. Chrisman-Campbell, 'Diagnosing the dress of the queen's train-bearers at the coronation of George III', *Costume*, 47 (2), pp. 145–60

CHRISMAN-CAMPBELL 2015
K. Chrisman-Campbell, *Fashion Victims: Dress at the Court of Louis XVI and Marie-Antoinette*, New Haven and London

CLEAVE AND WELBORN 2013
K.V. Cleave and B. Welborn, '"Very much the taste and various are the makes": reconsidering the late-eighteenth-century robe à la polonaise', *Dress*, 39, pp. 1–24

CLIMENSON 1899
E.J. Climenson (ed.), *Passages from the Diary of Mrs Philip Lybbe Powys, 1756–1808*, London

COCKBURN 1932
H. Cockburn, *Some Letters of Lord Cockburn*, Edinburgh

COLLINGS AND REDINGTON DAWES 2007
O. Collings and G. Redington Dawes, *Georgian Jewellery: 1714–1830*, Woodbridge, Suffolk

COLTMAN 2010
V. Coltman, 'Party-coloured plaid? Portraits of eighteenth-century Scots in tartan', *Textile History*, 41 (2), pp. 182–216

COLTMAN 2019
V. Coltman, *Art and Identity in Scotland: A Cultural History from the Jacobite Rising of 1745 to Walter Scott*, Cambridge

COMBE 1801
W. Combe (ed.), *The Life, Adventures, and Opinions of Col. George Hanger: Written by Himself*, London

COOKE 1799
J. Cooke (ed.), *A Voyage Performed by the Late Earl of Sandwich round the Mediterranean in the Years 1738 and 1739*, London

CORFIELD 1989
P. Corfield, 'Dress for deference and dissent: hats and the decline of hat honour', *Costume*, 23 (1), pp. 64–79

CORNER 1991
D. Corner, 'The tyranny of fashion: the case of the felt-hatting trade in the late seventeenth and eighteenth centuries', *Textile History*, 22 (2), pp. 153–78

CRILL 2015
R. Crill (ed.), *The Fabric of India*, London

CUMMIN AND TAUNTON 1994
G.E. Cummin and N.D. Taunton, *Chatelaines: Utility to Glorious Extravagance*, Woodbridge, Suffolk

CUMMING 1982
V. Cumming, *Gloves*, London

CUMMING 1989
V. Cumming, *Royal Dress: The Image and the Reality, 1580 to the Present Day*, London

CUNNINGHAM 1861–6
P. Cunningham (ed.), *The Letters of Horace Walpole Earl of Oxford*, 9 vols, London

CUNNINGTON AND CUNNINGTON 1951
C.W. Cunnington and P. Cunnington, *The History of Underclothes*, London

CUNNINGTON AND CUNNINGTON 1972
C.W. Cunnington and P. Cunnington, *Handbook of English Costume in the Eighteenth Century*, London

D'AMATO *ET AL.* 2016
M. D'Amato, W. DeGregorio, D. Ghelerter and M. Majer, *A Catalogue of Exquisite & Rare Works of Art Including 18th to 19th Century Costume Textiles & Needlework*, New York

DAS 1992
S. Das, *Fabric Art: Heritage of India*, New Delhi

DAVIDSON 2019
H. Davidson, *Dress in the Age of Jane Austen: Regency Fashion*, New Haven and London

DEANE 1957
P. Deane, 'The output of the British woolen industry in the eighteenth century', *Journal of Economic History*, 17 (2), pp. 207–23

DEBOW 1854
J.D.B. DeBow, *Compendium of the Seventh Census*, Washington

DEFOE 1725
D. Defoe, *Everybody's Business Is Nobody's Business*, London

DELANY 1820
M. Delany, *Letters from Mrs Delany (Widow of Doctor Patrick Delany), to Mrs Frances Hamilton, from the Year 1779, to the Year 1788: Comprising Many Unpublished and Interesting Anecdotes of their Late Majesties and the Royal Family*, London

DELPIERRE 1997
M. Delpierre, *Dress in France in the Eighteenth Century*, New Haven and London

DE MARLY 1987
D. de Marly, *Louis XIV and Versailles*, London

DE PILES 1743
Roger de Piles, *The Principles of Painting*, London

DE RÉMUSAT 1880
C. de Rémusat, *Mémoires de Mme de Rémusat 1802–1808*, F.C. Hoey and J. Lillie (trans.), 3 vols, London

DE SAUSSURE 1902
C. de Saussure, *A Foreign View of England in the Reigns of George I & George II: The Letters of Monsieur César de Saussure to his Family*, London

DIDEROT AND D'ALEMBERT 2021
D. Diderot and J. d'Alembert (eds), *Encyclopédie, ou dictionnaire raisonné des sciences, des arts et des métiers, etc.*, 28 vols, University of Chicago: ARTFL Encyclopédie Project, R. Morrissey and G. Roe (eds), <http://encyclopedie.uchicago.edu> (visited 16 May 2022)

DOWDELL 2015
C. Dowdell, 'The multiple lives of clothes: alteration and reuse of women's eighteenth-century apparel in England', unpublished PhD Thesis, Queen's University, Kingston, Ontario, Canada

DU MORTIER 1988
B. du Mortier, 'Men's fashion in the Netherlands (1790–1830), caught between France and England', *Costume*, 22 (1), pp. 51–9

DUNKIN 1844
J. Dunkin, *The History and Antiquities of Dartford, with Topographical Notices of the Neighbourhood*, London

EARNSHAW 1985
P. Earnshaw, *Lace in Fashion: From the Sixteenth to the Twentieth Centuries*, London

EHRMAN 2011
E. Ehrman, *The Wedding Dress: 300 Years of Bridal Fashion*, London

ELBOROUGH 2021
T. Elborough, *Through the Looking Glass*, London

EWING 1981
E. Ewing, *Fur in Dress*, New York

FAIRHURST 2017
A. Fairhurst, 'Women's shoes of the eighteenth century: style, use and evolution', *Journal of Dress History*, 1 (2), pp. 25–43

FAIRHURST 2019
A. Fairhurst, 'Eighteenth-century women's shoes: a valuable historical resource', *Costume*, 53 (1), pp. 20–42

FARRELL 1992
J. Farrell, *Socks and Stockings*, London

FARRELL 2016
W. Farrell, 'Smuggling silks into eighteenth-century Britain: geography, perpetrators, and consumers', *Journal of British Studies*, 55 (2), pp. 268–94

FESTA 2005
L. Festa, 'Cosmetic differences: the changing faces of England and France', *Studies in Eighteenth-Century Culture*, 34, pp. 25–54

FIELDING 1926
H. Fielding, *The Works of Henry Fielding*, G. Saintsbury (ed.), 3 vols, London

FLETCHER 1901
E. Fletcher (ed.), *Conversations of James Northcote with James Ward on Art and Artists*, London

FORDYCE 1766
J. Fordyce, *Sermons to Young Women*, 2 vols, London

FOREMAN 2008
A. Foreman, *The Duchess: Georgiana, Duchess of Devonshire*, London

FOSTER 1982
V. Foster, *Bags and Purses*, London

FRASER 2002
A. Fraser, *Marie Antoinette: The Journey*, New York

FRITZ 1982
P.S. Fritz, 'The trade in death: the royal funerals in England, 1685–1830', *Eighteenth-Century Studies*, 15 (3), pp. 291–316

GALE 2007
R.R. Gale, *'A Soldier-like Way': The Material Culture of the British Infantry 1751–1768*, Elk River, MN

GEFFROY AND VON ARNETH 1874
A. Geffroy and A.R. Von Arneth (eds), *Correspondance secrète entre Marie-Thérèse et le comte de Mercy-Argenteau, avec les lettres de Marie-Thérèse et Marie-Antoinette*, 3 vols, Paris

GERNERD 2015
E. Gernerd, 'Pulled tight and gleaming: the stocking's position within eighteenth-century masculinity', *Textile History*, 46 (1), pp. 3–27

GERRARD 1994
C. Gerrard, *The Patriot Opposition to Walpole: Politics, Poetry, and National Myth, 1725–1742*, Oxford

GOLDSMITH 1762
O. Goldsmith, *The Life of Richard Nash of Bath, Esq*, London

GOODMAN 2017
S.L. Goodman, 'Devil in a white dress: Marie Antoinette and the fashioning of a scandal', unpublished Master's Thesis, San Jose State University, CA

GOWER 1885
R.S. Gower, *Last Days of Marie Antoinette. An Historical Sketch … With Portrait and Facsimiles*, London

GREIG 1926
J. Greig (ed.), *The Diaries of a Duchess: Extracts from the Diaries of the First Duchess of Northumberland, 1716–1776. Edited by James Greig. With a Foreword by the Duke of Northumberland*, London

GREIG 2013
H. Greig, *The Beau Monde: Fashionable Society in Georgian London*, Oxford

GREIG 2015
H. Greig, 'Faction and fashion: the politics of court dress in eighteenth-century England', *Apparence(s)*, 6, <http://journals.openedition.org/apparences/1311> (visited 7 February 2022)

GRIFFIN 2016
M. Griffin (ed.), *The Collected Poems of Laurence Whyte*, Lewisburg, PA

HANSARD 1840
G.A. Hansard, *The Book of Archery*, London

HARRIS 1844
J. Harris (ed.), *Diaries and Correspondence of James Harris, First Earl of Malmesbury*, 4 vols, London

HARRIS 2006
J. Harris (ed.), *5000 Years of Textiles*, London

HASLAM 1996
F. Haslam, *From Hogarth to Rowlandson: Medicine in Art in Eighteenth Century Britain*, Liverpool

HAYDEN 1992
R. Hayden, *Mrs Delany and her Flower Collages*, London

HOLME 1688
R. Holme, *The Academy of Armory or, a Storehouse of Armory and Blazon*, Chester

HOME 1889–96
J.A. Home (ed.), *The Letters and Journals of Lady Mary Coke*, 4 vols, Edinburgh

HOSFORD 2004
D. Hosford, 'The queen's hair: Marie-Antoinette, politics, and DNA', *Eighteenth-Century Studies*, 38 (1), pp. 183–200

HUNG 2001
H.F. Hung, 'Imperial China and capitalist Europe in the eighteenth-century global economy', *Review*, 24 (4), pp. 473–513

JESSE 1844
W. Jesse, *The Life of George Brummell, Esq.*, 2 vols, London

JESSE 1867
J.H. Jesse, *Memoirs of the Life and Reign of King George the Third*, 3 vols, London

JIROUSEK 2019
C.A. Jirousek, *Ottoman Dress and Design in the West: A Visual History of Cultural Exchange*, Bloomington, IN

JOHNSON 1755
S. Johnson, *Dictionary of the English Language: In Which the Words are Deduced from their Originals, and Illustrated in their Different Significations by Examples from the Best Writers, to Which are Prefixed, a History of the Language, and an English Grammar: in Two Volumes*, London

JOHNSTONE 1817
A. Johnstone, *Johnstone's London Commercial Guide and Street Directory … Corrected to August 31, 1817*, London

JOLLY 2009
A. Jolly (ed.), *Furnishing Textiles: Studies on Seventeenth- and Eighteenth-Century Interior Decoration*, Riggisberg

JOLLY AND PIETSCH 2012
A. Jolly and J. Pietsch (eds), *Netherlandish Fashion in the Seventeenth Century*, Riggisberg

JONES 2014
C. Jones, *The Smile Revolution in Eighteenth-Century Paris*, Oxford

KARAMZIN 1803
N.M. Karamzin, *Travels from Moscow, through Prussia, Germany, Switzerland, France and England*, A. Feldborg (trans.), 3 vols, London

KAY-WILLIAMS 2013
S. Kay-Williams, *The Story of Colour in Textiles: Imperial Purple and Denim Blue*, London

KEAY, 2012
A. Keay, *The Crown Jewels: The Official Illustrated History*, London

KREMS AND RUBY 2016
E.-B. Krems and S. Ruby (eds and trans.), *Das Porträt als Kulturelle Praxis*, Marburg

LANGLEY MOORE 1971
D. Langley Moore, 'Byronic dress', *Costume*, 5 (1), pp. 1–13

LAQUEUR 1982
T.W. Laqueur, 'The Queen Caroline affair: politics as art in the reign of George IV', *Journal of Modern History*, 54 (3), pp. 417–66

LA ROCHE 1933
S. von La Roche, *Sophie in London, 1786, Being the Diary of Sophie von La Roche*, C. Williams (trans.), London

LEE-WHITMAN 1982
L. Lee-Whitman, 'The silk trade: Chinese silks and the British East India Company', *Winterthur Portfolio*, 17 (1), pp. 21–41

LEMIRE 1991
B. Lemire, '"A good stock of cloaths": the changing market for cotton clothing in Britain, 1750–1800', *Textile History*, 22 (2), pp. 311–28

LEMIRE 1992
B. Lemire, *Fashion's Favourite: Cotton Trade and the Consumer in Britain, 1660–1800*, Oxford

LEVEY 1983
S.M. Levey, *Lace: A History*, London and Leeds

LÉVY 1869–76
C. Lévy (ed.), *Oeuvres complètes de H. de Balzac*, 24 vols, Paris

LEWIS 1937–83
W.S. Lewis (ed.), *Horace Walpole's Correspondence*, 48 vols, New Haven and London

LISTER 2003
J. Lister, 'Twenty-three samples of silk: silks worn by Queen Charlotte and the princesses at royal birthday balls, 1791–1794', *Costume*, 37 (1), pp. 51–65

LLANOVER 1861-2
L.A.H. Llanover (ed.), *The Autobiography and Correspondence of Mary Granville, Mrs Delany: With Interesting Reminiscences of King George the Third and Queen Charlotte*, 6 vols, London

LLEWELLYN 1995
S. Llewellyn, '"A list of ye wardrobe" 1749: the dress inventory of John Montagu, 2nd Duke of Montagu', *Costume* 29 (1), pp. 40–54

LLEWELLYN 1996
S. Llewellyn, 'George III and the Windsor uniform', *Court Historian*, 1 (2), pp. 12–16

LOCKE 1693
J. Locke, *Some Thoughts Concerning Education*, London (*The Works of John Locke in Ten Volumes*), London 1812, vol. IX

LOCKHART 1837-8
J.G. Lockhart, *Memoirs of the Life of Sir Walter Scott*, 7 vols, Edinburgh

LOVELL 2005
M.M. Lovell, *Art in a Season of Revolution: Painters, Artisans, and Patrons in Early America*, Philadelphia, PA

MACDONALD 2004
J. Macdonald, *Memoirs of an Eighteenth-Century Footman*, London and New York

MACKRELL 1998
A. Mackrell, 'Dress in *Le Style Troubadour*', *Costume*, 32 (1), pp. 33–44

MACKY 1722
J. Macky, *A Journey through England. In Familiar Letters from a Gentleman Here, to His Friend Abroad*, 3 vols, London

MANNING 1954
F.J. Manning (ed.), 'The Williamson letters, 1748–1765', *Bedfordshire Historical Record Society*, 34, pp. 1–147

MANSEL 1982
P. Mansel, 'Monarchy, uniform and the rise of the frac 1760–1830', *Past & Present*, 96, pp. 103–32

MANSEL 2005
P. Mansel, *Dressed to Rule: Royal and Court Costume from Louis XIV to Elizabeth II*, New Haven and London

MARKIEWICZ 2014
E. Markiewicz, 'Hair, wigs and wig wearing in eighteenth-century England', unpublished PhD Thesis, University of Warwick

MARKO 1997
K. Marko (ed.), *Textiles in Trust*, Proceedings of the Symposium 'Textiles in Trust' held at Blickling Hall, Norfolk, September 1995, London

MARSCHNER 1997
J. Marschner, 'Queen Caroline of Ansbach: attitudes to clothes and cleanliness, 1727–1737', *Costume*, 31 (1), pp. 28–37

MASKIELL 2002
M. Maskiell, 'Consuming Kashmir: shawls and empires, 1500–2000', *Journal of World History*, 13 (1), pp. 27–65

MATHIASSEN *ET AL.* 2014
T.E. Mathiassen, M.L. Nosch, M. Ringgaard and K. Toftegaard, *Fashionable Encounters: Perspectives and Trends in Textile and Dress in the Early Modern Nordic World*, Havertown, PA

MCCORMACK 2017
M. McCormack, 'Boots, material culture and Georgian masculinities', *Social History*, 42 (4), pp. 461–79

MCNEILL 2022
F. McNeill, 'Toxic allure: did white lead make-up enhance beauty at a deadly cost?', <https://www.toxicallure.com> (visited 23 May 2022)

MEASURINGWORTH.COM
MeasuringWorth, 'Five ways to compute the relative value of a UK pound amount, 1270 to present', <www.measuringworth.com/ukcompare/> (visited 24 May 2022)

MEYER 1995
A. Meyer, 'Re-dressing classical statuary: the eighteenth-century "hand-in-waistcoat" portrait', *Art Bulletin*, 77 (1), pp. 45–63

MILES 1995
E.G. Miles (ed.), *American Paintings of the Eighteenth Century (The Collections of the National Gallery of Art: Systematic Catalogue)*, Washington and New York

MILLAR 1963
O. Miller, *The Tudor, Stuart and Early Georgian Pictures in the Collection of Her Majesty The Queen*, London

MONOD 1993
P.K. Monod, *Jacobitism and the English People, 1688–1788*, Cambridge

MONTGOMERY 1970
F.M. Montgomery, *Printed Textiles: English and American Cottons and Linens, 1700–1850*, London

MORAND 1964
P. Morand, *Le Prince de Ligne*, Paris

MOREAU 1822
M. Moreau (ed.), *Mémoires de M. Goldoni: pour servir à l'histoire de sa vie et à celle de son théâtre*, 2 vols, Paris

MOSER 1794
J. Moser, *The Adventures of Timothy Twig, Esq*, 2 vols, London

MUHLSTEIN 2003
A. Muhlstein (ed.), *Memoirs of the Comtesse de Boigne*, T. Waugh (trans.), 2 vols, New York

MULDREW 2012
C. Muldrew, '"Th'ancient distaff" and "whirling spindle": measuring the contribution of spinning to household earnings and the national economy in England, 1550–1770', *Economic History Review*, 65 (2), pp. 498–526

MUNDY 1885
H.G. Mundy (ed.), *The Journal of Mary Frampton: From the Year 1779, until the Year 1846*, London

NENADIC AND TUCKETT 2022
S. Nenadic and S. Tuckett, 'Colouring the nation: dyeing and printing techniques', <https://www.nms.ac.uk/collections-research/collections-departments/global-arts-cultures-and-design/projects/colouring-the-nation/> (visited 15 February 2022)

NICHOLSON 1998
R. Nicholson, 'The tartan portraits of Prince Charles Edward Stuart: identity and iconography', *Journal for Eighteenth-Century Studies*, 21 (2), pp. 145–60

NOAILLES AND CHAMBERS 1923
H.G.H. Noailles and A. Chambers (eds), *The Life and Memoirs of Count Molé (1781–1855)*, London

NORTH 2008
S. North, 'The physical manifestation of an abstraction: a pair of 1750s waistcoat shapes', *Textile History*, 39 (1), pp. 92–104

NORTH 2020a
S. North, *Sweet & Clean?: Bodies and Clothes in Early Modern England*, Oxford

NORTH 2020b
S. North, 'Indian gowns and banyans – new evidence and perspectives', *Costume*, 54 (1), pp. 30–55

O'BRIEN *ET AL.* 1991
P. O'Brien, T. Griffiths and P. Hunt, 'Political components of the industrial revolution: parliament and the English cotton textile industry, 1660–1774', *Economic History Review*, 44 (3), pp. 395–423

OGDEN 2018
J. Ogden, *Diamonds: An Early History of the King of Gems*, New Haven and London

PARMAL 1997
P.A. Parmal, 'Fashion and the growing importance of the *Marchande Des Modes* in mid-eighteenth-century France', *Costume*, 31 (1), pp. 68–77

PASTOUREAU 2000
M. Pastoureau, *Blue: The History of a Color*, Princeton, NJ

PAULSON 1997
R. Paulson (ed.), *The Analysis of Beauty by William Hogarth*, New Haven and London

PINDER 1785
P. Pinder, *More Lyric Odes to the Royal Academicians, by a Distant Relation to the Poet of Thebes and Laureate to the Academy*, London

POINTON 1999
M. Pointon, 'Valuing the visual and visualizing the valuable', *Cultural Values*, 3 (1), pp. 1–27

POINTON 2001
M. Pointon, '"Surrounded with brilliants": miniature portraits in eighteenth-century England', *Art Bulletin*, 83 (1), pp. 48–71

POINTON 2007
M. Pointon, 'Women and their jewels', in Batchelor and Kaplan 2007, pp. 11–30

POINTON 2010
M. Pointon, 'Liaisons dangereuses: buttons, button-holes and the materials of masculinity in eighteenth-century England', *Fashion Theory*, 16, pp. 1–30

POINTON 2016
M. Pointon, 'Accessories as portraits and portraits as accessories', in Krems and Ruby 2016, pp. 45–59

PÖLLNITZ 1737
K.L.F.V. Pöllnitz, *The Memoirs of Charles-Lewis, Baron de Pollnitz. Being the Observations He Made in His Late Travels from Prussia through Poland, Germany, Italy, France, Spain, Flanders. Holland, England, &c. in Letters to His Friend. Discovering Not Only the Present State of the Chief Cities and Towns; but The Characters of the Principal Persons at the Several Courts*, 2 vols, London

PREBBLE 1988
J. Prebble, *The King's Jaunt: George IV in Scotland, August 1822: One and Twenty Daft Days*, London

PRIESTLEY 1993
U. Priestley, 'Norwich and the mourning trade', *Costume*, 27 (1), pp. 47–56

PYNE 1808
W.H. Pyne, *Costume of Great Britain*, London

RAUSER 2020
A.F. Rauser, *The Age of Undress: Art, Fashion, and the Classical Ideal in the 1790s*, New Haven and London

REID 2012
S. Reid, *Cumberland's Culloden Army 1745–46*, Oxford

REYNOLDS 1842
J. Reynolds (ed.), *Seventh Discourse on Art*, London

RIBEIRO 1983
A. Ribeiro, *A Visual History of Costume: The Eighteenth Century*, London

RIBEIRO 1984
A. Ribeiro, *The Dress Worn at Masquerades in England, 1730 to 1790, and its Relation to Fancy Dress in Portraiture*, New York

RIBEIRO 1988
A. Ribeiro, *Fashion in the French Revolution*, London

RIBEIRO 1995
A. Ribeiro, *The Art of Dress: Fashion in England and France 1750 to 1820*, New Haven and London

RIBEIRO 2002
A. Ribeiro, *Dress in Eighteenth-Century Europe 1715–1789*, New Haven and London

RIBEIRO 2011
A. Ribeiro, *Facing Beauty: Painted Women and Cosmetic Art*, New Haven and London

RICHARDSON 1741
S. Richardson, *Letters Written To and For Particular Friends, on the Most Important Occasions*, London

RICHARDSON 1742
S. Richardson, *Pamela, Or Virtue Rewarded*, Dublin

RICHARDSON 1985
S. Richardson, *Clarissa; or The History of a Young Lady*, Angus Ross (ed.), New York

RIELLO 2006
G. Riello, *A Foot in the Past: Consumers, Producers and Footwear in the Long Eighteenth Century*, Oxford

RIELLO 2013
G. Riello, *Cotton: The Fabric that Made the Modern World*, Cambridge

ROBINSON AND CALVEY 2015
J. Robinson with G. Calvey, *The Fine Art of Fashion Illustration: Fashion Illustrations from the Julian Robinson Archive*, London

ROCHE 1999
D. Roche, *The Culture of Clothing: Dress and Fashion in the Ancien Régime*, Cambridge

RORSCHACH 1989
K. Rorschach, 'Frederick Prince of Wales (1707–51) as collector and patron', *Volume of the Walpole Society*, 55, pp. 1–76

ROSE 1989
C. Rose, *Children's Clothes since 1750*, London

ROSENTHAL 1996
J.W. Rosenthal, *Spectacles and Other Vision Aids: A History and Guide to Collecting*, San Francisco, CA

ROTHSTEIN 1990
N. Rothstein, *Silk Designs of the Eighteenth Century in the Collection of the Victoria and Albert Museum*, London

ROUQUET 1755
J.A. Rouquet, *The Present State of the Arts in England*, London

ROUSSEAU 2009
J.-J. Rousseau, *Emile, or On Education*, A. Bloom and C. Kelly (trans. and ed.), Hanover, NH

RUSH 1972
B. Rush, *Two Essays on the Mind: An Enquiry into the Influence of Physical Causes upon the Moral Faculty, and On the Influence of Physical Causes in Promoting an Increase of the Strength and Activity of the Intellectual Faculties of Man*, New York

RUSSELL 2004
F. Russell, *John, 3rd Earl of Bute: Patron & Collector*, London

SABOR 2011–19
P. Sabor (ed.), *The Court Journals and Letters of Fanny Burney 1786–1791*, 6 vols, Oxford

ST CLAIR 2016
K. St Clair, *The Secret Lives of Colour*, London

SCOTT 1853–4
W. Scott, *Waverley Novels*, 25 vols, Edinburgh

SCOTT THOMSON 1943
G. Scott Thomson (ed.), *Letters of a Grandmother, 1732–1735: Being the Correspondence of Sarah, Duchess of Marlborough with her Granddaughter Diana, Duchess of Bedford*, London

SHERIDAN 1781
R.B. Sheridan, *A Trip to Scarborough: A Comedy. As Performed at the Theatre Royal in Drury Lane. Altered from Vanbrugh's Relapse; Or, Virtue in Danger, By Richard Brinsley Sheridan, Esq.*, Dublin

SIMOND 1817
L. Simond, *Journal of a Tour and Residence in Great Britain during the Years 1810 and 1811, by a French Traveller with Remarks on the Country, its Arts, Literature, and Politics, and on the Manners and Customs of its Inhabitants*, 2 vols, Edinburgh

SMILES 2002
S. Smiles, 'Defying comprehension: resistance to uniform appearance in depicting the poor, 1770s to 1830s', *Textile History*, 33 (1), pp. 22–36

SNOWMAN 1990
A.K. Snowman, *Eighteenth Century Gold Boxes of Europe*, Woodbridge, Suffolk

SPENCER 2018
E. Spencer, 'None but *Abigails* appeared in white aprons: the apron as an elite garment in eighteenth-century England', *Textile History*, 49 (2), pp. 164–90

SQUIRE 1970
G. Squire, 'Liberty, equality and antiquity: dress 1785–1820', *Costume*, 4 (1), pp. 4–16

STANDEN 1964
E.A. Standen, 'English washing furnitures', *Metropolitan Museum of Art Bulletin*, 23 (3), pp. 109–24

STANHOPE 1889
P.H. Stanhope, *Notes of Conversations with the Duke of Wellington, 1831–1851*, London

STANILAND 1990
K. Staniland, 'An eighteenth-century quilted dress', *Costume*, 24 (1), pp. 43–54

STANILAND 2000
K. Staniland, 'Princess Charlotte's wedding dress', *Costume*, 34 (1), pp. 70–80

STYLES 2007
J. Styles, *The Dress of the People: Everyday Fashion in Eighteenth-Century England*, New Haven and London

TAYLOR 1983
L. Taylor, *Mourning Dress: A Costume and Social History*, London

THATCHER ULRICH 2009
L. Thatcher Ulrich, *The Age of Homespun: Objects and Stories in the Creation of an American Myth*, New York

THORNTON 1965
P. Thornton, *Baroque and Rococo Silks*, London

TUCKETT 2016
S. Tuckett, 'Reassessing the romance: tartan as a popular commodity, c.1770–1830', *Scottish Historical Review*, 95 (241), pp. 182–202

VAIL 1958
R.W.G. Vail, 'Our friendly enemies: the pro-American caricatures of a London woman printseller of 1776–1778', *New York Historical Society Quarterly*, 42 (1), pp. 39–46

VAN HORN 2016
J. Van Horn, 'George Washington's dentures: disability, deception, and the Republican body', *Early American Studies*, 14 (1), pp. 2–47

VIGÉE LE BRUN 1835
E.L. Vigée-Le Brun, *Souvenirs de Mme. Louise-Elisabeth Vigée-Le Brun*, 3 vols, Paris

VINCENT 2018
S.J. Vincent, *Hair: An Illustrated History*, London

WALKER 1813–14
G. Walker, *Costume of Yorkshire*, Leeds

WALKER 1992
R. Walker, *The Eighteenth and Nineteenth Century Miniatures in the Collection of Her Majesty The Queen*, Cambridge

WALPOLE 1927–8
H. Walpole, 'Journals of visits to country seats', *Volume of the Walpole Society*, 16, pp. 9–80

WALTON 1975
K.M. Walton, 'Queen Charlotte's dressing table', *Journal of the Furniture History Society*, 11, pp. 112–13

WATT 2013
M. Watt, 'Whims and fancies', in Peck 2013, pp. 82–103

WAUGH 2018
N. Waugh. *The Cut of Men's Clothes, 1660–1900*, London

WENDEBORN 1791
F.A. Wendeborn, *A View of England towards the Close of the Eighteenth Century*, 2 vols, London

WHITLEY 1915
W.T. Whitley, *Thomas Gainsborough*, London

WHITTAKER 1823
J. Whittaker, *Ceremonial of the Coronation of His Most Sacred Majesty King George the Fourth*, London

WILDEBLOOD 1965
J. Wildeblood, *The Polite World: A Guide to English Manners and Deportment from the Thirteenth to the Nineteenth Century*, London

WILLIAMS 2014
H. Williams, *Turquerie: An Eighteenth-Century European Fantasy*, London

WINE *ET AL.* 2018
H. Wine, A. Godyicki, V. Napoleone, L. Oliver, L. Packer, Y. Rimaud and F. Whitlum-Cooper, *The Eighteenth Century French Paintings: National Gallery Catalogues*, London

WITHEY 2021
A. Withey, *Concerning Beards: Facial Hair, Health and Practice in England 1650–1900*, London

WORSLEY 2010
L. Worsley, *Courtiers: The Secret History of Kensington Palace*, London

WORTLEY MONTAGU 1835
J.H.M. Wortley Montagu, *Letters of the Right Honourable Lady Mary Wortley Montague: Written during Mr. Wortley's Embassy at Constantinople; to which Are Added Poems*, Leipzig

# ACKNOWLEDGEMENTS

As is always the case, this book and the exhibition it accompanies at The Queen's Gallery are the result of the hard work and assistance of a large number of Royal Collection Trust staff. Such a project is challenging even under normal circumstances – a global pandemic and organisational restructure made it even more so, and I am truly grateful to everyone involved for their commitment and dedication. I hope the end result is something of which we can all be proud.

My thanks first go to Desmond Shawe-Taylor, a generous mentor and friend, whose encyclopedic knowledge and extraordinary synoptic vision has gradually encouraged me to seek broader connections and comparisons across disciplines and epochs. Both book and exhibition have been significantly improved by Desmond's advice and input during our years of working together, while his feedback on the manuscript was thought-provoking and thorough. My interest in dress history started at a young age; it was under the tutelage of Professor Aileen Ribeiro at the Courtauld Institute, however, that my eyes were fully opened to the value of studying the history of clothing and what it tells us about broader societal change. Her extraordinary legacy and depth of research remain a constant source of inspiration and awe. I would also like to thank Alexandra Kim for her considered and insightful feedback on the manuscript, which resulted in changes that greatly improved the book's structure, clarity and content. My questions have been patiently answered by a number of experts – here my particular thanks go to Paul Cattermole for his advice on military dress, Heather Toomer for her comments on lace and whitework, and Jenny Tiramani on construction and cut. I would also like to thank Jill Lasersohn for offering both her home and her exceptional textile collection to me so generously. Enjoyable and fruitful conversations with Misha Ewen, Neal Hurst, Montaz Marché, Tim McCall, Jonquil O'Reilly and Kirsten Tambling have directed me to new avenues of research within the field.

The source material for the breadth of subjects covered within this book is exceptionally rich and rapidly evolving. In a book of this type, whose ambition is to introduce the subject to a general reader, while also providing something of interest for the specialist, it is impossible to do justice to every nuance of interpretation. For reasons of space, only those publications specifically referenced in the text are included within the bibliography, although many other sources besides those listed here have influenced my thinking and led me down fascinating rabbit holes of research. For that reason, I very much hope interested readers will consider this book a starting point, inspiring them to explore new insights from emerging scholars, particularly those studying under-represented communities and identities traditionally overlooked in the scholarship, alongside those who are well established in the field of fashion history. The diversity of perspectives these researchers bring – and indeed the new questions they pose – offer fruitful and important contributions beyond the avenues considered here, encouraging further discussion about how we interpret visual material from this period and what its continued relevance might be for us all today.

I am grateful to the many people who have read draft versions of the text at different stages, and provided comments, corrections and encouragement. Within the Royal Collection Trust I would especially like to thank Elizabeth Ashby, Jeannie Chapel, Lexi Drayton, Kathryn Jones, Tim Knox, Isabella Manning, Simon Metcalf, Rachel Peat, Lucy Peter and Rhian Wong. Thank you also to Jane Simpkiss for helping with the initial research for Chapters 9 and 10, and to Kate Brennan and Abi May for assisting with the compilation of the bibliography, glossary and captions.

The beautiful design of the book is the artistic vision of Ray Watkins, while it has been both expertly copyedited and project managed by Linda Schofield. From the Royal Collection Trust publications team Polly Fellows and Kate Owen have offered guidance and support at every stage, while Tung Tsin Lam, Karen Lawson and Daniel Partridge have provided images of the very highest quality. Sarah Tucker's production expertise has been invaluable, and thanks are owed to Bev Zimmern, proofreader, and Nicola King, indexer.

Thank you to our partner organisations for lending their objects so generously to the exhibition, and for conserving and mounting them for photography. My particular thanks go to Sarah Glenn, Rosemary Harden and Eleanor Summers at the Fashion Museum Bath; Joanna Hashagen, Annabel Talbot, Jane Whittaker and Rachel Whitworth at the Bowes Museum; Tara Fidler, Adrian Phillips, Polly Putnam, Matthew Storey and Mika Takami at Historic Royal Palaces; and Jenny Tiramani at the School of Historical Dress. Thank you also to the other institutions who have allowed us to reproduce their images in the book.

As always, members of the conservation and art handling teams at the Royal Collection Trust have done a sterling job gathering and treating objects for both the exhibition and new photography. My thanks in particular go to Glenn Bartley, Ashleigh Brown, Claire Chorley, Nicola Christie, Allison Derrett, Tamsin Douglas, Michael Field, Megan Gent, Adelaide Izat, Chris King, Nick Kingswell, Sonja Leggewie, Francesca Levey, Simon Metcalf, Sarah Patch, Clara de la Peña McTigue, Rosanna de Sancha, Puneeta Sharma, Rachel Sharples, Claire Shepherd, Rachael Smith, Matt Stockl, Kate Stone and Sophy Wills. Thank you to my curatorial colleagues, past and present, for their suggestions and support: Alex Buck, Martin Clayton, Caroline de Guitaut, Emily Hannam, Stella Panayotova, Bill Stockting, Emma Stead and Oliver Walton.

For the production of the exhibition, my thanks must first go to Hannah Belcher for her vision, enthusiasm and impressive scheduling, along with Sarah Morris and Theresa-Mary Morton. Thank you to Ian Gardner for his endless patience designing the exhibition space as we tried to make everything fit, Zoe Harper for the mounts, Deborah Phipps for textile conservation and Michael Perry for his magnificent illustrations. Thank you also to Dee Vianna for her constant encouragement and wise advice.

The final thanks go to my family on both sides of the Atlantic, and particularly to John, Isabel and Ava. Ten years after the publication of *In Fine Style* in 2013, my daughters still love dressing up – albeit more often now in football kit or pointe shoes.

# INDEX

# PHOTOGRAPHIC CREDITS

Published 2023 by Royal Collection Trust
York House
St James's Palace
London SW1A 1BQ

Royal Collection Trust / © His Majesty King Charles III 2023

Published on the occasion of the exhibition *Style & Society: Dressing the Georgians* at The Queen's Gallery, Buckingham Palace, London, in 2023.

ISBN 978 1 909741 85 0
103240

A catalogue record for this book is available from the British Library.

Publishing Editor: Polly Fellows
Publisher: Kate Owen
Editor and Project Manager: Linda Schofield
Designer: Raymonde Watkins
Indexer: Nicola King
Production Manager: Sarah Tucker
Typeset in Bressay, Bliss and Didot
Printed on Magno Matt 150gsm
Colour reproduction by Altaimage, London
Printed and bound in Italy by Graphicom

Front cover: Detail of Fig. 8.11
Back cover and title page: British School, *St James's Park and the Mall*, c.1745. RCIN 405954
Endpapers and page 344: Detail of Fig. 8.10
Half-title page: Detail of Fig. 6.36
Page 4: Detail of Fig. 9.12
Page 328: Detail of Fig. 1.32
Page 336: Attributed to William Rought (active c.1790), *George III, Queen Charlotte and Six Princesses*, c.1795. Lamp black and gum arabic on glass. RCIN 452452
Page 337: Detail of Fig. 3.27